Praise

'If you're interested in pop histor
in fascinating detail the dizzy, con
'90s and '00s pop.' – **N**

'Never before has there been
first time I've really felt a true
A fantastic book!' – **Ni**

'A brilliant, celebratory, gossipy history of '90s pop. Great stories and interviews. If that's your era, you'll love it . . . a wonderful book for pop kids everywhere.' – **Richard Osman**

'It was the best time to be a pop star and it's great to be able to relive it all again in the amazing *Reach for the Stars*.' – **Duncan James, Blue**

'I can't think why anyone wouldn't love this book.' – **Greg James**

'So funny and detailed and, most importantly, such a clear love and understanding of the people in it . . . an entertaining balance of fan worship and camp detached wit.' – ***The Times***

'A hoot. You don't so much read it as inhale it.' – ***The Observer***

'A funny, bright, often poignant read.' – ***Sunday Times***

'An outstanding catalogue of oral testimonies from major and minor players in UK pop.' – ***New Statesman***

'A must-read for any pop fan. 5/5' – ***Classic Pop***

'Fantastic.' – **Xenomania Records**

'Cragg's knowledge and affection for the music shines through every paragraph.' – **BBC**

'Book of the millennium.' – **Popjustice**

'The definitive account of turn-of-the-millennium pop.' – ***Buzz***

'Joyful and eye-opening . . . an enormously entertaining read.' – ***Record Collector***

'Prepare to be left open-mouthed . . . some of the finest secrets from the pop-music landscape of those heady times.' – ***Heat***

'A book that does justice to an extraordinarily fertile period for British pop – Michael Cragg's assessment of new-millennium bubblegum is top-rate storytelling.' – **Bob Stanley**

'You won't find a more comprehensive and entertaining pop book than this.' – **Jordan Paramor**

'A truly hilarious pop-culture nostalgia-fest!' – **Jack Rooke**

'An outstanding music book. *England's Dreaming* for people with a working knowledge of 5ive.' – **Fergal Kinney**

'A gloriously funny, often shocking and occasionally poignant trip down memory lane . . . a must-read for any discerning pop fan.' – **Lucie Cave**

'Nobody buys books. No one's going to read this.' – **Louis Walsh**

MICHAEL CRAGG has been writing about pop music for over a decade and has interviewed everyone from Lady Gaga to Lorde, via Little Mix, Shawn Mendes, Miley Cyrus, Katy Perry and Britney Spears. He has written for outlets including *Vogue*, *The Guardian*, *GQ*, the BBC, *The Observer*, Popjustice, *Dazed* and *Billboard*.

During his three years as contributing editor at *Guardian Guide*, he interviewed '00s pop luminaries such as Steps, Emma Bunton and Nadine Coyle. He also edits the independent biannual music magazine *Beat*.

Reach for the Stars

1996–2006: Fame, Fallout and Pop's Final Party

Michael Cragg

NINE EIGHT BOOKS

NINE EIGHT BOOKS
NEB 015

First published in the UK in hardback in 2023
This paperback edition published in 2023 by Nine Eight Books
An imprint of Black & White Publishing Group
A Bonnier Books UK company
4th Floor, Victoria House, Bloomsbury Square, London, WC1B 4DA
Owned by Bonnier Books, Sveavägen 56, Stockholm, Sweden

@nineeightbooks

@nineeightbooks

Paperback ISBN: 978-1-7887-0727-5
eBook ISBN: 978-1-7887-0725-1

A CIP catalogue record for this book is available from the British Library.

Publishing director: Pete Selby
Senior editor: Melissa Bond

Nine Eight Books would like to thank
Peter Stoneman for additional editorial support.

Cover photographs: Girls Aloud © Ray Burminston/Comic Relief via Getty Images; S Club 7 © Hayley Madden/Redferns; Spice Girls © Mike Prior/Getty Images; Craig David © Tim Roney/Getty Images
Typeset by IDSUK (Data Connection) Ltd
Printed and bound in Great Britain by Clays Ltd, Elcograf S.p.A

1 3 5 7 9 10 8 6 4 2

Nine Eight Books is an imprint of Bonnier Books UK
www.bonnierbooks.co.uk

FSC www.fsc.org MIX Paper from responsible sources FSC® C018072

Contents

Spoken-word intro

I'm going to start with a confession. As a closeted teenager in the early '00s I did some things I am ashamed of. I went to see the Libertines. I was a fan of post-*Kid A* Radiohead. I once went to Ireland to see Travis only to be hit on the head by warm beer and, at one point, an inflatable armchair. For a while, I thought hiding in indie music would help me keep my secret for a bit longer when in fact it just fed my covert obsession; glorious, shiny, ludicrous pop. I'd secretly gorge on the Latin flavours of 'Spice Up Your Life' or get a delicious sugar rush from 'Don't Stop Movin''. Later I'd sit with my proudly pop-obsessed uni housemate and listen to 'hard-edged' ladband Five and the high street R&B of Blue, before hitting the local indie club. I'd carelessly align myself with the throng of *NME* readers trying to justify their love of Girls Aloud or the Sugababes via the prism of credibility ('It's pretty good for a pop song!!!'), when in fact I owned all their albums and distinctly remember singing along to the former's pearlescent six-minute epic 'Untouchable' in a full-length mirror, willing myself to be who I was.

Perhaps because I only lived this UK pure pop boom – instigated by the Buffalo boot-stomping swagger of the Spice Girls in 1996, which is where this book starts – on the periphery, when I started writing about music as a journalist years later, I immersed myself fully. As pop shifted through the gears over the following two decades, taking in post-ironic synthpop, Lady Gaga, gloom wobble dubstep, drop-obsessed EDM and Billie Eilish-adjacent mope-pop before settling on a sort of generic streaming-friendly dance-pop sound, I often found myself harking back to the weightlessness of, say, Liberty X's 'Just a Little' or Five's 'Keep On Movin'' or A1's 'Caught in the Middle'. Like most people, this rose-tinted nostalgia – hey, this book is about the late '90s and early '00s, get used to it – ramped up as a pandemic-ravaged world went into lockdown. Gazed upon from a modern world seemingly on fire, this prelapsarian era suddenly represented even more of a refreshing change. A time before the threat of nuclear war, climate crisis, global financial collapse, social media, culture wars, Piers Morgan's TV career, TikTok and, of course, the pandemic.

Musically, the shiny, irony-free, edge-less, story-telling '90s and '00s anthems also stick out among the darker, slower, generally heavier feel of recent pop. Featuring early input from some of today's biggest hitmakers, from Stargate (Beyoncé, Rihanna) to Steve Mac (Ed Sheeran, Sam Smith) to Max Martin (Ariana Grande, the Weeknd), '00s pop's uncomplicated perfection still feels imbued with more life than a lot of the Logic-created music that's lazily finessed for playlist domination today. The Spice Girls' ragged 'Wannabe', for example, turned the beauty of female friendship into a battle cry in a lad-heavy, post-Britpop

Britain. Their doctrine, critiqued ad nauseam in recent years, felt rightfully joyous away from the harping naysayers who years later could hop on the ubiquitous bird app to poke holes in everything.

Post-'Wannabe', Billie Piper harnessed the Spice Girls' bolshiness on her debut single 'Because We Want To', allowing young girls in particular a place to rebel, even if the stakes were as low as a stereo being a bit too loud. Boybands, buffeted by the success of Take That and lush enough to escape into, veered between mushy, love-hearts-in-your-exercise-book ballads (Westlife) and hip-thrusting, arm-waggling up-tempos either delivered by perma-smiling Ken dolls (A1) or rough-around-the-edges *EastEnders* characters (Five).

It was also a pre-social media world, untethered from the discourse, ruled over by long-lost cultural markers: music TV shows from *CD:UK* to *Popworld*; pop magazines from *Smash Hits* to *Big!*; by Radio 1 roadshows and the hysterical annual *Smash Hits* Poll Winners Party; by CD singles (the iTunes Store didn't launch in the UK until June 2004) sent skywards by the death of Princess Diana in 1997 and Elton John's hastily repurposed candle-based tribute. It was a time when a well-placed tabloid story could win an all-important chart war and, for better or worse, a misplaced quote (Lee Ryan, elephants, 9/11 – need I say more?) could actually help, not hinder (in the UK at least), a career away from the permanence of Twitter. Singles, aided by bargain-bin mecca Woolworths, were still king, with a top-ten placing paramount for fear of being dropped. It was also a time when January's quiet period would see a sudden influx of releases by acts desperate to improve on their previous single stalling at, say, number nineteen (I'm looking at you, allSTARS*).

A decade in pop is a lifetime, however. So this book finishes in 2006, a year when a lot of those previously mentioned cultural markers started to disappear. *Top of the Pops* was axed, as was *CD:UK*. Simon and Miquita left *Popworld*, while their irreverent forebear *Smash Hits* – grappling with a sudden dearth of pop stars and skewing towards TV talent – printed its final issue. As the internet began to swallow up print media and started creating a whole new stratum of disarmingly 'real' pop stars via sites like MySpace, the TV landscape also changed. Launched in 2004 by Simon Cowell – who had spent the decade moving from behind-the-scenes A&R for the likes of Westlife and Five to oddly dressed TV panto villain – *The X Factor* built on the success of 2001's *Popstars* and the following year's double whammy of *Pop Idol* and *Popstars: The Rivals*.

Suddenly, the mechanisms behind the manufactured pop juggernaut were being completely laid bare. Not only could we see the sausage being made, but we were in charge – or made to think we were in charge – of its ingredients. The power was with the viewers-turned-voters; where in the past pop stars such as Rachel Stevens represented the girl-next-door-done-good archetype, a beacon of relatability with a sheen of glamorous untouchability to keep the pop star mythos going, now the public decided which girl next door got their chance and that distancing, untouchable sheen had to go. Relatability was key, as was authenticity, which in the end would give way to the influx of chart-dominating, straight-faced singer-songwriters like Adele, Ed Sheeran and Emeli Sandé – what journalist Peter Robinson referred to in 2011 as 'The New Boring'.

The harsh critiques previously given behind closed doors by (mostly) men in suits were now being codified on TV talent shows into a new way of talking about wide-eyed hopefuls. Eventually those (mostly) men in suits became the true stars, eclipsing the show's winners and losers. The public, used to seeing warts and worse on the increasingly popular *Big Brother*, also needed (sob) stories, a journey, an angle. Years of drama school training followed by a sideways step into a pop band wasn't enough. The public needed to be there every step of the way and slowly became distrustful of slick, ready-made acts in matching outfits doing the same choreography (or ANY choreography: see One Direction). On the surface, *The X Factor* aimed at discovering unbridled talent away from the media-trained shiny pop of old, only to balk at any sudden movements lest it harm the brand. The light entertainment TV format also meant audiences were likely to forget about the contestants once the show was over and the conveyor belts cranked into gear again; a narrative established from the outset via Hear'Say on the original TV talent show experiment, *Popstars*. From that point forward, the permanent smiles started to fray at the edges and the pop bubble quickly calcified into a trap.

All of this shiny, happy, factory-formed pop, be it Steps, S Club or Same Difference, was catnip to critics who, in a pre-poptimism era, saw music loved by children, girls, gay men, large amounts of the population, as inferior. Something to be grown out of. Something certainly less worthy than whatever they were listening to, despite the fact that seemingly weightless music is far easier to anchor with your own all-important meaning than something defined as X or Y from the start. Rather than accept that two competing ideas can both offer up positives and negatives, the pop vs indie debate became a war. Frankly, in book-form at least, it feels like the indie side has had its say. Part of why I wanted to do this book in an oral history format was to add some extra weight to a hugely important period of UK music that often felt ignored in the stream of chin-stroking think pieces on Britpop, the post-Strokes UK indie resurgence or the post-MySpace Arctic Monkeys chatter.

Reach for the Stars is about celebrating not just the (often, but not always) immaculate pop but also the pop stars themselves at a time when pop really did mean '. . . as in popular'. The reason I focused solely on the UK (with a dash of Ireland) is because, post-Spice Girls, a wave of pop crashed onto these shores. Girlbands, boybands, mixed gender groups, solo artists – every week seemed to bring with it a new act to become obsessed with. And this was an era of proper fan obsession, too – none of this casual £9-a-month streaming nonsense; this was a time of hammering phone lines, queuing outside record-shop signings, cutting out clippings, snapping up merchandise.

I also wanted to give the pop stars themselves the chance to speak. Often asked in playful interviews at the time to discuss who they fancied or what colour best describes them or their favourite sandwich filling, their voices weren't always hugely important outside of singing. On these pages they can recall the highs, the lows and the endless hours spent in minivans being whisked to local radio stations. I wanted to reflect on the joy of that period – and nearly everyone I spoke to got misty-eyed remembering this incredibly unique, all-in-this-together time in pop – but also, with hindsight, to highlight some of the trickier moments, including the side-lining of Black artists into 'urban' categories, the lack of care around mental health and the climate of fear around pop stars coming out.

Obviously part of being a pop star in this period was to walk that thin line between characterful funster and media-trained robot. Everyone had to learn to whack on a smile, even if behind the scenes punches were being thrown (Five), inter-band alliances were being formed (Steps) and toilet windows were definitely not being climbed out of (Sugababes). Which is why, all these years later, it's fun to see the perma-smiling facade thrown onto the fire. Truth bombs are joyfully dropped from great heights, augmented by supporting input from a host of the era's defining songwriters, producers, music video directors, journalists, record label bosses, PRs, fashion experts, TV hosts and talent show judges.

In fact, it was one of the latter, Louis Walsh, who had this to say to me at the start of our tetchy ten-minute phoner: 'No one's going to read this.'

Please let's not live in a world where Louis Walsh is right.

Now here's a story from A to Z: Who's who?

Alex Needham: Formerly of *Smash Hits*, *The Face* and *NME*. Currently arts editor of *The Guardian*.

Alexis Petridis: Former editor of *Select* magazine and current head pop and rock critic of *The Guardian*.

Andy Margetson: Director of S Club 7's TV series *Miami 7* and *L.A. 7*, as well as various S Club music videos.

Andy McCluskey: Member of OMD and the co-founder, songwriter and producer behind Atomic Kitten.

Antony Costa: A quarter of Supersexual hitmakers Blue.

Ashley Bird: Former editor of hirsute rock bible *Kerrang!*

Barry Stone: Songwriter, producer and one half of Jewels & Stone.

Bradley McIntosh: The swinging one from S Club 7.

Brian Dowling: *Big Brother* season two winner and former co-host of *SM:TV*.

Brian Higgins: Songwriter, producer and head honcho of ludicrous hit factory Xenomania.

Cameron McVey: Songwriter and producer who basically rescued the Sugababes' *One Touch*.

Carolyn Owlett: One-third of the 'hip-hop Supremes', the 411.

Ceri Evans: Better known as UK garage producer and remixer Sunship.

Chantelle Fiddy: Journalist, editor and debut album-era Craig David stan.

Charlie Adelman: Manager and American Steps super-fan.

Chris Cowey: Television producer who worked at *Top of the Pops* from 1997 to 2003.

Chris Herbert: Manager behind Five, Girl Thing, Hear'Say, Triple 8 and more. Also put the Spice Girls together before being given the boot.

Christian Ingebrigtsen: The blond Norwegian one from excellently coiffured boyband A1.

Claire Richards: Steps' main vocalist and inventor of culinary classic, Pasta a la Clara.

Colin Barlow: Former co-managing director, Polydor.

Craig David: UK garage and R&B legend.

Craig McLean: Culture journalist who had the balls to pop Hear'Say on the cover of *The Face*.

Daizy Agnew: Former member of just-slightly-behind-the-curve girlband, Girls Can't Catch.

Dania Pasquini: One half of music video director duo, Max & Dania.

Darcus Beese: Former A&R director, Island Records.

David Lim: '00s pop super-fan and co-host of podcast *Right Back at Ya!*

Dean Piper: Former celebrity journalist for the *People* and the *Mirror*.

Emma Bunton: AKA the living legend that is Baby Spice.

Felix Howard: Songwriter and musician whose credits include the Sugababes, V and Amy Winehouse.

Geri Halliwell: AKA the living legend that is Ginger Spice.

Gregg Masuak: Music video director.

Hallgeir Rustan: Former member of ubiquitous Norwegian production team, Stargate.

Hannah Robinson: Songwriting icon.

Hannah Verdier: Journalist and former editor at *Smash Hits*.

Holly-Jade Johnston: '00s boyband super-fan.

Hugh Goldsmith: Former managing director, RCA, and founder of Innocent Records and later Brightside Records.

Iain James: Songwriter and former member of just-behind-the-curve boyband, Triple 8.

Ian 'H' Watkins: Mr Hyperactive and Steps' loveable class clown.

Jamelia: 'Window Shopping' hitmaker and living legend.

James Bourne: One third of baggy jeans enthusiasts, Busted.

James Masterton: Chart geek who runs the Chart Watch website.

JB Gill: A quarter of Jack the Lad Swing exponents, JLS.

Jenessa Williams: Journalist and long-term McFly stan.

Jenny Frost: Formerly of Eurovision contestants Precious before being snapped up by Atomic Kitten.

Jeremy Joseph: Owner of the G-A-Y nightclubs. Important to note that our forty-minute interview took place while he was running through London.

Jo O'Meara: The Voice in S Club 7.

Jodi Albert: Former Girl Thing member turned *Hollyoaks* actor. Also married to Kian from Westlife.

Joe McElderry: Winner of *The X Factor* in 2009 and Rage Against the Machine's biggest fan . . .

Joe Stone: Writer, editor and the Spice Girls' biggest fan.

Joel Babbington: '00s pop super-fan and co-host of podcast *Right Back at Ya!*

Jon Shave: Songwriter, producer and Xenomania alumnus.

Jonathan Bown: Former assistant editor at *Smash Hits.*

Jony Rockstar: Songwriter and producer famed for his work with the Sugababes.

Jordan Paramor: *Smash Hits* and *Heat* journalist who also penned a number of pop annuals.

Justine Bell: Former A&R coordinator, Innocent Records.

Karl Twigg: Songwriter and producer partly responsible for some of Steps' most incredible moments.

Keisha Buchanan: The Sugababes' longest-serving member and vocal powerhouse.

Keith Semple: Former One True Voice vocalist who now fronts two rock bands, SEMPLE Band and the Cyberiam.

Kelli Young: Cane-wielding member of Liberty X.

Kevin McDaid: Former member of actually-really-great lost boyband, V.

Kimberley Walsh: Sultry-voiced member of Girls Aloud.

Laura Snapes: *The Guardian*'s deputy music editor and '00s pop superfan.

Lauren Cochrane: Senior fashion writer at *The Guardian*.

Lee Brennan: Cute-as-a-button lead singer with 911.

Lee Latchford-Evans: Steps' much-needed everyman.

Lee Thompson: Former head of music at Viking FM and later at music TV channel, The Box.

Lisa Scott-Lee: Steps' chief cheerleader and post-irony icon.

Liz McClarnon: One third of Atomic Kitten.

Louis Walsh: Slightly tetchy Boyzone and Westlife manager turned TV talent show judge.

Louise Nurding: Former member of Eternal turned solo star.

Lucie Cave: Former Trouble TV presenter turned *Heat* magazine editor-in-chief.

Malcolm McLean: '00s pop super-fan and author of 2019's *Freak Like Me: Confessions of a 90s Pop Groupie.*

Mark Beaumont: Premier indie music journalist.

Marvin Humes: Former member of VS and linchpin of occasional condom manufacturers JLS.

Max Giwa: The other half of music video director duo, Max & Dania.

Mel B: AKA the living legend that is Scary Spice.

Melanie Blatt: All Saints' silken-voiced centrepiece.

Melanie C: AKA the living legend that is Sporty Spice.

Miranda Cooper: Xenomania's lyrical genius and former Gina G backing dancer.

MNEK: Producer, songwriter, singer and '00s pop fan.

Mutya Buena: Sugababe 4 Life and the greatest singer of her generation.

Myleene Klass: Former member of TV talent show experiment, Hear'Say.

Nadine Coyle: 'The Voice' of Girls Aloud.

Natalie Appleton: One quarter of All Saints.

Natasha Hamilton: Husky-voiced member of Gareth Southgate's favourite girlband, Atomic Kitten.

Nicola Roberts: Every cool person's favourite Girls Aloud member.

Nicole Appleton: Spoken word exponent and member of All Saints.

Nigel Dick: Music video director and auteur behind S Club's film, *Seeing Double*.

Nikki Whelan: '00s pop super-fan with a basement full of merchandise.

Oritsé Williams: JLS's most thoughtful member.

Paul Flynn: Journalist, author and advice-giving legend.

Pete Selby: Former music retail buyer who once peed next to a boyband member.

Pete Waterman: Music industry impresario who signed Steps and later became a reluctant TV talent show judge.

Pete Whelan: '00s pop super-fan with a basement full of merchandise.

Peter Bradshaw: *The Guardian*'s film critic.

Peter Loraine: Former editor of *Top of the Pops* magazine turned marketing genius at Polydor turned label and management company owner.

Peter Robinson: Journalist, editor, author, Girls Aloud super-fan and founder of Popjustice.

Richard 'Biff' Stannard: Responsible for some of the biggest and best songs from this period.

Richard X: Producer, songwriter and professional pop agitator.

Rick Nowels: Songwriter and producer who worked with both Mel C and Geri on their solo material.

Ritchie Neville: Five's biggest heartthrob, i.e. he had curtains.

Sam Bloom: Former member of TV stars and chart also-rans, allSTARS*.

Savan Kotecha: Simon Cowell's favourite songwriter.

Scott Robinson: Five's spiky-haired bad boy with a heart of gold.

Sean Conlon: The soul of Five.

Sean Smith: One half of *X Factor* 2007 third-place runners-up, Same Difference.

Shayne Ward: Basically saved *The X Factor* by winning series two in 2005.

Shirley Manson: Iconic Garbage frontwoman and eventual Spice Girls fan.

Siobhán Donaghy: The Sugababes' ethereal, most effortlessly cool member.

Simon Ellis: The former musical director for the Spice Girls turned S Club 7 hitmaker.

Simon Jones: Pop PR legend.

Sophie Ellis-Bextor: Indie darling turned slayer of Posh Spice turned excellent pop practitioner.

Stef D'Andrea: Jeepster records founder and Belle and Sebastian apologist.

Steve Anderson: One of the few people with a Girls Aloud production credit outside of Xenomania.

Steve Brookstein: (Rightfully?) bitter winner of the first *X Factor* series.

Stuart Kershaw: Member of OMD and the co-founder, song-writer and producer behind Atomic Kitten.

Su-Elise Nash: One third of R&B/garage crossover hitmakers, Mis-Teeq.

Tanya Boniface: Singer of above-average R&B-pop hits such as the 411's 'Dumb'.

Tisha Martin: Singer of above-average R&B-pop hits such as the 411's 'On My Knees'.

Tom Findlay: Co-creator of the immaculate 'Song 4 Mutya (Out of Control)'.

Tom Fletcher: Bespectacled leader of McFly and (very briefly) former member of Busted.

Tony Lundon: Former member of 'Move Ya Body' hitmakers Liberty X.

Una Healy: Irish *Popstars* survivor and former member of the Saturdays.

Yvie Burnett: Louis Walsh's sidekick and former *X Factor* vocal coach.

1

Glorious wannabes: The arrival of the Spice Girls

On 13 February 1996, in a nondescript conference room in Manchester, four twenty-something men deflated UK pop. Gary, Mark, Howard and Jason, resplendent in fifty shades of beige and with their grown-out boyband feather-cut fringes now grazing their eyebrows, confirmed Take That were over. 'Unfortunately the rumours are true, "How Deep Is Your Love" is going to be our last single together,' intoned designated band newsreader Gary. Sat in front of a suitably depressing makeshift backdrop resembling a hung-out-to-dry maroon bedsheet, he stuck the knife in deep: 'From today, Take That is no more.'

Having ushered in a new wave of boybands – from 911 to Bad Boys Inc to original Irish stool-botherers Boyzone – The That, as *Smash Hits* hailed them, were bowing out near the top. Long gone were the leather-clad, jelly-wrestling videos of yore. Having cemented their side-step into Serious Artistes with 1995's impeccable 'Back for Good' and having lost rogue member Robbie Williams to the wilds of Glastonbury, it had already felt like the fun was starting to drain away. That they bowed out with a cover felt like the ultimate 'will this do?' ahead of what many predicted would be Gary's swift rise up the solo ranks to be anointed the next George Michael.

Mired in Britpop's afterbirth, the UK music scene in 1996 was a bloke-heavy swirl of guitar-led authenticity, coke-sweat and lad mags. If women's voices were heard at all it was via the clutched pearls of media commentators' faux shock at the rise of ladette culture or through the prism of sex on the pages of magazines aimed at men. At the time, UK pop's biggest female artist was bop merchant and *FHM* regular Louise Nurding, a former member of Eternal whose credentials as the UK's biggest girlband at the time shouldn't be underplayed. Their New Jack Swing-infused R&B sound, however, was quickly bettered by American girlbands such as TLC, SWV and En Vogue.

By the summer of 1996, however, everything had changed. Pop's barren wasteland, still mourning the loss of Take That, was re-turfed by three pairs of Buffalo boots, one pair of scuffed trainers and the *click clack* of two black stilettos. Up against a tetchy pop climate, blinkered record industry groupthink ('girls don't buy music by girls!') and a wave of increasingly tepid dick soup, Geri, Emma, Mel B, Victoria and Melanie C created a global pop culture movement that shifted everything from pop to politics; merch to marketing; feminism to fashion. The Spice

Girls were the launchpad for everything that followed in the late '90s and early '00s, kickstarting a sugar rush of pure pop that brought back boybands, cemented the status of grade-A girlbands and, over in America, laid the foundations for the arrival of Britney Spears.

Like all great epoch-defining moments, it started in a modest semi-detached house in Maidenhead.

'There wasn't a girlband that was sassy, sexy, cool'

In February 1994, Heart management, AKA father-and-son duo Bob and Chris Herbert, put an advert in entertainment trade magazine The Stage. *They were looking for 'streetwise, outgoing, ambitious and dedicated' 18–23-year-olds for a 'choreographed, singing/dancing, all-female pop act for a recording deal'.*

Chris Herbert, Spice Girls former manager: I was interested in A&R and wanted to try to get myself a position within that department in a major label. That's when I thought about putting a band together and from there that should leap-frog me into the industry. So it was purely selfish reasons at the time. Looking at the marketplace off the back of the success of Take That and Boyzone, literally every record company was following suit. The message was loud and clear about just signing boybands. I was looking at it going, 'That's all very good, but boybands only appeal to 50 per cent of the market; it's female bias.' Up until that point you just had Eternal, but there wasn't a girlband that was sassy, sexy, cool, aspirational, fun.

'Geri is a self-confessed bullshitter and we were all along for the ride'

Approximately 400 women showed up for Heart management's auditions. Melanie C chose to cover 'I'm So Excited' and missed the second audition with tonsillitis. Geri, on the other hand, missed the first audition but managed to talk her way into the second. Eventually, Geri, Melanie C, Mel B, Victoria and Michelle Stephenson became the band, Touch. Three months into living, recording and rehearsing together, Stephenson exited stage right and a replacement had to be found.

Chris Herbert: I wanted to cast it like the TV show *Friends*. They were such a mismatch of characters but it covered the full spectrum. You'd never put them in a room together but they worked collectively anyway. So if you could cast it in the same way as those TV shows and get a girl that represented every single colour of the spectrum then you're going to open the net even wider.

Melanie C: I remember the very early days more clearly than I do the crazy days. We were all so ambitious and determined to succeed. And excited because things were starting to happen. All of our dreams were being realised.

Mel B: I didn't think about what was out there or what someone else was doing or what Britpop was. One of the biggest television highlights of the week was *Top of the Pops*. The biggest moment was when I saw this incredible mixed-race woman Neneh Cherry owning the stage singing 'Buffalo Stance' in 1988. I'd never seen someone who looked a bit like me on *Top of the Pops*. That was massive. I was just focused on what we were doing and how well we could do it, how different we could be and how good we could be.

Geri: Before the Spice Girls I was working as a solo artist. I'd met the other girls but we weren't a band yet and I remember thinking, 'What way do I go?' I went to ask this DJ, who was quite well up in the food chain, and he said to me: 'Girlbands never work.' He actually said that. But I went with what I felt. I really loved the girls and the idea of what we were doing.

Chris Herbert: Geri is just pure cheek and tenacity and charm. She missed that first audition. Every time I spoke to her it was all really positive and 'yeah, I'm going to be there'. Then the day before she'd come up with an excuse like she had laryngitis or she'd been on a skiing holiday and burnt her face. Whether or not that was tactical, it worked. I was so far through the process that I just said, 'Look, come down, we're doing a workshop and I've got it down to my shortlist.' She bowled through the doors and I thought, 'You make up for a lack of talent with your character and your campness and everything about you.' She added another element – it's not all about talent; it's about the full package.

Melanie C: Our original management had an investor and he had a house in Maidenhead of all places, so we all moved in. I suppose it was quite good because it kept us out of too much trouble. It was a pretty modest semi and we drove off every day to this little church hall to do choreography, vocal lessons and to have meetings with producers and songwriters.

Emma: I'd just missed out on playing Bianca in *EastEnders*. I was down to the last four. So I'd just found out about that and

I was devastated. I was at college and a singing teacher asked if I'd ever thought of being in a band. She said, 'Well, I'm working with some girls and one of them wants to go back to uni so they're looking for another girl.' She told me to go and meet these two managers, I sang for them and they asked me when I could move in with the girls.

Chris Herbert: Michelle was a very good singer but she didn't fit in. There was the girls and then there was Michelle. She had a lot on her plate – her mother wasn't well, which I didn't know at the time – but she was very introverted. We decided to let her go and look for someone else. Pepi Lemer, who was their vocal coach, mentioned she was doing coaching with this girl, who was really sweet. So I went and saw her and in walked Emma. I thought she was brilliant. Then the girls met her and literally as soon as she walked in they were like sisters.

Mel B: I remember after Michelle [Stephenson] left, we all went to meet Emma, who turned up with her mum Pauline. She looked really cute but also you could see she had this little edge and we all knew instantly she was the one to complete the band. And we were right.

Emma: As soon as I met them we had an instant connection.

Melanie C: When Emma came in, that's when the dynamic shifted and we started to believe we had something really special. It was a real chemistry between the five of us.

Geri: She was eighteen years old. There's a big difference between an eighteen-year-old and a 22-year-old; you've just seen a tiny bit more. So I've always felt very protective of Emma. She was instantly my little sister and I immediately felt like that towards her. I still do.

Emma: I'll never forget Geri driving and looking at me at the same time and being convinced she was going to kill me. Instant connection with Mel B; we ordered a takeaway that first night. But I got homesick very quickly and I was still really young. So I thought, 'Right, either hide this and feel a bit sad or just speak to them all.' Literally the first night I went, 'I'm really homesick and miss my mum,' and of course that bonded us and they were all amazing. I felt fine after that.

Mel B: I shared a room with Mel C. I'd done a season in Blackpool when I was sixteen and lived by myself for a few months but Melanie had spent a year at dance college away from home and she was really good at a lot of practical things. She taught me how to do my washing – to separate the whites from the coloureds for washes. And Victoria was always really good at looking after her clothes, hanging them up when most of us just had clothes in a pile on the floor. That's why me and Geri 'borrowed' her outfits when she went home at the weekend. She never said anything even though she must have known.

Melanie C: We did actually have a cleaning rota. I think I probably did the lion's share because that's my nature. But since I was twenty-two I've always had a cleaner. Also, being Sporty Spice, you don't really have to iron much.

Emma: Mel C or Geri would have taken the bins out. Practical Spice.

Mel B: We all took it in turns.

Emma: Mel B used to cook corned beef and rice, which was a step up from my beans on toast. We used to make Victoria clean the bathroom.

Chris Herbert: Geri was like mother hen; she had everyone organised and they had a routine in terms of what their schedule was every day. If you went into that house there were Take That posters everywhere, they were like young girl fans on a mission, living out a dream. There was an energy there.

Mel B: I remember going into nightclubs at pound-a-pint weekends with Geri. It would be just the two of us – always dressed in matching hot-pants and long socks. The thing that would make me die laughing is the way Geri would act as if we were stars already. At one point every evening, she'd go up to the DJ, get on the mic and announce to everyone: 'Ladies and gentlemen, Touch are in the house.' It was just me and her; no one knew who the hell we were. I'd just burst out laughing.

Melanie C: Geri is a self-confessed bullshitter, right, and we were all along for the ride. We would go to clubs and go up to the bouncer and say, 'We're a girlband, we're on the guest list,' and they'd say, 'No, you're not.' Somehow we'd convince them to let us in.

Emma: We'd go out on a Wednesday. It was drum 'n' bass night and we'd go to that. Me and Mel B used to love it and then Geri would come and try to get into it as well. Geri was doing all her voguing and we'd be like, 'What is going on?'

Biff Stannard, songwriter and producer: They were nurtured. It wasn't so much that they were told what to do but because they had time living together they figured it out for themselves. It's so rare. There were other bands that lived together, like Five did later on, and what they learned was which ones hated each other. So it can be counterproductive.

Chris Herbert: For this to be authentic and convincing they had to be like sisters. That was only ever going to happen by chucking them in a house together and seeing what manifested. It could have gone horribly wrong but actually it was the making of that band. During the best part of a year that's where Girl Power was really born and they just became this unstoppable unit. All the DNA happened there.

Emma: [We were] very confident together, like, 'We're going to make this happen.' We even wrote a song called 'We're Gonna Make This Happen'. So it was just thinking it, feeling it, going for it, having each other's backs; we just felt like we could do it.

Chris Herbert: They had the ability to sing and dance but they hadn't necessarily considered being in a band, so there was a lot of work to be done in terms of getting them to perform like a proper fully fledged act. I had to drill them every day: rehearsing the same four songs, the same choreography, doing vocal lessons. In Geri's case, she was a bit of a wooden horse in terms of her dancing ability, so she would go down to Pineapple Studios and have dance classes in the evening. I should think it was pretty bloody boring for them. But I'd still say to this day they were at their best vocally back then.

I needed to get them to the point where they could showcase that to the best in the industry.

Mel B: I had absolutely no doubt we were going to make it. Our original managers kept telling us we weren't ready and we'd be constantly pestering them to get people down from record companies to come and see us. When they did we'd be the ones taking phone numbers and networking.

Emma: We were asking for a contract and they were like, 'We're not sure how ready we are for that, we don't know how good you are yet.' By the time they wanted a contract we felt strong on our own.

Melanie C: We wanted things to be moving quicker. We wanted something solid. And we were skint. I was signing on and claiming housing benefit before we were put in this house. We wanted a little bit more stability.

Chris Herbert: My biggest tussle was with Geri. I love Geri to bits, I think she's brilliant, and I've not worked with anyone else who is as focused and ambitious, but she definitely lacked in other areas. I didn't think they were ready and Geri wanted the quicker route. I wanted to get them ready for a showcase, then I wanted to assemble their creative team, then once we had the writers and producers I wanted to get to the studio and craft the best part of the album. Then take that to a record label. As time went on, Geri was getting frustrated. She and I would argue because she wanted us to get a song off the shelf and take it to a label to get a singles deal. I'm not going to deny [this process] was very frustrating for them, but I felt it was necessary.

Melanie C: It was a really bold and brave move [to leave Chris and Bob Herbert]. But we just felt like they didn't understand what we had. I'm sure some of it was naïvety and maybe foolishness, but everything we ever dreamed of, we made happen. We needed management that shared that vision and we felt like we were maybe being held back because they were being realistic. They were like, 'Girls, don't run before you can walk,' and we were like, 'No, no, we're ready to go.'

Chris Herbert: I wanted to get them under contract and the girls wanted to be under contract. My partners at the time included my father and a financial backer called Chic Murphy. Chic was a bit of an old-school promoter and manager and his view was that any one of these girls is interchangeable. Do not make them feel secure. As long as they are feeling insecure, they're going to be fighting for their position and you'll be getting their A game. He was vehemently against putting them under contract and I was fighting for it. In the end, I got them to draw up a contract and we issued that contract to the girls and their lawyers. What I didn't realise was there was a bit of stalling tactics going on because during the course of that [process] the rot had set in and the girls were starting to think more independently. They had met people in the industry who were saying, 'You girls are the next big thing,' everything they wanted to hear, so that contract never got signed. That's how they got away. Big lesson learned.

Steve Anderson, songwriter and producer: I think the Spice Girls were so needed at the time. It was the anti to everything else that was going on. Biff tells a story of how he went for a meeting with Jason Donovan and it happened to be at the same studio the Spice Girls were at. He walked out of his meeting and Mel B literally jumped on his back and said, 'Who are you and what do you do?' A week later they wrote 'Wannabe'.

Biff Stannard: They interrogated everyone they met – 'Are you married? Gay? Straight?' Everything was asked. Like they were shining a bright light in your face. As soon as I said I'd done 'Steam' by East 17, which they loved, Mel dragged me into the showcase and introduced me as 'Biff – he wrote "Steam"', and it went from there. Everyone else was asked to leave, which was very flattering at the time, and they just performed three or four songs for me. It's a bit like that Adele thing; you're just really entertained by them instantly. Really funny. Watching their bond and how they got on was really magnetising.

'"Wannabe" is a punk record'

Hugely passionate, fiercely determined and brilliantly bonkers, the newly christened Spice (the 'Girls' bit was added later after record label bigwigs kept referring to them as 'those Spice Girls') needed a single that somehow encapsulated all those qualities. It was the job of Biff and his co-writer and co-producer Matt Rowe to try to keep up with them in the studio, with 'Wannabe' one of their first completed songs. Later, at new label Virgin Records' behest, the song would go through various different guises, even relegated from debut-single status at one point.

Melanie C: Matt and Biff had a tiny little writing room at [east London studios] Strongroom. All five of us bundled into this tiny space with them and we were just so full of energy and excitement. We were so close that we all had our silly little sayings and Biff just wanted to get that on tape. There were no rules; just go with it. 'Wannabe' was written very quickly. We didn't know it would ever see the light of day – it was us just experimenting, having fun and being the Spice Girls.

Biff Stannard: It sounds like a night out. I just remember thinking, 'If I was a straight guy, I would be so intimidated by them.' They were making me feel borderline uncomfortable because they were so in your face – and let's be honest, all gay men love women like that – so I idolised them instantly. I wanted them to write about that. About what a force of nature they were. 'Wannabe' is like a punk record. It's about how they make men feel. I remember having a lie-down after a session and waking up and Matt had written a Post-it note on the tape saying, 'Press play and listen to this.' I remember thinking, 'Bloody hell, that's good.' The demo pretty much is what the final version became.

Mel B: For the record, I wrote the rap in the toilet.

Geri: I remember Mel B coming out with 'zig-a-zig-ah'. She's got that fantastic thing as a writer where she can come up with the final bit that can give a song its personality. That *zing*.

Emma: For me, ['zig-a-zig-ah'] is definitely a bit naughty. It's not quite as naughty as what Mel B would say.

Mel B: Never going to tell. It's whatever you want it to be.

Biff Stannard: Of course 'zig-a-zig-ah' is about sex! I think people figured it out because whenever they'd perform it Mel B would always do that thing with her legs, which looks pretty sexual.

Geri: I remember thinking on the chorus it had to be 'got to get wid my friends' because 'wid' was just cool. I was much more about the cake of a song – the repetitive chant of the song. It was written effortlessly.

Biff Stannard: They were like the band you'd always dream of working with. They knew exactly who they were and what they wanted to be, so therefore I knew exactly in my head how it should sound. This was back when you'd get artists for three days or a whole week; it was a real pleasure. You don't get that any more. So we did the trilogy of songs – 'Wannabe' on day one, 'Feed Your Love' on day two and '2 Become 1' on day three. Then there was three or four sessions after that where we did 'Mama' and 'If You Can't Dance'. It was quite easy because they're all songwriters, then there's me and Matt, so you have seven songwriters in the room.

Geri: I can't remember who did what [on 'Wannabe']; it was more about the spilling of a vibe on the page. Writing by yourself fulfils you in a different way because you're really expressing how you feel and you can get more reflective, but when writing with the other Spicies you can feed off each other.

Biff Stannard: Victoria was there for the writing and the recording of the vocals on the 'Wannabe' demo, but she wasn't there for the mastering of the vocals. She was at the dentist, I think.

Geri: I think she was either shopping or . . . bless her . . . some of us . . . I don't know what to say. She wasn't there.

Emma: I thought she was at a wedding. One of them she was at a wedding.

Melanie C: She was there when it was written and demoed. I don't think she was there when we were mastering. There was an absence at some point.

Mel B: When we split from our first managers, we just didn't stop pushing and pushing. We found out Simon Cowell was a big deal in the industry, drove up to London really early and jumped out on him singing 'Wannabe' along to our tape. He said: 'Sorry, girls, I don't think you're quite right,' and went into his office. We've both laughed about that since because he was so very wrong.

Hugh Goldsmith, former managing director of RCA: We were actually very close to signing the Spice Girls before Virgin pipped us to the post. [Their new manager] Simon Fuller was a great friend of Mike [McCormack, RCA's former director of A&R], Jeremy [Marsh, former president, BMG Music Division] and I, and we were already working with him on other artists signed to RCA. As a result, we got to know the girls well when they were talking to potential label homes and, following a memorable Spice Girls showcase in Jeremy's kitchen, we were massively keen to sign them. However, it was a huge deal financially and unfortunately we weren't able to compete with the offer Virgin were prepared to make. We were gutted.

Geri: We'd written an album and ['Wannabe'] was the strange family member that was just there. We knew we had to either lead with it or it would never come out. The record company didn't want to go with it. I walked in on a meeting and heard them saying they wanted us to have a strong R&B flavour and I remember standing there saying, 'We want this song, we want this song.' It was scary, but we had the confidence to stand by it. I fought with [co-managing director] Ashley Newton, who wanted the production of 'Wannabe' to be very R&B. I remember having arguments on the phone time and time again, saying that we were dead in the water if we tried to compete with the Americans at R&B. We had to be who we were. It was very un-airbrushed. It was like a rabble and a collection of voices and feelings and expressions.

Emma: Geri came to me and she was like, 'I think we've got a bit of a problem, I don't think they want the first single to be "Wannabe".' I was adamant that 'Wannabe' had to be the first single. We loved 'Say You'll Be There', which I think they wanted, but 'Wannabe' was like getting a punch in the face. It was *pow*, it was the moment. It had to be first. It was Geri and I that really pushed for that and we did it. Of course we did. Our poor record company didn't have a leg to stand on.

Biff Stannard: We were really involved in those discussions because we were such good mates by that point. They were still learning [about the music industry] so they would ring us and Geri would say, 'They want this or that.' But they had creative control contractually. Simon Fuller got them such a great deal where they, along with Simon, got to pick the singles so they would have been able to override Virgin anyway contractually via lawyers. If you're in a room with them and they say the single is 'Wannabe', you're not going to say no.

Emma: That's what was so lovely about it, because we weren't corrupted by the industry. We didn't know who we should or shouldn't be speaking to. I loved that about us. It's about the heart of the Spice Girls. It still feels very pure.

Biff Stannard: They used to dress me up in the studio. They just got really bored and they'd dress me up in make-up while we were making '2 Become 1'. With that song, Matt Rowe and Geri were having a fling of sorts and I think Matt had written the first two lines lyrically. It was a very '90s thing of having the third single be a ballad. Then the ballads turned into a big thing for them. No one goes for a wee at a Spice Girls gig during the ballads, do they?

Joe Stone, journalist and superfan: I didn't massively care about the ballads, but definitely having that safe-sex message [in '2 Become 1'] fuelled my capacity at that age to be a know-it-all. They gave you the tools to really make adults uncomfortable, like I'd say, 'Obviously this is about wearing a condom, it's really important to practise safe sex.'

Biff Stannard: I think it was me and Emma who really wanted to get that line [about safe sex] in. Back then you'd think there would be some kind of pushback but the whole band thought it was great. I think it's really sweet the way she sings that line. I've often wondered if people did start wearing condoms more because of that.

'Suddenly we had something really important we had to do'

Having battled for 'Wannabe' to be the lead single, the girls faced another problem; a music industry with the adage 'if it ain't broke don't fix it' tattooed across its forehead in 60ft letters. The last pop act to truly cross over in the UK had been Take That, leading to a slew of oddly hairless boybands. Cute, energetic and prone to a perfectly timed hip thrust, they spoke directly to pop's core fanbase, AKA teenage girls and gay men. On paper, a new girlband who weren't making R&B were headed straight for the dumper. Even pop magazines were hedging their bets, with Big! *calling them 'a poppier version of Eternal' and predicting a chart peak of eighteen in an early review of 'Wannabe'. That would pale into insignificance compared to* Smash Hits' *initial reaction, however. For the Spice Girls, this only solidified a band mantra that would soon morph into a new religion complete with empowered devotees.*

Alex Needham, former deputy editor, *Smash Hits*: They came in one afternoon and did their act, were sort of flirtatious and full of energy, very in your face, and then they put 'Wannabe' on the cassette player and performed around us. I remember finding it so toe-curling. Geri might have even tried to sit in my lap.

Jordan Paramor, former features editor, *Smash Hits*: This wasn't unusual. One guy brought in his Bontempi organ to play us his music. And we'd get calls saying Ultra were waiting in reception or Bad Boys Inc would pop in. Robbie Williams popped in a lot, too. I just remember these girls coming in, putting their tape on and dancing and singing around us. They were just so confident. I remember sitting there thinking, 'Woah, I could never do that.'

Alex Needham: It became a scandal later because Kate [Thornton, then editor] didn't even come out of her office to watch the performance, which was obviously terrible diplomacy on her part. Anyway, they cleared off and we didn't hear much more about them. I was in charge of printing the song lyrics [in the magazine] and I don't think I even did 'Wannabe'.

Biff Stannard: They got a whiff early on that *Smash Hits* weren't interested. They sort of started the demise of *Smash Hits* because they ostracised them purposely and *Top of the Pops* magazine championed them.

Peter Loraine, former editor, *Top of the Pops* magazine: The record company were like, 'You must write about them, it's going to be huge.' And we were in two minds because other than Eternal there was no one else like that. We knew from our mail bag, and via research groups, that it was all teenage girls that liked boys; they liked boy pop stars. They saw it as 'they're going to get my boy'. So it was going to take something different.

Geri Halliwell: They said they couldn't put us on the cover of magazines because they wouldn't sell any copies.

Alex Needham: Kate's whole direction for the magazine was that she was interested in Britpop, so she wanted us to put the Bluetones on the cover. She was interested in Oasis; that's who she thought *Smash Hits* should be covering. It was a bit of a disconnect.

Peter Loraine: If you were a reader of that magazine and the Bluetones walked past you in the street you wouldn't have known who they were. So they were going in a different direction from us. But we were open-minded about the Spice Girls.

Jordan Paramor: Take That had split, East 17 were on the way out. It was all going a bit wrong. There were a lot of indie bands around, so Shed Seven, the Bluetones, Oasis, Blur.

Peter Loraine: Myself and Susie Boone, who was the deputy editor, went to have lunch with [the Spice Girls] one day at a restaurant in Portobello. We arrived first and it was a bit like a scene out of a film because there was a genuine screech of a car pulling up downstairs. Before [meeting us] they gathered around and did some kind of 'we can do this' chant. They were everything everybody always says they were – loud, funny, entertaining, very bullish. Then they burst into song. This was mainly led by Geri. At one point she leaned over to me and said, 'We know you don't like us.' And I was like, 'That's really not true.' 'Well, we've been told you're in two minds about writing about us,' and I said, 'Well, yes, but the reason is that at the moment most of our readers like reading about boys.' Then with 'Wannabe', and with Girl Power, they spun it and they very clearly knew how they were going to do something different.

Mel B: You have to remember, me, Vic and Mel C came from a dance background and Emma went to Sylvia Young, so all of us had been going to auditions since we were really young and you learn that rejection is just part of the job. I even auditioned to be part of the von Trapp family in a theatre production of *The Sound of Music* despite my mum saying, 'They will just want white, blond kids, Melanie.' We were all used to having to prove ourselves again and again and Geri was just a born hustler – she had so much drive and confidence so we just thought, 'Right, let's go bang on the next door.'

Melanie C: We always felt we were more like a New Kids on the Block or a Take That, but we didn't put two and two together and go, 'Oh, we're girls, that's an issue.' We went into it thinking it was a level playing field and very quickly we learned that it wasn't.

Lee Thompson, former head of music, Viking FM, Hull: There was a guy who I worked with, Steve Jordan, and he'd had these five whirling dervish girls come in one day to be interviewed for the evening show. They were talking over each other, it was like they'd had no media training whatsoever, but that was the charm of the Spice Girls. Steve's words to me as they left were, 'That's the last we'll see of those girls.' This was just before 'Wannabe' came out. When you spoke to people at Virgin at the time they had no idea that 'Wannabe' was going to be this massive global hit.

H from Steps: At the time, Britpop was dominating the charts – I mean I loved a bit of Britpop – and there was a massive knee-jerk reaction to pure, classic, cheesy pop. And that's what the Spice Girls did – they came out unashamedly with a massive Girl Power banger. Even though you couldn't use them as a template for us as a band, they definitely brought pop back. They made it much easier for us to knock on people's doors and go, 'HI!'

Jeremy Joseph, owner, G-A-Y: The first show the Spice Girls ever did was at G-A-Y. It's funny because they'd just got to number one with 'Wannabe' but they did five or six songs. We try to make sure the shows we put on are just the hits and the new single. But with the Spice Girls, it was really interesting that every song got this amazing reaction. People were going mad for songs they'd never heard before.

Joel Babbington, co-host of *Right Back at Ya!* podcast: I was five when the Spice Girls came out and for me growing up in a low-income household in Essex, which could be a bleak time, it made it all feel so optimistic. Just a beam of joy that was shone into my house. It was that pure escapism. Like, I want to live in the world they're in.

Melanie C: We never set out to be this feminist, Girl Power movement, but because record labels had mentioned [girlbands don't sell], magazines had mentioned it, we were like, 'Fuck this, we've got a point to prove.' We're here and we're going to do this for the girls. Thank God for that sexism because it gave us an opportunity to change things. We wanted to have fun, we wanted to go out there, we wanted to make music, we wanted to perform, we wanted to be famous, but suddenly we had something really important we had to do.

Biff Stannard: I was watching some old interviews they did recently where they would take journalists to task about some sexist remarks they made. It was very easy to mock the Girl Power feminism side but it was a big thing back then. And [especially] coming off the back of the whole *Loaded* generation with lad culture. They were fearless.

Geri: [Girl Power] was an organic thing that existed within us already. I'd heard Shampoo say [the phrase Girl Power] and I thought, 'Oh, that's good.' That phrase epitomised what we stood for. It was about celebrating each other and celebrating the generation. It doesn't have to be sharp elbows – it's pulling you up rather than putting you down.

Jordan Paramor: Feminism started to really come to the fore more – before that if you were a feminist you were just seen as an angry old woman. The Spice Girls gave women permission to go, 'No, it's Girl Power, we're amazing.' It influenced the whole next generation of girls growing up.

Laura Snapes, journalist, editor and superfan: A combination of going to a girls' school and Girl Power really bolstered my world view of 'boys suck and girls are much better'. A very seven-year-old way to see the world. I had no conception of what feminism was.

Jordan Paramor: Ladette culture was still going but it was morphing into something else. Ladette was more, 'You have to like Oasis, you have to go to gigs and drink pints and keep up with the lads.' Then the Spice Girls came along and changed the landscape. You knew they were going out and partying, but they were doing it in a different way. They weren't drinking pints; they were drinking really nice wine at the Met Bar.

Nicole Appleton, All Saints: I always saw [ladette] as meaning that you drank pints, and I didn't drink pints! That's why I didn't like it. I'd drink Champagne and margaritas. I was a Champette.

Jordan Paramor: Everything got a bit classier, because it had been a bit grubby and grimy. I think a lot of young people didn't feel cool enough to feel part of that Britpop, ladette world, but the Spice Girls came along and it was like, 'Okay, well I can be part of this.'

Paul Flynn, journalist and author: That was one of the beauties of the Spice Girls – they could appeal to girls but they also had a lad mag quality to them. They were the girls you'd see in clubs, or versions of that. There was something quite elite suburban about them; gobby, funny. And, apart from Geri, they were all regional.

Melanie C: We were at the BRITs in February 1996, so we still hadn't released anything, and Virgin Records invited us. We had a few drinks, as one does at the BRITs, especially in the '90s, and there were words between myself and Victoria. I think I told her where to go and so the next day I was in really big trouble. I didn't think I'd done anything wrong. That for me was a huge turning point because it made me very controlling of myself. This was my dream as much as anybody else's and to think I could fuck it up for me, fuck it up for the other girls, completely freaked me out. It set me on that road of not ever finding myself in that situation again. I became very disciplined, to the point of it becoming a bit of an issue later on in my career.

Laura Snapes: As I got older and I started reading about the Spice Girls in grown-up media, as opposed to kids' media, you'd get to see what their lives were, or supposedly were, and just the horrible ways they were treated in the media.

Melanie C: Early on, certain things were said, even before we were in the public eye, that made me feel very conscious about my size. It was something that never affected me until I was in the public eye and I became so hyper-sensitive being photographed, going to shoots and being criticised and commented on constantly. I was striving for perfection for fear of not being good enough. I went into a tailspin of trying to become what I visually thought a pop star should look like in the '90s.

Laura Snapes: I remember the tabloids' fixation with Mel C's sexuality very precisely. Reading about them through that lens gave me a more keenly developed sense of how women were expected to be in the public eye and that's a deeper seed sowing for a developed sense of feminism.

'You could see my nipples and the video was banned in India'

Released on 26 June 1996, 'Wannabe' spent seven weeks at number one in the UK, finishing the year as the country's second biggest-selling single behind the Fugees' 'Killing Me Softly'. On the European Hot 100, it was number one for nine weeks, eventually replaced by the band's second single, 'Say You'll Be There'. In America – the lucrative but often elusive market for most UK pop acts at that time – 'Wannabe' spent a month at number one, while global sales of their debut album, Spice, *quickly rocketed past the 20 million mark. Their household name status was assisted by their very own pop superhero nicknames; Posh, Sporty, Scary, Baby and Ginger. The ride to global domination was a bumpy one, however, with 'Wannabe''s messy, chaotic, backflip-heavy video – filmed in London's King's Cross after a proposed shoot in Barcelona fell through – nearly scrapped in favour of something more polished. Once again, the band knew best.*

Gregg Masuak, video director: I had actually been approached by the record company to remake the 'Wannabe' video, which they hated. As did I when I first saw it – I thought it was bullshit. They didn't want it to represent the girls. Now it's such an iconic video, we all love it, because it just was shit and stupid but in a really good way. And perfectly them. So I was bummed when the management and the band told the record company to fuck off; they weren't going to remake it. But I'm really pleased that stupid, shit video is out there.

Geri: We were protective of [the 'Wannabe' video]. Plus we were so busy by that point that we couldn't shoot another one anyway.

Jordan Paramor: They made pop fun again. It's that simple. Boyzone were really nice guys, but they weren't wearing Union Jack dresses or jumping on tables. They were sitting on stools.

Mel B: My hair caused controversy [in the 'Wannabe' video], because the stylists wanted to straighten it and I refused. I wanted to go out there in my 'fro. I wanted to be who I was. I was given some Alexander McQueen trousers and a designer top I hated. I ran out and bought a cheap yellow top for a couple of quid, came back with it and put it on – without a bra. The problem was St Pancras Station was pretty derelict at the time and freezing cold so you could see my nipples and the video was banned in India.

Brian Higgins, songwriter and producer: We'd just started Xenomania and I started to hear a murmur about the Spice Girls and, me being as competitive as I am, I didn't want to like it. But when I saw them interviewed I couldn't believe it. I thought they were incredible. I just thought, 'I don't know any girls like that.' So intimidating and sexy and frightening and confident. Once I put that with the record and heard 'Say You'll Be There', I just thought, 'Oh my God, this is incredible.'

Louise Nurding: I remember being in south-east Asia on tour and hearing about this new girlband that were releasing a record and going, 'I wonder how that will do.' I thought the video was interesting and exciting. Then a couple of weeks later I remember going, 'Oh my God, it's blowing up.' I thought it was so good for young girls and women in the pop industry, that they were shifting that amount of records and creating that amount of excitement.

Paul Flynn: It just exploded in a way that hadn't happened before – Take That were such a slow burn. When the girl version of it appeared, it was right out of the box enormous. What I thought was so clever about 'Wannabe' was that one line about 'getting with my friends'. That as a message to send out to school-age kids was always going to have repercussions for years. Pop songs were all about heartbroken women, or women chasing love, and 'Wannabe' was like, 'No, my friends are more important.'

Geri: I think when you're in a girlband you suddenly feel bulletproof. I think women naturally like hanging out with each other, like a pride of lions. I think it's much easier to defend someone else rather than yourself. Still today, I feel protective over our friendship.

Melanie C: I think because we had each other, and the dynamic of the band, it made us very courageous. When you're in a band like that and you become successful, all of a sudden you feel very protective over each other. Especially at the time. Women were being spoken to in a way that would never happen today. Because I had that strength from, say, Mel B and Geri together, we all just got carried along with that. We wouldn't stand for anything. We were Spice sisters.

Chris Cowey, executive producer, *Top of the Pops*: 'Wannabe' was brilliantly written, brilliantly produced. The video was superb. And *Top of the Pops* played a massive part in that whole marketing thing because their nicknames were down to Peter Loraine, who was the editor of *Top of the Pops* magazine.

Peter Loraine: During that initial lunch in Portobello I said that we would write about them and, to do something that's bespoke to the magazine, why don't we give them nicknames? They loved that. Fast forward a few weeks later and we were doing our first photoshoot with them and [all the nicknames] slotted into place. But we didn't make a big deal out of it – we were working on a piece and there were a few of us in the room, probably about three or four people, and together we all came up with the names. So it was my idea that we would do the nicknames but the names just came about from what we were calling them among ourselves.

Emma: I loved mine. I'll say it a thousand times, I really love mine. I've always been like that.

Mel B: I thought Scary Spice was funny. I didn't feel it defined me because I knew who I was and I also thought it was quite handy to have people being a bit scared . . . but that's not who I really am.

H from Steps: We tried to kind of do that – so I was Hyperactive Steps, Claire was Smiley Steps, Lee was Sporty Steps, Faye was Curly Steps, Lisa was Party Steps. It was like, 'Why are we trying to do this?' They had to put you in a box to appeal to that young audience.

Paul Flynn: It was pop working at its most potent. It's the people that look like you, that sound like you, but a bit better. And the possibility of fame and riches, of hanging out with important and powerful people and going to amazing places – all those dreams that the '80s instilled in us. Oasis were the same; they wore the same clothes as their fans but slightly better. It was very working class, too. Even Victoria Beckham is what you'd call nouveau riche. I always thought that Posh Spice was a really funny name for her. I remember my friend slept with someone and said, 'Oh my God, he was so rich he's got more than one type of cheese in his fridge,' and that's what Posh Spice is.

Peter Loraine: There was not a moment where any of us thought it would ever mean a thing to anybody outside the pages of the magazine. But the late Linda Duff, who was the gossip editor of the *Daily Star*, was an old *Smash Hits* journalist from the mid-'80s and she loved pop music. She phoned me up and said, 'I've just read your Spice Girls piece, it's hilarious, I'm going to use these nicknames in the *Daily Star* this week.' So they started calling them by the *Top of the Pops* names. Fast-forward about six months and Simon Fuller phones and says, 'We've just landed in New York and there are hundreds of kids at the airport and they're all just screaming "BABY", "SPORTY", "SCARY".'

Melanie C: With some of us, they don't know our real names.

Peter Loraine: People always say, 'Did the magazine get paid for the idea?', and no, we didn't, but what did happen was that the band were so ferociously loyal to the magazine. We could ring up Virgin Records and say, 'We'd really like Mel C to wear a football shirt because it's the World Cup and would she do it with Spike from 911?' It was great for the magazine – we beat *Smash Hits* and we became the UK's biggest-selling music magazine and the UK's biggest-selling teen magazine. Everything changed as a result of the Spice Girls. Before them our magazine had a ceiling – we couldn't really sell more than 200,000 copies because I believed we were getting almost every teenage pop fan that was interested. Then with the Spice Girls it suddenly went really young.

James Masterton, UK chart geek: From the late '80s to the early '90s, the whole idea of a singles market was in decline. The CD revolution had arrived and the music industry was very excited and had jumped on it straight away. But the idea that kids would purchase CDs wasn't really being contemplated. What you start to see around about '93 and '94 is this gradual transition away from vinyl. By 1995, things gradually started to move in the direction of the CD generation and there was this realisation that the music industry couldn't take for granted the idea that a generation would simply grow up buying pop music. So the industry did need to skew younger and focus in on that. The Spice Girls fit perfectly because they were dressed in primary colours, very bright, very bubbly, and they were nicely poised to take advantage of the fact that the CD single revolution was just about getting into gear.

Peter Loraine: The record sales in that demographic went up; the magazine went from selling 200,000 copies to a Spice Girls cover selling 300,000. So we started putting them on the cover for consecutive months.

'She said she tied her hair up with a pair of knickers'

By the start of 1997, the Spice Girls were the biggest pop culture phenomenon since the Beatles. Their first three singles had all peaked at number one, as had their album. The rate of their success meant they were asked to become the face of nearly every product imaginable, even helping to launch an entire new TV channel.

Gregg Masuak, video director, 'Who Do You Think You Are': My first meeting with them was a wardrobe call and they just exploded like a barrel full of monkeys into the room. You'd never heard so much chatter coming from every angle, from every direction, about everything possible known to mankind. They were really fun. But they were so pressed for time and management were busy building in all these deals. In fact, it was announced that the girls had all become millionaires on the day of the shoot. So that added to their joy.

Peter Loraine: They were so entertaining to speak to. You'd get an hour to interview them and what you'd try to do is three interviews. So one for September, one for October, one for November. Then we'd have five minutes left and it would be, 'Right, let's see how posh Posh Spice is.' Things like, 'Has your dad got a lawnmower that he drives around the garden and sits on?', and she'd go, 'Oh, actually, yes, he does.' If only two of them were available you never thought, 'Oh, please don't let it be X or Y because they're boring.' They were all as brilliant as each other.

Gregg Masuak: When Channel 5 launched it was the Spice Girls that were the first thing shown on the channel and so I did all those initial commercials. But it was only Posh Spice who wanted to have a bucket of water thrown at her. She was like, 'I'll do that, no worries.'

Peter Loraine: We used to divide it up, who would interview each person, and I used to do Victoria. She was so funny. Half the time I'm not even sure she knew she was being funny. She told me one day she'd got up really early and had been pulled over by the police because she was driving too fast. She said she tied her hair up with a pair of knickers as she had to get out of the car.

Chris Cowey, producer, BRIT Awards 1997: They were so clear about what they wanted to do. But they had this veneer of carefree fun about them. None of us knew Geri was going to come out in *that* dress. I got a real roasting from someone at a lecture I did at an American university for over-sexualising women because of the crotch shot of Geri. I had to explain that it wasn't intended as that – there was a ramp that led up onto the stage and the camera was at the bottom looking up. We genuinely didn't know Geri was going to come out in that dress so the camera configuration was arranged in advance. It was then unavoidable we'd see her knickers.

Geri: Charging around the world and being interviewed and all those things, that can be draining. I remember going to Asia and we'd be so jet-lagged that we felt drunk. We'd go straight into promo and we were so tired we'd just laugh.

Melanie C: [The schedule] was absolutely insane. I found an old Filofax – so '90s – and I was having a flick through it and it was like, 'New York, London, Dublin, Taiwan'. The amount of countries and continents we were in in a week was ridiculous. Obviously it's one of those situations where the more experienced people around you were like, 'This isn't going to last forever,' so it was go, go, go.

Gregg Masuak: There was so little time [shooting 'Who Do You Think You Are'] that we needed to race through it. We had to send over an incomplete edit to management to say, 'This is what we still have to do,' and they just went ahead and approved it. Without my approval. To this very day what the world has seen is an incomplete version. It's indicative of the arrogance of hubris; of managers of pop stars who actually don't have the creativity to make things as good as they should be, and could be, with the power to say, 'Yeah, this is done.' Simon Fuller can go fuck himself. Like he cares.

Biff Stannard: We wrote [second album *Spiceworld*'s lead single] 'Spice Up Your Life' in two hours and we recorded it and had it confirmed as the first single in four. There were five mics in a row and I recorded it Motown-style with them all singing. So if Mel B was a bit loud – ha! – I'd get her to step back a bit. And Emma could come forward a bit. We sent it to Simon and he came back within an hour saying, 'That's the first single,' so the pressure was off. But then they said, 'Oh, we're going to make a movie at the same time.'

'We were in danger of becoming a joke musically'

Everything about the Spice Girls' early success felt like it was on fast-forward. Released just fourteen months after their debut album, November 1997's Spiceworld *(14 million global sales) was quickly followed a month later by the Golden Raspberry-winning film of the same name. In America, where* Spice *had only been released in February that year, it meant they had two albums on the* Billboard *Hot 100 at the same time, a fact that led to criticisms of money-grabbing. An accusation not helped by the fact that their perma-smiling visages adorned everything from lollipops to cameras to mopeds. Around that time the band also sacked Simon Fuller as their manager, a move that tipped mounting criticisms over into a very British build-them-up-and-tear-them-down backlash. In the UK, it had been brewing ever since Geri had the temerity to not only plant a big red kiss on Prince Charles's cheek – breaking royal protocol – but also squeeze his bum.*

Biff Stannard: They had announced the second album was coming that November [in 1997] and we hadn't even started.

Melanie C: We were shooting the movie, so we had a mobile studio onset. I remember 'Stop' was written [with Andy Watkins and Paul Wilson, AKA Absolute] onset. The movie took six weeks to film, which is crazy. The album took longer.

Biff Stannard: They'd turn up in the outfits from the film. They were soldiers one day or they'd come as Spice Girls in their full get-up. It was really weird. Then we'd have to create that mood where we had to write a song.

Melanie C: I love speaking to Biff because he fills in so many gaps, because that time was crazy.

Biff Stannard: We were at Abbey Road for about three or four months, but we only did three or four songs in that period because you'd sometimes only get them for an hour. There are frog sounds on 'Never Give Up on the Good Times' because we were so bored, so we'd embellish and embellish. I'm a massive New Order fan and there's a frog on their *Low-Life* album and I remember thinking, 'I really want to put frogs on this song.' There were big burly security guards in the studio literally tapping their watches, waiting to take them to shoot the film. It was like, 'Hang on a minute, the reason you're here and they're making the film is because of what we did in a tiny room a year ago.'

Melanie C: Biff's so mild-mannered, he's such a big softie, so for him to lose his rag was a big deal. That would have made us all sit up.

Biff Stannard: I asked them really politely to leave and then thought, 'Fuck this,' and we moved to a smaller vocal room and sat on the floor with a guitar and wrote 'Viva Forever'. That's the only time I got frustrated with the situation. It had all got so big and we were all going a bit mad.

Lee Brennan, 911: I dated Emma around the end of 1997. It all had to be perfectly timed with her tour manager and my tour manager. She'd fly in from somewhere and be like, 'I'm landing here, you need to be at that gate at that time and there will be paparazzi so you need to duck down.' It was crazy. With 911, we didn't have people chasing us all the time. But as soon as there was any inkling of 'Is this guy seeing a Spice Girl?', they were following me everywhere. We went to Ireland for a week and that was mental. There were a few fights with photographers because they just don't give a shit, half of them. I think they sent an undercover guy to stay in the same hotel as us.

Melanie C: I think in the initial meetings we had with Simon Fuller we talked about wanting to do a film. Some of the first trips we took to LA were to have meetings with Disney and different studios.

Mel Blatt, All Saints: For me, that was the main thing with the Spice Girls that I had a problem with. It's a way of life now, but they were kind of the first people to put their names on everything, like every day, everywhere, everywhere, everywhere. Using that to promote themselves as well. That's what I had a problem with, so when we were being compared to them I was like, 'No, no, no.' We write our own music, we're here to perform, we're not selling anything. We wanted to be a band, just a band.

Shirley Manson, Garbage: I felt that the creation of the Spice Girls was a hideously cheap effort by a bunch of old white men in the music industry, invested in exploiting the injection of female rebellion into mainstream pop. The whole campaign felt very manipulative, transparent and cynical to me at the time. It wasn't ['Girl Power' as a slogan] that bothered me at all, but the pretence of it. I never felt that these girls were in charge of their songwriting, their style or their imaging. The power remained solely with the men who were managing, writing and producing their career. The 'girls' held no power whatsoever from where I was sitting. It all felt so fake to me.

Melanie C: One of the big factors in leaving Simon Fuller was to do with the endorsements. Each of us girls have different reasons, but for me I've always wanted to sing and make music and perform live, but there was a point where the endorsements had just completely overtaken everything we were doing music-wise. We were in danger of becoming a joke musically. That was part of the reason I started to lose faith in Simon as a manager because it was taking us in a direction I didn't feel was right for the band.

Alex Needham: It's the acts who have a sense of joy about it, and authenticity, which the Spice Girls had in spades, that do well. I feel like it was their own creation, as much as they were marketed heavily. Looking retrospectively, you can tell the ones who were being ordered about from the ones who did have some agency. The Spice Girls were selling so many records that they felt confident in sacking Simon Fuller right in the middle of it and taking ownership of it – they had the moxie to turn around and say, 'I don't think it should be done like this.'

Melanie C: Things became really difficult once Simon had gone. For whatever reason, whether it's a patriarchal thing of 'the man that made you' – which isn't true because we came to Simon fully formed and he helped facilitate what we wanted to achieve – it was a very interesting turn from the tabloid media. They really tried to knock us down, like, 'How dare they succeed without a man at the helm?'

'I took myself to bed for at least forty-eight hours'

At the start of 1998, the Spice Girls embarked on their first concert tour, starting off in Europe before eventually heading over to America. On 26 May, the band landed back in the UK after two shows in Helsinki. Promo for new single 'Viva Forever' was scheduled for the next day via a performance in front of Carol Smillie on the National Lottery Live *show. Only Geri didn't turn up. She was, according to Melanie C at the time, not feeling great but would be back soon. The next day, however, as the rest of the band flew to Oslo to continue with the tour, Geraldine announced via her lawyer that she had left the Spice Girls. Consequently the news meant that the official England World Cup song, '(How Does It Feel to Be) On Top of the World', released a day later and featuring the girls alongside the dulcet tones of Space, Ocean Colour Scene and Echo and the Bunnymen, was to be the last Spice Girls song recorded with Halliwell until 2007. It peaked at number nine.*

Emma Bunton: It was odd. Jade [Jones, Damage vocalist and Emma's husband] was on the flight [back to the UK] with us and I remember [Geri] saying, 'I'm going now. Bye, everyone.' I actually thought, 'That's weird,' and Jade picked up on it, too.

He was like, 'You never say goodbye to each other, you'll be seeing her again in four hours.' I didn't know, obviously, but I thought it was odd.

Melanie C: I got the bloody short straw, didn't I, having to fucking say, 'Get well soon, Geri' [on *National Lottery Live*]. I'm the worst person to do that because I'm the worst liar, but we truly believed she'd come back. We thought she was having a bit of a wobble. There'd been times in the past where people had walked away from the band in the heat of the moment. So we hoped she'd be back, but no, she was definitely gone for good . . . Well, until 2007.

Simon Ellis, musical director on the Spiceworld tour: I was walking the streets of Oslo at about 4 p.m. and I got the call saying, 'Geri's left,' and I was like, 'What do you mean she's left?' They were like, 'She's left the band.' We had a show that night, so I said, 'Right, get the girls down to rehearsals,' and we literally sat around the piano, the four girls that were left and me, and we went through the songs saying, 'You're singing that bit, you're doing that bit.' The girls all knew Geri's parts anyway, so it was kind of easy. The main concern was that somebody was going to forget that Geri wasn't there and they'd look around and think, 'Why isn't she singing her part?'

Mel B: It felt very weird but the four of us had these real showbiz backgrounds and we all knew the show had to go on, but of course it just didn't feel right on that day.

Chris Cowey: Before Geri left, we did their final performance on *Top of the Pops* and you could tell she didn't want to know. She was looking all frumpy and disinterested. It was very obvious that there was some kind of schism going on there.

Alex Needham: It's an inevitability with bands, isn't it? You're tired, you're spending all day with each other, you're getting on each other's tits. It's just a fact of life. Then there's all the other unpleasant stuff – like their ex-boyfriend speaks to a paper about what they were like in bed and their family sells stories – and all of that takes its toll. You can't trust anyone.

Emma: We talk about it now and I've had it out with her, because I love Geri. We have a great relationship and we did back then, but I just felt like she'd left me.

Joe Stone: Geri leaving was truly devastating for me. I'd lost two or three grandparents at that point and it had really not touched the sides in comparison. They had played such a massive part in my childhood. It also felt in conflict with everything they'd led me to believe, which was friendship never ends. I took myself to bed for at least forty-eight hours. I was having food brought to me – I was inconsolable. To try to soothe me, my mum was like, 'Oh, there will be something else that you love just as much as the Spice Girls,' and she suggested that I could become a B*Witched fan. I remember fucking losing it at that point.

Melanie C: It was really hard to come to terms with and we were all very upset by it. She had her reasons and she was very unhappy and having a hard time, so of course with time we've come to forgive her. And she has since apologised . . . On stage at Wembley in front of 70,000 people. Very Geri. I think she might have felt her time was done with the Spice Girls, but we didn't. Also, we had an American tour to fulfil. Our biggest fear at the time was that it would jeopardise that tour because they were expecting five girls.

Biff Stannard: I'm a massive Pet Shop Boys fan, especially lyrically, and we always thought it would be great to call the last song on an album 'Goodbye'. And that felt like quite a Neil and Chris thing to do. I think that's initially what [1998 single 'Goodbye'] was, rather than about Geri, but later when we met up with them [on tour] in Nashville and we were talking more, it changed. The middle eight that Victoria sings is definitely about Geri.

'I feel like a lot of the pop girls we know and love owe part of their career to them'

Recording for the band's third and final (SO FAR!) album started in mid-1999 with long-term collaborators Biff Stannard and Matt Rowe. Sessions with Eliot Kennedy (who previously co-wrote Pepsi advert soundtrack 'Step to Me' in 1997) and white-hot R&B futurist Rodney Jerkins followed, but recording was interrupted by various solo endeavours and an eight-date 'we're still friends, you guys!' UK Christmas tour. The album was finally finished in July 2000, with fans voting via the World Wide Web to call the album Third Time Around. *Ignoring democracy, the band went with* Forever *– a title anchored by cover art featuring the band members desperately gripping each other's hands as if tied to a chain-link fence – and it was released on 1 November 2000. In a much-publicised chart battle, the album was beaten to number one by sensible coat enthusiasts Westlife. In America the album stalled at thirty-nine. A month later, promotion for the album ceased, bringing* *the band's whirlwind four-year career to an end . . . That was until they reunited in 2007 for a greatest hits album, which included a new single, 'Headlines (Friendship Never Ends)', and world tour.*

Melanie C: I think we all felt that whatever came next needed to have a change of direction. That's when we worked with Jimmy Jam & Terry Lewis and Rodney Jerkins, so we felt it was time to try something a little different with *Forever.*

Laura Snapes: I barely remember any of the songs on *Forever* outside of 'Holler'.

Emma: 'Holler''s a banger.

Joe Stone: I just thought *Forever* was dog shit. I've never been the type of fan where you just uncritically consume everything they do.

Gregg Masuak, director 'Let Love Lead the Way': There were two singles and I got the ballad, which sucked. I was in the States when they asked me and it always felt like, 'Can Gregg do it? He's got two days and £100k less than the other videos.' It was nice to see them but it was much more grown-up than my previous experience. When I did the Channel 5 commercials with them, Victoria was talking about this footballer she had a crush on; then by the time I did that video she's on the phone talking about what designer shit Brooklyn was going to wear that day.

Lucie Cave, editor-in-chief, *Heat* magazine: Victoria and David were just unbelievable. Her and Jade Goody would be our biggest sellers. You wanted to know everything about her life. I remember Geri fuelled many a *Heat* interview and cover. You'd follow these people through their love lives and their bodies.

Dean Piper, former celebrity journalist: I cocked up once with Emma Bunton. We were in ['fancy' central London club] Funky Buddha and we were drinking. I remember we smoked half a packet of B&H and she was quite pissed and we had an open chat about the Spice Girls. They'd not long broken up, so I was like, 'Come on, when are you going to get back together?' I then went into the loo, took out my Nokia 3210 and I wrote down the whole thing and texted it to one of my colleagues and said, 'Just keep this for me tomorrow.' Then I did an exclusive in the *People* newspaper like, 'Emma Bunton opens up about the Spice Girls'. She was furious. Obviously. I'd completely broken her trust.

Gregg Masuak: I always thought Emma got the short end of the stick in terms of the persona she had to play. Just be really cute and innocent. The others got to let loose and they had the ability to be more physical. So I nicknamed her Grumpy Spice because she always had to be aware of herself and not swear or go wild in case somebody blew the lid off the fact she's not a baby. But when I saw her on set for this video she was much more comfortable presenting herself. When Emma's stylist got the whole brief wrong we had to improvise and so she's just wearing a roll of fabric that's all safety-pinned together. It's not a dress; it's just a piece of fucking fabric that's been draped around her. She's fucking awesome. She didn't complain.

Emma: I was at a difficult point [during the reunion in 2007], because I'd literally just had my baby. I took Beau on tour at three months. I didn't know what to expect really. My body wasn't back in shape; my hips weren't in the right place to be up on stage performing. I look back on it fondly but I probably wouldn't do it again with a three-month-old.

Biff Stannard: We wrote [2007's final single] 'Headlines' separately, so we never had that chemistry. Matt had to fly to America to record Mel B and Victoria and then I did the other three in the UK. It was very difficult at that point to get five people back into that headspace again.

Joe Stone: I think the biggest shock when you talk about their legacy is that they've got the legacy they've got. They're still such a part of popular culture. I don't think any other band has been so globe-conquering but lasted for such a short period.

Laura Snapes: My hope is that it remains a legacy. They're not an act that should have any purchase with seven-year-olds today, because it is of its time. It depresses me when they try to elongate it and stretch it into something it's not. There's always this 'was it feminist or was it capitalist?' thing, but it can very easily be both. They created a world and a sense of belonging that you really wanted to be part of. Especially if you were a shy little kid. All you could see was five women becoming the biggest thing on the planet. They seemed funny and naughty and everywhere and it just implicitly says that you too can be funny and naughty and have mates and be everywhere.

Shirley Manson: I feel differently about them now, looking back. I realise how much they influenced an entire generation of young girls into embracing the idea that they were powerful and could embody any identity within the spectrum of their gender. I realise it was a timely and beautiful experiment that served its purpose with thrust, joy and vigour; I also realise how influential a pop band the Spice Girls were and the immense love they engender to this day. At the time, I couldn't see the positives. I was too obsessed with judging the artifice.

Geri: The music is the legacy – if it's still being played and still being liked then that's wonderful. Let's look at talent shows, for example, you sometimes get amazing voices but it doesn't connect. Why is that? It's because if you don't have that real connection with a personality that's dripping into the song, it doesn't stay with you and it doesn't stick. The testament of a great song is: 'Does it still sound good twenty years later? Do you still want to hear it?'

Melanie C: The best thing for us girls is seeing the change in how female artists are viewed and the opportunities that seem to have opened up for women in music. Now feels like the golden age of being a Spice Girl because so many amazing female artists were Spice Girls fans. It's lovely to hear how they were inspired and empowered by us.

Mel B: Our legacy is our audience. We brought fun back but we also had something to say by celebrating everyone for their differences; gay, straight, Black, white, brown, bi, small, whatever you were, you were welcome to our party. We were – and we still are – all about inclusivity, about Girl Power, about standing up for who you are. In a way we were quite ahead of our time when it came to mixing music and feminism and that makes me proud. Our fans make me proud, the girls make me proud.

★ ★ ★

After 2007–08's hugely successful, full-band line-up comeback tour (the 47-date jaunt made over $200 million), each member continued with their solo projects, be it TV, fashion, more albums or *Strictly Come Dancing*. In 2012, the band reunited to perform at the closing ceremony of the London Olympics as part of the *A Symphony of British Music* celebrations, whizzing around the Olympic Stadium on top of five black cabs to a mash-up of 'Wannabe' and 'Spice Up Your Life'. That heady rush was quickly punctured by Beady Eye covering Oasis's 'Wonderwall'. Posh, Baby, Scary, Sporty and Ginger reformed again briefly later that year at the premiere of their ill-fated jukebox musical, *Viva Forever!*. Written by their 'Who Do You Think You Are' co-star Jennifer Saunders, it was panned by critics and closed after seven months.

The band then almost destroyed any lingering post-Olympics goodwill via the ill-fated GEM project, announced in July 2016 to celebrate the twentieth anniversary of 'Wannabe'. Featuring Geri, Emma and Mel B (hence that acronym), the accompanying video – seemingly filmed on three iPhones – had all the high-gloss production value of a fan-made YouTube tribute to a recently deceased pet. A day later a new song called 'Song for Her' leaked, but, as Emma would later tell me, 'We'd been in the studio again but that was not our focus.' In 2019, and minus Victoria this time, the band reformed for a sold-out UK stadium tour that grossed over $78 million from just thirteen shows. The reunion chimed with a slew of famous fans waxing lyrical about their childhood heroes, be it Adele, Emma Stone, all of HAIM, Charli XCX and Little Mix.

While their biggest hit spoke of dismissing nostalgia – if you want a future, forget the past, etc. – its timelessness lives on. In December 2020, Spotify released a list of the ten most streamed '90s songs by female artists in the year 2020 and nestled above Britney's '. . . Baby One More Time' sat 'Wannabe'. A knockabout, curiously unhinged belter created by a bunch of wannabes that ended up shifting the world on its axis.

* Geri Halliwell quotes taken from my interview for *Beat* magazine, issue 19, summer 2016
* Emma Bunton quotes taken from my interview for *Guardian Guide*, 23 March 2019
* All Saints quotes taken from my interview for *Guardian Guide*, 21 July 2018

2

Who do you think you are? The Spice Girls go solo

Unlike most bands that split up – sorry, 'go on hiatus' – all five members of the Spice Girls embarked on solo careers. For Mel B, Emma, Victoria and Melanie C, releases were scattered in between recording and releasing the final Spice Girls album. In fact, for Mel B – who was the first member to go solo with 1998's excellent, Missy Elliott-assisted banger 'I Want You Back' – this caused a problem when her R&B-leaning album *Hot*, featuring production from Rodney Jerkins and Jimmy Jam & Terry Lewis, arrived less than a month before the Spice Girls' R&B-leaning album *Forever*, featuring production from Rodney Jerkins and Jimmy Jam & Terry Lewis. *Hot* stalled at number twenty-eight.

They also all had to try to steer clear of Geri, whose debut album *Schizophonic*, unleashed in 1999, spawned three number-one singles. Melanie C, meanwhile, had to balance flogging her rock and alt-pop-leaning *Northern Star* album, released in late 1999, with recording and promotion for *Forever*, while Emma and Victoria both sensibly waited until 2001 to properly launch their respective solo adventures. Both did, however, release collaborations in 1999 and 2000, with Emma's Tin Tin Out-assisted cover of 'What I Am' battling with Geri's 'Lift Me Up' for chart supremacy (Geri 'won') and later Victoria's garage anthem 'Out of Your Mind' featuring True Steppers and Dane Bowers going toe to toe with Spiller and Sophie Ellis-Bextor's 'Groovejet (If This Ain't Love)'. In the end Victoria's tune didn't punish enough people, peaking in the runner-up spot.

Between them the five members of the Spice Girls scored twenty-eight solo UK top-ten singles, which even the sniffiest of critics will agree is not to be sniffed at.

'Someone threw a Weetabix at me'

Jeremy Joseph: Geri wasn't sure who her fanbase was going to be but she knew she had an audience at G-A-Y who loved her. [Her performing 'Look at Me'] was an amazing moment. George Michael came to support her. The reaction was phenomenal. I think she felt that security that she needed. When you're in a band, the other members are your security blanket; leaving a band, you lose that.

Joe Stone: Around the time of single releases, I got a lot of nerves for Geri. They'd had such a run of success that things like [lead single] 'Look at Me' only getting to number two did seem devastating.

Simon Jones, Geri's former PR: There was so much hype. I think everyone was overly confident – Geri was on the cover of every paper every single day – that the label assumed it would be number one. They didn't feel like they needed to do [the classic singles trick] of releasing two CDs and in the end Boyzone kept it off the top. It was super close and, if we had had a CD2, it wouldn't have even been a conversation. I remember getting the midweeks on a Tuesday morning and it not being number one and thinking, 'This is a disaster.'

Laura Snapes: I do think Geri Halliwell is a Dadaist pop genius for some of the stuff she came up with. Like that time at the BRITs [in 2000] when she came out in between the inflatable legs or the video for 'Look at Me', which Taylor Swift must have seen before making the 'Look What You Made Me Do' video, because she also has a funeral for herself.

Simon Jones: The 'Look at Me' video is genius. I remember being in a meeting and Geri said, 'We're going to kill off Ginger Spice in the video,' knowing that those images would then be picked up in all the papers.

Malcolm McLean, author of *Freak Like Me: Confessions of a 90s Pop Groupie*: We went to Geri's house the day after her twenty-seventh birthday. She came out to see us and it had rained loads so she went in and got a T-shirt and towel out. I had to get changed in front of her. I loved the fact that Geri Halliwell was giving me a towel and a T-shirt from her house, but I also had to take my top off in front of her. I still have the T-shirt. But it's really shit and I wore it to death and people would be like '. . . that's the T-shirt'.

Simon Jones: With Geri, there always had to be a stunt and an angle. Geri is the best PR of all time. She doesn't need the money, obviously, but if Geri ever needed another career she could be a PR. Her ability to get herself talked about was amazing.

Dean Piper: I heard on the grapevine that Geri decided she wanted to go through Soho on a unicorn. And her PR at the time went, 'Right . . .' And she went, 'What do you mean? I've seen them in films, just get me a unicorn.' She allegedly thought unicorns existed. She's absolutely brilliant.

Simon Jones: As far as I know that's not true. There are so many stories about Geri. She's incredible. There *was* an Old Compton Street moment around [2004's] 'Ride It' single. It was, 'What are we going to do?' And she was like, 'Why don't I ride a horse down Old Compton Street?' We were going to arrive at G-A-Y so Jeremy [Joseph] was part of it all.

Jeremy Joseph: I think I can take credit for this one. We were looking for mad ideas and I knew she was obsessed with horses, so the idea was 'How about riding a horse down Old Compton Street?' The whole point was to bring London to a standstill. You wanted to maximise everything. If Geri is front page of every paper riding a horse or performing at G-A-Y, then other artists are going to go, 'I want to do that.' It's a snowball effect.

Simon Jones: I had to get a sign made that said, 'Ride It, out now', or something. Awful when you think about it now – so cheap. So I'm standing there trying to fix this sign when she's on the horse and she says, 'Right, let's go,' and I'm like, 'Hang on, the sign's not attached.'

Rick Nowels, songwriter and producer: Working with Geri was fabulous. She's as fun as you'd imagine her to be. She's got a great wit, a great mind. A lot of the sort of conceptual stuff in the Spice Girls' songs came from her – she's a big-picture, positive person. I love our song 'Scream If You Wanna Go Faster'; it should have been the hit. It was going to be the first single and then she did a dance version of 'It's Raining Men'. 'Scream If You Wanna Go Faster' would have given her more of an identity as a cool artist and as a singer-songwriter. 'It's Raining Men' is a cheap shot.

Melanie C: I loved my time with the Spice Girls but it was quite intense and overwhelming and there was always an element of compromise. For me to go out and do things my way was really refreshing for me. At that age, you're discovering who you are and very quickly I was thrown into this arena where lots of people were having an opinion on who I was. I'd read something and I wouldn't recognise that person. I'd be like, 'Is that me? Is that who they want me to be? Is that who I should be?' Sporty Spice in an interview was very different to Sporty Spice on stage. There were all these different things to get your head around.

Biff Stannard: I remember I was really drunk and I was trying to copy Blur's 'Beetlebum' on the guitar. Badly. [Melanie C] walked in when I was playing and just started singing that melody [to debut solo single] 'Goin' Down'. Matt [Rowe] was drunk on the floor. It's quite a sleazy song. The choice of that song as the first single would have been intentional.

Melanie C: I had a bit of a bee in my bonnet at the time. I was quite frustrated about being put in a box. Now I'm older and wiser I get it, but at the time I was really frustrated because I knew there was more to me than just being Sporty Spice.

Biff Stannard: To be fair to Mel, she was a massive fan of Blur, which is probably why I was learning that song. It was a natural sound for her to make. It didn't feel contrived to have loads of guitars on songs with her.

Rick Nowels: I had a manager named Steven Budd in the UK and he called me and said, 'You've got a meeting with Mel C.' I was pretty starstruck. That's a Spice Girl. They were big like the Beatles. She came over to LA not too long after and we sat down and we wrote, and the first song we did was 'Northern Star'.

Melanie C: It was phenomenal. I was having this opportunity to work with these people who'd worked on my favourite album of all time, which was Madonna's *Ray of Light.*

Rick Nowels: *Ray of Light* was a culturally iconic album. So everybody who worked on that album was golden for a bit after that. All cool artists looked at that album for a source of direction and inspiration. It's easy for the record company, like, 'Let's go to the hippest people'. Any project there is you always want the coolest names and the coolest people.

Melanie C: You were not allowed to get out of your lane in the '90s. I was quite naïve – I went out [at V99 festival] thinking, 'My band's great, I'm great, the tunes are great,' and then just had a really divided appreciation from the audience. It was probably the hardest gig I've ever done – someone threw a Weetabix at me, and you need a bloody strong arm because those Weetabix are light – but I'm really grateful for it. It was like a baptism of fire, you know. It set me on this road of earning my stripes as a live performer.

Rick Nowels: I call Geri and Mel C the Lennon and McCartney of the Spice Girls. They're both fantastic songwriters.

Joe Stone: People talked about the Spice Girls as a band being overexposed, which is fair, but I think fatigue really set in with the solo careers. There were five campaigns running simultaneously. There was a real drop in quality because they're the best example of a group being more than the sum of their parts. And that was incredibly exposing when they fractured off into their solo careers.

MNEK, songwriter, producer and '00s pop fan: I grew up at a time when one of the Spice Girls was always releasing something. If Mel B wasn't here doing her solo single, Mel C was with Lisa Left Eye, Victoria was wearing a lip ring, Emma was in the fucking desert and Geri was out there going rogue.

Melanie C: Obviously, starting my career in the Spice Girls, you go from zero to a hundred in no time. We were flying first class, private jets on tour, five-star hotels. Then it came to my solo career and my first album was very successful; second album the troubles started, and then when I was dropped from Virgin Records it was like, 'What now?' So I set up my own label. I wanted to do the exact opposite of everything I'd done so far. I did get in a tour bus and stay in shitty hotels and play some dives. I think it was the making of me as a performer. That made me feel worthy of my position.

David Lim, co-host, *Right Back at Ya!* podcast: That Victoria versus Sophie [Ellis-Bextor] chart battle was brilliant. Obviously the Posh machine was turned up to 100. It was so crucial to be in the tabloids, as well as the constant TV appearances you had to do. Now it's like, where do we get a performance? Where do we get fun personality stuff? It's just BuzzFeed challenges.

Sophie Ellis-Bextor: It was insane. It was even on the news.

Joe Stone: It felt high stakes. My favourite factoid about that is that apparently Victoria was demanding the sale figures were faxed to her every three hours. That feels incredibly late '90s, early '00s.

Laura Snapes: I cried when Groovejet beat 'Out of Your Mind' to number one. Very unfair. I would copy everything they did, even down to their crushes. I've never found David Beckham attractive but, because Victoria did, he became my de facto crush.

Sophie Ellis-Bextor: I think the worst bit was that, when I was number one, I'd agreed to do a Radio 1 roadshow in Plymouth on my own. When I finally got home, I didn't have any food or drink in so I went to the local pub and asked for a glass of Champagne but they didn't have any, so I had a pint and then I started to fall asleep halfway through it. That's how I celebrated.

Joel Babbington: Victoria Beckham had one of the biggest-selling singles of that year, and in any other week it would have been number one, but she was labelled a flop.

Joe Stone: For her first solo single proper, 'Not Such an Innocent Girl', they tried to manufacture another chart battle between her and Kylie with 'Can't Get You Out of My Head', but by that point there was no battle. It got to number six. It really quickly went from everything looking like it could be number one to settling for a top ten.

Nigel Dick, director, Mel B's 'Tell Me' video: You had to stick a pin up [Mel B's] bum a bit because I remember she kept arriving saying she'd only had two hours' sleep. She also told me a few other things that perhaps being a gentleman I should not share. So you just go, 'Yes, thank you very much for sharing, now let's get to work.' She was part of this band of bubbly, sexy girls, so the minute it starts rolling she starts delivering. The trick is to focus her on delivering the maximum Mel B-ness, whatever that is.

Mel B: On 'Tell Me' I had a 10-foot wind machine and complete creative input so it was fantastic.

Nigel Dick: I think subconsciously if you get the brief and they say we've got five loaves and two fish then you come up with an idea that suits that. If they say we've got £350,000, or whatever it was for Mel B, then automatically you go bigger. You want to show the bucks on the screen. I think I stole the idea of the big wind machine from a fashion spread I saw. It's a prop; it gives you something to use to direct – 'Okay, darling, stand here, look fabulous and sing the song.'

Emma: I worked with Tin Tin Out first, which felt like a nice stepping stone.

James Masterton: November 1999 and it was Spice Girl versus Spice Girl, Geri [with 'Lift Me Up'] vs Emma. That was the most extraordinary week because by some strange coincidence the tabloids found out that Geri was having a fling with Chris Evans. It started at the beginning of that week and then magically they split up around the Thursday or Friday. It was a great example of the synergy at play, where the antics of these people were suddenly on the front pages of newspapers with a chart battle going on behind it.

Emma: To be able to get back in the studio with Biff [for 'What Took You So Long'] was really enjoyable.

Biff Stannard: 'What Took You So Long' was really good fun. I'd had that title for a while. It wasn't because she was late; she was always on time. I remember that being a really happy moment when it went to number one. We went out and celebrated.

Gregg Masuak, director, 'What Took You So Long': Poor Emma. We kept on wanting to go to the tropics, but we always ended up somewhere so fucking cold. It was the desert but it was winter time and she was dressed in nothing. I had this idea she would be there at night and all the wolves were going to come and find her and gather around. They were trained but wild. It was only afterwards that she came to me and said, 'This is great, because my biggest fear in the world is dogs.' When you're terrified of dogs you jump in the middle of a ring of wolves – that's Emma.

★ ★ ★

As the chart placings started to diminish, the artists forever known as Scary, Baby, Ginger and Posh gradually shifted their focus away from music. Families were added to, TV careers were cemented, successful fashion labels were launched and a library's worth of books were written. Only Sporty has remained fully committed to the pop grindstone, releasing her eighth album, *Melanie C*, in 2020. It became her first album since 2003 to enter inside the UK top ten.

* Emma Bunton quotes taken from my interview for *Guardian Guide*, 23 March 2019
* Sophie Ellis-Bextor quotes taken from my interview for *The Guardian*, 12 March 2014

3

A slam dunk? Five make a splash

Having helped form, and then been sacked by, the Spice Girls, managers Bob and Chris Herbert quickly turned their attention to boybands. With no Take That and with the ballad-obsessed Boyzone hogging the spotlight, the pair felt pop was missing a proper all-dancing, all-singing, attitude-heavy ladband. In America, where Spice Girls mania was still just around the corner, the precisely curtained Backstreet Boys – who had started their careers in Europe in 1996 pushing big-chorused, R&B-lite bangers created by Swedish hitmakers Max Martin and Denniz PoP – were starting to take off. Keen to fill the gap in the market in the UK, while gliding along in the transatlantic slipstream of the Backstreet Boys, the managers placed an advert in *The Stage* in early 1997. While Take That and the recently signed 911 had slogged it out on schools tours and at club nights before landing major label deals, Five (or 5ive if you're a purist) signed with BMG/RCA under the watchful eye of a certain Simon Cowell.

'Boyzone were going to bring you flowers and Five were going to fuck you down the side alley'

Formed in May 1997, Five, AKA Ritchie Neville, Scott Robinson, J Brown, Sean Conlon and Abs Love, released their debut single 'Slam Dunk (Da Funk)' *– created, like half of their 1998 debut album,* Five, *by Martin and PoP in Stockholm – just six months later. Their eleven UK top-ten singles, three top-five albums and two arena tours spanned less than a four-year period. That it ended in burnout, depression and fist fights was hardly surprising given their lightspeed ascent. But it all started out via five lads – including singers, rappers and novice dancers – standing out from an initial crowd of 3,000 wannabes that featured a pre-fame Russell Brand among their number.*

Chris Herbert: When I did the Spice Girls I actually made a mood board and I pretty much had all the characters you see today on that board. I did the same with Five and it was urban, more street, a bit more hip-hop-influenced, rappy. In terms of styling it was baseball and basketball, very American influenced.

Hugh Goldsmith: In my last few months at RCA, I introduced Simon Cowell to Chris Herbert, who I'd met socially one weekend. Chris, of course, had put the Spice Girls together and seemed quite down at the time, having been left by the girls, who then went on to find new management and become hugely successful. We gave Chris £10,000 to spend on sourcing talent for a new act that we all agreed he would eventually manage. That act would become Five.

Chris Herbert: The idea really was Boyzone were going to bring you a bunch of flowers and Five were going to fuck you against a wall down the side alley. Girls love a bad boy and boys could relate to it. Musically it was going to be harder and tougher and more appealing to girls and boys alike.

Scott Robinson: It was an audition I'd found in *The Stage* and it was looking for the Spice Boys. I remember wearing a grey Kappa tracksuit – I'm from Essex – and some white Reebok Classics. I had a cropped haircut that I gelled down, which looked horrific. Also, despite being seventeen, I had been out drinking the night before and my dad came into my room to wake me up saying, 'You've got to go to this audition.' I was like, 'Dad, I can't go, I'm hungover, I don't want to be in the Spice Boys anyway.' He thought it could be my big break.

Ritchie Neville: I didn't look it, but I was a little grunge-y kid; I was into Nirvana, Pearl Jam and Stone Temple Pilots. It was either that or I was into dance music. Pop was a bit of a dirty word to me. I turned up and it was a media circus. There was press there and a Spice Girls tribute band performing. I was in this queue just going, 'What the hell is this?'

Sean Conlon: I saw Abs at my audition. He had some sunglasses on and looked a little bit like how Peter Andre used to dress. He really stood out from the whole queue.

Scott: I went to London and auditioned at Pineapple Studios. There were thousands of people and I was number twenty-two and J was number twenty-one. I heard his audition and then I went in and did mine. Next we went into another room where we had to dance and that's where I thought it was game over.

Ritchie: The audition process itself was like a cattle market. Ushering ten in at a time, super rushed. I walked into one of the dance studios and some music came on and I turned around and there were people windmilling and going for it. I felt really awkward. So I just very lightly moved, feeling very self-conscious about it all. Within a minute they turned the music off and if you got a piece of paper it meant you went to the next part, which was singing.

Scott: I remember thinking, 'But I can't dance.' It looks like I could in the videos and on stage but that's because a choreographer has drummed it into me. So I just stood there nodding my head a little bit as if I had a pint in my hand. J was breakdancing right in the middle, which is hilarious because he went on to really not like fame and stuff like that. He was never as confident with the singing, because he's a rapper, so he wanted to prove himself with the dancing. Everyone was standing in a semi-circle and J was in the middle doing head-spins.

Sean: I performed one of my own songs. At the time, that's all I was doing, just writing songs. I never really had any aspirations to be in a band or even to be famous. I had no idea the band was going to be as big as it was. I thought it would be an introduction into the industry, like I'd meet somebody and be able to write songs. I never thought about being famous. Plus I was only fifteen so it was more like a stepping stone for me.

Ritchie: I did George Michael's 'Freedom', which was a bit of a speciality as I'd done it in a singing competition at school.

Scott: [Russell Brand] was there. He denies that now. Which is funny because he's done some dodgy things in his career and auditioning for Five isn't the worst thing he's done.

Ritchie: After that first audition it was a kind of, 'Don't call us, we'll call you.' I thought they were going to call the house phone and so I remember one lunch time about a week after the auditions, I called Mum from the payphone at school to check to see how quickly she would answer. And she didn't answer! I got home that night and told her. She laughed and was like, 'Rich, do you honestly think if they wanted you in their big new band that they're only going to call once?'

Sean: When we got into the second audition and they put us together as a five, something clicked. You could feel it.

Scott: The second audition was at a place called Nomis Studios and that was where it started to hot up. They put us into groups. Every other group was a group of four, because the original idea was for the band to have four members. We were the only group of five. They were trying to see which one of us they could kick out. I remember J in tears in the toilet thinking it would be him to go. He was like, 'I'm the oldest, I'm more of a rapper than a singer.' They gave us a track to learn so that every group did the same song and Abs very cleverly wrote a rap for it and J did the same. We were the only band that had done something different.

Ritchie: At the time, pop bands had always been five people, so they wanted to do something different and have four people. But they couldn't decide which one of us to lose, so they kept it as five. Which is one of the reasons we called ourselves Five.

Scott: That audition process was meant to go on for weeks and weeks, but on that very day they sent everyone else home.

Sean: You did start to get a feeling like, 'Hang on, this could be a little bit bigger than I thought.'

Scott: I remember Simon Cowell was there and he said, 'You're the band, I'm signing you to RCA Records on a five-album deal, this is happening very soon.'

Ritchie: He was definitely a presence and a character. I remember whispers of like, 'Yeah, that's the guy from the record label.'

Sean: We didn't have the struggle that other bands have where they're gigging for years and trying to get a deal. It was on a plate for us really.

Ritchie: I could see the potential in every single one of us and I knew the fire I had in my belly, so when the songs started coming and they were really good I was like, 'We could seriously take the world here.' We had everything we needed. We could have set up our lives forever.

Scott: We auditioned in the May and by Christmas we were top ten in the charts with 'Slam Dunk (Da Funk)'. Our first show ever was the Radio 1 roadshow in Weston-super-Mare. When we pulled up, Peter Andre was at the gate signing autographs and I remember wondering if anyone would want our autograph one day. Then after we'd done our performance people were asking for our autograph and we didn't have one. I was just using the one I put on my bank card. Our second ever performance was the *Smash Hits* Poll Winners Party in front of 15,000 people. We never looked back from that moment. It was so quick that it was too quick actually. That's why it didn't last.

'I'd ask for a score to get some Stellas from the offie'

A key element in the Spice Girls' early success was their genuine bond. It was one fostered via months of living together in a small terraced house, a literal move organised by Bob and Chris Herbert to set a solid foundation. Keen to see if lightning would strike twice, the Five boys – aged between fifteen (Sean) and twenty-one (J) – were quickly moved into a council house in Surrey. In terms of the narrative around the band as 'the bad boys of pop', the move was genius. In terms of their relationships and their health vis-à-vis cleanliness and sanitation, it was a disaster.

Sean: I didn't think anything of it when I first moved. I just thought, 'I'm going to do music, it all makes sense.' So I had my clothes packed in one hand and my keyboard in the other. Then I went on the train, met Scott and J at Euston Station and the next minute we're in the house. Then it starts to become pretty daunting.

Ritchie: I nearly didn't move in. I was doing my A levels, it was the last year, so I was a bit like, 'I've come all this way, I should really finish them.' My parents agreed. But I didn't want to be left behind if I moved in three months later – they would have had a lot of experiences already and I'd be playing catch-up. One day I put on Radio 1 and Ultra Naté's 'Free' came on. Being a little spiritual, I was like, 'That's a sign': you're free to do what you want to do. I went home and told my mum I had to go and she understood.

Scott: I wasn't particularly an old seventeen-year-old. I'd been away from home once for Edinburgh Festival when I was in a musical and I struggled then. You didn't really have time to catch your breath. It was a three-bedroom house, so me and Abs shared, but he was never there because he had a girlfriend at the time. I would see my girlfriend Kerry, who is now my wife, at the weekends. Sean had a tiny little box room and then Rich and J shared. It was funny but it was mental. Put five young teenagers in a house with no parents and see what happens. There's a lot of drinking, but also a lot of work. We worked so hard.

Sean: We had a lot of moments when we really did get on but there were bits of testosterone and bits of friction here and there. Just lads living together trying to find their feet. It wasn't always great but we did have some laughs.

Scott: Individually, people had problems with J. He was going through the same pressures but at a different age and dealing with them differently. It was difficult for all of us. I'd looked up to J for quite a while until I started to realise he was manipulating and using me a little bit.

Chris Herbert: They probably became caricatures of themselves because we said this is what we're doing and this is the image, so their reputation started following them wherever they went.

Scott: We were the band that liked a drink. But so did Westlife. They're Irish boys; they can fucking drink. They were just not saying they were having a drink; they were being good boys. So we got tarred as the ladband, but we were still a boyband. We were just a bit cooler. And we still are.

Pete Whelan, '00s pop superfan: I think a lot of it was image and gimmick. I know there was a bit of fighting between them but I think there was an element of, 'If we present them as tough, they're not just another generic boyband like Westlife.'

Peter Robinson, journalist and editor of Popjustice: I wonder how much of the bad-boy image was real. You had Take That and East 17 and then you had Westlife and Five, which is basically the same thing. The difference the second time around was Five and Westlife were A&R-ed by the same person, Simon Cowell, and on the same record label, so it's very easy to manage it. Having them knocking around at the same time probably did each of them a favour.

Lee Thompson: It was contrived, but then actually they started living up to that persona and then some. They came in for an interview one time, probably about '98 or '99. We were in a Mexican restaurant afterwards and they were fighting with each other. The guy from the label was like, 'I can't do anything about this, that's the way they are.' I remember two of them going outside to fight.

Sean: [Management and label] wanted the edgy style of band for sure. A lot of boybands were really contrived and controlled. Because the fans that were into boybands were predominantly young teenagers, they were very conscious about what parents would think. But then with us I think initially they wanted an edgy band but they tried to contrive it in another way with the TV show.

Chris Herbert: We launched them off [ITV documentary series] *Neighbours from Hell.* It was all about warring neighbours. I had put them into a house in a place called Heatherside in Camberley and the boys were warring with this gang there. We were like, 'This is brilliant.' There were neighbours up in arms and I thought, 'This is perfect for this show.' So we rung them and said, 'Look, we've got this band, do you want to put them on?', and that's how we did it. It fed perfectly into the narrative we were trying to create.

Ritchie: They wanted a band with edge and that's what they bloody well got. None of us are people that will be bossed around. So then if you put five of those people together all the time and then they start annoying each other . . . We're all very strong characters so eventually there's going to be those eruptions. We were young, we didn't have that level of maturity.

Scott: I'm not even joking, at one point we ran out of plates because no one was washing them so we chucked them away. Then we went to the supermarket and bought paper plates and plastic cutlery so that we could dispose of it. So you'd have a microwave meal and then dash the plate in the bin. People would say juvenile but I'd say genius. That place was a cesspit.

Chris Herbert: It was dreadful. I sent my cleaners down there and they refused to clean the place.

Ritchie: We were travelling around a lot so it wasn't like you could stay in and cook. We put on loads of weight later on as we'd just be having McDonald's and KFC. I was getting tubby. I remember there was a piece in the tabloids calling me 'beefy'. I remember that really hitting home, like, 'Beefy?!' I didn't realise. I went and looked in the mirror and I'd definitely put on weight.

Sean: I didn't have a clue [about living alone]. I hadn't cooked, I hadn't washed my own clothes. I was literally just a child.

Scott: Later they moved us into a really plush five-bedroom house. But it's funny because we were fucking paying for that house. We were thinking, 'Look at us, wahey,' and we'd get picked up in nice cars and say, 'Can you wait an hour, mate?', and they'd keep the meter running.

Ritchie: Even our parents didn't understand [our record contract]. It was a recipe for disaster because music industry contracts are really complicated. I had the perception that if you make it big enough you will be a millionaire. I thought I would end up with £50 million and a yacht.

Scott: We had a lawyer but I didn't really know what a lawyer was. I'd seen one on the telly, so we asked a couple of questions. But basically when we got into that band, even when money was coming in, we were given £100 a week to live on. I had had a couple of jobs as a pot collector at a local social club, then I ran a burger wagon, so I was always trying to make money. Sean was fifteen. He'd never seen £100. I remember him going, 'Have I got to share it?'

Sean: I thought I'd won the lottery then.

Ritchie: Sean was quite good with money and he was also quiet about it. He wouldn't advertise the fact he'd saved it; he'd keep his mouth closed. I would always hit up Scott, like, 'I can't even eat.' That first year was a struggle.

Scott: Sean used to hoard it. After about five weeks I'd spent all my money on beer. I would go into Sean's room and he'd go, 'I've not spent any, still got £500.' I'd ask for a score to get some Stellas from the offie.

Sean: I wouldn't say I hoarded it. But I was careful with it. Scott enjoyed it a little bit more, I suppose.

Scott: It wasn't until we started to get a bit wiser – not wise enough, I might add – that we'd say, 'Have we got any money?' They'd say, 'You've got some coming in,' and I'd look at my bank account and be like, 'You weren't joking.' So I'd go and buy a Merc.

'We weren't saying that it wasn't a hit record, but it just sounded like everybody else'

With the Backstreet Boys joining the Spice Girls in kickstarting American radio's renewed interest in pure pop, Five were flown out to Cheiron Studios in Stockholm to work with Denniz PoP and Max Martin. Known for fusing top-tier ABBA melodies with a very Swedish approximation of R&B, PoP and Martin – alongside songwriter and rapper Herbie Crichlow and producer Jake Schulze – crafted a sound that suited both Five's penchant for rapping over more hard-edged 'funk' beats (the word 'funk' appears approximately 678 times on debut album Five*) and, via the ballads, highlighted Scott* *and Ritchie's doe-eyes. In the UK, the band worked with Biff Stannard and Julian Gallagher, as well as Tim Lever and Mike Percy of '80s synthpop experimentalists Dead or Alive fame. The latter two, alongside Eliot Kennedy, co-created the album's second single 'When the Lights Go Out', which would later become the band's first (and only) US top-ten hit. Along the way they also turned down a boyband classic and very nearly got their hands on one of pop's biggest ever singles, '. . . Baby One More Time'.*

Sean: I didn't even have a passport. I had to get one really quickly so I could even go [to Sweden].

Scott: It's so difficult because you're seventeen so you don't really know who these [producers] are. I knew they were a big deal. I knew I was in the room with people who knew what they were doing.

Ritchie: We didn't understand it at all. We knew they'd worked with Ace of Base. The Backstreet Boys were big but they hadn't had the mega hits like 'I Want It That Way'. We knew 'Quit Playing Games' and actually that was one of my guilty pleasures.

Sean: If I'm brutally honest I didn't really know who they were. Scott was into Backstreet Boys but I'd never sort of got into that.

Scott: I remember talking to Denniz and he was playing me some of the new songs the Backstreet Boys had coming up. I remember phoning one of my mates and going, 'You'll never guess what, I've just listened to the new Backstreet Boys album before it's even been finished.'

Sean: I listened to Seal, Roachford, Sade and singers like that. I wasn't the type of person who read interviews and I didn't even always know who the people were that sang the songs. I was only interested in the music.

Scott: We had to fight [to be able to write songs on the debut album]. We wanted to have our stamp on the music. We were the only boyband out there at the time that it was okay to like if you were a guy. It wasn't that embarrassing to go, 'You know what, Five are pretty cool.' I've got no problem with Westlife's music, I think it's very good, but if you were a lad and you were a Westlife fan you would take that to the grave. You're not shouting that from the rooftops and saying, 'Oh, yeah, I love "Flying Without Wings", what a tune.'

Biff Stannard: They were bad boys, like East 17. It was almost like anti-pop. They were just so naughty. Sometimes people have said to me, 'Was it a sort of casting couch thing?' But they're not my type at all. I just remember thinking they were feisty, really good writers as well, and there was friction in the studio and sometimes that leads to really good results. That was the first thing Simon [Cowell] threw at me that I thought was really good.

Scott: Denniz was a big part in nurturing what we were doing and the rapping. Him and Herbie Critchlow pretty much invented the way Abs and J went on to rap. J was a Tupac-type rapper when he joined the band and then him and Abs started doing these phone raps like the Beastie Boys.

Biff Stannard: I remember J was a bit self-conscious about [the rapping]. It was different with Tony in East 17 – you could get away with that kind of cadence of rapping. I still hear a lot of people who sound like J in modern rap actually.

Scott: When Denniz passed away [of stomach cancer in August 1998, aged thirty-five] it was quite hard to pick yourself up after that. We still worked over in Sweden with Max [Martin] and he had learned everything from Denniz. He then did alright for himself.

Biff Stannard: Lovely Denniz. That hit them quite hard because they were getting there with him. It was hard for me to fill his shoes, because I was a massive fan. I was intimidated by that. I was the first person they'd met afterwards and they were a bit, not wary, but, 'What's this going to be like?'

Sean: It was sad, although I never got terribly close to Denniz, if I'm brutally honest. They were quite business-like [in the studio] and quite mechanical. I'm not saying that's a bad thing – that's how they've got success – but that's just the truth.

Scott: At one point Simon offered Max Martin his Aston Martin to have '. . . Baby One More Time' [for us].

Chris Herbert: I'll tell you the story. Clive Davis had signed the boys in America to Arista and Clive had also signed TLC. Max was trying to pitch the song for TLC and he asked us to give it to Clive. We played it for him and he was like, 'It's not right.' We were listening to it and we were like, 'You could make this into a guys' song as well.' So we said to Max that we'd love to use it for Five. It took some convincing. Even to the point where Simon said, 'Look, I'll buy you a brand-new 500 Sl Mercedes for the song.' So Max agreed.

Ritchie: We were that tougher boyband, so you could imagine guys singing that chorus and it being a tougher pop song.

Chris Herbert: We played it to the guys and at the end it was deathly quiet and we said, 'What do you think?' In front of Max, they went, '. . . It's fucking wank!' Max was so insulted by it. I managed to convince Max again that we could win the boys over, but by this point Max was like, 'I've got this other girl who is going to sing it.' I asked who it was and he said it was a girl called Britney and that she was an up-and-coming new artist. I said, 'But the boys have just had a top-ten hit in America [with 'When the Lights Go Out'], you must be mad not to give us this song.' Anyway, Britney Spears did it.

Scott: Everyone always goes, 'Oh, do you regret you didn't get it?', but just because it was a hit with Britney didn't mean it would have been a hit with Five. I think Rich would have looked good in a school uniform, but I don't think it would have had the same effect.

Ritchie: I thought that was quite brave of Max because it was a guaranteed hit with us. Britney had only just been signed. All is fair in love and war. Simon would have probably said, 'Okay, well what else have you got, then?'

Biff Stannard: There's another really good story about Max using a massive snare sound and Simon telling him to turn it down. Apparently Max just hung up on him. 'Isn't the snare a bit loud?' 'No, bye.'

Hallgeir Rustan, former member of Stargate: Simon Cowell always knew what he wanted. At that time, we used DHL to send the mixes and every delivery took three or four days. There was one mix where Simon wasn't happy with the snare drum sound. Several mixes were sent via DHL but Simon still didn't like it. He got on a plane and flew to our studio in Trondheim. We listened to fifty or sixty different snare drums. Finally we ended up with the snare drum that was in the first mix. Everybody's happy.

Chris Herbert: Five didn't learn from their mistakes because we had almost the exact same scenario with 'Bye Bye Bye'.

Scott: The hook was there but the rest of the chorus was different. I said, 'Do you know what, this isn't a Five song. It doesn't sound like us, give it to NSYNC.' They did and obviously they finished the verses without us. Could Five have sung it in that vein and done quite well? Probably. But it wouldn't have felt right to us.

Sean: When we first went to Cheiron, it was a bit Backstreet Boys but edgier, with some rapping and more of a hip-hop influence. When we got further on, we started doing some of the writing and we started to stumble on something boybands hadn't really done before. Songs like 'If Ya Gettin' Down', 'Let's Dance', 'Keep On Movin''. Although we had some songs that were still very American and boyband-y, we were also creating something British. We were just putting our foot down at that point. We weren't saying that ['Bye Bye Bye'] wasn't a hit record, but it just sounds like everybody else. Give it to one of them.

Peter Robinson: Five were the sort of band, a bit like Girls Aloud later, who felt like they could do all sorts of nonsense and do something exciting. So, if they sample Joan Jett or do a song based around the *Battlestar Galactica* theme or do a song that samples *Grease*, it makes sense. I went to Simon Cowell's office during Five's reign and he played me a cover they'd done of 'Pour Some Sugar on Me' by Def Leppard, which never came out. They seemed like the kind of band where you'd go, 'Okay, fair, that makes sense.'

Scott: Our first single in the States, 'When the Lights Go Out', went top ten.

Lee Brennan: 'When the Lights Go Out' was written by John McLaughlin for us. It was meant to be the first song from our second album, but Simon Cowell got his mitts on it. I don't know how. We'd learned the song and then suddenly we were told it was no longer our song.

Scott: I remember being too exhausted to be overly excited [by US success]. We could have been massive in the States if we'd have been given enough time. We were spread too thin over too many territories.

Ritchie: They wanted us everywhere all at once. Most bands take off in the UK, then Europe, they might go to Asia, and then after a few years, if they get really successful, America comes knocking. Whereas the whole world knocked for us at the same time. It sounds like fun and it was, but it was genuinely us waking up on a coach and not knowing what continent we were on.

Chris Herbert: It burnt them out. In hindsight, I would never do that again. We took on too much too soon. There was a point where you looked at the world and there wasn't a territory they weren't selling records in. We got a Disney special, which was the holy grail. They'd done it with NSYNC, they'd done it with Britney, and we got one along with B*Witched.

Sean: I look back on that time with a little bit of sadness really because we could have been so much bigger in the US. We had the top-ten record, we played Times Square, it was really starting to happen. We just couldn't find our feet and that's when everything started to become dysfunctional and there were frictions within the band. And then frictions between the band and management. Then the band and the label. Frictions everywhere.

Ritchie: Some of the guys, who will remain nameless, would piss high-level people off. Like high-level ITV producers, high-level BBC producers. Radio 1 people. You'd be like, 'Boys, keep it together.' We had America on a plate. But it was like a self-destruct button with some people. Like, 'I'm going to do everything I can to fuck this up. I'm going to be obnoxious and rude, I'm going to disappear at a huge photoshoot with a major US magazine.' To the point where the label came in and were like, 'You fucking British guys are a bunch of twats and you can fuck off.'

'I would say there were a few tussles and other times I was physically attacked'

From the very start, Five's bad-boy image always seemed to co-exist with the music. In fact, an advert for the Five *album, in conjunction with Woolworths, played into this sense of major label-endorsed rebellion. Billed as the 'I've seen the light' promotion, fans were encouraged, while buying Five's debut, to hand in an old CD by a rival band ('Let's face it we've all made mistakes', ran the blurb). In return, fans would get a free four-track bonus CD and a signed certificate. The reality of this ladband image, however, would slowly start to take over. Strangers thrust into a house together a week after being told they were in a band, their early disagreements soon grew into full-blown fist fights. What had started as a spark for creating exciting pop songs soon morphed into a situation where they would have to be kept apart in the studio. Suddenly the age gaps between various members became insurmountable chasms.*

Biff Stannard: Part of being a producer is being a babysitter; it's not just about doing beats. They'd lived in the house together and they were fighting like dogs from the beginning. Just at each other's throats. To the point where you'd work with a three and a two, never all five at one time. I don't think I ever worked with them as a five-piece more than once or twice. They did have a security person with them, but he was off getting them drugs or whatever.

Ritchie: No drugs. There was occasionally, possibly a little bit of spliff.

Hallgeir Rustan: When we had a meeting with Simon Cowell he told us about the boys and that the chemistry inside the group was perhaps not the best. He recommended we work with the vocalists, Scott and Ritchie, first because if we took the whole group in the studio it could lead to fighting.

Scott: You're overworked and everything starts to fracture because you're tired. You put teenagers and early twenty-somethings together and it's carnage. So yeah, there would be rows that would break into fights. And J would always be in the middle of that. There were points where a couple of us would be recording and then we'd go and the other three would come in.

Ritchie: I personally harbour no ill-will or resentment to J or Abs. I would want nothing more than to hear that they're happily getting on with their lives and that they're cool. J was quite a domineering character and he wanted things done his way. He was willing to get that point across in a physical way sometimes. Sometimes.

Simon Jones, former PR for *SM:TV* and *CD:UK*: They definitely had fist fights down at *CD:UK*. They had to be separated a couple of times. And it would always be threatening to kick off with other bands as well. They were punching each other. I remember watching it in the corridors. You had the two studios and in between there was the café area where loads of the bands would just hang out. So stories would naturally occur, which we'd then give to the tabloids. I'm sure I gave that story about Five having a fight to them because it mentioned *SM:TV* and *CD:UK*, so I'd done my job.

Ritchie: I would say there were a few tussles and other times I was physically attacked. There were fist fights and tussles that spilled out into corridors. Some physicality went on.

Biff Stannard: They were just really laddy. It was drinking and it was banter. They kind of gave the impression they didn't really give a fuck whether it was a hit or not or whether it sold.

Jeremy Joseph: At first I was a bit wary of doing [Five at G-A-Y]. I didn't know whether they were suitable. They started a bit rough around the edges and then, as it was getting a bit poppier, we started doing them and it worked. But it wasn't actually until I'd spoken to Ritchie I realised their attitude wasn't as bad boy as they were being portrayed. That's what changed my view of them.

Paul Flynn: Things are so massively different now, but when I worked at *Attitude*, there were two conversations you'd have with the straight acts we'd put on the cover; one was, 'How much flesh are they willing to show?' A hot boy would sell the magazine like nothing else could. It was pre-internet, pre-being able to see everything you want all the time. The other question was, 'How are they with gay people? What do they think about gay people? Are they going to feel uncomfortable?' You literally had to gauge the temperature. Can you imagine having that conversation now? The one we loved in the office was J. So we just did him on the cover [in May 2000]. He didn't show flesh, but he did do vest. It was quite Russian roulette as to what would happen on the day [with straight pop stars]; you had to go through a little dance each time.

Dania Pasquini, one half of video directors Max & Dania: We did lots of videos for them, from the beginning right through to their last ever video. In general they were a good bunch of guys. I never personally saw or witnessed anything other than good fun and them being up for it. They were clever, funny, witty, up-for-it guys. They had attitude when a lot of boybands didn't at that time.

Max Giwa, the other half of video directors Max & Dania: They were these bad boys who just wanted to be raucous and have a great time with girls so we were like, 'Brilliant, bring it on.' We just created a world around them.

Hannah Verdier, pop journalist: Five were always problematic from the start. They hated it all. Ritchie was alright, but they hated each other. The first time I met them I was at *Just Seventeen* and we had to play five-a-side football against them. The writer who was supposed to do it was sick on the day because she knew what they were like and I was a keen sub-editor so I said I would go. They were utterly horrible.

Alex Needham: They always seemed massively overworked. When it's something you really believe in and you're putting your heart and soul into it, you're probably a bit more cheerful. When you're just turning up and you've got to be a certain whacky character when you're eighteen and you find it all totally cringeworthy, then you turn up, do it and clear off.

Scott: We wanted to be the band that were honest. We wanted to be the band that said, 'Yeah, I was pissed last night, I've got a hangover.' Just be real because people connect with that much more. When Westlife are on the TV going, 'No sex before marriage and I've never had a drink in my life,' and then it would cut to an interview with Five and me going, 'What day is it because

I was hammered last night, what's going on?' That was more relatable.

Ritchie: Bearing in mind we came from the generation that were drinking cider down the park, it was like, 'Well, where did you grow up?' Obviously they were lying.

Jordan Paramor: Five didn't hide the fact they didn't get along. If you interviewed Take That or Boyzone, they might have had a blazing row beforehand, but you wouldn't know that on the shoot. But Five didn't tow the party line like other bands did. If one of them was annoying, they'd snap at them and they wouldn't really care if we put that in *Smash Hits*. They were always arguing. You could tell J was really uncomfortable about it all.

Holly Jade-Johnson, boyband super-fan: They were a bit rough. I remember on the *Smash Hits* roadshow they definitely seemed more like they were going to go to jail pretty soon. Or had been in jail.

Biff Stannard: I used to like it when they argued; it would be interesting to try to work it into the songs. That energy. You did them so quickly and you'd play them back to Simon Cowell and he'd go, 'That's shit,' and your heart would sink. Then the next one he'd go, 'Single.' So ruthless. But it worked and 'Keep On Movin'' is still one of my favourite songs I've ever done.

Paul Flynn: I don't know how I know this, someone must have put it on as a joke or something, but 'Keep On Movin'' sounds amazing on ecstasy. The chord progression is built for ecstasy.

'Westlife, Five and A1 were all gauging who got the biggest screams on the tour'

While their boyband peers had been shlepping up and down the country doing gay club nights or popping up in shopping centres in order to get attention, Five appeared fully formed, backed by industry heavyweights and with a string of early hits under their elastic waistbands. It meant there was a certain confidence about them that didn't always go down too well. That arrogance and immediate success drew the attention of not only the pop magazines, but also the tabloids, a situation that was sent into overdrive by the fact that Ritchie – the band's heartthrob – was in a relationship with fellow pop star Billie Piper.

Scott: Back in the day, there was a little bit of arrogance, like, 'Oh, no, I'm better than them. We're number one and they're not.' I get on really well with Peter Andre now, but I remember back in the '90s when we first met thinking, 'You're a twat.'

Lee Brennan: They came on the *Smash Hits* Poll Winners Party tour with us and won the Best New Act award. It was like, 'Who the hell are these guys?', just creating chaos backstage. Right from the start, before they'd even released a song, they were sure of themselves and didn't give a crap who anybody else was, even if you'd had number-one singles. They were groomed, they were styled, their hair was bang on, plus they had the songs.

Lucie Cave, former presenter on Trouble: We used to cover the *Smash Hits* tour and I remember Westlife, Five and A1 were all real rivals because they'd be gauging who got the biggest screams on the tour. There was loads of jealousy behind the scenes. Everyone just got really pissed every night. They would do their thing on stage and then everyone would go back to the hotel and stay up until 5 a.m. Then there would be fans there, so God knows what was going on.

Christian Ingebrigtsen, A1: There were definitely boyband rivalries. With Five in particular because they were the tough guys. So we were always happy if we headlined over them. Obviously. We weren't really good friends with Five back then; we never really spoke to them. Westlife were as big as they were but they were always nice backstage.

Lucie Cave: Five could get away with being moody with you and you sort of expected that from them, but Westlife had to be switched on all the time. They were getting pretty tired by the end of the tour because they had to be these golden boys in all white.

Nikki Whelan, '00s pop superfan: Scott from Five was always rude.

Scott: Back then, the fans didn't want to have a conversation with you as if you were a normal person. I had my face and my neck scratched, like I was bleeding because they just wanted to say, 'I've got Scott's hair under my nails, yay!' Once I had my shoe stolen by a fan. We were on tour in Italy and we were about to go on stage and the stylist is going, 'Scott, where's your shoe?' I knew whoever stole my trainer was in the audience. So I went out on stage and said, 'You might have noticed I've got one shoe on, but I am not going to sing "Until the Time Is Through" until I get my trainer back.' From the very back of the arena, followed by a spotlight, this trainer got carried across people's hands.

Sean: I was so overwhelmed with the fame and the people dressed as pop stars, I sort of went into my shell. I just didn't feel comfortable with it, so I'd sit quietly on my own a lot. It was only when we did *The Big Reunion* [in 2013] and we got to meet other bands that I started to feel more comfortable. I realised they felt like me too but everyone responded differently. I was more withdrawn. Like, this feels out of control so I'm just going to sit in this corner.

Ritchie: In the environment I was in day in day out, it wasn't always a very nice place to be. It was aggressive and there was a lot of confrontation. Then you've got the pressures of learning to be famous at seventeen and eighteen. I've never felt as lonely as I felt at that age. Every day was: 'You've got to get through this, this is the beginning of your life, it's not always going to be like this, one day the band won't exist.' Billie was going through the same thing, but alone. More often than not the people that work for you, they don't give a fuck about you. At least with Five, when we weren't rowing, we might have a deep conversation in the van and talk about stuff. I don't think she had that.

Scott: The record company wanted you to hide [relationships from fans] but I didn't want to. I was so in love with Kerry that I wanted to shout it from the rooftops. They were saying, 'You're going to alienate the fans,' but I wanted them to know that I wasn't there for them. So, after a while of them saying no, I just announced it in an interview. I was bored of being told what to do.

Ritchie: I remember being backstage in Germany somewhere in a corridor and having this really odd moment with Billie. We didn't really know each other, we just walked up to each other, said hello and hugged. But neither of us let go. We ended up standing there and having this tender, lovely hug for about four minutes. We were each other's solace. I knew I could trust her and I could tell her anything and she's not going to sell her story. I moved into a flat and I remember being absolutely made up. Five had lived together for nearly two years and I was like, 'I can't spend another moment with these boys, they're doing my tits in.' Billie was still living out of a hotel and it was doing her head in so I suggested she move in with me while she was looking for her own flat. We ended up living together for two years; she never left.

Laura Snapes: I was aware Ritchie Neville went out with Billie Piper and that that made her unpopular. Looking back, he looks like Julian Clary – hardly a teen heartthrob.

Nikki Whelan: When I was younger I did get defensive about [them having relationships]. I went through a phase of not liking Billie because of it, which is ridiculous. But I love her now. It was that immaturity.

Ritchie: Our management knew, her management knew, the labels knew. Cowell and [director of Innocent Records, Billie's label] Hugh Goldsmith knew each other, because Hugh was part of RCA when we signed with them. So they were friends. They had conversations about it and it was about controlling how it came out. It was a case of, 'This is going to come out, so instead of them doing it how they want to do it, why don't we work with them?'

Hugh Goldsmith: In her book [2006's *Growing Pains*], Billie says I advised her that 'going out' with a popular boyband member could potentially harm her popularity and also attract unwanted aggression from jealous fans of whoever that artist might be. Naturally, we were all concerned about the impact Billie dating Richie might have on her career, but, more importantly, we most certainly did not want to see her get hurt in any way.

Jordan Paramor: I remember [Billie] coming on stage at the *Smash Hits* Poll Winners' Party after the news broke and getting booed.

Ritchie: We were nervous about it. We knew the first show after coming out about the relationship would be bad, but actually it was worse than we thought it would be. The booing was awful. It wasn't just a few people – most of that arena booed her. When you really love someone, it's hard. You have a couple of those relationships in your life if you're lucky and, at the time, especially with what was going on in our lives, I totally loved her. That was really difficult to watch. It was hard for her, but actually it didn't affect her record sales and it didn't affect her career.

Hugh Goldsmith: Innocent was a small, tightly knit team and we had a strong family vibe between us and with our artists. So we were all absolutely gutted to witness Billie being booed by a sector of Five fans on the *Smash Hits* tour and our hearts went out to her. Understandably, Billie was devastated by what happened and things got even worse, in the next few months, as jealous fans started sending hate mail to her fan club and to the teen magazines. Billie's confidence was knocked badly by the whole experience. Our label view on all the nastiness was that it would eventually die down if Billie lay low for a while. So her focus then swung primarily on to starting the next album as well as doing promotion outside the UK.

Jeremy Joseph: For a nightclub, the licence was eighteen and over, but on stage the licence doesn't apply. We did Billie when she was sixteen. She had her head screwed on. She was older than her years. She started with this teen girl market, but girls were never really going to like Billie because she's competition. Our audience didn't care that she was dating someone from Five. She was an example of the label going, 'Right, we're losing this audience, what audience will work for her?' You watched her go from bubblegum pop to more adult dance.

'Simon basically shut down the entire Eiffel Tower for Girl Thing'

By the summer of 2000, Five were the biggest boyband in the country. Their first two albums had shifted 6.5 million copies worldwide, they'd sold a million albums in America alone and 1999's Invincible *had given them two UK number-one singles in the shape of ecstasy fave 'Keep On Movin'' and the ludicrous Queen collaboration, 'We Will Rock You'. Happy with the success of the so-called Spice Boys, and perhaps still smarting from their sacking from the Spice Girls, in 1998, Chris and Bob Herbert set about forming Girl Thing, recruiting Jodi Albert, Michelle Barber, Anika Bostelaar, Linzi Martin and Nikki Stuart. Signed to RCA by Simon Cowell – who had once turned down Scary et al., let's not forget – they were pitched somewhere between the rebellious Five and the personality-packed Spice Girls, but with an All Saints 'edge'. They launched in the summer of 2000 with shouty anthem 'Last One Standing', which, thanks to the truckloads of cash being poured into the project, was assumed to be a given for the number-one spot. The band even recorded a number of radio interviews and idents pre-emptively heralding their debut chart-topper. In the end, the single peaked at eight, while the follow-up single, 'Girls on Top', crashed out at twenty-five. Their self-titled album, which featured their original version of the soon-to-be-massive 'Pure and Simple', was only released in Australia.*

Chris Herbert: We were incredibly arrogant by this point. We'd had a real run of success, Simon Cowell and I, and we believed our own hype. I think we had all the characters in there and the songs were pretty good, but we overhyped it. The expectations of this band were that they were going to eclipse the Spice Girls and Five combined.

Jeremy Joseph: They were playing off a sort of, 'Let's do a girl version of Five.' Actually, all you're trying to do is copy one success and move it onto another and it doesn't work.

Biff Stannard: It just felt really contrived. I thought Simon was really interesting, but wasn't sure about the band. So I produced two songs on their album. Simon is unlike any other person I've ever met. His whole thing is trying to capture the zeitgeist just after it's happened but he was a bit late with them. He got better at it as time went on.

Jordan Paramor: I did their media training. It was too transparent. Too contrived. You could see what they were trying to do and you can't take the public for fools. It's no different to

Boyzone slipping into Take That's shoes or Westlife coming along later to replace Boyzone. But Girl Thing missed the boat.

Jodi Albert: We got to appear on the cover of *Smash Hits* magazine before we even released our first single. That was incredible.

Hannah Verdier: We went all out with the build-up a few weeks before, like, 'Hey there's this new pop band,' and then put them on the cover. I can remember really clearly the midweeks coming in and they weren't anywhere near number one.

Chris Herbert: We had all the front covers of the magazines booked with them celebrating their number one before we'd even charted.

Hannah Verdier: The management wanted us to be best friends with them. Like, 'Right, you're going to go in and make friends.' We had to hang out with them.

Jodi Albert: We went to Paris to launch the band in front of the world's press. They basically shut down the entire Eiffel Tower for Girl Thing. Journalists were flown in from across the world and put up in an amazing hotel in Paris. We performed five tracks and then we sat down to do interviews. The treatment was amazing.

Chris Herbert: We had the girls performing at the top with Union Jacks flying off it. It was a bit cringey.

Alex Needham: Girl Thing were just a catastrophic, million-pound flop, weren't they? Not a bad first single, though.

Chris Herbert: Because the first Girl Thing single hadn't charted at number one it was deemed a failure. Simon was in a tailspin because it had knocked his ego. Mine, too. But he'd taken it quite badly and was probably getting the wrath of the label because he'd spent so much money on the launch of this band.

James Masterton: It's always thrown back at him as his greatest failure. They released one single that went in at number eight in their first week and for any brand-new act that would be a good achievement, but Simon Cowell said that was a disaster. There's an example of how it was all focused on that first week.

'I just needed a little bit of help'

When sessions for what would become Five's third album, 2001's Kingsize, *started, it was clear that the band were disintegrating. While the album's lead single 'Let's Dance' gave them another chart-topper, the video only featured four members. The two follow-up singles – 'Closer to Me' and the* Grease-*sampling 'Rock the Party' – featured videos made up of cobbled-together footage and animation, respectively. A perfunctory greatest hits album called* Greatest Hits *followed in November and peaked at number nine.*

Hallgeir Rustan: I think the friction within the band made it difficult to hold together. When everyone thinks they are the alpha male then it's going to cause problems.

Chris Herbert: I knew the band were exhausted. But they were also becoming hard work as well. I couldn't recognise whether it was pure exhaustion, whether they were suffering mentally, or whether they were just playing up. It was a combination of all those things. There was also a bit of bullying going on.

Sean: For me, it was a struggle from the beginning unfortunately. We had some really good laughs in Sweden when we were recording the first album, then after it came out there were internal struggles. We had just come back to do a new album and I was really struggling with anxiety, feeling overwhelmed. We didn't really have any help, you know, so the other guys in the band said I should go and see a counsellor. Back then, it was unheard of. It's not like now. So I went to see a counsellor, saw a psychologist and they were the ones who signed me off and said he's not mentally healthy enough to come back and work.

Ritchie: We'd started the promotion for 'Let's Dance' and they paired me with Sean to sit with the journalist. The journalist asked, 'How are you guys doing?', and you don't go, 'To be honest with you, mate, I'm fucking tired,' you just go, 'Yeah, I'm good, thanks.' Sean sat there with his head down and he was like, 'Yeah, yeah, I'm fucking good, man,' and he just kept repeating, 'Soooo fucking good, I'm soooo fucking good.' Then he got up and walked off. He didn't come back and I did the interview. Afterwards I went to the tour manager and he was like, 'He's in the van, he's going home, he needs a bit of time.' I still didn't understand it at this point. We were specifically told not to call him. We were told he didn't want to be bothered by anyone or anything, he just wants space. So we respected that. Then he never came back.

Chris Herbert: Sean comes across as a hard northerner but is really really soft and he's the youngest in the band, so, although externally he was playing a character, internally he was in real turmoil. Trying to come to terms with this newfound success and fortune and fame and schedules. I knew he was going downhill but it came very suddenly.

Scott: We had to lie and tell anyone that asked that Sean had glandular fever. We knew that he was having a breakdown and he'd left. But the label wanted to make sure that *Kingsize* was going to sell so they said we couldn't tell anyone.

Sean: Now they would have said it was to do with mental health and you'd get a bit more care, but back then it was more, 'Mental health issues? Hang on a second, you're selling millions of albums, you're making money, how could you have any mental health issues?' That's how it was.

Scott: If that was now, the single release would have been put back and we would have had a break. And the band would never have broke up.

Ritchie: Most people only see the videos, where you're selling a dream. It's a happy place. But you might have been crying before that take and the make-up artist says, 'Come on, you've got puffy eyes, let's get that sorted,' and then you're back in dreamland. That's where you realise that money ultimately means absolutely nothing. It's about where you're at inside yourself as a human being that dictates how happy you are.

Sean: The label were in a rush and they didn't want to wait, so they convinced the band to use a cardboard cut-out of me [in the video for 'Let's Dance'].

Dania Pasquini: At that time, we were playing with what we do and we were taking the mickey out of ourselves, the whole industry, out of Simon. [That video] opens with the band going in to meet someone who was meant to be Simon Cowell. You can see their sense of humour in that video because they created those characters, they brought that to the table. You can't fake that.

Ritchie: We had a bit to say about that video idea because that was our life. We'd go into these meetings and be like, 'Who the fuck are these people?' We'd be in Simon Cowell's office and he'd go off to speak to someone and so we'd be like, 'Go on, go through his desk.' We were taking his drawers out and he had all these books on psychology and body language. Or you'd be in the room and just when you'd catch eyes with him he'd give you the quickest little wink. It was as if that wink was to say, 'You're my baby.' Unbeknown to him, afterwards we'd all get in the van and be like, 'Did you get a wink today?' If someone didn't, you'd be like, 'Yeah, I'm his baby today.' Everyone got a wink at some point. That's why the spoof thing happened in the video because that was how it felt.

Max Giwa: Sean wasn't available so we had a cardboard cut-out of him. That was a send up. They all embraced it and took it on board.

Dania Pasquini: [The cut-out] was our idea. We were paying homage to the fact that he couldn't be there. We wanted to include him and, because the whole video was about irony and poking fun at the industry, we thought it was fitting. But I didn't understand that he was having a hard time then. I have a different view of it now.

Sean: It did hurt a little bit. It was kind of like the label saying, 'Well, he's so miserable anyway and he's not smiling and he's so quiet that he might as well have been a cardboard cut-out.' That's what it felt like to me.

Scott: It was awful. Sean can't even watch that video because that's just fucking wrong.

Sean: From the video directors' point of view, they had a job to do. What are they going to do? There's a band member missing, they've got their career and they've just got to carry on. They didn't know me personally.

Scott: I was also struggling. My eldest son was in intensive care because he was born six weeks early. He was really poorly and I remember a call when I was at the hospital looking after him saying, 'You've got to go on *CD:UK* and perform,' and I was like, 'I couldn't give a fuck, I'm not doing it.'

Chris Herbert: I can't remember that, no. Towards the end, there was trauma most days. It was very, very difficult. The ending of that band was really messy. I realise now that Scott was also really struggling mentally.

Scott: In the end, I ended up doing the performance. I was crying in the corridor and I think Rich looked at the boys and said, 'This is done.'

Ritchie: There was a lot going on. We'd also done a show in Belgium and I had sprained my ankle. So we were a band called Five with four members, doing a song called 'Let's Dance' but I was doing it on a stool. Then Scott just broke down in the corridor and I remember him saying, 'I just can't do this any more.' He was crying so much that he couldn't really talk. And J and I sat either side with our arms around him and I distinctly remember looking across at J and going, 'It's done, isn't it?' You can have as many number-one singles as you like but we were looking at two out of five members being basically unwell.

Sean: Simon Cowell was quite bitter about it back then. I don't hold anything against him; he was younger and he had his eye on the prize. There wasn't any mental health awareness. I'm sure he would deal with it differently now. Or I'd like to think he would. But back then he was quite bitter. I think he looked at me like, 'How could I not appreciate everything I'd been given by him?' He thought I was throwing it back in his face and being unappreciative because so many other kids would have loved to be doing what I was doing. But I just needed a little bit of help. I literally went from school to the next minute being on TV and really famous, but still a child. I handled it the best that I could, but it didn't go too brilliantly.

Chris Herbert: Richard Griffiths, who headed up BMG at the time, later went on to manage One Direction and I remember sitting down with him and he said, 'We're treating One Direction in a very different way to how we treated Five, because we learned how not to do it with them.'

'Liam Gallagher got a Bop It! out of his bag'

While Five's pop-star journey ended horribly, the band have continued in various guises throughout the years. After The Big Reunion in 2013, which J only appeared in briefly, they continued as a four-piece, before Abs left in 2014.

In 2022, Scott, Sean and Ritchie released a new album, Time, *still under the Five moniker despite the obvious numerical discrepancy. Like a lot of the pop stars from that era, for Scott, Ritchie and Sean it's the positive memories that have slowly drifted back to the surface. A time of huge concerts in front of hundreds of thousands of fans, of unexpected collaborations and of drunken evenings playing inane games with the lead singer of Oasis.*

Scott: The first memory that jumps out is being on stage with Queen at Party in the Park in front of 200,000 people, performing 'We Will Rock You', which obviously went to number one. The Queen version only got to number two, so Five beat Queen at their own game. Just coming off stage and Brian May saying he prefers our version because it's faster. I remember he said to me, and I'll never forget it, 'I always knew that "We Will Rock You" was a number-one record, I just didn't know it would happen now.' Really cool.

Ritchie: My ultimate favourite moment was actually a private one. We were doing 'We Will Rock You' and we were at Roger Taylor's house. He had this rehearsal studio and we'd done a few passes at the song and were having a tea break. The mic was still up so I just sang the opening lines of Jimi Hendrix's 'Hey Joe'. Then Brian started joining in with the guitar, then Roger's picked up the sticks and the three of us jammed the entire song. It was such a lovely moment. Yes, it's Rich from Five, the number-one boyband, and it's Queen, the absolute legends, but we were just three guys that really loved music.

Sean: This is going to be a bit of a let-down because most people talk about things like playing in front of 250,000 people, but my moment is laying in the little house we had in Surrey. We'd just signed the record deal and been to a label party. I remember laying in this little box room, still getting my £100 a week, and I couldn't believe we'd actually signed a record deal. For me that was it. It felt like anything was possible. All I wanted to do was music and it felt like it was really going to happen.

Scott: The other memory that sticks out is being very drunk with Liam Gallagher in Rio, where we'd performed on the same stage in front of 250,000 at Rock in Rio. I was with Sean, Rich, my wife, Kerry, and Liam Gallagher. He was playing an Oasis album that was about to come out and every song he had written he was like, 'Ah, fucking hell, man, this is an absolute banger, this is amazing.' Then every one Noel had written he'd say, 'This one's fucking shite.' Noel didn't speak to us at all – we weren't cool enough. But Liam was down for it, he invited us into the room for a few drinks.

Sean: Do you know what, I really, really liked Liam. He gets a bit of a bad rap from back in the day, but what I liked about him was, given the genre of music he's in, like the indie music, he could have been snobby with us. There was a lot of that at the time. He wouldn't get any sort of medals from the serious music press for hanging out with Five, but he didn't care. He just said, 'Sit down, have a drink.'

Scott: This is so not rock 'n' roll, but Liam then got a Bop It! out of his bag and was like, 'Shall we have a fucking bang on this, it's a brilliant game?' So we're standing around playing Bop It!, pissed. It's my favourite pub story. My mates will go, 'Tell the Bop It! Liam Gallagher story.'

Ritchie: At the time, it was really hard, but it's almost like it's giving back now. It's nice now.

Sean: I definitely don't regret being in the band. I wish that I could have found the strength to not have to leave. I wish we could have carried on. But it's not a regret because I had to do it. If I could change anything, I would put myself in a better place to handle it, you know.

4
Thank Steps for the Music

The Spice Girls' all-encompassing success instantly broadened pop's appeal, making consumers of a pre-teen, or tween, market who had previously ignored the lure of two-track cassette singles. It also made space for something more cartoonish in UK pop, while also making unfathomable success seem more attainable. Their sense of carefree magic wasn't necessarily as evident in the boybands that also peppered the pop landscape, however. Irish balladeers Boyzone would shortly usher in Irish balladeers Westlife and, while they both knew their way around a key change and looked delicious in a sensible black M&S roll-neck, the heady bounce and pep of that sugar-rush pop was absent.

That is until Steps – AKA Ian 'H' Watkins, Lee Latchford-Evans, Claire Richards, Faye Tozer and Lisa Scott-Lee – arrived in November 1997 via the ludicrous fiddle-heavy, line-dancing techno curio '5,6,7,8'. If the Spice Girls seemed like a gang you might want to join, Steps were the Butlin's Red Coats you initially wanted to avoid. Six months after '5,6,7,8' swept the UK school disco scene, Irish leg-wagglers B*Witched unleashed their own fiddle-heavy banger 'C'est La Vie' and suddenly fun was back in dysfunctional pop.

Keen to find a 'mixed Spice', AKA a pop act with both male and female members, '5,6,7,8' scribes Steve Crosby and Barry Upton, alongside manager Tim Byrne, had turned to pop's post-Spice Girls Bible, *The Stage*, in order to find their band. What was initially supposed to target the burgeoning line-dancing market (!), with little hopes of longevity, soon expanded into a hugely successful, ABBA-aping success story that's still going strong twenty-five years later.

'One of the girls, who was quite deep and spiritual, said it hurt her soul to sing "5,6,7,8"'

Claire from Steps: I actually signed my first record deal for a girlband called TSD on my eighteenth birthday. I had been doing karaoke every weekend at a pub and it was through people I'd met and knew that I heard about this girlband that was being put together. I went [to the audition] with my mum because I was only seventeen. We just chatted for ages and at the end they said, 'Do you want to do it, then?', and I said, 'Yeah, okay.'

H from Steps: Back then there was no *X Factor*, there was no *Britain's Got Talent* or *The Voice*, so the way we used to get jobs was via *The Stage*. Everyone was auditioning for either girlbands or boybands. So this one advert jumped out because it was looking for boy and girl members. I've got the original advert somewhere and it says, 'auditions for sassy, sexy twenty-year-olds'. I thought, 'Well, I can do that.' We all sent our CVs in and I embellished mine quite a lot because all I'd done was been a Red Coat at that point. So through a process of elimination Lisa and I plus three other members got the audition. That was the first line-up that was shopped around. Nobody took any interest.

Claire: When [TSD] didn't work out, I was devastated. I was temping at the time, doing reception work, and my mum said, 'Right, come on, you're miserable, let's start sending out your tapes and photos.' So I kept buying *The Stage* and looking at the adverts and sending off my cassette and picture to everybody. Most of the time using the Burger King head office's franking machine to send them.

H: The original three members left, basically because they didn't want to be line-dancing pop stars. We were so uncool. I love cheesy pop and I couldn't believe my luck. I'd come from a very small village in Wales and to me I'd hit the jackpot even though we hadn't done anything at that point.

Claire: I don't know how many applications I sent off but, I am not joking, Steps is the only one that called me for an audition. Myself, Lee and Faye were all at the same audition. H and Lisa had been in the band with three other people for about six months. For whatever reason, all three of those people decided it wasn't for them. I remember H telling me later that one of the girls, who was quite deep and spiritual, said it hurt her soul to sing '5,6,7,8'. Clearly I'm not that deep.

H: Claire has always been a lot more mature, so I thought she was twenty-eight when we first met.

Claire: Little shit.

H: I always thought she was an old soul, which is ridiculous because she's actually the baby of the band.

Claire: I do think he thought I looked older because I had really short hair and it probably aged me a little bit. But I was bloody nineteen! How dare he.

'I remember going from **Blue Peter** *rehearsals straight to the dole office'*

Once the final line-up was secured, the five-piece initially went their separate ways. There was no group house and, unlike other bands that followed later, there was no record deal in place. 'Normal' jobs still needed to be done in between showcases for labels. After dominating pop in the UK in the '80s and early '90s via his PWL label, be it with Kylie, Jason or 2 Unlimited, music impresario Pete Waterman was somewhat cast adrift by 1997. Kylie had gone indie, Jason had gone completely and 2 Unlimited had found there were indeed limits. After one very short showcase led to a very low offer, however, the fortunes for both Steps and Waterman were about to change.

H: Some of us couldn't afford mobile phones – I think Claire had one – but the rest of us wrote postcards to each other. We were penpals, basically. We weren't on a retainer, because we weren't signed. The people looking after us at the time didn't pay us a wage. It was all up in the air; we didn't know what was around the corner, so we were all rabbits in headlights when it started. It was pipe dreams.

Claire: Lisa was finishing a job at Butlin's, Lee was still at college. I don't know what H was doing. Faye was working at the Hilton on Park Lane, and actually she carried on for a while. There was no money at the start. Then we started rehearsing at Pinnacle leisure centre in Epsom. Believe it or not we rehearsed for the showcases for two weeks. Two weeks for one routine.

H: We had our showcase in Nomis Studios. We invited lots of record companies and heads of A&R – Simon Cowell came to see us on that same day and said no to us. He didn't want us. Years afterwards when we were doing the same show as Westlife, Simon came over to me and said, 'I made a mistake, I'm sorry.' But Pete [Waterman] just got it.

Claire: I think Simon had been to see the other formation of the group. I think they'd done a few showcases and hadn't been signed. The only showcase [the new line-up] did was at Battery Studios and that was for Tina Wisby and Steve Jenkins, who were the head of Jive, and Pete Waterman. Pete had a licensing deal with Jive at the time, so technically we were signed through Pete's label Eastern Bloc Unity Label and it all went through Jive.

Pete Waterman: An old friend of mine rang me and said he'd got a group and they wanted to audition for us. To be honest, I went out of politeness. One thing I can tell you now is I wasn't interested in a line-dancing group. My mother-in-law at the time had been telling me for at least a year that the way to make money was a line-dancing record and when your head of A&R is your mother-in-law you've got a real problem. So I had avoided it like the plague.

H: Pete was this legendary figure that shaped my childhood. My bedroom wall was Bananarama, Kylie, Jason, and Rick Astley. All of these icons, their careers were launched by this man, this god. And he was a pop god.

Claire: I was a PWL kid. That was exactly the kind of music I listened to and was obsessed with as a teenager. Pete just seemed to get it immediately. We'd all raided our wardrobes and found matching outfits and basically just mimed and did the dance routines. We didn't even pretend to sing it. I've heard him tell the story that as soon as he heard me sing he just knew – but he didn't hear me sing on that day!

Pete Waterman: They did '5,6,7,8' and instantly I'd forgotten about the line-dancing thing, I just watched them and Claire was brilliant.

Karl Twigg, Steps songwriter and producer: Straight away you could tell they were stars. 911 came in as well and you had the main guy who looked like one of Ant and Dec, don't know which one. Straight away you thought, 'Hang on, these guys are going to make it.' But Pete didn't take them on.

Lee Brennan: I don't think Pete had much time for us really. I think he just thought, 'Here's another act trying to do it.' Didn't want to sign us.

Pete Waterman: [Steps] had done the rounds of all the record companies because Tim [Byrne], who was their manager, was packaging them as Mixed Spice. I guess what worked for me was because I had just gone in to be polite, it sort of whacked me and I went, 'Wow, that's amazing.' I forgot all about the cowboy hats and I just thought they were really good. But I was in a hurry, so I said to Steve, 'Listen, sign 'em, give him £500 for the record and I'll make it at the weekend.' If they'd have had another offer they wouldn't have taken mine because I was so matter of fact about it. So I went back to the office, played the demo [of '5,6,7,8'] to a couple of producers and members of the staff and they all thought it was awful. Dreadful. I said, 'Sorry, but it's a hit.' The two producers wouldn't put their name on it at first; they wanted nothing to do with it. So I said, 'Put Pete Waterman on twice the size you normally would, then.'

Karl Twigg: That is complete and utter . . . truth. I tell you what it was, when Mark [Topham, Steps songwriter and producer] and I first got to PWL we'd been in jazz funk bands. And we'd gone from that to '5,6,7,8'. We still knew all the guys from those other bands, so we were like, 'Fucking hell, what are they all going to say when they hear this?' The funny thing is, when we did [Steps' 2000 number-one bop] 'Stomp' later on, all the musicians we knew played on that song. So even they succumbed to the lure of Steps.

Pete Waterman: There was so much belligerence against me putting this record out that the producers really wanted to take the mickey out of me. But you can't wind me up – once I think a record is a hit the more perverse you want to be the more I'm going to like it. So when I went in they'd really modernised it, and really techno-ed it as opposed to line-dance-ed it. Thinking they were going to offend me. If anything they'd made it more palatable for me. I did come up with the techno idea, but not as techno as they went.

Karl Twigg: I would never have made a record to piss him off. You put your heart and soul into it.

H: We're opening up old wounds now – I'm over it, I promise – but in the original version of '5,6,7,8', I sang the whole middle eight. Lisa did the answer phrase bit. But the lyrics were so bad, oh my gosh. I'm so glad it was cut in the end.

Karl Twigg: There were some parts in the middle of it that Pete wanted to keep that just sounded like 'I Should Be So Lucky'. I had a massive row with him while we were making it. I took that part out. I just ripped the original version they brought in to pieces.

H: The label saw us as a one-off novelty record. Like 'The Birdie Song' or 'Agadoo'. They didn't believe in us that much to invest money in the future. But our peers, like B*Witched or Five or S Club, they had millions of pounds invested in them as groups that would have longevity.

Claire: I was lucky I still lived at home with my mum and dad, so any money I got I spent on clothes. Everybody else had to pay rent. Every now and then we'd get per diems, so the first time someone handed us that little wad of cash it was like, 'Oh my God!' For a long time, that's all we really lived on. If we earned any money from any gigs we did, it just covered our expenses.

It was a good year and a half before we earned any proper money at all.

H: I remember going from *Blue Peter* rehearsals straight to the dole office to get our Jobseeker's Allowance, me and Lee. We lived together. We weren't getting paid. So yeah, we were on TV but we were also signing on. Nobody recognised us back then so it was fine.

Claire: By this point, H especially had so much faith in the fact '5,6,7,8' was going to be a massive hit. And, being signed to an actual label, we felt like there was something behind it. Even at that point, it was still just meant to be a line-dancing band. Pete knew it was going to be the hit that got us noticed, but it wasn't his intention to follow through with that sound. We've got a stash of line-dancing hits just waiting to be released!

Pete Waterman: The real gem of the story is one of my mates was Tony Wilson from Factory Records. He did evening shows for Granada and I did [ITV's late-night clubbing show] *The Hitman and Her*. We had a mutual respect for each other. He rang me and said, 'Waterman, everybody's after your guts,' and I went, 'Why?', and he said, 'Because you've killed country music, you're a pariah.' Then he said they'd got so much hate mail, could we do a programme with you? It was a Wednesday-night slot on Granada and it was like, 'You bring your band on and let these people have a go at you.' So we did the show, everybody was having a go at me, but the audience just went through the roof. By Saturday I had a call from the lady who ran Saturday morning TV for the BBC saying, 'Could we have this group on?'

H: All I knew was that I was in a pop band and I was going to be on the front of *Smash Hits* magazine and on *Top of the Pops* and that's all I cared about.

Claire: [At that time] there was Aqua and the Vengaboys and we could have gone down that road, I think, but Pete managed to change it to become something in between all of that. Even though it was all very upbeat and up-tempo, if you listen to our songs they're all quite depressing. It was our image that meant people really saw us as that kiddy band. We'd perform everything with a big smile and a dance routine. People just hadn't seen anything like it. There is a very big element of escapism when it comes to Steps.

H: Also, don't forget, Pete had spent a long time in the pop wilderness – he'd had major hits in the '80s, but there'd been a spell of time where there were tumbleweeds. He didn't know where he was going. He had a lot to prove.

Karl Twigg: He was a byword for bad music. When we got [to PWL] it was the uncoolest place to be.

Pete Waterman: ['5,6,7,8'] sold 500,000 copies. It's probably the biggest-selling single never to enter the top ten. The whole fact it was selling was staggering. We kept looking at it and thinking, 'This is incredible.' It was selling right across the board, not just the stores that reported to the charts. Steps were the only group where we never discounted any of their records. We never did discounts to Woolworths or anybody. We kept that right up until the very end – if you want it, you've got to buy it.

Claire: In those days, everybody worked hard to break an artist because back then you had to. In a night, we'd probably do an under-18s, then do something early evening and then do a nightclub. Imagine being in a nightclub and that fiddle starts up. The outfit I wore in the '5,6,7,8' video was the outfit I wore for every single club gig for months and months. Bearing in my mind my outfit was red PVC trousers and a red mesh top, neither of which are very washable. So yeah, you could probably smell me coming most of the time. When we got *Top of the Pops* we begged them, 'Please please please can we have a new outfit.'

H: '5,6,7,8' became this monster nobody could stop. We released the record in November and it stuck around for a few months and it was in January when Pete said, 'Right, we can do something more with this.' Then negotiations took place. At the time, we were line-dancing pop stars but it was Pete's idea to turn us into, and I quote, 'ABBA on speed'. He always saw us as more than 'The Birdie Song'. Everyone laughed at us, everyone wanted to get rid of us, but we kept coming back. It was like COVID; you couldn't get rid of us – it was a pop pandemic.

'All of S Club 7 were sleeping underneath the make-up tables'

Given Steps' manager Tim Byrne had started his career working on the Smash Hits *Poll Winners' Party and its associated tour, Steps were quickly thrown into the 'live' circuit of nationwide roadshows. With six-week lead times for singles and a plethora of magazines (*Smash Hits, Big!, Top of the Pops, J-17, *etc.), regional radio and TV shows to appear on, pop acts would often* *find themselves bumping into each other multiple times a week. A community slowly built; a petri dish of bonding and bickering between power naps.*

Claire: The vibe was very different [back then]. Everybody knew everybody. I remember at the *Smash Hits* Poll Winners' Party, it was always the girls in one room and the boys in the other, so obviously H and Lee would be in with Five and 911 and Westlife. We'd be in with B*Witched and Billie Piper and the girls from S Club 7. Everybody got on really well. We all had a laugh. I find that in pop now everybody keeps themselves to themselves. No one really mixes any more.

Lee Brennan: They'd set up little curtained-off areas and we'd all be chatting over the curtains. We'd all be in a sports hall getting changed together. I think once everybody got really, really busy it would be like passing ships in the night. You'd see someone coming offstage and be like, 'Hey, how you doing, mate? Can't stop, going to another thing somewhere else.' It became this crazy whirlwind.

H: I still class some of my dear friends now as people I met from bands during that period. I've known some of them for twenty-five years and unless you've lived it you don't understand it. We shared dressing rooms at the *Smash Hits* Poll Winners' Party, so we'd be with S Club and we were all knackered getting our make-up done. They were sleeping underneath the make-up tables. I remember Tina and Jon literally sleeping on my feet. It was crazy. I remember Adam Rickett coming in to change – my ears pricked up then, I can tell you. It's a cliché but it was an incredible rollercoaster that will never happen again like that.

Bradley McIntosh, S Club 7: When we were around other bands at, say, the *Smash Hits* afterparty, we always felt like they all knew each other and we didn't know them as well. We were often in America doing the TV shows. So we'd feel like outsiders.

H: All Saints were the coolest band. They'd walk in a room and everybody wanted to see them, whereas we'd be changing behind a cardboard divider with our coat-hanger head mics.

Claire: For a while, I definitely thought I was cooler than I was. I'd be like, 'I wear Maharishi trousers and I wear shell-toed trainers, I must be cool.' I *so* wanted to be in All Saints. I think it took me a long time to realise what Steps is. I think I was fighting against what Steps was but now I'm not at all. Steps is exactly us.

H: We had a record company and we had people looking after us, but we didn't have people throwing money at us. Honestly, I think that's why we did so well [financially], because we were young but we weren't stupid. We knew that money was going to have to be coming from somewhere. That money was going to be recouped. Whereas, no disrespect to other bands, maybe they weren't as savvy and sassy as us. We weren't teenagers, we'd had jobs and we'd worked in the business, so even though we didn't understand record contracts we knew somebody was paying for it and that was probably going to be us.

'Her mum's ringing up saying, "You're not taking drugs, are you, Claire?"'

While '5,6,7,8' peaked at number fourteen and dug its scootin' boots in by hanging around the UK top forty for over three months, Steps were still dismissed as one-hit wonders in waiting. While a bank of line-dancing songs gathered dust in a cupboard somewhere, there was one song that was about to change everything. August 1998's 'One for Sorrow', which 'channelled' ABBA's 'The Winner Takes It All', became their first bon-afide smash (it would have been number one were it not for those pesky Welsh polemicists Manic Street Preachers and their snappily titled 'If You Tolerate This Then Your Children Will Be Next'), setting a template of hi-NRG yet wistful pop that the band would become synonymous for. Oh, and covers – lots of covers.

Claire: ['One for Sorrow'] started to prove to people that we weren't going anywhere and that we could release serious music.

Pete Waterman: Karl [Twigg] and Mark [Topham] played me 'One for Sorrow' at a meeting with the management and the band. I was very worried about whether we were ready to go with that song at that time. So I said, 'No, we need something before that,' so we did 'Last Thing on My Mind', which should have been a hit for Bananarama [in 1992], but at that point they were past their sell-by date. It was a long way from outside the top ten to a number one, so we needed an interim record. When 'One for Sorrow' came out, it was just a record that was like, 'Wow.'

Jeremy Joseph: With Steps you're watching a band evolve at G-A-Y. There was a moment where suddenly we saw an enduring pop act and it was with 'Last Thing on My Mind'. They performed '5,6,7,8' and got an okay reaction. Then they did 'Last Thing on My Mind' and the reaction was stronger. You could see for an adult audience that they were turning into a proper band.

Claire: I used to just hang around the studio and wait until I was needed because I was told, 'Don't go home.' But I didn't really have a life either because I didn't have a boyfriend and I lived at home with my mum and dad.

Karl Twigg: Their schedule was insane. We were trying to finish Claire's vocal [on 'One for Sorrow'] because the next day they would be off and we wouldn't see them again for sixteen weeks. [One night] she was recording at 2.30 a.m. and her mum's ringing up saying, 'You're not taking drugs, are you, Claire?'

Claire: She was saying, 'What are they giving you? What is it that's making you stay awake?' I was like, 'Mum, I'm twenty, I think I can stay awake.' Most of the time we'd have little naps during the day. I used to have this coat that looked like a sleeping bag so I'd put the hood over my head and you'd just have this little lump of duvet.

Karl Twigg: [Mark and I] did used to have the odd spliff, one every sort of fifteen minutes . . . No, it wasn't that bad.

H: Oh, that would explain a lot. I would have flagged that. I was such an angel back then. But I was smoking cigarettes a lot, just because at the time everybody knows we weren't singing live. It was the thing to do – we were basically pop drag queens. We used to lip synch for our lives.

Karl Twigg: All we did was muck about and laugh [in the studio]. That is it. H would come in in the morning and fucking nipple-cripple me. I'd be like, 'You fucker.'

H: Yeah, just little nipple cramps. That was my general good morning, to the girls as well . . . I'm joking!

Claire: With ['One for Sorrow'] I always thought it was because I was the only one [in the studio], so that was why I sang the whole song. But I've been told different since.

Lisa from Steps: Years ago it was difficult when somebody was given more [lines], but how I look at it now that I've had kids and grown up, I'm proud of the vocal and it's a great song. I'm proud that she's in our band.

Karl Twigg: I don't want to say that she carried the band, but I think at the beginning her voice was so unique and powerful. To the point where after recording '5,6,7,8' we said to Claire, 'Give us a call if this doesn't work out.' But the minute we finished ['One for Sorrow'], we were just looking at each other like, 'Let's have another listen, is it really what we think it is?' I love that record.

Claire: Pete used to do this thing where he'd sit us in the studio and listen to the whole album back to back and then he'd play what the next single was going to be. It was 'One for Sorrow' and I started crying.

Pete Waterman: We could have had a number one with that song if we'd have done discounting. If we were number one or number three we didn't care because we wanted to build the fanbase. If you didn't like Steps you didn't like Steps full stop. It wasn't like we were going to convince you by knocking 10p off the price of the record.

Claire: Later I was trying to make a point that every time we released a single we would be number two but we would have sold more copies than most other number ones of that year. It was probably my mistake for using Westlife as an example – well, it obviously was – and I just said, 'Next week Westlife could release a song and sell 10,000 and they'll be number one.' They took it that I was specifically picking them out. Then Louis Walsh was on the radio going into one about Steps and then Westlife wouldn't talk to us for ages. It was really weird.

H: [Follow-up] 'Tragedy' was also a really strange one because it was another single that stuck around, so we were in the pop consciousness. Probably for the wrong reasons because they just wanted us to go away. 'Tragedy' was chosen because it was part of the TV show *Bee Gees Mania* and our manager at the time, Tim Byrne, he bagsied 'Tragedy' for us. The dance routine originally was more like Kevin McAllister in *Home Alone*, like slapping each side of our faces, but we said no.

Claire: ['Tragedy'] was the first number one of 1999, so that made it more special. It had felt like it was never going to happen. Back then those chart positions were so important. It was the difference between your record company keeping you or getting dropped.

Peter Loraine, former artist development manager, Polydor: For my first job at Polydor I was tasked with putting together a Bee Gees tribute album. So I spoke to Tim and together we decided they would do 'Tragedy'. Very exciting. Two days later Tim phones back and he says, 'It's not going to happen, I can't get Pete Waterman to do it, he thinks it's a terrible idea, sorry.' My boss was Lucian Grainge, who is now head of Universal for the world, and he asked me how I was getting on with the Bee Gees album and I said, 'Robbie's in, 911, Louise, but Steps have said no.' Lucian picked up the phone, ordered a car and we drove to PWL and we went in for a meeting with Pete. Lucian said, 'This is my new person, he's doing this, you need to do this for us, at least try it out.' So Pete kind of rolls his eyes and agrees. And it went to number one!

Pete Waterman: I was never not behind it. Not true. I was approached to do this album with the Bee Gees and we agreed to do a Steps track as long as it was 'Tragedy' and that we could have the single rights and they could have it on the album. That was the only negotiation. I can even tell you when I did that deal – I was walking down the platform at Euston Station to catch the train to Liverpool. I know exactly where I was when I rang Tim Byrne and said, 'Right, I've agreed that deal, we've got the singles rights and they can have the track for the album free of charge.'

Peter Loraine: Then *Abbamania* [the ABBA tribute album] came after the Bee Gees one.

Pete Waterman: The thing was, ABBA were like [production hit factory] Stock Aitken Waterman. People hated ABBA. The whole thing came about because Elvis Costello and myself were on a very late-night television show and Bono made this derogatory remark, which he always denies, about ABBA. And we just said, 'Sorry, this is one the greatest pop bands of all time.' At that time, nobody played ABBA. I then got called by London Weekend Television and we talked the producer Bob Massie into using pop groups like B*Witched, Steps and all that [for a TV special] and that's literally how that whole ABBA thing broke open. It was huge and I think there were four singles taken from that album that were hits. ABBA saw us as these outcasts that history had almost erased, so [it was comforting for them] when one of these guys, Pete Waterman, comes along and says, 'Welcome to the club, I know what it's like to be hated because I'm hated more than you are.'

Steve Anderson: When 'One for Sorrow' came out everyone was like, 'Oh, it's a bit like ABBA,' but what that did was remind people about ABBA. A few weeks after the release of 'One for Sorrow', ABBA's *Greatest Hits* went to number one. It was before *Mamma Mia!*, all of that. He did it again when Steps did 'Stomp' and there was a sticker on the sleeve like 'respect to Nile Rodgers and Bernard Edwards'. It was a Chic record. But then people started getting more interested in Chic.

Karl Twigg: Yeah, I think that [sticker] might have been Pete's idea. They still sued us anyway so we probably shouldn't have put the sticker on there. I think that drew more attention to it. 'I'll show you how to get past this, lads.' Yeah, cheers, Pete. They got a percentage of the song.

Pete Waterman: You can't just put this record out without paying homage to the person you've nicked it from. I'll sort the publishing out with Nile Rodgers, but you've got to credit the fact it was their idea. You can't just take somebody's track and then say, 'Well, it's in homage.' If it is then great, but pay the bleeding bloke.

'The reaction was, "Who the fucking hell is Belle and Sebastian?"'

*The BRIT Awards have always prized themselves on their unique collaborations, and the 1999 show was no exception. In years to come, we'd witness Florence Welch twirling around Dizzee Rascal and Rihanna looking perplexed near the Klaxons, but on that chilly February night an ill-fated supergroup made a right old racket that would go down in award show infamy. But enough about David Bowie and Placebo's 'unique' take on '20th Century Boy'; let's focus instead on Steps, Cleopatra, Billie Piper, B*Witched and Tina Cousins donning their finest highly flammable satin flares for the four-part medley 'Thank ABBA for the Music'. If that riled up the 'real music' gatekeepers, they would soon get their own back when milky tea-drinking students Belle and Sebastian caused the biggest award show controversy since Jarvis Cocker waggled his bony posterior near a Jesus-aping Michael Jackson.*

Claire: There was a real snobbery around pop, and us, and what they think we are. People like the Spice Girls, you can't ignore that volume of success, so they had to acknowledge them in a way, but everybody else was doing really well behind them but was never given as much attention. We were selling more records and selling out more arenas than quite a lot of those acts who got their moment.

Pete Waterman: They used all the acts doing ABBA to get the audience, because that was the big thing at the time – B*Witched,

Steps and all that, it was enormous. They knew there were no big acts to get the kids watching TV so they put them on. But it was more, 'Get them on and get them off as quick as possible.'

Louise: When you were in that environment it wasn't so much about the music. It was about your ability to draw a crowd on the red carpet. I'm sure your cooler bands would look down their noses a bit more, but ultimately there is no difference. If you're selling enough records to keep on making albums then you're doing something right, regardless of your style of music. Also, everyone loves a good pop song.

H: That night was crazy. It was definitely us versus them. The room was full of the coolest people in the world and there was us. I filmed all the rehearsals, so there's Lisa and I watching Cher. Backstage footage of Stephen Gately playing the slot machines and us rehearsing with Billie Piper. I just couldn't believe my luck – this iconic show and they had us on there. And they didn't really do pop. Those cool cats, the bigwigs, they don't like pop.

Claire: It was one of the first public votes using the internet [for British Breakthrough Act]. We were being told constantly that we were going to win. No one told us what order the awards were going to be done in and I'd been ill with tonsillitis so had missed most of the day's rehearsal. Everybody that was in that category was in our performance pretty much. So we were all stood backstage [ready to perform] and someone went, 'Is that our award [being read out]? We found out we hadn't won and then we had to go out and do ABBA Mania.

Peter Robinson: I was there that night and I don't think the problem with that performance was the lack of rehearsal. In terms of saying thank you to someone, it's a bit like putting a ribbon on a shit and posting it through a letterbox.

Stef D'Andrea, joint owner of Belle and Sebastian's former label, Jeepster: We got an invitation from the BPI. We thought it was a bit peculiar. Radio 1 were promoting [the award] and saying you can vote for your favourite via phone voting and via the very new form of internet voting. A lot of Belle and Sebastian's fans were fourteen to twenty. The two youngest people at Jeepster at the time were nineteen or twenty years old, and a chap who worked with us called David understood where the internet was going. He had started Sinister List, the band's mailing list, which the fans would join and have these great long chats. So the suggestion came from one of these chat rooms – why don't we spread the word to all the Belle and Sebastian fans to vote via Radio 1's website?

Mark Beaumont, indie scribe for *Melody Maker* and *NME*: It was the first show of strength of the internet because the BRITs were the establishment stronghold and here was Belle and Sebastian using the weight of their fanbase to break the stranglehold of pop. I think it was the first high-profile example of the internet being used to shift culture. There was a real feeling that [the alternative indie scene] had broken through over the course of Britpop in the mid '90s. With the alternative music scene at that point, there was a sense that they did deserve to be there and at that top table. We got used to that feeling that we could break the charts on a regular basis. There was a certain amount of entitlement there.

Claire: No one had even heard of Belle and Sebastian.

H: Who were they again? Who?!

Pete Waterman: Had I heard of them before? No. Had anyone? No. Did I care? No. I felt sorry for Steps.

Karl Twigg: I was there. I was on the table with them. The reaction was, 'Who the fucking hell is Belle and Sebastian?'

Stef D'Andrea: Technically Steps had more fans, but as we know with pop fans they're very overnight things and they don't tend to maintain fans. Belle and Sebastian have still got a strong fanbase twenty-five years later, but Steps, like most pop bands, didn't last.

Claire: I remember Pete Waterman and Steve Jenkins going crazy and causing a real stink because if it wasn't us who should have won, Five were in that category, Cleopatra. It was all the new pop of the time. No one could believe it.

Peter Robinson: I remember a sort of pandemonium. Not because Steps hadn't won it but just the fact that Belle and Sebastian had. And they weren't like [fellow nominees] Cornershop, who had had a hit record. The way they galvanised their fanbase was the sort of thing a band like Steps would be doing years later.

Pete Waterman: I wasn't surprised [when Steps lost]. I'd made it quite plain that I thought the BRIT Awards were basically the major labels patting themselves on the back and that was proved.

Stef D'Andrea: We were literally one man and his dog. Me and my friend started [the label]. We were in a tiny rented office in west London, we had two teenagers working for us and that was it. It was probably the last shocking moment at the BRITs really, after the Jarvis incident and the John Prescott Chumbawamba thing [Prescott received a cold shower at the 1998 awards]. It was going to be on the front page of *The Sun* the next day but wound up on page three because some other celebrity nonsense happened, but it was on the front page of *The Sun* in Scotland.

Pete Waterman: To me [the BRITs] shot themselves in the foot because you couldn't deny it – everybody could see it at that point. I didn't have to say anything any more, did I? Steps not winning – how does that work? Sometimes you stay quiet because it looks wrong if you say anything because the public can see it for themselves. Everybody that year just went, 'What?'

Stef D'Andrea: There were various people either congratulating us on the night or saying snide things. Just, 'Who are you? I've never heard of you?' I realised how much it mattered to people. It's harder to imagine that now because award ceremonies just go over people's heads, like the charts do. In the '90s, the charts and award ceremonies were so big. We did end up on *Top of the Pops* in 2000 when we had a single called 'Legal Man'. We came into view of the pop artists again because that pop group with seven people in it were there. I realised by standing next to them that all seven of them seemed to be identical in height. They must have gone, 'Right, we want it so that when they're on screen you don't have to go from small to tall.' It was like they were made by a machine.

H: There was a lot of controversy around it and Pete went to town.

Stef D'Andrea: We then went back to our office and suddenly all these phone calls started coming in from the *Mail* and *The Sun*, asking for comment. It was like, 'What? Who is Pete Waterman? What is he saying?' When I told the band about it they all pissed themselves laughing. After all the stink started with Pete Waterman and the newspapers, they thought they'd really cracked it. They thought they'd uncovered a con because 12 per cent of the votes came from one computer and that was basically old men not understanding the internet. If you go back to 1998 and you're at a university like Glasgow or Edinburgh, there's like 25,000 students there and you've got a library with these things called computer terminals you can go on the internet with. So 25,000 students would have access to a handful of terminals. They didn't understand how the voting worked.

Pete Waterman: To apologise for the year before, you then dream up a new category [Best Live Act]. How does that work? I thought that was nonsense. That was an even bigger insult than not giving them the award in the first place.

H: When we did win that award a year later, they told us to pay to get a physical copy of it. So it was £500 each and everyone paid for their one, but I said, 'No, stick your BRIT Award,

I don't want one, thank you.' I'm not paying for something I've won.

Mark Beaumont: It was fantastic Belle and Sebastian managed to bag the award through canniness and the passion of their fans, but if you see the indie versus pop thing as a bit of a battle, which to some degree it was, it woke the pop world up to the potential of what could be done with the internet. Over time, they certainly weaponised that.

Pete Waterman: If nobody loves you, you don't care, do you? If people hate you, then you know there will be no good reviews written about you so you don't have to read reviews or care what people think. There's no point, you know where you stand.

Mark Beaumont: I remember Steps came to the *NME* Awards in 2001 and I was sent on a ridiculous job by the editor. There was a programme on at the time called *Banzai* and there was a guy on it called Shakey-Hands Man and his job was to shake hands with people for as long as possible. So I was sent out to be the Shakey-Hands Man at the *NME* awards and Faye from Steps – what a lovely woman – she literally shook my hand until I wanted to stop. She had no problem whatsoever with very lengthy handshakes. I was quite fond of Steps really. At that time, as much as there was a sense of triumph in the underground alternative music reaching the charts, there was also a bit of respect there.

Chris Cowey: You have to park your own personal musical tastes to one side and do what's right for the audience. I had to learn to appreciate S Club 7 and Steps and try to find the television gold in it. Even getting bands like Steps to sing live, you know, some of them had great voices. Also, I used to always try to focus on *Top of the Pops* refuseniks, of which there were a few. I would say to the Radioheads of this world, 'Look, every time you don't do the show, that means I have to put Steps on.'

Claire: *Top of the Pops* was my absolute dream come true. When I was a kid my nan's husband worked as a security guard at the BBC and he took me there one day and showed me round. I remember watching Bonnie Tyler rehearsing in the studio and just thinking, 'This is everything I've ever wanted.' Then we went to the canteen and had beans and chips and that is exactly what I ate the first time we did *Top of the Pops*.

Lee Thompson, head of music, The Box: One of our biggest acts were Steps. They were brilliant because they knew that if you put a simple dance routine in the video and then when the single comes out you open up the booklet and it tells you how to do it, it's that perfect synergy. Very clever. That's why Steps were so huge and so successful without Radio 1 play. You'd never find a Steps song on the Radio 1 playlist or even on a commercial radio playlist at that point.

Paul Flynn: I was reviewing Steps for the *Manchester Evening News* and I took my friend who really loved them. It was a bit of a step too far for me. Quite literally. But, you know, I'd take Steps over Travis any day of the week. They were playing the Manchester Apollo and I was the row in front of Pete Waterman and he had a banner that said, 'Steps we fucking love you'. And it looked like he'd made it himself.

Pete Waterman: What? No, not me. Definitely not me. Let me tell you, I've done a lot of things in my life, but a Steps concert with a banner? Definitely not. It was my doppelgänger.

'They probably thought, "Are they children's entertainers? Is this comedy?"'

By the summer of 1999, Steps had scored five top-ten singles in the UK, while debut album Step One *had shifted close to 1.5 million copies. They also found themselves on the same label as both Britney Spears and the Backstreet Boys. It made sense, therefore, for Steps and their matching outfits to traverse the Atlantic and see if their easily digestible dance routines and hi-NRG pop could seduce audiences used to pneumatic precision and Swedish-made, high-gloss bangers. The fact that they were all wearing yellow pedal pushers wasn't going to faze them.*

Charlie Adelman, US Steps fan: I first heard the music of Steps when I was eleven years old at my first Britney Spears concert. Steps opened and it was 'One for Sorrow' that got me into them. I remember hearing it at the show and being like, 'Oh, I love this.' Then they did 'Tragedy' and my dad said, 'This is an abomination, they've ruined the Bee Gees.' I had never heard the original at that point.

Claire: We didn't want to go [to America]. We were doing so well in the UK and we were quite savvy when it came to what things were going to cost us. They wanted us to re-shoot videos and we didn't really want to do that. I'm glad we did it. It was good for us, but it was a weird experience.

H: We were bonafide pop stars . . . Actually, I hate that word 'stars'; I prefer tarts. So we were pop tarts in our own right by 1999. We were riding high, we'd had massive success, so I didn't think of Britney as anything different to somebody that was doing the same job as us. When we were just starting out, we were headlining a gig in Singapore for the record company and Britney was our support, which is crazy. She was so lovely and I remember we were dicking around in the pool after, just being stupid. And because of that she asked us to support her on her American tour.

Claire: H loved that tour . . .

H: I became great mates with her. For some reason, she took a shine to me – probably because I've got a big gob. She loved the British accent. I wore pedal pushers at the time and she loved them. She also loved the Paul Frank T-shirts that I used to wear and I remember drawing a little map for her to tell her how to get to the Paul Frank shop in Covent Garden. We got on really well, so [on the tour] she invited me to fly on her private jet, which didn't go down very well with the others. Come on, I'm not going to turn that down! I'm not going to go on a sleeper bus, with no sleep.

Claire: We didn't really have to sleep on the bus anyway, because by the time we came off stage we would drive a couple of hours and be in the next place. H never really wanted to do that so somehow he got himself well in there with old Britney.

H: I remember [the US] reaction was horror. They were used to NSYNC, the Backstreet Boys and obviously Britney. We'd turn up looking like tropical fruits in banana yellow doing 'Love's Got a Hold of My Heart' and they'd be like, 'What the fuck is this?' They probably thought, 'Are they children's entertainers? Is this comedy?' But we did a big Disney special and there was a massive spike and 'Tragedy' did really well, I think.

Charlie Adelman: I remember on the sticker for the *Step One* album here the quote was from the *New York Times* review and it was something like, 'If the '90s belonged to the Spice Girls, the '00s belong to Steps.' But if Steps had blown up in the US my passion for it may not have sustained. I was far less into S Club 7 because they were on TV every week and everyone knew who they were. They were cheesy and lame and everyone knew that. Steps I could get away with because people didn't really know.

Claire: Do you know what, some audiences were great, but in the middle of America I'd say nine times out of ten there'd be lots of open mouths. People just not entirely sure what was going on.

Charlie Adelman: Britney was the first modern pop artist I was into and Steps were just so different from that. It was fun to have Britney, this over-the-top, promiscuous pop star, who for an eleven-year-old boy felt very edgy, but then Steps were like a modern take on the old queens I'd grown up listening to.

Pete Waterman: I stepped away at that point because I knew the Americans wouldn't understand Steps, and they didn't. They went and did some very strange things and I wasn't prepared to do that. I just didn't get it. The Americans saw Steps and thought they were a cabaret band.

H: Because we'd spent so much time in America, the other territories that we were riding high in suffered. So we had to make a decision between carrying on in America or maintaining what we have. The general consensus was to maintain what we had. At this point we were knackered, we were burnt out. We'd just started to realise that we could say no to things. We were very much pop puppets. But we were workaholics as well. We all knew that if we didn't work hard we wouldn't get results. Other bands rested on their laurels or they'd take months off because they were knackered, but we were literally on the whole time. We used to do two weeks at Wembley arena with matinees. No other band did matinees.

Jordan Paramor, author, *Steps: In Private*: Quite often Faye and Lisa would be up for a drink afterwards, maybe H, so we'd go to the bar. Claire not always. Lee was a bit more head down. Faye loved a party. There were hilarious times where I would be chasing Faye down the corridor trying to get her to speak to me. They were so easy and lovely to deal with. I've been around some people that I would not like to go on tour with, quite frankly.

Sam Bloom, all STARS*: I don't remember us spending that much time with Steps when we supported them. They are a bit older than us so they were in a slightly different age bracket. They were also in a different fame bracket, too.

Claire: There were a lot more magazines and more TV shows to do back in those days and we would do absolutely everything that we could.

H: I remember it was the 1999 MTV Europe Awards in Dublin and I was hanging out with Britney and Christina. I had a stinking cold, I was so ill. So I was going home early. I was in the limo rank and next door to me was Missy Elliott and then Alicia Silverstone was the other side of me giving me tissues. Missy Elliott had her arm around me at one point saying, 'You'll be okay.' I was like, 'This is fucking some surreal shit.' I'd just been chatting to Britney and Christina and now Missy Elliott's got her arm around me and Alicia Silverstone is giving me tissues. What the fuck? And I went home to a Lemsip.

'It's not enough to say, "Oh, the tabloids were homophobic"; everyone was'

The idea of 'manufactured pop' heavily implies laser-focused, conveyor-belt perfection. Band members have jumped through hoops, passed various tests and been selected based on their ability to make uncomplicated sense to as many people as possible. It's a straight line from the band to the fans; no tangents, no kinks, no sudden movements. The platonic ideal of a pop act is that everyone is available to be fancied at all times. This is very important for men whose attractiveness and constant availability snares the core female pop fans who, it was heavily assumed, would not accept a deviation from the single and straight. For H – who saw friend Stephen Gately come out via The Sun *in 1999 ('Music experts and fans are predicting Boyzone's career will continue to prosper' ran a worried BBC article at the time) – that meant living as a gay man within the band but not being publicly out until 2007, six years after the band split. For Lee, and the female members of Steps, it meant hiding relationships.*

H: There came a time when the band all knew [I was gay], where I'd told them, and from then onwards they had my back.

As we were evolving as a group and getting more well-known, the interest from the tabloids was growing. Also, magazines like *Smash Hits* and *Top of the Pops* would always ask, 'Who do you fancy?', and Lisa would always go, 'He's only got eyes for me.' It was a way of shutting the conversation down. To make a joke out of it. In hindsight, you could still say Britney Spears was fit and mean it, but not want to play with her boobs.

Claire: We all just backed him up, whatever he said. Firstly, it wasn't our situation to discuss. It was very rare that we were asked [about our sexuality], if ever really. But we all knew, so within the five of us we didn't need to keep things hidden. But it was all a bit more sneaky in those days, so nobody would come out and ask him in an interview. We all know now what went on back then with people getting stories and things, so I think we all did well within us to keep a lid on it. And quite rightly he told his story himself when he was ready.

H: We lived in a very different day and age. We had to appeal to our market, which was perceived as the teen market. I kind of got away with it – I was never a sex object. I was never a sex bomb. I was always the cheeky blond one with blue eyes and big gob, so I masked a lot of the interest in me with that. I deflected it.

Alex Needham: Sexuality was almost irrelevant because the audience was so young. We probably would ask people who they fancied, which is slightly cringey that we would do that to people we knew were gay. Although we didn't always know. I remember asking Ricky Martin whether he fancied Mel B, which is quite embarrassing now.

Jordan Paramor: We all knew [H was gay]. There was so much stuff we were privy to. Obviously we hadn't put it in the magazine. We weren't out to stitch anybody up. We were mates with them, we'd go out with them. There was a really nice element of trust between magazines and pop stars because when we were on the roadshow the things that went on in terms of people getting off with each other, people sneaking into people's bedrooms. It was hilarious. But none of it went into the magazine. People weren't privy to what was going on behind the scenes because it was the happy, joyous world of pop. You didn't do that. That's why we got such brilliant access and people trusted us.

Joel Babbington: It felt like Steps were the band where we didn't know anything about their personal lives. They were literally Steps the pop stars and nothing else.

Claire: We all had to pretend we were single and we weren't allowed to tell anybody if we did have partners for fear of upsetting the fans. I think back then they never really gave people enough credit to understand that people like us had lives outside of work. Faye had a boyfriend, Lisa had a boyfriend, Lee often had a girlfriend. But the general rule of thumb was that if you were in a band you had to pretend you were young, free and single. That's not reality. We have come a long way since then thankfully. It doesn't feel right for someone to tell the world whether they're straight or gay. Why should you? But back then it was such a burden for so many people. I remember when it happened to Stephen Gately, you're forced in a way to tell everybody about your private life.

Jordan Paramor: It still breaks my heart when I think about Stephen Gately. It kills me that he was forced into coming out in the papers. He then wanted to do a second interview to talk about it, with a magazine. So I did an interview with him for *Smash Hits* and we sat and had a glass of wine just the two of us in this bar. He spoke to me really emotionally about it and I ran everything past him afterwards to make sure he was happy. He wanted to explain things more to the fans and expand on what had been said in the paper. He was such a young boy to have that happen to him.

Paul Flynn: The broad thinking was, up until Gately, that if you had a gay member of your band it's going to damage the brand. The girls aren't going to like it. Of course we know that's nonsense and has been proven to be nonsense since. But around then George Michael came out, famously with the LA sting, and that did kill his career in America. American radio did stop playing his records. When I started working at *Attitude* the industry was openly homophobic. It almost wore it as a badge of pride, and that spills down to people's lives in very direct ways. It's not enough to say, 'Oh, the tabloids were homophobic'; everyone was. The country was terrible, the climate was terrible.

H: It's sounds really vacant, but I'd always wanted to be a pop star. It was the thing I always aspired to because I loved pop music. It was the place I went to lose myself, because I was a young gay boy in a rural village and there wasn't anybody like me. I was bullied and I was made to feel very different and I lost myself in my bedroom wall. That's all I knew. Getting a mention in *Smash Hits*, let alone being on the cover or being on

Top of the Pops, was a massive middle finger at all of the bullies who taunted me and called me names because I was different. It was a massive fuck you, to be fair. And it's still a massive fuck you. After twenty-five years, I have a huge smile on my face and they're doing fuck all.

'In hindsight we should have gone on a break, like Ross and Rachel'

Steps' third album, Buzz, *released at the end of 2000, saw them start to experiment with new producers, specifically Max Martin affiliate Jörgen Elofsson, who gifted them the immaculate 'It's the Way You Make Me Feel'. Despite that album adding four top-five hits to their tally, the band spent most of 2001 denying they were splitting up. Things weren't helped by the announcement of a greatest hits album and accompanying tour, a chapter-ending move that typically foreshadowed the end for any pop band. Despite hearing constant denials and receiving another tranche of Steps merch for Christmas, fans had a rude awakening on 26 December 2001. As the front cover of* The Sun *put it: 'STEPS SPLIT'. Little did they know at the time, H and Claire had actually informed the band of their decision to leave four days earlier.*

H: We were going to keep it quiet for a few more months and work it all out and then do a statement. But the tabloids leaked the story, so that was the news everyone woke up to that day. We were scrambling for damage limitation because it was 'Steps ruin Christmas'. Crazy, right? The fucking *Sun*.

Joe McElderry, winner, *The X Factor*, 2009: Steps was my first concert ever. It was the last tour they did before they split up. I remember just being in complete awe. Now I live not far from Faye Tozer and we're friends, so I like to tell her on a regular basis that I am still an obsessive stalker fan of hers.

H: An element of it was that we were very tired and we needed a break. The real story was we hated each other. Not hated, that's a strong word, but we were sick of each other. We were tired. And we didn't want our surnames to be Steps. We wanted to live and enjoy what we'd worked hard for. In hindsight we should have gone on a break, like Ross and Rachel. But you can't re-write history.

Claire: When you're in that kind of world there are highs and lows anyway, but it's quite a toxic environment to have to live in twenty-four hours [a day], seven days a week. Anybody that lives their job 24/7 is going to come a cropper at some point.

Lisa: I woke up the next morning thinking, 'I'm not in a pop group any more.' I didn't have a job; I didn't have the guys. It was really scary.

Lee from Steps: I was like, 'They'll change their minds.'

Lisa: H and Claire went off to form a duo, so there was the three of us who were like, 'What the fuck happened?'

Claire: I also had the pressure of basically starving myself for four and a half years because I was told I had to lose weight on day one of being in Steps. I always felt like I was the fat one because I'd been told I was fat. I was nineteen, I was a size 12 and I had a bum and hips. When you're that young you don't understand that, no matter how much you try, if you don't look like Kate Moss naturally, you're never going to look like Kate Moss. You're just going to be ill. If anybody told me to lose weight now I would go and order a burger and a cake. But I was in my early twenties and that is the age of a person where you develop your adult personality. However you experience life then is how you carry it forward as an adult. I got to twenty-four or twenty-five and I had no clue who I was. I had no clue how I could continue doing what we were doing. A really good rest might have done the job, but then if we hadn't stopped when we did there wouldn't be Steps now.

Karl Twigg: It was a shame. I thought that if Steps had got through that album and held it together for a bit longer they could have carried on.

Pete Waterman: Towards the end the management were completely ruling the roost. They broke the group up. That was just simply the management wanting to break the group into two things – H & Claire and then Steps. And it never worked.

H: No, [splinter group H & Claire] was a natural progression. There were lots of people's noses out of joint that thought that was planned, but no.

'I thought something else would start pretty soon'

While H and Claire, AKA H & Claire, scored three top-ten singles, their debut album, 2002's Another You and Another Me, *stalled at number fifty-eight and they were dropped. While Faye Tozer scored a UK top ten with Russell Watson, and Lee Latchford-Evans starred in an Edinburgh fringe play called* Wolfboy, *a 'psychological sexual thriller', the only other person to properly try their luck with music outside of the band was Lisa Scott-Lee, whose perceived edginess – she often matched her chunky multi-coloured hair dye to her dental braces – had won her a legion of fans. In 2003, she unleashed electropop behemoth* Lately, *which peaked at number six (number four in the midweeks). After her two follow-up singles stalled outside the top ten, however, she embarked on an MTV fly-on-the-wall documentary in 2005 called* Totally Scott-Lee *(subtitle:* Desperately Seeking Fame*). The now ironically reappraised cult classic, complete with desperate in-built catchphrase '. . . but I'm B-List at Capital', focused on new single 'Electric', which, as per the show's rules, had to go top ten or she'd quit the music industry. It peaked at number thirteen and that was that.*

Claire: The year of H & Claire was great. We had such a great time. We achieved a lot and we earned a lot of money as well.

H: I remember at the time we had the biggest record deal for people from an existing band. It was crazy. We set records for that deal and we didn't have to pay any of that back; it was great.

Lisa: I just wish [the MTV documentary] would go away. I'm a performer; that's all I want to do. It wasn't about me trying to be a big solo star. It's weird because when we do our signings now, people have T-shirts on with this 'B-List at Capital' thing, which I don't understand.

Claire: [H and I] had worked really hard, we were co-presenting *SM:TV* at the same time, we were gigging constantly, but the album just didn't connect, we did a gig at Euro Disney and then we were dropped. I was devastated. It was great to feel like we had a career beyond Steps, but I don't know if I realised that would be it for pretty much ten years. I thought something else would start pretty soon.

★ ★ ★

A decade later, in 2011, the band reformed for a no-holds-barred four-part Sky Living documentary, *Steps: Reunion*, in which they went over every detail of their career and eventual demise. In October, they chucked out another greatest hits album, *The Ultimate Collection*, which included all the hits plus a gloriously on-the-nose version of ABBA's 'Dancing Queen'. The album entered at number one, with the band also scooting around the UK on a thirty-date arena tour. High on the excitement, they released 2012's unloved Christmas album, *Light Up the World*. After another tour, the band finally did a Ross and Rachel and took a break, returning in 2017 with new management (via Peter Loraine's Fascination) and new music in the shape of the thundering, *Vice*-approved single 'Scared of the Dark'. The accompanying album, *Tears on the Dancefloor*, as well as 2020's *What the Future Holds*, both showcased the DNA of Steps – big melodies, big vocals, even bigger key changes – but with a semi-modern twist. They also both peaked at number two and were both accompanied by huge arena tours. In 2022, their third greatest hits, *Platinum Collection*, released to celebrate their twenty-fifth anniversary, entered at number one.

* Lisa Scott-Lee and Lee Latchford-Evans quotes taken from my interview for *Guardian Guide*, 6 January 2018

5

From Billie to Blue: The influence of Innocent Records

In early 1992, Take That were alarmingly close to being handed their P45s by their label, RCA. Their debut single, 'Do What U Like', complete with a homoerotic video featuring jelly being vigorously applied to bare buttocks, had peaked at eighty-two. Their two follow-up singles, 'Promises' and 'Once You've Tasted Love', hadn't fared much better. With budgets extended and the all-important media demanding a hit before they'd feature the band again, a new tactic was needed. For Hugh Goldsmith, former songwriter turned publisher of pop-culture magazine *Sky* turned newly appointed marketing director at RCA, the band needed a way of speaking directly to their fanbase.

Utilising the then-untested database marketing business, Hugh and RCA encouraged fans at Take That's shows to hand over their addresses. Over 8,000 fans signed up and were swiftly sent information on the band's next single, 'It Only Takes a

Minute', in the hope the move would reach enough people for the band to land an all-important top twenty and therefore a *Top of the Pops* appearance. The plan worked and that fourth single – complete with a look that was less G-A-Y foam party and more fingerbanging behind the boxing gym – entered at sixteen. After an appearance on *Top of the Pops*, the song crashed into the top ten, eventually peaking at number seven. The rest, as they say, is history.

When Virgin Records, coffers bulged by Spice Girls swag, were looking to launch their own pop label imprint from scratch, they turned to Goldsmith, who had also helped, along with Simon Cowell, turn two lantern-jawed *Soldier Soldier* actors into hitmakers, Robson & Jerome. Launched in 1997, Innocent Records' first signing would arrive a year later in the shape of Billie Piper. From there, Goldsmith would sign ex-*EastEnder* Martine McCutcheon, whose immaculate ballad 'Perfect Moment' topped the charts in 1999, before scoring more chart success with '00s pop mainstays Atomic Kitten and Blue.

With no existing catalogue to fall back on and knowing full well the amount of money needed to launch pop acts, Goldsmith knew he had to avoid the Take That grind and hit the ground running.

'Even before Billie was famous, when you were with her, people looked'

Hugh Goldsmith: My first call from Paul Conroy, Virgin's President, came in March 1997. At this point, I was managing director of RCA. Paul explained that Virgin wanted to expand more into the world of pop, having had a hugely successful time with the Spice Girls, who were now fully established as a world-dominating pop phenomenon. Paul asked me whether I would be interested in setting up a new pop label and I jumped at the chance. My first task on setting up Innocent was to put together my team. Even though I was keen to have a more hands-on involvement in A&R than I'd had at RCA, it was imperative that I should find a great head of A&R and I did, in the form of Cheryl Robson, who I poached from Chrysalis Publishing. It was Cheryl's idea that we should look for a young solo female and she mentioned Madonna as a reference. Quite soon after we started our search, I was reading the latest issue of *Music Week* and leaping out from a *Smash Hits* ad was someone who seemed to embody the essence of Girl Power in every fibre of her being. I had a strong feeling she might be the person we were looking for.

Jodi Albert: Getting a record deal at that time was like winning the lottery. It wasn't like now where there are so many social media and music platforms. Back then I was working so hard [at Sylvia Young], really trying to learn and prove myself. The only girl who had a record deal in my class was Billie Piper. She was so beautiful, she really looked and sounded like a pop star. A record company executive was opening up *Music Week* and he saw her and thought, 'She's the pop star we need.'

Laura Snapes: This is definitely the era when pop becomes product. It's funny – the Spice Girls were formed from an ad and they worked so well because of all their vibrant, conflicting personalities. But when labels tried to replicate that, they took all the craziness out and just tried to create something unthreatening that would appeal to kids and not cause their parents any undue worry. If any of the Spice Girls had tried to get into pop just a year or two later, they probably would have been counted out because they weren't necessarily blandly cute and obliging in that way. That said, whoever spotted Billie did a good job as she was obviously hugely talented.

Hugh Goldsmith: Understandably, Sylvia wanted the two of us to meet in advance of me meeting Billie. I remember Sylvia telling me that Billie was one of her most talented students and, in today's terminology, a triple threat, with great expertise in acting, dancing and singing. To my ears, this sounded like a fantastic combination, all of which would be invaluable if Billie was interested in diving into the world of pop. At the second meeting, I met Billie and her dad, Paul. Billie had a wonderful brightness and positive energy about her and Paul was clearly, and understandably, a very protective and straight-talking dad.

Jodi Albert: Billie was so talented. I was delighted for her. She wanted me to be her backing dancer but unfortunately it wasn't possible as I wasn't yet over eighteen.

Hugh Goldsmith: In the first instance, we agreed it would be a good idea for Billie to record a demo track to see how she felt in the studio. At this point, Cheryl and Billie started working together on the music and they bonded brilliantly. In addition to Cheryl, I had other female colleagues at Innocent – Justine Bell, Deborah Lynam and, later, Sara Freeman – who I knew would help Billie feel at home. Because, even though Billie and I got on great, it was important to me that on a day-to-day basis she would always feel a strong sense of female support and care within the label.

Justine Bell, former A&R coordinator, Innocent Records: My first impression of Billie was super positive. I liked her a lot straight away. Billie always had a vibe about her that you wanted to be around. She was never over the top and thirsty for attention. She was just cool and friendly and funny and magnetic. Even before she was famous, when you were with her people looked. She had something that you couldn't quite put your finger on.

MNEK: Billie Piper was Britney before Britney; let's start there. She's the template. I've read a lot about the story of Billie and it's really interesting because there was no intention of her coming in as a pop singer.

Hugh Goldsmith: Cheryl Robson oversaw the A&R on Billie's first album and her focus was on making a pop R&B album, reflecting the mood of the moment and also Billie's personal taste.

MNEK: She started recording these demos and did a cover of Changing Faces' 'G.H.E.T.T.O.U.T.' [on the B-side of 'Because We Want To']. She's an R&B head. But then the *Honey to the B* album is this teen pop record.

Hugh Goldsmith: 'Because We Want To' was a bit of a red herring because it was a much younger-sounding track than the rest of the album.

Laura Snapes: It undersold the other singles from *Honey to the B*, which were more sophisticated – more R&B-influenced,

definitely bridging that gap between Robyn and Britney Spears, who was months off launching.

Hugh Goldsmith: The media frenzy and profile Billie received as a result of being the youngest female to ever enter the UK charts at number one was incredible. However, topping the charts on debut really is a blessing and a curse. It's a blessing because the artist becomes a household name overnight but a curse because, after having reached those dizzy heights, it's not unusual for unnecessary pressure and expectation to kick in on subsequent releases.

Justine Bell: I had no clue what was going to happen [with 'Because We Want To']. I'd been working at a label for five years [before Innocent] where everything had failed so the idea of having a number one with a brand-new label seemed impossible. But I was really hoping it would be successful – Hugh had offered to buy me a new motorbike jacket if it was, so I was buzzing when we got the midweeks!

MNEK: 'Because We Want To' could only have been a first single. It's her 'Wannabe'.

Laura Snapes: Billie definitely slid into a lane that the Spice Girls created. And she was always on kids' TV so you couldn't help but know who she was.

Hugh Goldsmith: Billie's follow-up singles from that first album were a much more accurate reflection of the sound of the album and closer to Billie's preference for R&B.

MNEK: The single edit of [second single and number one] 'Girlfriend' by Cutfather & Joe is one of the best teen pop records ever. Fun fact about Billie: 'Girlfriend', 'Saying I'm Sorry Now' and 'Whatcha Gonna Do' were all covers of songs by a failed R&B girl group from the UK called First Class. Their version of 'Girlfriend' is still on YouTube.

Hugh Goldsmith: After Cheryl left Innocent to go to Warner's, I took over Billie's A&R [for 2000's *Walk of Life*] and, with her being older and the sound of pop having moved on following the arrival of Britney, we focused on making a more mature pop album. Happily, the album's first single, 'Day and Night', was a triumphant comeback for Billie, debuting at number one with 100,000 sales.

Justine Bell: It's really tricky [transitioning to an older audience] and we definitely spent a lot of time trying to figure out how to make it work.

Laura Snapes: You grow up so massively between the ages of fifteen and eighteen. Obviously she's going to want to express herself differently. I think it also reflects the turbo-ing of pop more generally. On the one hand it's the Americanisation, but on the other it's the Scandification – you can trace such a direct line between NSYNC's 'Bye Bye Bye', which came out January 2000, produced by Cheiron, to 'Oops! . . . I Did It Again', released that April and also produced by Cheiron, and 'Day and Night', released that May and produced by Stargate. They all sound the same!

Justine Bell: Much of what we did with Billie was successful, but not everything. The 'Walk of Life' single was quite different both in terms of styling and sound because we were trying to find a way to grow her musically. The single didn't connect.

Laura Snapes: She got loads of grief from fans of Ritchie Neville for dating him. Then she got the really nasty tabloid coverage once she turned eighteen and was dating Chris Evans and treated as – gross – 'fair game'. And even though she had that globalised pop sound by her second album, a tinpot British pop star was never going to be able to compete with the Britneys and Christinas of this world, though I imagine she was still worked nearly as hard. It must have been thankless and pretty lonely.

Justine Bell: Was I surprised when she retired from pop? Not really. She had stepped into a new life with Chris [Evans] and that had offered her new opportunities. Plus it meant she could have a rest. The schedule had been full-on for a long time.

Hugh Goldsmith: I didn't foresee some of the challenges that lay ahead for Billie as a young solo female in such a demanding environment and, to this day, I remain relieved and happy she got through the difficult times and went on to become such a brilliant and successful actor. In spite of the tough times, Billie writes in her book [2006's *Growing Pains*] that she would do it all again but knows that I wouldn't, and she's right.

'I actually credit Kraftwerk with inventing Atomic Kitten'

Post-Spice Girls, the hunt was on for a girlband that could replicate their success. Or even just 10 per cent of it. While Girl Thing aimed for pure mimicry, the Sugababes for something cooler, while in Liverpool an unlikely amalgam of the Spice Girls, All Saints and Oasis was being haphazardly constructed by two members of '80s experimental pop practitioners OMD. Originally called Exit, then Honeyheads, then later Automatic Kitten (the change to Atomic Kitten happened after a mishearing that stuck), the three-piece initially included Kerry Katona, Liz McClarnon and soon-to-be-Sugababe Heidi Range.

Andy McCluskey: I continued as OMD through the '90s but I realised I was banging my head against a brick wall. I was conceited enough to still feel like I could write good songs, I just felt like the vehicle was considered beyond its sell-by date. Everyone thinks this is the most bizarre thing, but I actually credit Kraftwerk with inventing Atomic Kitten. I'd become quite friendly with Karl Bartos. I was talking to him about the fact I was going to stop doing my own music and write for other people. He said, 'Don't be a songwriting whore and give your songs to your publisher, just create a vehicle for the songs.' He asked me what the best pop group was and I said a three-piece girlband. Boybands are usually terrible because they sell records largely because love is deaf as well as blind. Girlbands have to have good music. So Karl Bartos said to me, 'Okay, create a three-piece girlband.' So Kraftwerk invented Atomic Kitten.

Stuart Kershaw: We'd actually talked about doing an electronic boyband. Almost like a Kraftwerk thing, but with boys. I know that sounds nuts, but no one had ever done it. We'd write all the music and they'd front it, but it would be us carrying on OMD, basically.

Andy McCluskey: We put an advert in the *Liverpool Echo*, just asking for girls who could sing and dance. It started, however, with an acquaintance of mine called Davy T, who is a DJ. He had a techno band called the Porn Kings. He came in the studio one day and said, 'Are you still trying to do a girlband?' His actual words were, 'There's this girl in my band who is a star and she's wasting her time waving her tits around behind me.' He showed me a video of them playing this techno festival in Cologne and there was Kerry [Katona] in this pink one-piece trouser suit, miming keyboards and clapping along and I just went, 'I've got to meet her.'

Stuart Kershaw: She had this incredible energy. She kind of took your breath away because of how energetic she was, a real presence, and you need someone like that in a band.

Andy McCluskey: She was only seventeen. In she comes to the studio, a bundle of energy, and within sixty seconds she goes, 'Do you want to see me photos?', and she gets out her topless photographs. I thought, 'This is a very interesting interview technique.' She wanted to be a page-three girl, but she'd been in foster care so she couldn't do it until she was eighteen. I said, 'Right, give me a year before you become a model and I'll try to make you a pop star.' She couldn't sing. I was always sat in the corner running the computer and Stuart and our engineer were always at the desk looking at her and whenever she got frustrated she'd just lift her top up and go, 'I'm only in this band for my tits.'

Stuart Kershaw: When she did get it right, [her voice] was a really lovely thing. But it was getting her to focus. She was far more interested in doing other things. People had told her she couldn't sing but it was more a lack of pitching.

Andy McCluskey: It was Marilyn Monroe syndrome – she'd been through a lot of problems, she was unhappy in her own skin, but she had something about her that was infectious. I just thought, 'She's going to be a star'; she will bang her head through a wall to be a star, because she thinks being rich and famous will make her feel better. As it turned out, it didn't. I had no idea what I was letting her in for. In manufactured pop they take these kids and they squeeze them through a bunch of shapes and go, 'You're the square one, you're the round one, you're the pretty one, and we're going to dress you like this.' With Kerry, I just thought, 'You're in and now I'm going to find some singers.' That's when I met Liz and Heidi Range.

Liz McClarnon: I went to a stage school and my singing teacher was like, 'Somebody wants to start a band and I know him and he was really famous in the '80s.' So she introduced us. I'd never done an audition before so I was quite wet behind the ears. It was very on trend to wear really crazy contact lenses at the time. I had these bright blue contact lenses and I walked in and Andy was like, 'I hope you can sing because you really look the part.' I sang 'Right Now' for him and he put me in the band. Kerry was already in the band then.

Stuart Kershaw: Heidi was fourteen or fifteen and she had this amazing voice. We weren't sure in the end if she was going to be old enough to do it and she left before we signed. That meant we had to re-vocal everything she had done and we'd based the whole thing around her, so from a production point of view it was a nightmare.

Andy McCluskey: Heidi Range has got one of the most incredible voices I've ever recorded in my life. This meek little schoolgirl would come in and then you'd put her in front of a microphone and Shirley Bassey would come out. She left and then regretted it for two years, so I was delighted for her when she did get into the Sugababes [in 2001]. So we had to re-audition and met Natasha.

Natasha Hamilton: Andy put an advert in the local Liverpool paper called the *Echo*, looking for girls with attitude.

Liz: And he got one!

Natasha: My mum saw the advert and so she phoned up and booked it. I was doing auditions left, right and centre, because my path was definitely wanting to be a singer. I turned up on the Friday afternoon and there was supposed to be a full day of auditions, but I was the first one in and everyone else got sent home. It was quite a strong audition for me. I ended up singing Atomic Kitten songs and they had me there for hours. Apparently Andy said that some of my vocals from my audition ended up on the actual 'Right Now' single.

Andy McCluskey: Quite by accident we had a blonde, a brunette and a redhead. I realised that effectively myself and Stuart Kershaw were kind of like parents in absence. We felt an obligation to those girls. Liz McClarnon and Natasha Hamilton are smart girls. And we persuaded their parents to let them join a pop group.

Liz: Our mums had to sign our record deals. I do remember the conversation my mum had with my sixth-form teacher, who was just like, 'Wait, she's what? She's leaving school to, what, be a pop star?' I was doing four A levels at the time. My mum was like, 'I'm going to give it a year and that's all she's got.'

Stuart Kershaw: When I wasn't in the studio I was taking them to do PAs up and down the country, so I got to hear whether they were happy or not with things. To be a big brother to them sort of thing and help them with problems. When I was in a band you'd make up and get on with it, but blokes are different to girls. Guys would go, 'Right, I'll hit you in the face and we'll all be fine,' but I don't think it works like that with girls.

Liz: It was very much in the Spice Girls mould because they had opened the door for girlbands. When we were kids it was all boybands, we didn't really have anybody, and then the Spice Girls came along and once you got over the, 'Oh, it's girls and they're being really loud,' you absolutely went, 'That's the same as me.' From a business point of view people were thinking, 'That's going to make money, let's do more of that', but from a young woman's point of view we were like, 'Yes, I want to do this, they look so empowered.' Personally, looking at the Spice Girls, I loved that they weren't polished and I think that worked for us as well. From a fanbase point of view, especially a same-sex fanbase, you can look up at them and aspire to achieve what they have.

Natasha: I think one of the draws with Atomic Kitten was that we were not polished at all. It was literally just go and do what you want to do. We didn't know how to do our hair or our make-up. We didn't have a stylist. I'll never forget Andy taking me, Liz and Kerry shopping around the markets in Liverpool to get our stage clothes. I ended up with a pair of flared jeans with an oriental patterned skirt that went over the top, massive platform shoes and a yellow hi-vis vest. That was my stage outfit. It was so ridiculous, it was brilliant. We were just three normal girls. I'd come from very humble beginnings so for me to be taken shopping around town and not have to pay for it, I was like, 'This is AMAZING!' It was the best day of my life.

Andy McCluskey: We spent a long time recording what would become the bulk of the first album. I went to my publishing company, who I had made millions of pounds for, and I said, 'I've got a new project, can you take it to labels.' They came back and basically said, 'We don't think it's good enough.' But they said they would waive their ownership of it, meaning that if we took it somewhere else and got a deal it would be ours. So we set up some showcases in London via my lawyer.

Natasha: I'd done so many auditions and been in other 'bands', working out of someone's shed recording music, so to then turn up at a recording studio with Andy who had already had the fame, for me it was like, 'This is special.' I knew it wasn't just someone trying to make it. I was like, 'We are going to make it.' I knew from day dot, deep down in my soul, I knew it was for me. This is the golden ticket.

Stuart Kershaw: We knew what we wanted and we targeted Hugh when we were marketing it to the record companies.

Hugh Goldsmith: I first became aware of Atomic Kitten when I received a demo tape from their manager, Martin O'Shea. There were a lot of girlbands around at the time and I wasn't actively looking for one for the label. However, there was an energy in the music on that demo that was totally compelling and the songs were brilliant. It was a breath of fresh air to find a new act that already had great songs in place. So I arranged with Martin for the band to come down from Liverpool to put on a showcase at Nomis Studios in Shepherd's Bush.

Stuart Kershaw: Hugh had done things with Billie and he had this pop sensibility. You knew he'd be able to get the right people in the right jobs to do the right pushing in the right places.

Hugh Goldsmith: I will never forget the immense blast of Girl Power that hit me when meeting Atomic Kitten for the first time. They were like the Spice Girls on steroids! Martin later told me the intention was that Atomic Kitten would channel 'the spirit of Oasis in a girl band'. The girls were down to earth, hilarious and full of energy and I was so impressed by their showcase I stopped them halfway through the second song to tell them I wanted to sign them there and then. Not something I'd done before or have since.

Andy McCluskey: He goes, 'Girls, come here, come here,' and they came down to the front and he said, 'I'm going to sign you.' They were just bouncing off the walls. I was gobsmacked. But I kept saying to them, 'Getting a record deal doesn't mean you're there.' It means someone's going to give you the ladder but you still have to climb it.

Justine Bell: Initially I didn't love everything about them. It was Hugh who saw the potential. In time I came to appreciate their hustle. They were full-on and Kerry was a massive character who always kept things interesting. We had some run-ins but I liked her a lot. It was a wild time. We had lots of girls on the label. All big characters – Martine [McCutcheon], Billie, Atomic Kitten.

Simon Jones, Martine McCutcheon's former PR: I remember with Martine we were going through some requests and it was like, 'Oh, you've been offered the cover of *Cosmopolitan* magazine,' which was a big deal. I can remember her saying, 'I don't know if I want to do that.' Then she said, 'What you need to do, Simon, when a request comes in, you need to think, "Would Barbra do it?"' Now I know you're thinking Windsor, but it was Streisand. So the benchmark that we were supposed to live by was 'Would Barbra Streisand do this?'

Andy McCluskey: The reality was that the first Atomic Kitten album came out after they had three top-ten singles, but only went to number thirty-nine.

Natasha: I remember being absolutely gutted. I really wanted it to be better than that. We knew we had a last chance with 'Whole Again', and from the minute we sang that song we knew it was special, but we steered away from the ballads. It was about the high-intense pop or the middle of the road. I think everyone was nervous to take a punt on such a slow song for a pop band.

Andy McCluskey: Paul Conroy at Virgin said to Hugh, 'You've spent a few millions on this and it's not selling, pull the plug now.'

Hugh Goldsmith: I'm someone who worships at the altar of the song because the game-changing impact of a truly fantastic song can never be underestimated. A game-changing song has the power to rescue a doomed career, sustain a successful career or indeed launch a career that would never have happened without it.

'In my ear was my wife, who had always felt "Whole Again" was the strongest track on the album'

Just as he'd had to do back in 1992, Goldsmith found himself offering up one last roll of the dice to a struggling pop act that had exhausted media goodwill. Originally released in Japan in March 2000, their debut album Right Now *featured the original, spoken-word-heavy version of 'Whole Again'. After Atomic Kitten performed its new, more radio-friendly incarnation night after night during the band's support slot with Steps to an increasingly rapturous reception, it was decided 'Whole Again' would be the song to gamble everything on. It would eventually spend a month at number one in the UK and sell over a million copies. All that, despite the band having to halt promo to quickly find a new member . . .*

Hugh Goldsmith: In A&R terms, Andy McCluskey and I had a difference of opinion as to how 'Whole Again' should be arranged. I want to stress here that I have the utmost respect for Andy as an artist and songwriter. He is brilliant in both fields and, in 'Whole Again', he and Stuart wrote a fantastic song. However, their original version of the song featured spoken vocal verses all the way through in addition to a spoken vocal in the middle eight.

Natasha: It was actually Kerry's song and me and Liz just sang on the chorus. It was a great album track but we needed a top-three hit.

Hugh Goldsmith: I was concerned, as were our radio pluggers, that [the spoken-word verses] might hinder the song's uptake at daytime radio because this aspect made it similar in style to 'Never Ever' by All Saints, which was still receiving significant airplay at that time. So I asked Andy if he would consider adding melody to the verses so they could be sung not spoken. However, understandably, he wasn't too keen on reworking his original composition but he did agree that it would be okay for me to experiment with other writers. As a result, I reached out to a number of other songwriters. Eventually, Bill Padley and Jeremy Godfrey came through with the solution and the million-selling number one, 'Whole Again', as everyone now knows it, was ready to go.

Natasha: When they made the melody to the verses and we heard it, we were like, 'Oh my God, this is mega.' It totally lifted the song up to a level that was like, 'Wow.'

Andy McCluskey: We couldn't understand why they weren't more successful. I think Virgin thought they had the new baby Spice Girls. So myself and Stuart and their manager Martin O'Shea got together and said, 'Right, let's go back to Innocent and Virgin, we still believe in this band.' They hadn't given us the second half of the advance for delivering the album, which was £50,000, so we said, 'You keep that and give us the catalogue back.'

Hugh Goldsmith: At the point we released 'Whole Again', the project was haemorrhaging money and I came under a lot of pressure from Virgin's financial director to drop the band.

I even told Martin that this was the case. However, he did a brilliant job of persuading me to put pressure back on Virgin's FD to release me enough budget to fund one final throw of the dice with the new 'Whole Again'. Also, in my ear was my wife, Carrie, who had always felt this was the strongest track on the album and that we should somehow try to get it released.

Andy McCluskey: So Hugh is straight off to Paul Conroy going, 'They've obviously got another contract, they want to release "Whole Again" as a single, please don't let them go to another label.' But we didn't have another deal. We were going to waive £50,000 and try to release 'Whole Again' ourselves. What we ended up doing was accidentally bluffing Virgin into giving them one more chance. They went from spending £150,000 on videos to making a video for 'Whole Again' for £25,000. And that was basically just a cheap copy of the Sugababes' video for 'Overload'. And bang it goes straight in at number one.

Hugh Goldsmith: Martin did indeed offer to waive the final £50,000 advance the band were owed if we would consider allowing them to release 'Whole Again' independently. There was no way I wanted to let this happen, especially after all the hard work that had gone into the new version of 'Whole Again', and in a way Martin did me a favour with his request. It gave me the ammunition to go back to my bosses and put them under pressure to let me try one more single release. Thankfully, they agreed, but I was given a massively reduced marketing budget to do the job.

Justine Bell: ['Whole Again'] was a complete game-changer, which I can take absolutely no credit for. By this time I thought we were dropping the band and to be honest I'd moved on. Hugh wouldn't let it go, though. He was obsessed with making the song a hit and giving them one last chance. He pulled in all kinds of favours to make sure the single was properly stocked in-store and that the girls got decent promo. He totally made it happen against the odds.

James Masterton: January in the music industry used to be defined by the exhaustion factor. So music sales would plummet. But that opened the door to acts being able to sneak in and have hits when they wouldn't have normally. The great story from that January period was the resurgence of Atomic Kitten, who had spent 2000 flinging out singles with nobody paying them much attention. So one final throw of the dice was 'Whole Again', which was released in early 2001 when not a lot was going on.

Lee Thompson: Atomic Kitten, number one with 'Whole Again', and Radio 1 wouldn't play that song. They just wouldn't touch it. But it was huge for The Box.

Andy McCluskey: Before that we were approached by our publishers saying, 'Listen, this hasn't been a global hit yet, there are two artists who would like to cover "Whole Again" for America and the rest of the world, would you give it to them?' And we said no. We wrote it for Atomic Kitten and we only write for Atomic Kitten. We saw ourselves as part of the group. The whole thing was the industry – the girls were the shop window and we were creating it.

Stuart Kershaw: We had calls from Clive Calder [at Jive] saying, 'Can Britney have it?' And we said, 'Well, the girls are doing it and so we have to give them a chance to do it really.' It was crazy. We didn't even want to write with other acts because we thought we might dilute what we had.

Andy McCluskey: Not only did we turn down Britney Spears but we turned down Celine Dion.

Natasha: Celine Dion?! I knew Britney [wanted it] but I didn't know Celine did.

Liz: I think it's a little bit simple for Celine. She would have belted it.

'I'm a blagger, basically. I just thought, "Why not? Just go for it." I winged it'

With all the signs pointing to 'Whole Again' being massive, and with the video on heavy rotation, Kerry Katona announced she was leaving the band in the weeks leading up to the single's release. Having ridden the pop roller-coaster through a corkscrew's worth of twists and turns, Liz and Natasha knew they couldn't let the momentum die and so set about finding a replacement. At the same time, Eurovision Song Contest 1999 fifth-place runners-up Precious were splitting up, meaning one member, Jenny Frost, was about to become a free agent.

Stuart Kershaw: It felt like walking into a wall every time you try to open a door. But the reason we were successful was because our mentality was, 'If it's a wall then we'll either knock it down or climb over it or walk around it.' We were so determined.

Andy McCluskey: We had persuaded Kerry to stay on and do ['Whole Again']. So the single was coming out and they were all getting together for the *Pepsi Chart Show* in London. Kerry got in the van and basically had a breakdown and went, 'I can't do it.' Natasha just went, 'Right, fuck her.' She'd already been in touch with Jenny Frost, who was in Precious, but they'd just finished. So Natasha calls up Jenny and says, 'You're in the band from today, get in a taxi and go to the ITV studios, you're on the *Pepsi Chart Show* in two hours, and on the way learn the words to "Whole Again".' It was ruthless. To be honest, Natasha and Kerry always had a fairly fractious relationship.

Natasha: What actually happened was I already knew [Kerry was leaving]. Me and Kerry were really close and she confided in me that she was going to leave but she told me not to tell anyone. I was seventeen and I'm a very loyal person, so I didn't want to ruin our trust. But I knew that we needed to prepare. In the end, I spoke to Martin and said he couldn't tell anyone else. He was like, 'Everyone needs to know!' I'll never forget, we were in a Chrysler Voyager in Edgware and Martin was like, 'Kerry's leaving the band,' and Liz, who was always dead quiet, literally screamed. She opened the door of the Chrysler and ran down the street and I remember running after her, grabbing her and hugging her. I said, 'Listen, Atomic Kitten isn't just about Kerry. It's about three girls. We're going to make this work.' We were both crying and I was like, 'We're going to do this.'

Jenny Frost: I was with the girls from Precious – in a club called Pop – and we were out to be like, 'We had a good run, we all love each other, but let's call it a day,' and we were saying cheers with a bottle of Champagne. Tash was next to us. She was like, 'Babe, I need to talk to you,' and I was like, 'Give me a minute, we're just having a toast because we've split the band up.' Then she went, 'Well, I *really* need to talk to you then.' She dragged me off to the loo.

Natasha: She asked what was going on and I told her Kerry had left and we were due to be on the *Pepsi Chart Show* and we needed someone tomorrow. 'Whole Again' was already being played on the radio with Kerry's vocals. It was right in the middle of our promo trail. One day I spoke to Jenny, the next day she was having a meeting with us and then the following day she was at the *Pepsi Chart Show* singing. She had the words to 'Whole Again' on a piece of paper.

Jenny: It was like, 'Listen, we're releasing this song, if it goes well then great, but if it doesn't we'll be dropped so it's a bit of a risk for you.' I didn't care, I was like, 'Let's go for it!' It worked out very well. Literally fast-forward about sixteen hours and I was performing it live on TV. I'm a blagger, basically. I just thought, 'Why not? Just go for it.' I winged it.

Andy McCluskey: That's why whenever 'Whole Again' was performed on TV it all had to be live because we didn't have a track with Jenny Frost on it because she'd only joined the band on the day of the first TV show.

Stuart Kershaw: We'd gone from the luxury of having weeks with the girls singing and practising and getting things right to getting them for two hours on a Wednesday afternoon.

James Masterton: For the first time ever, they were newsworthy and so you could put on the front page of the newspaper:

'Kerry Katona leaves Atomic Kitten and is having Brian from Westlife's baby'. And the record flies to number one and stays there for a month and it made Atomic Kitten.

Andy McCluskey: Kerry started her connection with Brian quite early on and it was like a millennial pop version of Romeo and Juliet. The two of them were followed everywhere they went by security. Westlife and the Kittens were never allowed to turn up at a hotel at the same time, because it was always the boyband fans outside. They had to close the curtains to the bar downstairs so fans couldn't see in. Kerry and Brian used to have to sneak off to either the ladies or the gents to have a fag in a cubicle and talk to each other. The bodyguard used to have to kick the door down and go, 'Get out, you can't be together.'

Hannah Verdier: It was really heartbreaking when Kerry Katona left. She was a good old girl. Her life could have been so different. When she got together with Brian she was so happy. They tried to give them Atomic Kitten names and she was like, 'I'm Sex Kitten.' She'd put herself out there as the sexy one.

Jenny: I think if I hadn't been in Precious before it would have been more difficult [to join an existing band] because everybody did love Kerry. But the fans were happy that the band was continuing, so that made the transition smoother and easier. I've got such a gung-ho attitude that I kind of just went for it. But I think that throughout my time with Atomic Kitten I did always feel like I was blagging it. I felt that. For the other girls, that's all they've ever wanted to do is be performers from when they were young. I never did. I did always feel like maybe somebody else deserved to be there more than I did. There was quite a bit of inner turmoil throughout the band era, but I managed to drink my way through it.

Andy McCluskey: The next thing, the album was re-released and it sold 1.5 million worldwide.

Hugh Goldsmith: People thought we were crazy pulling the album from the shops at the point that 'Whole Again' was a huge hit. There's no doubt we sacrificed a level of album sales in the January to March window, but by re-releasing the repackaged album in August 2001 on the back of a second number-one single [the band's cover of 'Eternal Flame'], it flew to the top of the album charts before going on to sell 600,000 copies. Kerry had left the band and, with Jenny joining just as 'Whole Again' took off, it was a no-brainer to get her involved vocally across the updated album. This process also gave us the chance to add songs to the album in a similar vein to 'Whole Again', thereby giving new fans of the band a better listening experience. The first edition had been primarily quite young-sounding up-tempo pop.

Brian Dowling, *Big Brother 2* winner and co-presenter of *SM:TV*: I got to sing with Atomic Kitten. I did the talking part from 'Whole Again' with Jenny Frost.

Jenny: When Brian was in *Big Brother* he used to sing 'Whole Again', so when he won and he came out we got him to perform it with us at G-A-Y. Everyone went wild.

Jeremy Joseph: There was one time [at G-A-Y] where we got soldiers in and we abseiled Atomic Kitten from the ceiling.

That was quite funny. One of the girls chickened out last minute and ran down the stairs, one managed to do it and the other got stuck halfway. That was during the first track.

Natasha: Oh my God, it was the worst idea we've ever had for a show in our lives. Firstly, the three of us are absolutely terrified of heights. So why we thought abseiling from the rafters of a very high theatre would be a great idea, I don't know. In rehearsals Liz's harness snapped so she was hanging upside down. So Liz said she wasn't going to do it but me and Jenny still had to do it. Then Jenny's rope was twisted so she was still stuck at the top. I was stuck halfway down. The intro music had finished and everyone was looking as if to say, 'This is crap.'

Jenny: That was absolutely ridiculous. You were always trying to outdo other bands at G-A-Y. You used to do it to get your picture in the paper to then try to get the sales up in the week. The outfits couldn't get any smaller so it was like, 'Let's abseil from the ceiling!'

'We did have musical differences . . . We wanted them to do our songs!'

After re-releasing 'Right Now' in August 2001 and watching it sail to the top of the UK charts, Atomic Kitten were one of Europe's biggest pop acts. Finally the good ship Kitten seemed to be on smoother waters. Behind the scenes, however, a messy and protracted divorce centring around money and publishing splits was taking place between Andy and Stuart on one side and the band's management on the other. Despite this, Andy and Stuart would get three songs on the band's second album, 2002's chart-topper Feels So Good, *but their contributions, none of which were selected as singles, would fight for their place alongside some of pop's biggest hitmakers, including Stargate, Ian Masterson and Steve Anderson.*

Andy McCluskey: Because Stuart and I had created the band we saw ourselves as part of it. We created them to be the vehicle for our songs, so we weren't like other songwriting units. We participated in part of the record royalty and obviously we had the publishing royalty, too. This started to cause problems in the band because the manager could only commission what the girls were earning and they weren't earning a lot. This is part of the problem in manufactured pop – all of the record royalty goes to pay off the advances, which include massive amounts of money for production, video, promo costs, clothing, hairdressers, tour support. The publishing money is free to go to whoever wrote the songs. And because the girls didn't write the songs, they had no income stream. They were just on a wage to live on and the manager was commissioning 20 per cent of not very much, so he was unhappy.

Stuart Kershaw: [On the second album] they wanted more publishing or the manager decided he wanted more of the publishing, so he wanted more writers. It was a good opportunity for them to wrestle control away from us. It's a sad thing but that's business. That's how it happens, with people whispering in people's ears. The band are no longer down the road for you to have a chat with; they're off on tour.

Andy McCluskey: 'Whole Again' broke the mould and then of course became the mould. Because the next thing is that Hugh Goldsmith calls me into his office and says, 'Right, we want a new album and I don't like the new direction, in fact we don't want a new direction.' He said, 'I want "Whole Again", "Whole Again" and more "Whole Again" and, if you don't write it, I'll find someone else who will.' And, in the end, he did.

Hugh Goldsmith: Atomic Kitten had found their place in the market with 'Whole Again' and it would have been crazy not to follow through with more songs of a similar nature. However, I certainly didn't want them to be exactly the same! One of our mantras at Innocent was a phrase coined by Justine to sum up the pop market and what fans primarily wanted from their artists: 'More of the same but different.' And that's what we were after in this situation.

Andy McCluskey: We actually had our [production deal] contract torn up [by the band's management]. For the next four years after that we were told we couldn't speak to the girls other than through lawyers. Which was a painful experience.

Hugh Goldsmith: Andy's falling out and parting of the ways with Atomic Kitten was not something I was involved in. I was aware that there was tension between the two parties but I was still quite taken aback when Martin called me one day to say he and the band had terminated their agreement with Engine, Andy's production company.

Stuart Kershaw: We gradually drifted apart. Which is a cliché, like 'musical differences'. But we did have that because we wanted them to do our songs.

Hugh Goldsmith: Also, it's important to mention that the girls had begun to co-write songs themselves and these songs also needed to be considered for inclusion on the records.

Steve Anderson, songwriter and producer, 'Feels So Good': We were writing for Kylie's *Fever* album. It was a really sunny day and we wrote this big pop song. She demoed it and it sounded great, but it was too pop for *Fever* so it got to one of the guys at Innocent and they took it for Atomic Kitten. I remember going in with them and in those days with these bands the music bit was given the least amount of time in any of their schedules. Even to the point where, when I did Jenny's vocals, she was in the middle of guest-editing some magazine and she came in and said, 'I've literally got fifteen minutes to do this.' About 1 per cent of their life was spent on making the records.

Andy McCluskey: The reality is that we wouldn't have had the time to crank out a whole new album that quickly. The subsequent albums were made more like other band's albums were – the whole thing was written, all of the backing vocals were done by session singers because the band didn't have enough time to go in and sing all these harmonies. You go in, you sing your topline and then you get out because you've got to be on *Top of the Pops*. Those girls never stopped.

Natasha: One time our tour manager said we had two days off in one year. It was crazy. It was constant. It was exhausting. We were still kids really and you just wanted to go and hang out with your mates or be with your family, but you couldn't because you were working. You're living an intense adult career still as a child. There were times when it clashed, you'd be exhausted or not well or having a bloody breakdown.

Jenny: The schedule was ridiculous and it was really stressful, but compared to actual real life it's not. You've got somebody booking your flights, somebody carrying your bags, somebody doing your hair and make-up. At the time, you think, 'Oh my God, it's sooo difficult,' but it really wasn't.

Lucie Cave: My very first four-page interview for *Heat* was with Atomic Kitten. It was the Jenny Frost era and Natasha had just had a boob job and Liz was going out with Lee Ryan, who had just crashed his car because he was pissed. There was a lot to talk about. Anyway, it was the most hideous experience I've ever had because Jenny was really moody. I'd ask questions and every time she'd say, 'Next question.' She would stare and make me move on. Jenny wanted me to ask them something about the music. But they couldn't even remember songs that were on their album anyway.

Jenny: I was quite worldly wise and quite protective of the girls, so I often came across like the bitch in interviews. I was in a relationship so there were no scandals to talk about, but they were always digging at Tash and Liz's romantic life. They didn't want to talk about it. If someone had just had their heart broken and I knew that they'd been crying before the interview then the journalist would be pecking, so I'd be like, 'No, we're not talking about that.' So I came across like a bitch, but I was just being protective. There are some people that probably think to this day that I am a bitch but I don't actually give a shiny shite. I was always protecting the girls.

Lucie Cave: I told Mark [Frith, then *Heat* editor] what happened and he said, 'If you don't feel like you got anything, we'll pull the interview.' And they needed us back then. So our features editor phoned their PR, who was like, 'She's really sorry, she knows she was in a bad mood, can we do her bits again?' We said no. Then Mark came up to me later and he said, 'Write it as it happened – how excited you were to go and interview them, just talk to the reader through that whole experience and let them be there with you and keep everything in.' So I did. If someone's going to be moody they shouldn't be able to get away with it.

Jenny: I can remember the exact interview. Liz had just broken up with somebody and she was so upset she was shaking. I was saying, 'She doesn't want to talk about it.' In the end, I said, 'Listen, we're not fucking talking about it.' I remember seeing [Lucie] on *Loose Women* once and she said Atomic Kitten were the worst interview she'd ever had and I was like, 'Well, thank you.'

Hannah Verdier: I remember once with Atomic Kitten we were trying to get a cover shot and they were at each other. Jenny was ill and she was saying, 'This can't happen,' and she kind of had me pinned up against the wall in the studio. I was begging for ten more minutes to get the shot and she was like, 'This is my life; you can't do this.' Obviously then the bosses come in and tell them to get on with it. They were exhausted kids.

'I was a mum, trying to be a pop star'

At the end of 2003, Atomic Kitten released their third album, Ladies Night, *a fairly anodyne collection of soft-focus pop that felt increasingly staid in comparison with the DayGlo music being made by the likes of Girls Aloud and the Sugababes. It peaked at number five, their first album to miss the top spot. It was also their first album since Natasha Hamilton had given birth to her first son in October 2002. By early 2004, the band were falling apart and a 'hiatus' was announced ahead of a greatest hits album and a farewell tour. Behind the scenes, Innocent was also entering its final phase, with Hugh Goldsmith leaving at the end of 2003 to start the Brightside label.*

Liz: Now I know why it started because Tash and I have become a lot closer and I understand where she was. But at the time, I was told that Tash just didn't want to do it any more. I was like, 'Really?' I also did want a bit of time off myself. At that time, that's how I saw it. Now, looking back, it wasn't like that at all and I can totally see what Tash was going through.

Jenny: We weren't given a lot of information. I remember being in a hotel room and being told Tash has gone home, she can't do it any more, and then we sat down with her and she just said she needed a break. There was never any drama or anything.

Natasha: It was difficult because I had postnatal depression. I was very sick actually. It wasn't getting dealt with because I wasn't admitting to anyone what I was going through because in my head I was being ungrateful. It was like, 'I've got the world at my feet, I'm in the biggest girlband on the planet, I've got money, I've got a home, I should be happy.' But I wasn't. Back then with postnatal depression there were no young, twenty-year-old women discussing it. No one was discussing it. How it made you feel. That it was normal. I literally thought there was something wrong with me. It went on and by the time I was finally diagnosed, it was too late, I think. A lot of relationships had fractured because of me not saying my truth and people not understanding.

Liz: You can't blame yourself in that way.

Jenny: I think we saw it coming. Tash was struggling. Now as a mother myself I can see why she was struggling. At the time, I totally got it and there wasn't one moment where I was like, 'Ugh.' I just thought, 'It is what it is.' At that point, we were all getting a bit weary anyway.

Natasha: It was very much, 'The show must go on regardless, we don't really care what's wrong with you.' My doctor was saying, 'She needs six months to a year off,' and I was told, 'Well, you've got two [months] to get better and when you come back we want to know whether you're in or you're out.' It was very much like a threat and I couldn't live like that. We didn't have anyone who we could confide in and who could help. Quite often any help was, 'Send them to a doctor and put them on Prozac and everything will be fine.' I was a mum, trying to be a pop star. I was on one side of the world and my baby was at home with my mum. I missed out on those integral moments to bond. I had six weeks' maternity leave. I remember my first gig back after having Josh was the Disney tour. I had an emergency C-section, so I'd had my tummy cut open and I'd been stitched up. When you have a C-section, you have six weeks' downtime and back into light exercise. But with me I was back on stage in heels doing full-on dance routines. That had a psychological effect because I didn't feel glamorous. I didn't feel like a pop star. I felt fat. I just felt like an exhausted mum. Presenting yourself to people as a happy pop star when actually you want to go home and cry and be with your baby. Living that life continuously for months on end breaks you down.

★ ★ ★

In 2005, the band reunited briefly to release 'Cradle 2005', an updated version of a song from *Right Now*. A year later, they reunited again to record a cover of the Farm's 'All Together Now', which became a charity single associated with the 2006 FIFA World Cup. Years later – after a brief return to the original, Kerry-era line-up for *The Big Reunion* in 2012 – Jenny, Liz and Natasha would have another brush with football after 'Whole Again' was transformed into 'Southgate You're the One (Football's Coming Home Again)' during England's run to the final of the 2020 Euro football tournament. The updated version peaked at number fourteen.

'I had come up with LADS, as in Lee, Ant, Dunc and Si'

By 2001, the traditional boyband bubble was close to bursting. In America, the Backstreet Boys were about to enter a hiatus following 2000's lacklustre Black & Blue, *while NSYNC were essentially laying the foundations for Justin Timberlake's solo stardom. Five, meanwhile, were flying the flag for the UK boybands, but by that point the flag was on fire and the band members were using it as a weapon on each other. Even A1, whose music (and centre partings) skewed closest to the US boyband archetype, were about to regenerate as Travis. In this context, Blue, AKA Lee Ryan, Simon Webbe, Antony Costa and Duncan James, felt like a breath of fresh air. Musically, like Damage and Another Level before them, they skewed closer to R&B, but, via their work with the increasingly ubiquitous Stargate, it always landed with a huge pop thud. While their boyband predecessors favoured slick choreography, Blue's dance moves were slightly more rudimentary, the kind you might see around the bar at a Slug and Lettuce after the fourth shot of sambuca. Their sound, mixed with their propensity to smize in pictures and say what they wanted in interviews, gave them an air of cool that was often missing from their more controlled peers. It wasn't all plain sailing, though, as what started as a five-piece suddenly became a trio . . .*

Hugh Goldsmith: Blue was formed when I offered Daniel Glatman the same deal Simon Cowell and I had given Chris Herbert a few years earlier [with Five]. I thought Daniel was a very smart young guy with lots of drive and ambition so offered him a drawdown fund of £10,000 to seek out talented young singers that might form the basis of a cool new pop act, which he would then manage. Our original intention was that this new act would be mixed gender and that it might include a couple of people playing instruments. However, soon after starting the process, we decided to make our new group a boyband and changed our brief to Daniel.

Antony Costa: Me and Duncan knew each other from my local area of Golders Green. I used to see him with his bandmates when I was with my bandmates and we'd always chat. To cut a long story short, we became really good mates. Later I found a guy, Daniel Glatman, who was looking to put a band together, so me and Duncan went for it. We went to a place called Nomis Studios for the audition. I knew Lee from various boyband auditions and so did Dunc, but me and Dunc didn't know that we both knew Lee. If that makes sense. So I called Lee up and told him about the band and he wanted in. Then that grew to a five-piece with these two guys called Richard and Spencer.

Hugh Goldsmith: The five-guy line-up was finally in place and contracts were about to be signed. However, after Justine saw the band together for the first time and gave us her comments, we agreed that something wasn't right with the line-up. So, literally moments before the signing, we changed our minds. The band was too similar to a lot of boybands already in the market.

Justine Bell: I didn't like two of them. It seems incredibly harsh but it just didn't feel right and I'm glad we went with our gut.

Antony: We were a five-piece for literally two weeks. I've had longer three-course dinners, you know what I mean. It was horrible. When we got the phone call that day, we were in Dunc's Fiat Cinquecento and Daniel rang and said, 'Look, wherever you are, you need to get to the office, we need an emergency meeting.' We were like, 'Fucking hell, it's done, the dream's over.' For the two lads it was devastating. An acting agent friend of mine said to me, 'It's show business and not show friends.' I will take that to the grave. There's a time when you've got to think about yourself. I was eighteen years old and I had one GCSE. My whole life was based on getting in this band and trying to make it work. I spoke to my mum and dad and they said, 'Look, it's great you're a loyal person but you don't want to live with regrets.'

Hugh Goldsmith: It was an incredibly difficult thing to do and, to this day, I feel bad about dashing the hopes of two young guys about to sign a life-changing record deal. However, we knew we had to make the change and Blue would not have come about if we hadn't done so.

Antony: Because I'd seen what had happened to the other two lads who hadn't made it, I was always worried I wasn't good enough. The first year or so I was constantly living life on an edge because I was scared the other three would turn around and go, 'Look, Ant, it's not really working, we're going to look elsewhere.' Even though I was one of the founding members so to speak.

Hugh Goldsmith: This took the band back to a three-piece and created room for Simon to join and for the line-up to finally be complete.

Antony: Lee kept talking about a guy called Simon that he knew who'd come down from Manchester that could write, rap and sing. Simon also knew Duncan from another boyband audition so it all intertwined into one really.

Justine Bell: It just worked. Four great voices, four decent-looking lads. Cool, but not trying too much, and they worked exceptionally hard charming everyone they came into contact with.

Antony: At the time, P!nk was really smashing it and we were just talking about names and I think it was Simon who said, 'What about Blue?' We were all like, 'Yeah, what is that? It doesn't make sense.' But the thing is it doesn't mean anything; it's just a colour. But then you look at bands like Simply Red, Black Sabbath, Deep Purple. I had come up with LADS, as in

Lee, Ant, Dunc and Si. But that never worked because you can't be sixty years old and be called LADS.

Hugh Goldsmith: We definitely wanted to move away from the squeaky clean, overtly good-looking vibe of many other boy groups around at the time. We wanted them to have a bit of edge, humour and attitude.

Antony: I think Another Level were sort of dying down and from what I gather they wanted to put something like that in the market. Like an R&B boyband. One that blokes and girls can like, and dads and mums.

Jordan Paramor: I loved Blue. They were hilarious. They took it seriously but they were also just having a laugh. I really enjoyed hanging out with them. They treated me like one of the lads. All these girls would be screaming at them and completely in love with them and I'd be thinking, 'I just sat in a car with them for three hours farting constantly and sitting on my face.'

MNEK: The music was older, it was cooler, but also it wasn't an all-white band. Simon absolutely helped give the group a bit of a weight and an ability to do the more R&B-leaning records.

Chantelle Fiddy, journalist: If you look at how they were putting the bands together, there was often that consideration. 'Have we got a balance?' Look at S Club 7, Blue – it's like, 'Let's get a good mix so we can cover all bases.' Blue couldn't have sampled half the songs they sampled, like Biggie's 'Hypnotize' on 'Fly By II', without having Simon in the band.

MNEK: Controversially, I think their version of 'Too Close' [released as their second single] is superior to Next's original. I think Lee sings the hell out of it; the production is sleeker. The Blue one is tuned and Y2K polished.

Hugh Goldsmith: Billie's 'Day and Night' was the first record I worked on with Stargate, whose talent I'd previously admired from afar, and I also brought them in to work on Blue.

MNEK: Stargate were doing all the hits then. They were clearly inspired by R&B music but they knew they didn't have the culture in them to do it from a rough point of view. So they were like, 'Right, let's polish it up, let's make it really bright and really intentionally pop. Let's take everything we know from Scandinavia and blend the best of both worlds.' R&B and hip-hop were massive parts of teen pop, but it was more the groove of it or the musicality of it.

Hallgeir Rustan: We realised immediately that there was something special about Blue. Hugh Goldsmith had found these guys who were all really good singers – perhaps not the best dancers – and when they came to Trondheim [to record] all the girls fell head over heels. They were so fun to work with and full of ideas. 'All Rise' was basically written and recorded on a tough hip-hop track. We wanted the vocals to be tough and tight, especially in the chorus. We joked that they should be as tight as a marching band so we made them march while recording.

Antony: For me, when we first recorded 'All Rise', it was never a first single. It was too hard, very military. I was like, 'What is this song?' My first single choice was always 'If You Come Back'. But, when we came back to London, Hugh Goldsmith said, 'Guys, I've got some great news. I've got the mix of your first single.' When we sat down in his office and he said, 'It's "All Rise".' We just looked at each other like, 'Really?' Then he played the finished version and we were like, 'Oh, wow.'

'Lee calls me and says, "I think I might have said something . . ."'

By September 2001, Blue were one of the UK's biggest bands. 'All Rise' had peaked at number four, spending two months in the top twenty, while follow-up 'Too Close' earned them their first number one. Pulling the classic '00s pop trick of following two upbeat bops with a ballad that would lead into the album, their third single was 'If You Come Back', a top-tier emotional wind tunnel powered by Lee Ryan's vocal. With their debut album due for release at the end of November, AKA during the all-important Q4 period, the band travelled to New York to film 'If You Come Back''s video. The first day of filming took place on 11 September 2001.

Hugh Goldsmith: Justine and I were in New York with Blue and Atomic Kitten when the 9/11 atrocity took place. It's important to remember that Blue were actually standing on the Brooklyn shoreline, about to start shooting a video, when they witnessed the second plane hitting the World Trade Center.

Antony: It was traumatic because our families couldn't get in touch with us for twenty-four to forty-eight hours. It was a tragedy and it changed the world to this day, but to be there was just mind-blowing. It was like being in a blockbuster movie where people were running around and there was smog and smoke everywhere. We ended up getting evacuated to Tarrytown with Atomic Kitten for ten days. They were filming the video the day after, so on the 12th, and we were filming on the 11th. So we saw the second plane hit and saw the building collapsing from over near Brooklyn Bridge. From there we got evacuated.

Jenny: It really affected me. When we got back to the UK eventually, I wasn't sleeping at all and I was hospitalised for a few days. Every time I slept, I'd have these screaming nightmares. They just put me in hospital for a few days and knocked me out so I could sleep. I was a wreck. They said I had PTSD and that I needed to sleep. I had therapy afterwards. It was one of those moments I couldn't talk about for a really long time. Some of the things that we saw that day, you know.

Antony: I think we were [suffering from PTSD] in a way that we never really spoke about. We never shared a bedroom but that night when we were evacuated I remember sharing a room with Dunc and sitting up all night. It was a crazy time.

Jenny: Everybody was fucking traumatised. It affected us all for a long time. We used to fly so much. Before that, I never had an issue flying, but still to this day I'm not a good flyer.

Antony: We managed to fly back to the UK and I remember going straight to Southampton to do an outdoor gig.

Hugh Goldsmith: Fast-forward to the end of a long day of interviews back in London, with the same question being asked over and over again, and Lee snapped, saying something he deeply regretted, which resulted in huge levels of hatred being aimed at him for many months. Lee was only eighteen and what he wanted to say came out all wrong.

Simon Jones, Blue's former PR: They'd had a PR and they weren't happy so they brought me in just before that single and the album. We'd started doing press and we'd done a little bit of media training, but not much. I can remember sitting at my desk and for some reason they had gone into *The Sun*. I didn't even know they were doing it. Someone on their digital team had taken them in to do some sort of live thing for *The Sun* and didn't think to tell me or the PR team they were doing this. They walked over to the Bizarre desk and Dominic Mohan and he's like, 'Can I have a quick chat with the boys?' Why they thought it was a good idea to have a chat with *The Sun*, I don't know.

Antony: I think it got to a point where the trauma of it had built up and it felt like no one was really interested in our music. It was about, 'What did you see? How did it happen?' One of the lads, he just said, 'Look, can we just not talk about this any more, it's really hurting us emotionally; if you want to talk about something serious, let's talk about other stuff like whales being killed or dolphins being executed' – I don't know, I can't remember the exact words he said. From that it was the front-page headline you see today. [Lee Ryan is quoted as saying: 'Who gives a fuck about New York when elephants are being killed? Animals need saving and that's more important. This New York thing is being blown out of proportion . . .']

Simon Jones: They got in a car afterwards and Lee calls me and says, 'I think I might have said something.' It's my favourite line ever: 'I think I might have said something.' There are certain individuals that you don't want to hear that from. He told me and the colour drained from my face. I knew instantly it was going to be a disaster. I know Dominic, I know Bizarre, I know *The Sun*; they're going to want to turn this into something. So I rang Dominic and said, 'Oh, I understand that Blue were in,' and he said, 'Yeah, I was going to call you, Lee said some pretty horrific things.' Then it went into overdrive.

Justine Bell: Hugh was away at the time and I recognised this was dangerous and needed to be contained. I went into the office at about 7 a.m. and wrote a statement, which I got Lee to sign off on and post online apologising. It was a difficult time. Hugh pulled in a million favours to dampen down the impact.

Hugh Goldsmith: After having finally finished overseeing the making of the Blue album I was exhausted and decided to take a short break in a remote part of the Scottish Highlands with my wife and three kids. We were so remote I didn't even have a mobile phone signal. What could possibly go wrong?! So there I was, in the local pub, enjoying a whisky, when the phone behind the bar started to ring. It was Steve Morton, Virgin's director of promotions, who had somehow tracked me down to alert me to the interview and the fact that the story would run on the front page of the next day's *Sun* newspaper. We were told there was no way *The Sun* would change their minds even though our press people had done everything they could to persuade them not to run the story.

Simon Jones: There wasn't really anything we could do. I was trying to explain to Dominic that he didn't mean it disrespectfully; he just meant he didn't want to talk about it any more. Obviously Dominic felt he came across as disrespectful to the victims. I can remember it coming out. The label thought it was going to ruin them. You can imagine the ramifications for the online person who took them into *The Sun* without telling the PR.

Hugh Goldsmith: I was completely gutted and my immediate instinct was to call my contacts at media outlets like Radio 1, Capital Radio and breakfast TV to try to stop the story running on all their news bulletins the next morning, thereby limiting the damage somewhat. So I set up a 'war room' in the pub and started making the calls. Thankfully, the radio and TV stations were totally sympathetic and, to this day, I feel so grateful they didn't make matters much worse than they already were by running the story in all their bulletins.

Simon Jones: The next day *The Sun* ran a poll saying, 'Should Lee Ryan be fired from Blue, ring this number'. It was a big story in America: this UK band are saying, 'Fuck New York and fuck what happened'. It was made out to be that he didn't give a shit about the people that died in the Twin Towers, which to be fair to Lee is not what he was saying. He was just not very eloquent at that point in his life and wasn't expressing his thoughts in a clear way. *The Sun* knew what they were doing. Lee was being asked about serious things like 9/11.

Justine Bell: I had to go on tour with them for a week to make sure Lee didn't get cornered by journalists who might encourage him to say something else that could damage the band. Thank God there was no social media.

Antony: I think that was a defining moment. From that point onwards in a weird sort of way it put Blue on the map in terms of being in the bigger picture. All of a sudden people were interested in our relationships. And you just think, 'Wow, we're interested in making music and having a good time and making people happy.'

Justine Bell: It felt awful at the time but it probably helped them in the long run. Everyone knew who they were because of the tabloid stuff so it probably helped them monetise their profiles after the band split.

Simon Jones: There wasn't a day that went by where they weren't in the tabloids. They were just great fodder. They were out shagging girls, they were falling out of nightclubs, they were getting drunk, they were having arguments. They were always saying things that were cheeky. Once the papers realise a band is giving them stories, it almost becomes a self-fulfilling prophecy because every day they go into conference and go, 'Anything on Blue?' It felt relentless. They'd say, 'I heard Lee shagged this girl last night,' and I'd be like, 'How do you know that?' Things were leaking from inside the camp all the time. People on the inside were being paid to give stories. Sometimes I would feel like people were suggesting I had leaked stuff, but why would I? It's much easier to think I was doing it than say someone from their families. Often it is family.

Hugh Goldsmith: By now, there was already a very strong brotherly bond within the group and Lee was given the full support of his fellow band members at an extremely difficult time.

Jordan Paramor: We were at a gig somewhere with them and they were being asked to promote a male cancer charity. There was a 'Balls to Cancer' T-shirt and Lee put it on and said, 'I'm okay to wear this, aren't I?', and everyone shouted, 'No, no, take it off.' Just in case people thought he wasn't coming from a helpful place. Because it was out of context. Management were worried people might think he was taking the piss. Lee was devastated by the 9/11 thing. It haunted him and I think it still does.

Iain James, Triple 8: Artists are so much more switched on now with everything – their finances, their artistry, their marketing. In my day we did not have a clue. It's a blessing that we didn't become successful, because if Lee Ryan said what he said, God knows what *we* would have said.

Peter Robinson: Blue were a very Capital FM band. They made sense in that time where Capital FM was the biggest station in London. You'd see people that looked like Blue out and about in London clubs. They had an incredible vocalist in Lee as well. He was a brilliant pop star and a terrible pop star at the same time.

MNEK: Lee is an OG vocalist. Let's be clear. 'If You Come Back' and 'Fly By II' are proper classic boyband records regardless of region, because they sang the fuck out of those songs.

Antony: Lee also had an obsession with fire extinguishers. I remember being at the Copthorne Hotel in Newcastle and after a gig we went back to the hotel for a drink but it was Newcastle United's Christmas party, so Alan Shearer was there. And my good friend Dale Winton, who is no longer with us any more, he came up to see me and we were all having a laugh. That was the first time I got Dale Winton pissed on tequila. He was loving life, he was dancing and singing. Fabulous man. Miss him terribly. Anyway, Lee got a fire extinguisher out and hosed all the Newcastle team and the people in the bar. Dale was like, 'Oh my God, what's happening? This is fun! This is rock 'n' roll!' They tried to do us for the dry-cleaning bill but Lee ended up paying it all, I think.

Simon Jones: [Getting a 2004 feature in *Observer Music* magazine] was a big deal for the record label. They always loved it when a music broadsheet got on board.

Alexis Petridis, journalist: You were seeing that transference of power in terms of music journalism. Broadsheets didn't really cover pop music in its broadest sense really until the '90s. We were probably to blame to a certain degree for the collapse of things like *NME* and *Q*, because we were doing what they did but with a broader remit. We didn't have to service any particular tribal demographic or anything like that. You could cover anything you wanted.

Simon Jones: We took them to Dubai for the piece. Beforehand with the boys I was like, 'This is really important; don't say anything stupid, don't fuck this up.' We go to the gig and then there's an afterparty at some rich guy's house. I was nervous about it. Then one of the girls that was with us who shall remain nameless thought it would be funny to get sugar out and line it up as if it was lines of coke. I thought it *was* coke so I was panicking. I was trying to clear it up before anyone saw it and it became 'my night of coke with Blue'. I had a massive row with this girl like, 'That's not funny, it could have ruined this piece with *The Observer*.'

'You had two blond guys, an ex-model and a Greek geezer, do you know what I mean?'

A boyband is a delicate ecosystem. Built to be lusted after via cheeky magazine articles in everything from Smash Hits *to* Attitude, *it can be tricky for the members who perhaps don't get the full glare of the spotlight. For Blue, whose first two albums had both gone four times platinum in the UK, the tabloid focus was Duncan and Lee, while Simon – a former model and often the band's anchor – rarely struggled to get attention. It meant one member often felt sidelined.*

Simon Jones: I didn't get on with Antony. At the time, I think it might have been based on insecurity, but the problem was all the magazines were interested in Lee, Duncan and Simon. They'd say things like, 'Well, we'll do four covers but we don't want to print the Antony one.' I'd be like, 'Well, you have to – I can't go to him and say that.'

Hannah Verdier: When we were doing the covers on the very left-hand side you'd always put the ugly one. So you'd put, say, Gary Barlow there because you'd have a flap with a free gift covering his face. The boring one goes behind the free gift and the good-looking one goes in the middle.

Jordan Paramor: I was twenty-four when Blue started and I remember my friends saying, 'God, I fancy Lee from Blue.' She'd never said that about anybody from 911 or Five. They weren't dressed in Technicolour boyband outfits; they were the cool face of boybands. I remember another friend having a real crush on Antony because she thought she'd have more of a chance.

Antony: I felt like I was an easy target. I wasn't the blond-haired, blue-eyed boy or the one with the big muscles and the six-pack and the chiselled jaw. You had two blond guys, an ex-model and a Greek geezer, do you know what I mean?

Jordan Paramor: We used to call the ones that always stood in the back behind the main guys the plumbers in pop. No one knew what they were called or what they did. All bands had one that was slightly less popular.

Simon Jones: Often these magazines would take it upon themselves to just stick someone on the cover if something fell through. So it was fine when you were controlling it and saying, 'It's got to be all four boys,' but there were eight or nine of these mags; you couldn't control every cover they did. They'd just email and say, 'We've made a decision, we're putting Duncan on the cover this month.' But it was always Lee, Duncan or Simon. Antony is a lovely bloke, but at the time this tension built up where it was like, 'You're doing a shit job . . . for me.' I couldn't change the game we were in.

Antony: Because you don't feel that you're good enough to be in a band, you don't feel like you're good enough to be on stage and you don't feel like people like you. So you're always worrying. It got to a stage where I didn't feel confident and I used to make excuses. It wasn't me. So I thought, 'You know what, only you can change this,' so I came out of my shell a bit.

Simon Jones: For the last era of Blue, Antony had his own, separate PR. Obviously it was a waste of money and time, but I think it was the manifestation of the insecurity that developed from not resonating in the media as much as the other three boys. Just wanting to blame somebody for that, which I do understand because that was my job. He didn't think I was delivering for him.

'She gave us this weird dirty look as if to say, "Who the fuck are these four boys?"'

A clear reflection of Blue's impact came via the rarified company they kept. Not only did they release singles with both Elton John [2002's 'Sorry Seems to Be the Hardest Word'] and Stevie Wonder [2003's 'Signed, Sealed, Delivered, I'm Yours'], they were also invited to spend time with fashion goddess Donatella Versace. Apparently a huge fan of their oeuvre, in 2001 Donatella extended an invite to her show at Milan Fashion Week. Only, well, there was a breakdown in communication and Donatella actually wanted Blur. Blur not Blue.

Simon Jones: I remember them going to the Donatella Versace thing, but I didn't hear until way after the fact what had happened.

Antony: Her PR company over here phoned up our press people at the time and said, 'Donatella wants Blue to come over.' We thought it was amazing. We got kitted out in Versace in Mayfair.

Simon Jones: The boys were made up, like, 'Donatella has personally invited us.'

Antony: Then we got flown over by private jet. We were lining up after the show and she gave us this weird dirty look as if to say, 'Who the fuck are these four boys? Why are they wearing my gear?' I said to Simon that it was a bit weird. He went, 'Maybe she doesn't smile, who knows?' Anyway, we get home and our PR company phoned back and were like, 'We're so sorry, but she wanted Blur and not Blue.' She Instagrammed a picture of her and Damon [Albarn] the other month and tagged me in it saying, 'I've met my man.' It was great.

Hugh Goldsmith: They were the hottest new act in the UK by early 2002, so when I reached out to Lucian Grainge to see whether Elton would be interested in duetting with the guys on their version of 'Sorry Seems to Be the Hardest Word' I was hoping for a yes and, happily, that is what I got.

Antony: Elton John said that *All Rise* was the best album of 2001. He's quoted as saying that. We'd already finished the *One Love* album and I think it was Lee who said, 'What if we do a cover of Elton John?' We went in and did 'Sorry Seems to Be the Hardest Word', but originally Elton was only going to play the piano on it and not sing it. Then he heard our version and he came down and he said, 'Would you mind if I just laid the vocal down?', and we were all like, 'You crack on, mate.' These are his words: 'If it's fucking shit, I won't be offended, just take it out.' Anyway, he did it and it's what you hear today. One take.

Hallgeir Rustan: We arrived well prepared in the studio in London and Sir Elton John was to arrive at midday. We thought he would probably show up in the evening. But at 12 p.m. he was in the studio ready to work. Before the London session, we had rented the fattest grand piano in Trondheim and recorded the piano track on 'Sorry Seems to Be the Hardest Word' ourselves. After all the vocals on the song were finished, we asked Sir Elton John if he could play on the grand piano that was standing there in the studio. He sat down and played through the song once and, oh my God, it sounded ten times better than what we had worked on in Trondheim. Also, if he didn't have music, he could easily have been a comedian – so funny.

Justine Bell: Blue were perceived as a cool act and Elton John always seems up for that. He seemed to genuinely get on with the boys, too, when they recorded together. Initially he said he couldn't do a video with them. It took Duncan about five minutes to talk him into it. We shot the video the next week.

Hugh Goldsmith: A year later, I made another call to Lucian and this time it was to see whether we could interest Stevie Wonder in duetting with the band. As a result, I was able to enjoy one of the most memorable experiences of my career in the shape of two nights in Dr Dre's recording studio with Stevie Wonder. The surreal experience was topped off at about 3 a.m. on the second night when Stevie, who I was sitting next to at the desk while we were mixing his vocals, called his assistant and started singing his version of 'Happy Birthday' down the phone to her!

★ ★ ★

After the release of their third chart-topping album, *Guilty*, at the end of 2003, Blue were starting to fracture. Tellingly, it was their first album to sell below a million copies in the UK. A year later, they released the *Best of Blue* compilation, led by the pointedly titled single 'Curtain Falls'. By 2005, the band were on hiatus, with each member dabbling in solo material to varying degrees of success. Somewhat hampering their abilities to properly cash in on a reunion, Blue were one of the few pop acts of the time to treat the hiatus as exactly that, often cropping up in tabloids, on the nostalgia tour circuit and occasionally in the charts every few years. In 2011, they reunited for Eurovision, finishing in eleventh place with the single 'I Can', co-produced by Hallgeir Rustan (that role was almost thrown into doubt after Antony, displaying a deft ability to multi-task, was papped urinating while getting some cash out and texting on his phone). A fourth album, *Roulette*, followed in 2013, with another, *Colours*, arriving two years later. In 2022, they returned for an arena tour and released their sixth album, *Heart & Soul*, which was compromised slightly by Lee being arrested after allegedly becoming abusive on a flight. *Heart & Soul* entered the charts at number twenty-two, their lowest-peaking album so far.

6

Don't stop movin': How S Club 7 became pop's hardest-working band

While Chris Herbert healed his wounds after his Spice Girls sacking via Five's relentless drama, Simon Fuller – who had been handed his P45 in November 1997 – immediately started work on what would become S Club 7. In fact, the neat story goes he dreamt it all up the day after he saw the underside of Geri's clomping Buffalo boot. Having witnessed the global dominance of the Spice Girls first-hand, Fuller was keen to make his next move similarly all-encompassing. There were somc important tweaks on his mood board, however: where there was five before, let there be seven. Just girls? Come on, let's mix that up too; think Steps but glossier. Sure, we could shlep them around radio, TV and magazines for months upfront of the debut single or we could launch them via their own children's BBC TV show in which the band/brand play (slightly) fictionalised versions of themselves and debut music in every episode? So that's what he did.

Auditions started via *The Stage*, with Jon Lee, Paul Cattermole, Tina Barrett (who was at that point one third of Face2Face, later Mis-Teeq) and Hannah Spearritt all plucked out of 10,000 hopefuls. Rachel Stevens, meanwhile, was separately approached by two producers from Fuller's 19 management and asked to record a demo. Those five only became S Club 7 after three of the original hopefuls were fired. In the end, Jo O'Meara and Bradley McIntosh completed the picture and the UK gained its first fourteen-legged, all-purpose, sugar-pop behemoth.

'At the time, I was working at Pizza Hut in Chessington World of Adventures'

James Masterton: The biggest cultural shift, the tipping point for the revival of the pop music industry, was Princess Diana dying. Elton John performed his new version of 'Candle in the Wind' at the funeral and then rush-released it. In its first full week on sale it became the first song in history to sell a million copies during a week. The majority of those were on a CD single. That cemented the idea of the CD single being a mass-market consumer product. Supermarkets saw this demand and so music went from being a niche interest to something you could get your hands on absolutely everywhere. The CD single became a pester product in the same way a bar of chocolate might be. The record industry realised this by pushing forward acts who had distinct appeal to children. Sales started to shoot through the roof. This was to the benefit of every single pop act that emerged in this period.

Peter Loraine: It was at a time when Polydor's main acts, aside from Boyzone, were Cast, Shed Seven, Gene and a bunch of guitar bands. We were coming out of Britpop, the Spice Girls were ginormous, All Saints were doing really well, and [Polydor] didn't have anything pop. The first real thing we did was we went to Simon Fuller and asked what he was doing next.

Chris Herbert: Simon Fuller had been sacked by the Spice Girls and he was taking refuge down in Portofino in Italy at Sophia Loren's villa. He got a message to Simon Cowell and said, 'Look, you, me and Chris should get together to talk about our war stories.' So we went and spent about three days hanging out. Fuller said to me at one point, 'If you were to do another band, what would it be?' I said I had this idea of doing a mixed group, boys and girls, with more than five members, and it would be multi-cultural. At the time, I had a working title of United Colours because of the United Colors of Benetton adverts. Fuller was like, 'This is a great idea, we can build a TV show around it.' We left it that we were going to explore the idea more but nothing came of it. Then all of a sudden S Club 7 pop up. Make of it what you will.

Colin Barlow, former head of Polydor Records: The TV show for S Club 7 was absolutely revolutionary. What Fuller realised was that if you had a pop band and Radio 1 don't like them then it's not going to work, but if you've got a TV show then you don't have to worry about Radio 1. Everything with S Club 7 was built around the fact that Simon wanted to get an act to an audience, rather than have a gatekeeper at Radio 1 telling him that his act wasn't cool enough to be on the radio.

Peter Loraine: Simon had three ideas; he had 21st Century Girls, who were four rocky girls who played instruments and drove tanks in their videos; then there were three brothers who were like the British Hanson; and we were like, 'We want S Club.' At that point they were just called S Club and there were only five of them, so no Bradley and no Jo.

Jo O'Meara: I was singing in a country-and-western-themed restaurant in Guildford. I'd wait tables and then the music would start and whatever you were doing you'd have to stop, run to the stage, sing the song and carry on waiting the tables. A member of 19 management was in that evening having dinner. They approached me and said I'd be perfect for this new project Simon Fuller was putting together. So I went along to the audition.

Sam Bloom: I actually auditioned for S Club 7 and I got down to the final rounds with Hannah and Jon. I think I got replaced by Bradley at the end, just before they all got together.

Bradley McIntosh: I wasn't sure if they were 100 per cent keen on me. I did the audition and at the time I was working at Pizza Hut in Chessington World of Adventures. I didn't hear anything back for a while.

Jo: I was petrified going into the audition because the queue was so so long. I remember walking into this really horrible little room and I had to sing a couple of songs and then they got me to recite an acting piece. When I was auditioning for the band, I thought it was just a band; I had no clue there'd be a TV show alongside it. I sang Fleetwood Mac's 'Dreams' and then they wanted something up-tempo, which I didn't really do back then, so I just burst into 'I Wanna Dance with Somebody' by Whitney Houston. Then I got recalled to go and meet Simon.

Bradley: Funnily enough I got fired from Pizza Hut about a week after the audition, so I was on my way to get my P45 when I found out they wanted me to go and see them again. I remember going back to Pizza Hut and saying, 'Yeah, I'm going to be in a band,' and them being like, 'Yeah, whatever, mate, sure.'

Jo: The first time we all met was at [PR legend] Nicki Chapman's house and that's when we were told we were officially S Club 7. That was the start of a brand-new pop adventure. I found it tricky because the other five members had already bonded.

Bradley: Because of that [me and Jo] always had a strong bond together. We always ended up being in the studio for the longest as well.

Jo: Back then you all either lived together in a house, like the Spice Girls did, or you would get taken on days out. We would go to the Trocadero in London and we'd play arcade games or go bowling. Go for dinner, go to the cinema. That was all bonding exercises to get us working together as a unit, so it was quite tough because they all knew each other. Me and Bradley felt like the odd ones out at first. We went to Italy and stayed at the most unbelievable villa that Simon had hired out. He took us out on a private boat and we went shopping in Capri. We had a private chef. It was different to what I was used to back home, that was for sure.

Bradley: We had three-course meals and lots of wine. He could see the bond. Then he sat us in this room and started to explain that there would be a TV show. I knew some of the other guys were from stage school and I'm thinking to myself, 'Do they know I have no experience in acting?' I wasn't going to say anything, I didn't want to lose the job.

Jo: The shock was, 'Oh, by the way, you fly to Miami in two weeks to film your own TV show.' I'd never done any acting in my whole life. All of a sudden I had a hundred pages of script to learn in ten days. It was so frightening. That was first mentioned when we were all together in that room for the first time.

Bradley: I didn't know [Jo had never acted before either]. I felt like I was the only one who had come straight out of Pizza Hut. From that moment on it was full speed ahead, but obviously you go through all the legal stuff with contracts and get all the parents together. That process took a few months. There was an advance. I can't remember how much it was – maybe £50,000 or £100,000. I didn't really care about those things back in the day. I was just living the dream. I never once checked my bank account when I was in S Club 7. All I knew was that this card gets money out of the wall. That's it. Whenever I needed money, it just came out. I was sixteen when I first started.

Jo: So many people have asked me, 'What does the "S" stand for?', and I've tried to come up with theories. 'Simon' is the obvious choice. But then I was thinking, 'Is it some sort of a connection with the number nineteen?', because 'S' is the nineteenth letter of the alphabet. It's not even a secret thing we can never disclose because we don't know what it is.

Bradley: We just came to the conclusion that it's Simon's Club. S is the nineteenth letter of the alphabet and that's Simon's company, 19 management. Why wouldn't it be anything other than Simon's Club? If I was Simon, it would have been called B Club 7.

'We were in a villa in Barbados and in between waterskiing we went through all the scripts'

For the first series of the S Club 7 TV show, Miami 7, *the band travelled to, well, Miami, where they shot thirteen episodes in no time at all. The show's scripts were overseen by Simon's brother and* Spiceworld *pensmith Kim Fuller, who created a fairly depressing world around them. Promised fame and fortune by their management, the fictional band move to Miami only to find themselves penniless and performing for scraps. Each episode would feature a new song, while the opening theme tune to* Miami 7 *– launched in April 1999, two months before any music was officially released – was the (real) band's debut single and first number one, 'Bring It All Back'. The format was repeated in subsequent series, with 2000's* L.A. 7 *– in which Linda Blair co-stars as rollerblading landlady Joni, who accidentally runs Bradley over – led by number-two hit, 'Reach'. The show, which also featured various spin-off TV movies, was sold to 100 countries, attracting 90 million viewers worldwide.*

Colin Barlow: Simon wanted it to look like programmes like *Saved by the Bell* and *Sweet Valley High*. He wanted sunshine. They wanted to film it in America so it didn't just look like a parochial,

UK-based programme. It made people think of it as a global proposition.

Peter Loraine: I can remember sitting in a meeting room trying to explain how it was such a fine line between aspirational and too young and baby-ish. I remember saying, 'It can't look like *Grange Hill*.' We knew we had the slot on BBC at 5.10 p.m., which was the *Byker Grove* slot or the *Grange Hill* slot or the *Blue Peter* slot. I knew it couldn't be like those things; that it needed to have a gloss to it. Simon Fuller turned to me and said, 'Okay, we'll film it in Miami, then.' Literally the colour drained from the face of the person from the BBC as the budget for each episode went through the roof.

Andrew Margetson, director, *Miami 7* and *L.A. 7*: I knew that Simon Fuller and [TV producer] Malcolm Gerrie, who were the main players in the S Club project at the time, were struggling to agree on a director, and someone who worked for Simon put me forward. At the time, I was signed up to do another series of [Channel 4 kids' drama] *Renford Rejects*, which was fun, but shooting in Kensal Green compared to going to Miami . . . I was a young guy. Also, Simon was very charming, very persuasive, he sold it very convincingly. He played me the music, which I liked. I said to him, 'Here's the deal, I want to do the TV series but I also want to make the music videos. I wanted to be 360 on it.' Looking back, I think Simon was very shrewd because he wanted his team helming that project – he didn't want the BBC to control it.

Peter Robinson: It was really well put together because not only was this happening in the UK but the show was in dozens of other countries as well. That plan was done by somebody else first. It was done with [boyband] North & South by [manager] Tom Watkins [in 1998 and 1999]. That was the same sort of idea really – let's have a kids' TV show, *No Sweat*, and then let's launch a band off it. But it didn't really work and maybe it's the songs or the band.

Andrew Margetson: I'd grown up on *The Monkees* and it was always Simon's [reference point] because he'd look up to that show. It wasn't a radical idea, but it was smart to do it with a modern pop act. To use TV to sell records.

Jo: We were often compared to the Monkees and Micky Dolenz came on set one day and we all had a video made of us doing the Monkees walk along the beach.

Andrew Margetson: For me, the challenge was that some of them had done some acting but most of them had done nothing. And there was no casting involved; they're there, that's it. I spent a week with them workshopping, just to build their confidence. I got some actor friends involved. From where they came from to where they ended up is something I'm really proud of. We worked so hard. To run a whole show for thirteen episodes was brutal. I had to stick to the punishing schedule, but we were all kids and we did it.

Jo: [In the show] I was always the tomboy that was good at fixing cars and didn't take much nonsense from anyone. That was given to me but then I did kind of create it myself because it's always fun to play that kind of a character. Because I'm more cockney and the Essex one, it was a natural fit for me to become an *EastEnders* character, I suppose.

Bradley: I wouldn't say the character version of myself was accurate. I was willing to play that role. Only aspects were right, like I might be more sleepy, but that was because I was a party guy. That was never explained in the TV show. They made me a ladies' man as well, which I was, but not in that cheesy way. It was like I was Pepé Le Pew.

Andrew Margetson: Kim [Fuller, Simon's brother] controlled the scripts and they were written by a number of people, one of whom was Georgia Pritchett, who is now doing *Succession*. Quite the trajectory. There was a great writers' meeting before the shoot, where Simon flew the writers and me out to Barbados. We were in a villa in Barbados and in between waterskiing and whatever we went through all the scripts. I also remember after shooting one summer, I was with Simon in a villa in the south of France and Lucian Grainge was there. I remember showing them the music video for 'Bring It All Back' and them being wowed by it and thinking, 'Right, this is it, this is how showbiz works.'

Bradley: We did get the job done but there were a lot of times where people would say, 'Right, stop the laughing, guys, stop messing around.' It's like with any group of friends, all you need to do is look at them and you start laughing. We messed about a lot. It didn't feel like work.

Andrew Margetson: [Filming] was going to be difficult because the way I wanted to shoot it, partly because there's seven of them, involved a lot of long takes, so they had to remember a lot of lines. I couldn't break it up into small pieces because the nature of the beast meant that if you gave Jo a close-up you had to give everyone a close-up. Everyone was equally weighted. It put a bit of pressure on them because you'd shoot a three-minute take and then Bradley would screw up the last line. They learned very quickly.

Bradley: [The schedule] was constant. It was five or six days a week. Up at 4 a.m. most days because you had to start shooting at sunrise, so at 6 a.m. It was tough.

Jo: It was easier to just move us all as one, which could be really annoying if on the TV show I might not be in a scene until 2 p.m. but I still had to be picked up at 3 a.m. I'd literally sit around the whole day waiting for my scene, which might be one line.

Andrew Margetson: I remember there were some things in the script they didn't like. Simon had this idea, or maybe it was Kim, that they would have their own language. In those early episodes, there was this word 'parp', which was meant to be like 'rubbish' or 'poo', and they hated saying that. They had this idea that it would spread and every kid in the playground across Britain would be saying 'parp'. That was one of the few things they weren't enthusiastic about, to be honest.

Bradley: Eventually I made friends in LA so after work they'd come to my apartment. I made myself right at home – I bought a PlayStation, I got a music system. We stayed in this place called Oakwood Apartments, which was quite big. Stevie Wonder's son was staying in one of the other apartments and I made friends with him. I was just up until late and then I'd say, 'Guys, you've got to go, I've got two hours until I'm being picked up.'

Andrew Margetson: The constant worry was that they would run off and go crazy. We went into Miami at the end of filming series one and we stayed in a nice hotel on South Beach and I remember Jon, who was only sixteen, got a tattoo. Obviously he just lied about his age. Simon always had someone in charge of looking after the band. I remember later in LA we were put up in the Standard and the first night they went out on Sunset and partied and by the second night they were in a different hotel away in the valley somewhere. They were young so of course they wanted to have fun.

Jo: I shared a room with Rachel. We always wanted to share because we didn't like staying on our own, so we'd be together drinking cups of tea and learning scripts for the next day. I didn't drink and I never went out. I was a bit of a geek.

Bradley: Jo and Rachel were boring. Well, not boring – they were professional, that's what it was. They'd go to bed nice and early and be the first ones in the van in the morning. I'd be the last. But it's not because I was unprofessional – I was living the dream. I was having so much fun.

Andrew Margetson: [The TV show] was very valid and I was always proud of it and of the band. Of course we all want to be the Beastie Boys, but they were credible in a different way. Also: great singles. The target age group is younger, but it's still a valid audience. And it still gave a lot of pleasure to a lot of people.

Jo: We found out really late on the Saturday [that 'Bring It All Back' was number one] because the next day we were performing one of our first ever shows in front of 100,000 people at Party at the Park. Then when we were on stage they stopped everything and Dr Fox came on and announced it and 100,000 people just erupted. It was unbelievable. We were all running around the stage like loonies. Our first album was recorded primarily in Sheffield, but then once the TV show hit off and we were in America we had to keep the albums going at the same time as filming. That's why when we would have a day off from filming it wasn't a day off because we'd have to go straight to the studio.

Bradley: I remember we used to count the days off we had per year and it was less than a week's worth. We had days off but we wouldn't class them as proper days off because we'd be in LA, in our apartment. That's not a day off to me. A day off to me would be with my family and friends at home, not just in a cell.

Jo: We once flew to San Francisco to perform a show and we were literally on stage for fifteen minutes. We then flew straight back.

Hannah Verdier: They worked so hard. I saw them so exhausted that some of them were napping while the other ones were doing the interviews.

'In some way, S Club 7 weren't naff enough'

While the TV show pointed the band at the right audience, the music was key. The band had, after all, been put together as a pop act, with the TV show a surprise addition for many. Their debut album, S Club, *released in October 1999 featured a classic mix of hi-energy, frictionless bops and syrupy Hallmark card ballads. Follow-up album 7, which was somehow recorded and released just eight months later, became the band's only number-one album (it stayed in the UK top forty for thirty-eight weeks), with classic ballad 'Never Had a Dream Come True' later giving them their second UK chart-topper and only US top-ten single. They also won a BRIT Award for Best British Breakthrough in 2000, beating the likes of Phats & Small and the Wiseguys. The success was, as ever, well-earned, with the band squeezing in celebrations in the back of minivans.*

Peter Robinson: It's not as simple as saying, 'If you put something on TV then people will definitely like the record.' There was something else about S Club, which was the members of the band and the fact that the music was really good.

Andrew Margetson: The way it had worked was when I came on board they had already made that first album. So we made that series and then they made the second album. I know Simon found those songs from the top songwriters – [ex-pop star and songwriting legend] Cathy Dennis was involved. I don't know how they fitted recording in because it seemed to me that we were filming constantly.

Hallgeir Rustan: Our managers Tim Blacksmith and Danny D knew Simon Fuller well and they had a couple of meetings where they played some demos including [what became second single] 'S Club Party'. The brief was short – make songs that would work for the TV series and on the radio. This was a brand-new show, with completely unknown artists, so the second verse of 'S Club Party' [which features a description of each member, à la 'Wannabe'] was made so you got to know them in a funny way.

Simon Ellis: Simon called and said, 'I've got this new band called S Club 7, do you fancy writing some songs for them?' I hadn't really written songs professionally before. So I was like, 'Yeah, I'll give it a go.' Then he said, 'Do you fancy writing with Cathy Dennis?' I knew who she was but Cathy was just starting out [as a songwriter for other people]. We were two relative unknowns in the songwriting world. We got together and wrote [third single] 'Two in a Million' on that first day. We played it down the phone to Simon, with me on piano and Cathy singing, and he said, 'That's a hit.' We looked at each other like, 'This is crazy, it can't be this easy.'

Peter Loraine: It sounds really arrogant but there was no consideration that it wouldn't work. The music was so brilliant, the seven of them were so amazing, the backing from having the TV show was so great. When we started talking to people months before we were going to launch, *Smash Hits* would be like, 'Yeah, we'll put them on the cover.' When you work at a record company you have these planning meetings that are bespoke to an act and you go round the table and ask, 'What have we got at press? What's happening at radio?' With them we'd get to the TV person, who was Nicki Chapman at the time, and she'd say, 'I've confirmed fifty television appearances for them for the first single.'

Paul Flynn: S Club 7 came into the office of my first London job at the *Daily Express*. I worked on a very short-lived men's section for a newspaper called XY. It was the first newspaper response to the massive success of lad mags. [S Club 7] did that thing that I imagine everybody did with newspapers post-Spice Girls, which was they would come in, everyone stops working for a minute, they lip synch to the single and that guaranteed them top spot on the celebrity pages. By Sunday they were number one.

Bradley: With a lot of this stuff, it takes a while to sink in. A lot of the accolades I appreciate more now than I did then. There was so much going on and we were so busy back then. We were really proud to be nominated and to win a couple [of BRIT Awards].

Andrew Margetson: Halfway through filming *L.A. 7* they got a BRIT Award [for British Breakthrough Act] and I remember someone arriving on set with the awards and them having to do a little speech remotely. They were so excited and so happy. It was amazing to see that journey for them.

Simon Ellis: 'Never Had a Dream Come True' very nearly didn't happen. Cathy and I had written a bunch of songs for S Club and we were on a bit of a roll. The day we wrote that song, I pitched up at Cathy's house and the way we do it is I would start playing piano and Cathy would 'la, la, la' some melodies. We started about 11 a.m. and by 7 p.m. we had nothing. All I wanted to do was go home. Cathy said, 'Look, let's just give it another ten minutes and see what happens.' So she went downstairs to make a coffee and while she was doing that I started playing the 'Never Had a Dream Come True' melody and Cathy shouted, 'What's that? That sounds great.' By the time she'd made the coffee and walked up the stairs, she had half the lyric for the chorus, the title and all of the melody for the chorus. We finished it in about twenty minutes.

Jo: We didn't get that much time to digest how big a deal that [US top-ten hit] was. We were already on to the next thing. It is an amazing song and I definitely appreciate it more now.

Simon Ellis: Jo's not only the best singer in the band, she's one of the best singers this country has ever produced. Simon thought it was such a massive hit that no one else was going to sing it; it had to be Jo.

Jo: I would have been happy to share the vocals – it would have been a lot easier for me. Those songs were given to me and you can't say, 'No, I'm not doing it.' But yeah, I did feel a little bit like, 'Ooh, I hope they don't get the hump.' I think every single band in the world has a lead singer. It's very rare that you get a completely mixed band.

Malcolm McLean: In some way, S Club 7 weren't naff enough for me. Even if they had slightly matching outfits they would never do the whole flammable, everyone's wearing turquoise version like Steps. S Club definitely thought they were a lot cooler than that and they probably were. Relatively.

Bradley: Like best friends do, you have your bickering moments over little things. You're tired. I was definitely the little bro of the band.

Jo: It was very hard to get space because we were always together working. Or travelling to the next thing. Sometimes it would be really hard to just get half an hour sitting in a room by yourself. When we were in tour buses – or that famous radio bus, which was horrendous, because it was really cramped and small, like an old tin bus – Jon would put his headphones in, I would put mine in, and we'd all make out we couldn't hear if someone was talking to you. We were known for being very loud, our band, and I'm not naturally a loud person, so sometimes I'd think, 'Please, I need a bit of peace.'

Peter Loraine: If you think of the cycle of a band, they record an album, they tour an album, they promote an album – they did all those things but within it [S Club] were always recording a TV series as well. It was really intense.

Jo: If you didn't get number one it was classed as a failure. When you think back at artists who were dropped when they only made top twenty – it's harsh. There was a lot of pressure on us to get number-one singles and number-one albums, which we did get.

Jordan Paramor, author, *S Club 7: 7 Heaven*: I forgot I did that [book] because I wrote it in a weekend. I did all the interviews over the phone, all in one night. It was a Friday night, one after the other, bang bang bang, and I wrote it all over the weekend. They were in LA so I had to stay up until about 3 a.m. because of the time difference and I'd have an hour with each of them. It was no *War and Peace*.

Jo: We used to feel quite hard done by sometimes, but we were young. Jon was only fifteen. When I think about it that's a baby really.

Paul Flynn: I once went to Venice Beach and interviewed Jon, Bradley and Paul for *Attitude*. *FHM*, who were on the same trip, did the girls for their cover. We were supposed to do the boys on the cover but because Jon hadn't talked about his sexuality in the interview we did them inside. It was completely up to him to talk about it. Our thoughts at the magazine with Jon was that if he doesn't want to talk about it that's fine, it's up to him, but we're not going to cover it up or do any fucking beards. No telling stories about made-up girlfriends.

Nigel Dick, director, *Seeing Double*: It took me about five minutes of meeting [Jon] to suspect that he batted for the other team, as they say. He sort of personified a certain character, a certain personality, which I loved. It was never mentioned. It wasn't like, 'Okay, lads, let's go down the strip club, Jon won't be coming.' There was none of that. No whispering behind backs.

Paul Flynn: With S Club, you can't hide that fizzing energy pop music gives you, particularly in your adolescence, because it dovetails so perfectly – here are these people presented for you to fancy, here's this music that's made to react with your nervous system, and in the middle of that, 'Oh my God, am I having weird feelings about Paul Cattermole? Yes I am, but I can talk about everything else pop is giving me and not about having a sly wank about Bradley.' That's pubescence and that's the way pop music works really brilliantly with it.

Nigel Dick: Subsequently I read an article with him discussing being gay [Jon came out in 2010] and I was like, 'Good for him, I'm happy that he's happy.' The whole theory of a pop band when it's crystallised down to its essence is that you want to have thousands of screaming girls running after you. We weren't quite so emancipated all that time ago [to think] that there might have been a few screaming boys as well.

Jo: We used to like being in America because once we did get famous in the UK it was hard to go out and be free and be yourself, because there would constantly be paparazzi around. You didn't get much time to yourself. The only time you could be 100 per cent yourself was when you were indoors. So when we were in America we loved it over there.

Bradley: As someone who always wanted to be in a band and sing, I'd say a small percentage is actually singing. You're promoting. You're on *Top of the Pops* and it's not because you don't want to sing live, you just haven't got the time to do the rehearsals. You've got seven people, so if you haven't got the right sound engineer you could sound awful. We probably would have anyway. But with a tour you have months of rehearsals and vocal coaches, you work out all your harmonies, you're doing stage rehearsals and you get this beautiful blend. Being on tour was the reason I wanted to be in a band.

Jo: All of our favourite parts of the whole experience were being on tour. I always said I was a singer, but singing was only 20 per cent of my job in S Club. Going on tour was when I was at my happiest. I didn't do a lot of singing in the band, even though I did. If that makes sense.

'We were just about to sign a contract with a certain breakfast cereal . . . Sugar Puffs'

S Club 7's second BRIT Award arrived in 2002, winning Best British Single for stone-cold party starter, 'Don't Stop Movin''. It was a song – their third number one, chart fans – that seemed to elevate them in the eyes of critics and more 'discerning' pop fans from perma-smiling brand ambassadors to something approaching the parameters of credible. That trajectory was helped by the fact that on 20 March 2001 the boys in the band were caught smoking weed and cautioned by the police on the way to the Pepsi Chart Show. *Having been ignored by the tabloids, they were suddenly front-page news.*

Bradley: 'Don't Stop Movin'' was the one where we moved beyond the young kid, teenybopper audience. That one made us cool all of a sudden. Even older people were like, 'It's got a good feel to it, a bit disco, a bit "Billie Jean".'

Simon Ellis: Everybody loves that song. It's one of those timeless classics. Obviously it's a bit of a pastiche of disco and of 'Billie Jean'. Very similar drumbeat and bassline, which me and [co-writer] Sheppard Solomon had for a long time.

Hannah Verdier: I don't know how [S Club 7] got through the net of becoming famous because it felt quite late for that sort of [pop act] in a way. I think 'Don't Stop Movin'' buoyed them, obviously. I remember when they did 'Don't Stop Movin'' we were at *CD:UK* and Paul was telling everyone it was behaving like a number-one record. He was going into the mechanics of it.

Jo: That was our breakthrough single in a lot of ways. We were all kids when we started but then we became adults in the band, so we wanted to do cooler music and be a bit more edgy.

Simon Ellis: The 'Don't Stop Movin'' sessions are legendary in the S Club world. I was working in a studio in Farnham in Surrey. Jo had already been down to sing her bits the day before and the other members had done the backing vocals. I got Bradley in and he turned up about 2 p.m. I turned around to the recording desk and pressed play, but heard nothing from Bradley. He'd obviously been out all night and was fast asleep. So I thought, 'Shit, this is really not going to happen.' We got him to start singing but he sounded like he was still asleep. It was awful. I even thought about getting someone else in to sing it and try to impersonate Bradley. Anyway, I sent Bradley home. Then it got to about midnight – this was the last day in the studio – so I called somebody at 19 management and I said, 'Find Bradley and get him down here.'

Bradley: They needed me to vocal the song, but I was at the club. So they sent a team from 19 management to track me down. I remember someone walked in and said, 'Bradley, we need you at the studio.' I jumped into a car, straight out of a nightclub, and went to the studio.

Simon Ellis: He pitches up with this carrier bag full of beer and goes into the vocal booth. He was out of there by 2 a.m. and went back to the club. Great.

Bradley: The first take is what they ended up keeping. It's me after I'd just woken up, half tipsy.

Colin Barlow: They were really good people. Pop music at that time hadn't yet got to our version of the Gallaghers. We did have Brian Harvey in East 17 but that was as mad as it would go. They were always seen as very pure and that show was always very positive. They were really good role models for kids.

Nikki Whelan: I was a bit more sensitive to everything as a teen. Like when the S Club boys were arrested for smoking cannabis. Find me a boyband that doesn't do that. So tame.

Jo: Do you know what, how silly, for one. I think they were literally walking through Leicester Square. They weren't even supposed to be there because we were filming for the *Pepsi Chart Show* at the Roundhouse in Camden and we had to be on stage in forty-five minutes. Then we got a phone call from someone in the office saying the boys have been arrested and they're at the police station. I remember sitting there thinking, 'What is going on here?'

Nikki Whelan: I'd bunked off school – I was about fifteen – and had gone up to see them at the *Pepsi Chart Show*. There was this little paparazzi guy – I hated him – and we were just wondering why they hadn't turned up. He was like, 'I've just seen them. They went down the road in a police car.' I just thought he was trying to wind us up.

Jo: I don't know how they did it but they let them go and they got to the Roundhouse and we got on stage on time.

Andrew Margetson: I remember thinking, 'Smoking a big spliff in public, come on.' That's pretty mad.

Bradley: There's something really funny around that story. Believe it or not we were just about to sign a contract with a certain breakfast cereal . . . Sugar Puffs. That's why I think people started to say it was a publicity stunt because we lost our deal with Sugar Puffs after we got caught smoking puff. We were just young.

Jo: We went straight back to number one with 'Don't Stop Movin'' after that and we developed the new nickname

Spliff Club 7 for a little while. We went from being a really cheesy band to people thinking we were cool and starting to buy our records.

'I took S Club Juniors trick-or-treating once and we went to Sophie Ellis-Bextor's house'

Keen to keep control of his brand and aware perhaps that it's trickier to control exhausted young adults, in September 2001 Fuller launched a TV show, S Club Search, *to basically find the next S Club 7. The resulting band, S Club Juniors (later rebranded S Club 8 after S Club 7, later S Club, split), were all in their early teens or younger. They scored six UK top-ten singles with Polydor and two of their members – Frankie and Rochelle – later went on to make up two-fifths of Polydor's quite good girlband the Saturdays.*

Jo: To me, we were just filming another TV show. It was all auditions and getting the babies prepped. Not babies, Juniors.

Bradley: There was a competition on BBC for young kids to get the opportunity to sing alongside S Club 7 and perform with us. Then with the last fifty kids we went to meet them and pick the last eight. There were nine in the beginning but then one of them got a scholarship and it became eight. I hope that scholarship turned out well for him, you know.

Jo: It's when you saw [the final line-up] you started thinking, 'Which one is meant to be my little mini me?' That's what we all thought – we're being ousted here. And there was one more member!

Barry Stone, songwriter and producer: With S Club Juniors, the first thing we did was a song, 'Automatic High', we had written for another band. At the time it came out, it was a bit like, 'Is this suitable for children to be singing?', because it had lyrics about being ready any time. It obviously didn't bother Simon Fuller so we were happy to go with it. I don't think we were that bothered about the lyrical content back then. It didn't really occur to us; we just wrote what sounded good.

Hannah Robinson, songwriter: ['Only You,' from 2002's debut album, *Together*] was my first cut as a songwriter. I knew they were after that '60s pastiche-y sound, which I find quite easy to do. You know what you're trying to achieve. I never met them at all. We just sent the song off and then my publisher called to tell me they'd recorded it.

Colin Barlow: It was hilarious because you had a meeting with mum and dad, plus child, and all of 19 management. I don't think there have been many kiddy bands. They were a lot better than people give them credit for. It was great when we later did the Saturdays because Rochelle and Frankie already had the understanding of how it all worked, so they were on a different level when they went into the band.

Barry Stone: At that time, myself and Julian [Gingell] had a studio – well, a programming room – in the corner of a very big rehearsal building called The Depot on Brewery Road in north London. It was used by people like Blur and Oasis, Elastica, to rehearse for their big tours. So all the indie rock people and we were in the corner making this fun pop music. It was really bizarre when S Club Juniors used to come in because you'd have Chrissie Hynde in the café with all these kids running around. And they had their chaperones and their teachers.

Hannah Verdier: It's difficult to interview kids. It felt weird. Also, they were taking it more seriously than the adults were because they wanted to seem more grown-up.

Peter Loraine: It was done completely by the books. They were allowed to work four hours a day, or six if you got special permission from the council. They were chaperoned, looked after properly, did schooling. It was as good as it could have been.

Barry Stone: They'd have their tutors and all the kids would have their lessons in a separate room. Then we'd grab one of them for our allotted time, which we couldn't go over because we'd get a knock at the door. They couldn't sing with us for too long; I think it was twenty-five minutes at a time. Then we'd have to do the next one. It was a different way of working but we'd get into the rhythm of it. A lot of the times they would also come with a film crew so some of your allotted time would be taken up by pretending to record in front of the cameras. Which was slightly annoying because you needed to get on with stuff but you'd have to push faders up and down for a camera shot.

Peter Loraine: I took S Club Juniors trick-or-treating once and we went to Sophie Ellis-Bextor's house. I remember one of them was cheeky to her.

'It was like spending Saturday morning in Claire's Accessories with a migraine'

A month before S Club Juniors' debut single, the Cathy Dennis co-penned 'One Step Closer', their S Club mothership lost a member. On 28 March 2002, Paul Cattermole quit to return to his musical roots, AKA nu-metal noise merchants, Skua. Under contract to finish filming the fourth series of the band's TV show, Paul's departure was written into the script for the Barcelona-based Viva S Club. *For the remaining members, now rebranded S Club, the work continued and they went straight into filming their first (and only) film,* Seeing Double. *A £3.4 million global box office 'smash', it centred around an evil Svengali figure who creates a cloned robot version of the band because he's losing his vice-like grip on the real-life originals. Once again, it was co-written by Simon's brother, Kim Fuller.*

Bradley: Paul wasn't quite feeling it and he wanted to go off and do his own music with his rock band. We were prepared for it. I think we made the right decision in calling ourselves S Club and not S Club 6. It was cool; we're still friends now. We did it the right way, so there wasn't any animosity in the band.

Jo: I think it was the beginning of the end when Paul left. We did go on for another year, but it wasn't the same when he went. S Club 7 is S Club 7, innit, so when you've spent that amount of time as a unit and then one flies the nest it just didn't feel the same. People did have relationships in the band. We weren't told to keep them secret, but we were away a lot. It's not my place to talk about [Paul and Hannah's] relationship. I will say that when they were together they were very happy.

Nigel Dick: One Monday afternoon my phone rings and it's Alan Barnette, who had produced the S Club TV series and was very much in bed with Simon Fuller. He said he was making an S Club movie and asked if he could send me the script that afternoon. Then he said, 'If you like it, I want you to get on a plane to Barcelona on Thursday.' Then he added, 'By the way, the script isn't very good but we're going to make it better.' An hour later, a messenger was on the doorstep with the script. I had a word with my agent, who told me not to do it, but I was like, 'Fuck it, if I say yes, I'm going to spend three months in Barcelona and somebody else is paying for it.'

Bradley: [Filming] was really quick. We could have done a lot more with it, to be fair.

Nigel Dick: The interesting thing when you get to meet a bunch of people who have been together for years is that they have their own internal dialogue. Even if they don't like each other, they still have a common experience. Gradually as you start to spend time around them you start to see the friction between certain band members, but the point is you try to become part of their circle so you can enhance the good parts and cover the less fabulous parts. You want to understand them. And you want them to have trust in you because you're going to be working with them in a very intense environment.

Bradley: Nigel didn't make it feel like work. He'd make us say these funny things before every take, like, 'I am wearing no pants.' Just to get us into this character or whatnot.

Nigel Dick: Kim is a very nice guy, lovely chap, but he felt that he really had the essence of S Club running through his veins. It was clear he didn't. There's one scene where Bradley gets out of the car and there are dogs barking in the distance and he says, 'Who let the dogs out?' I remember questioning this line and Kim said, 'Oh, this is total Bradley.' Of course, on the first day of shooting the movie, Bradley comes up to me and goes, 'I would never say that.' If there had been time I would have said we needed someone else to come in and make the script cooler.

Bradley: Yeah, it was a little bit out of touch right there.

Nigel Dick: Gareth Gates was in it. God knows what stage his career was at at that point. It was like, 'Hey, Gareth, how would you like to play Gareth Gates in this movie?' One afternoon at Heathrow [for a scene featuring cloned pop stars] there was an Elton lookalike, a Madonna lookalike, a Michael Jackson lookalike and actual Gareth Gates all climbing on the same plane. For the band, the trickiest thing was the clones. 'Okay, in this scene am I a clone or am I my real movie self?'

Bradley: I didn't know who I was from time to time. At one point in the film, I can see it now, I'm playing it almost robot-like when I'm in the shower and I definitely played that wrong. If it wasn't for the clothes we were wearing, I wouldn't know which character I was.

Nigel Dick: To be fair to them, if you were Robert De Niro or Meryl Streep, you walk on set on the morning and you've got three Meryl Streeps to worry about – there's Meryl, there's

Meryl in the movie and there's Meryl the robot version. You could go to RADA for twenty years and not come up with a good solution for that. If it was confusing for them, I can guarantee it was confusing for me. In some scenes, half of them were the S Clubbers and half were the clones. So you had robotic Jon and real Jon in a scene with himself.

Jo: At that time, I had disintegrating crumbled discs in my lumbar twelve and thirteen. One of them was crumbling and the one underneath was under pressure so it was bulging, which caused it to sit on the sciatic nerve. The last few months of the band I was very highly medicated. I was on a lot of painkillers. I had to stop dancing. I could just about walk. That was a tough time because I was in agony for a lot of that last bit.

Nigel Dick: We had to come up with an endless bunch of gags to explain why Jo wasn't with the rest of them. It was a very strange dynamic because it would be like setting up the opening of 'A Hard Day's Night' and the four guys are running towards the camera, only Ringo's in a wheelchair.

Bradley: It was easier for her because there were scenes she didn't have to film. There's a scene where we're running through the streets of Barcelona and, when we get to the place, Jo's just waiting there on the side of the road. They had to write that in because she couldn't do all the running.

Nigel Dick: Essentially the speed with which I became the director and the movie went ahead was because they'd just finished shooting their last series, so all the machinery was in place – the art department, the art director, the AD, the cameraman. For some reason, the director who had been working on the last series got let go or jumped ship. If we shut it all down and turned it on again later, it would cost a bunch of money that people didn't have. These external forces govern the making of these things.

Jo: I have watched [the film] since. It's a cracker, innit . . . I tried to get my little boy to watch it and the first time he was too young to care and now he's too old to care. He's not one bit interested.

Bradley: Apparently that film is great hangover TV – we're trying to get it on Netflix.

Peter Bradshaw, film critic, *The Guardian*: Watching *Seeing Double* was like spending Saturday morning in Claire's Accessories with a migraine, or like witnessing the origin myth of a tween supervillain combo or pre-adolescent fascist dictatorship.

Pete Whelan: We wanted to go [to the *Seeing Double* premiere]. Not just stand outside, but actually go. The daytime soap *Doctors* was filmed in Birmingham where I lived at the time and so I phoned up S Club's record company and was like, 'I'm Christopher Timothy from *Doctors*' agent and he wants to bring his two kids to the S Club premiere.' They asked how many tickets we wanted and where to send them.

Nigel Dick: It played in Leicester Square. My two goddaughters, who were in their teens, were in the movie, so they came to the premiere with me. We arrived in a limo and there were loads of screaming fans. It was nice to have that moment. Then the next day the band fucking disbanded. Guys, could you not have waited! Could you not have sucked it in for a few more days?

'The level of their popularity is so hard to come by'

On 21 April 2003, almost four years to the day since they launched with Miami 7, *S Club announced they were to split while on stage in London during their S Club United tour (support came from, you guessed it, the newly christened S Club 8). Despite recently signing a contract extension, the warning signs had been there for a while. The previous November's fourth album,* Seeing Double, *had stalled at seventeen, while the album's disco-tinged lead single, 'Alive', had peaked at number five. The pep and infectious enthusiasm of those early singles had been replaced by something more undeniably desperate. In June, the band released a thirteen-track 'best of' called* Best: The Greatest Hits of S Club 7, *which peaked at number two.*

James Masterton: Downloading took off between 2002 and 2004 and you see that in the way the CD single market precipitously dropped. Newer music fans came along and said, 'Why do we need to pay for music? I can just click onto Napster and there's my music collection.' You then saw that with the steady decline of the cheery, chirpy pop acts. What always tends to happen is whenever the younger audience goes missing, the charts start to skew older. That was why acts such as the Killers, Keane and Coldplay were the people who were dominating the charts around that era.

Jo: I think there was a sense of relief because I needed it to be over. I'd had enough. I just wanted to feel normal again. I didn't know what feeling normal was, actually. I didn't really know who I was as Jo O'Meara. I was always Jo from S Club and I was always that character. You do then want peace. I hadn't had that for nearly six years.

Bradley: I think a lot of us were exhausted by that point. We were so tired, we were so overworked, we were ready to see what was next. Some people wanted to go into TV, some wanted to do their own albums, some just wanted to go on holiday for six months.

Simon Ellis: For me personally, after 'Don't Stop Movin'' it felt like things were coming to an end. Simon [Fuller] called me and said, 'We need another "Don't Stop Movin'".' That's always a mistake, because you'll never better the original. There are so many elements that come together when you're writing a pop song that have to be right and if one element is off then it misses. 'Alive' is a little bit like painting by numbers. It went to number five and everyone was like, 'Meh, it didn't go to number one.' It didn't go to number one because it wasn't as good as 'Don't Stop Movin''.

Peter Loraine: It made me really sad when S Club wanted to break up. I understood why, but I wondered at that time if maybe they couldn't see the wood for the trees. The level of their popularity is so hard to come by. When you step out of the group, whatever group it is, it's very hard to maintain that as a solo artist. Very few people have.

Jeremy Joseph: We always wanted to be part of a band's history. We did the very last thing S Club did together. They split on stage at G-A-Y. When you're no longer making money for a label or management, they don't care about you any more. They were just going to finish it on a low and we said, 'Come on, let's finish it on a high.' And as a band they said, 'Yes please.'

Bradley: We always had a great relationship with the G-A-Y audience and the guys there because it was pretty much the only club gigs we'd ever do. We were so busy we didn't have time to do that stuff, so it was either do a tour or do your TV stuff. It was great and we always got a great response from the crowd.

Jordan Paramor: S Club 7 worked so hard, my God. I think the sad thing is now, they're looking back and going, 'Where's the money?'

Jo: You can look at it in all different ways. All I can say is we probably could have done better [financially], but we could have done a whole lot worse. I've had a career out of it and I still have a career out of it today.

Bradley: It's up for debate really. I did a lot with my money. I invested it and still do today. My dad was the one who put me on to that because he saw I was spending a hell of a lot. I'd fill up two or three taxis with my mates and I'd pay. Then when we got to the club I'd put my card down. My dad was like, 'At the end of all this, what are you going to have to fall back on?' I bought my first property in 2000 and from there it just grew. We earned a lot of money. Maybe in comparison to Simon Fuller it doesn't seem a lot.

Jo: Not knowing what was next, or what I was supposed to be doing, was a huge shock. I'd just come out of something that was so military and then it stopped so quickly. I didn't know how to be without it. We were told what to do, told where to go, told when I'm eating. Literally everything was done for me; the only thing I had to think about was the job I had to do.

Bradley: I always wanted to do music. I always thought I would be in music, which is why I didn't take school too seriously. When you're that young, the world is all a bit of a dreamland. This little south London boy who wasn't sure where he was going, one day ends up in a band and then ends up performing for the Queen at her Golden Jubilee [in June 2002]. I was in disbelief, like, 'How did I get here?' Everyone was in the room – the Queen, the prime minister, Prince Charles, William and Harry. It was so intimidating, all these grand paintings. Who gets the chance to go to the Queen's palace?

★ ★ ★

Five months after the split was announced, Rachel Stevens released her debut solo single, 'Sweet Dreams My LA Ex', which peaked at number two. Between 2003 and 2005, Rachel scored four more top-ten singles and landed two top-thirty albums (including 2005's cruelly ignored *Come and Get It*). In 2006, Bradley briefly joined Upper Street, a boyband hybrid featuring members of Steps, 911, Another Level and New Kids on the Block, while Tina took a break from music. Hannah and Jon, meanwhile, moved into acting. In the ensuing years, various iterations of S Club would go on to perform at clubs and universities, before S Club 7 reunited for an arena tour in 2015. Tragically, on 6 April 2023, two months after the band had announced another reunion tour to mark their twenty-fifth anniversary, Paul Cattermole died of natural causes aged forty-six. The following month, Rachel, Bradley, Tina, Jon and Jo confirmed that the arena tour – now renamed the Good Times Tour after a 2001 fan-favourite album track sung by Paul – would still go ahead, though Hannah, while still a member of S Club, isn't joining them.

7

Re-rewind: UK garage's pop absorption

Pop absorbs, recontextualises and manipulates the genres around it, hoovering up the best bits and bolting them on. By the late '90s, UK garage, incubated in south London, was starting to move from an underground movement and into the top ten. Inspired by garage house and taking elements from R&B, jungle and dance-pop, UK garage, with its percussive bounce and sun-kissed, chilled Champagne feel, was the perfect playground for pop. It's where Victoria Beckham ventured in 2000 and the genre Liberty X dabbled in for their debut single a year later. But the genre's truly defining mainstream crossover star, Craig David, emerged in late 1999 via 'Re-Rewind (The Crowd Say Bo Selecta)', an effects-laden, catchphrase-heavy garage mega-banger that would later come to define him. A number-two smash, it saw him collaborate with fellow Southampton residents Artful Dodger, AKA Mark Hill and Pete Devereux, with the former going on to produce Craig's classic debut album, 2000's *Born to Do It*. Evidence of both UK garage's pop appeal and the influence of Craig's success arrived swiftly, with labels quick to commission chart-friendly garage remixes for the likes of new pop-R&B crossover girlband Mis-Teeq, AKA Alesha Dixon, Sabrina Washington and Su-Elise Nash.

While Craig's first single proper, 'Fill Me In' (a UK number one) carried the fluttering rhythms of two-step garage, the rest of *Born to Do It* cast its creator not as a soundsystem MC, but as an edge-free, pop-leaning, R&B impresario ready to take on his US counterparts.

'The closest thing I can link it to would be riding a surfboard on top of a wave'

Craig David: The first garage record I can remember is a song by Scott Garcia called 'It's a London Thing' in 1997. It came onto my radar in one of the Southampton clubs I was performing at called the Old Oriental. Mark Hill and Pete Devereux were playing upstairs in the house and garage room and I was downstairs in the R&B/hip-hop room with DJ Flash. I was an MC at the time. I was hearing this song and I was like, 'What is this?' Then I started getting into more of the vibe that the Artful Dodger were playing, where it was sampling R&B tracks and putting them over this new rhythm, which was going through a phase of being speed garage or garage or two-step. It was still trying to find its feet.

Chantelle Fiddy: At that time, I lived in Bedfordshire, in a little village, but I used to live in Southampton. So when Craig

David first appeared it was like, 'Oh my God, someone famous from Southampton, who is also good-looking.' I thought he was the shit.

Craig David: I had put out a song with the Artful Dodger called 'What Ya Gonna Do' [in 1998] and that was my first experience of going to London and hearing pirate radio stations as soon as I hit the M25. It was R&B but it was over a garage beat. There were these great R&B sampled vocals that were being used. It was just a euphoric time.

Chantelle Fiddy: The thing you have to remember about garage, and I don't know how to say this in PC terms, but there was a big part of it that was very Essex. Very cheesy. There was this idea that the cheesier you made the vocals, i.e. sped-up R&B vocals, you're going to get the women in the dance and the more women in the dance the more men you'll get. A lot of it was played with that view in mind.

MNEK: Garage was a real home-grown sound and it was able to take all the best things we love about pop music and make it faster. Before then we'd seen house and we'd seen techno and we'd seen disco, but it was usually four to the floor, but garage was more rhythmic and it spoke to Black people. Of course we've seen homogenised versions of it over the years, but everyone knows the real thing when you hear a So Solid record or a Craig record or the Artful Dodger or Mis-Teeq. Anything produced by Sunship, that's the real stuff. Everything else is garage lite.

Ceri Evans, AKA Sunship: The one thing that really attracted me to UK garage was that it was a little bit of everything. The more commercial stuff was obviously less dark. Something like the Artful Dodger stuff that crossed over is quite bubblegum, feel-good. It's got that throwaway, happy-go-lucky feel, like [Sunship's remix of Sweet Female Attitude's] 'Flowers' to a certain extent.

Craig David: I didn't know ['Rewind'] would be as successful on a commercial level. That people would hear it outside of my circle, which was Artful Dodger and my mum, basically. I was living at home at the time.

Chantelle Fiddy: It wasn't like you heard all these stories like, 'Oh, yeah, Craig David's been rolling with drug dealers, he's a bad boy, he's got a long list of offences.' He was a nice guy. You had these two scenes running parallel. You always had this underground. I went to Aya Napa with So Solid and that was my first experience of being in the club with people buying up all the Champagne just to pour it on the floor so you could dance in it. That was the excess of UK garage in that world. So if you don't want to be in that lane you've got the more innocent, commercial lane.

Craig David: ['Fill Me In'] was the song that once I played it to the record label I was so proud. That song to me has all the sensibility of my roots in garage but at the same time this infectious guitar. I think originally Mark was playing [the guitar riff] as part of a remix for a song by a boyband. I had to say to him, 'Woah, what's this?' I was like you need to give them a different guitar riff because that's mine.

Chantelle Fiddy: If you look at the lyrics it was very of the moment. He was definitely appealing to – and we don't use the word 'urban' any more – what was deemed at the time as this 'urban' audience and I think that was quite a new thing in the UK. In inner cities you'd always have pockets of Black music that wasn't popular elsewhere, but this was taking it outside of that. He's not from London; he's from Southampton. Every teenager could relate to that story [in 'Fill Me In'] of the parents coming home. It was a bit naughty.

Craig David: I adopted this [story-telling lyrical] style while I was listening to the R&B of that time, but also before that it would have been Terence Trent D'Arby and Michael Jackson. Then also a lot of the reggae that my dad would play to me. It was like, 'Take me by the hand and walk me through what you're trying to portray,' but then at the same time having the ability to keep it generic enough so it doesn't feel like my story and no one else could tap in.

Max Giwa, co-director, 'Fill Me In': The one thing [the label] stipulated was that they wanted a narrative-driven music video as opposed to just a normal video where it's him performing with loads of girls. Craig came from the pirate radio scene so [the video's intro] was a homage to that. A nod back to where he started from. It was their moment. The pioneers of a British movement were these kids: Craig, So Solid, Wiley, Dizzee.

Craig David: To have a number one, to be on *Top of the Pops*, to have artists I was a fan of be fans of my music, it was so surreal. It was like, 'Someone pinch me.' The closest thing I can link it to in terms of a metaphor would be riding a surfboard on top of a wave and never feeling like you were coming off of it. The view was beautiful, the vibe was great. Everything I had felt was being mirrored back to me in the world. It was incredible.

Hannah Verdier: Craig David was the first [UK garage star] we covered [in *Smash Hits*]. We did a double cover with him and Samantha Mumba. We had Luck and Neat on the cover, and Oxide and Neutrino as well. That is the last time, around the early '00s, where music was homogenous. Pretty much it was all one genre and you'd know the words to everything. You couldn't escape it.

Jamelia: I had to do shows with [the pop stars of the time] but I wasn't really a fan. I think I was fighting inner demons because I knew I didn't want to be a pop artist. I did love a couple of songs by All Saints and a couple by Girls Aloud, but they weren't me. I wanted to be like Mary J. Blige.

Su-Elise Nash, Mis-Teeq: The idea was we'd be an R&B girlband. That's where we thought we were going to go. [Late '90s girlband] N-Tyce and Eternal had been pretty big in the UK at least and definitely in my atmosphere and my environment. They would have been groups I would have looked up to. So that girl-group model is kind of what we were looking at at that stage.

Lee Thompson: The Box played everything that was doing well in the chart. We had a very good relationship with Relentless, who were putting out Daniel Bedingfield, DJ Pied Piper, So Solid. They were huge Box crossover records, absolutely.

Chantelle Fiddy: It was at that time in the industry where if you got the right remix – like Mis-Teeq did with [debut single, 2001's]

'Why?' – everything changed overnight. They went top ten with their debut single.

Su-Elise: 'Why?' was a really beautiful R&B song, but that remix [by Matt 'Jam' Lamont and DJ Face] really put us on the map. There weren't any other girl groups doing garage music. It was something we were all listening to in the clubs and partying to, but it wasn't something that had been done. It was very male-dominated, garage music, at that time. There weren't a lot of female artists exploring that genre. How it took off was absolutely amazing. It was what we all wanted but it wasn't anything we had ever thought would come so quickly as it did.

Chantelle Fiddy: I think the thing that really stood out for them was having Alesha [Dixon] MC-ing. It wasn't always the best, but you could easily get people involved with it, which is half the battle with pop.

Ceri Evans: She sounded like the real deal.

Chantelle Fiddy: The only other female MC around at that time was Ms Dynamite and she was very very authentic. Alesha wasn't that – she was from Welwyn Garden City.

Su-Elise: Alesha had been experimenting with MC-ing from the beginning so we were like, 'Yeah, let's do that, that's a cool touch.' We would all go out, we would party at TwiceasNice, that was the rave to be at back then. That was all garage. Guys like Mikee B and [DJ] Spoony are the ones that championed us at the start. In order to get that first hit we had to do so much graft. We were going to every PA in every club in every corner of the UK. Giving the DJs the track, saying, 'Please can you play this.' Of course we had help from our team, but we were signed to a pretty small independent label at that stage. When we then got to work with Sunship on [UK number two] 'All I Want', it was such an honour.

Ceri Evans: I also did [remixes for Craig David of] 'Rendezvous', 'Fill Me In', 'Walking Away', '7 Days', too. I very largely contributed to keeping him credible. There was a big divide between the signed pop stuff and the real underground. [Pop stars] were literally queuing up to have the remixes from me. I made the most of it financially: I was getting up to £15k a remix, which in those days wasn't bad. I could turn them over in three or four days. I did Christina Aguilera and Mary J. Blige remixes, too. I think that was more the labels wanting to get some more sales in the UK – it was all about money, money, money.

Chantelle Fiddy: When you look at [Daniel Bedingfield's] 'Gotta Get Thru This', there's a bit of beef around it. The version that was really popular originally said 'DND Edit' and that's Artwork from Magnetic Man. I remember interviewing Daniel and he got very angry about it – he felt like he'd done all the work and they'd added a few touches and they were getting the credit. But I wonder if the idea of putting 'DND Edit' at the end was to give it that co-sign – that this is someone on the garage scene.

Ceri Evans: [Pop absorbing UK garage] probably did upset the purists. I'd been making music since 1980, so the top of my list is survival. If you can say you're a purist then fantastic, good for you, but very few people can afford to be. Why am I going to complain about the way a scene's going if people are putting sustenance my way for myself and my family?

Su-Elise: You've got to remember R&B in the UK, apart from Craig David, hadn't really crossed into the mainstream that much. It was more American artists. So to be doing something really left [with UK garage] felt really good. We had our own niche and we were putting our own stamp on things.

'Craig David is a legend, so no BRIT Award can define him now'

By the time of the 2001 BRIT Awards, Born to Do It *– the fastest-selling debut by a British solo male artist in the UK and a million-seller in America – had spent over five months in the UK top ten. Having side-stepped away from garage thanks to musical sex diary '7 Days' and MOR ballad 'Walking Away', Craig was one of pop's biggest superstars. As a result, he was the most nominated artist at the BRITs, with six nods, including Best Single for '7 Days' and Best Album. In the end, he walked away (apols) with zero awards, losing every category to a white artist. To make matters worse, he'd also been booked to perform, with the leaked results at least allowing him to work a jibe at the snub into his live version of 'Fill Me In'. It felt like the music industry had welcomed Craig to the party – in fact, they'd sold tickets to the party off the back of his success – only to piss in his Champagne. For the BRITs, and their sporadic use of the Best Urban Act award category, it wouldn't be the first time they'd be accused of ignoring the successes and cultural dominance of Black artists.*

Marvin Humes, VS and JLS: One of the biggest music industry scandals of all time was Craig David not winning a

BRIT Award. He's one of the most influential, pioneering artists. He created his own music. Look, it's not the be-all and end-all, but Craig was so original when he came onto the scene. It's not spoken about enough how important and influential Craig David was to the music industry in our country.

Craig David: It was a strange period because firstly I was shocked I'd been nominated for that many. I will say that Bono going up on stage and singing 'One' and then going into 'Walking Away' was a huge moment for me. The original of 'Walking Away' had used a sample of 'One', which we couldn't get cleared, but then for him to show homage performing it to me as an eighteen-year-old kid at the BRITs was incredible. People like Elton John were on stage saying, 'If there's a better singer in the UK than Craig David then I'm Margaret Thatcher.' Dane Bowers had gone up and said a piece about how it was a travesty. It was front page of *The Sun* because it had already leaked that I hadn't won. If I'd have ended up winning just one, it would have been like, 'Okay, cool,' but to be nominated for six and get nothing and for that to happen around it – it was more memorable than actually winning.

Jamelia: Being nominated for a [BRIT] was just as great as a win [Jamelia was nominated eight times with no wins]. It meant that I was being recognised. As you get older and wiser, you do start to recognise things like [being nominated for Best Urban Act in 2005]. I think one of the really interesting things when it comes to Black artists behind the scenes, especially at that time, is we had a shared experience that was not only unique to us but that we had to keep a secret. We didn't want to lose our jobs. There were many conversations about things like that: 'Why is there an urban category? What does "urban" mean?'

Su-Elise: I didn't have a problem with that categorisation. I owned that. R&B music didn't come from pop music; that's not where it originated from, you know. It's its own weapon and I think acknowledging that is not a negative thing. Maybe you don't want to be pigeon-holed into a category and that I can understand, because it can be hard once you're seen as something to branch out.

Jamelia: At the time, 'urban' translated as 'Black'. So anybody doing any type of music that had a Black person singing was thrown into the urban category. But all the other categories were singled out by music.

Su-Elise: As we were taking this journey with Mis-Teeq, everything was starting to open up. Garage music stopped being seen as underground. When we're talking about urban, we're talking about music coming from the streets.

MNEK: The importance of those award shows was much greater then. It felt like that's all that mattered. If you had a BRIT or a Grammy, it could change your life. Craig David is a legend, so no BRIT Award can define him now. He's done wonders for any Black boy doing R&B music from the UK.

Chantelle Fiddy: [Craig] was the first time I'd heard somebody who was Black-British doing something in that R&B world and making it really cool. It was uplifting.

Tisha Martin, the 411: We were touted as the 'hip-hop Supremes' with our first single [2004's 'On My Knees'] and there really wasn't anything like our sound coming out of the UK at that time.

Carolyn Owlett, the 411: I think behind the scenes we were a bit of a risk. Our A&Rs really had to push hard for our deal. The head of Sony at the time didn't believe we would work at all so getting the green light to even make an album was a struggle.

Tisha: For our first single to go in at number four shows there was obviously some acceptance of UK R&B girlbands!

Jamelia: People like Craig and people like the Sugababes, I saw them as doing the same thing I was doing, which is, 'We know we want to do R&B but we can't because we're British and we're in the UK.' So it was kind of like pop/R&B. But I wanted to be an R&B artist. I grew up in inner-city Birmingham. My ambitions included being a forensic scientist first of all, until I realised I'd have to deal with dead people. Then I wanted to be a midwife until I realised I had to deal with the downstairs of every female. Then I went to Notting Hill Carnival for the first time when I was fifteen years old. I used to record tapes of myself singing and pretend they were my album. My London cousins took the tape and put it into the hi-fi system to embarrass me, but they were like, 'This is really good.' The next day at Carnival my cousin spoke to one of the DJs and told him I could sing. I was horrified. I ended up getting on stage and singing 'Right Here' by SWV. Weirdly an A&R man who worked at EMI was in the crowd and he approached my mum and asked if she would be okay with bringing me in for a meeting. That conversation ended with him offering me a record deal that was more than my mum's annual salary.

MNEK: Every Black artist has to ask, 'What do I have to do to get to the next level?' There is a limit with R&B music both sonically and also commercially.

Tanya Boniface, the 411: Americans do R&B really well because it's where true Rhythm and Blues originated. They pump a lot of money into their acts to help break them and it shows. The belief is there. For example, we had to drop two top-five singles before [Sony] would sign off on our album! If we had the same level of investment and nurturing and label support that the US acts get, I am certain we would have had a really long and fruitful career.

Jamelia: There was an element of code switching, like, 'If you want to be here, this is what you have to do.' I was okay with that because I still got to make R&B records, they just weren't the singles. The songs that were chosen as singles were always pop/R&B. 'Superstar' wasn't my favourite choice. People are always surprised when I say I was literally crying in the studio when I was told I had to record that song. I hated it. It was so pop. Also, it had been number one for a Danish *Popstars* contestant [Christine Milton], so for me it felt like I was taking something from someone. That didn't sit well with me.

Carolyn: I think the label struggled with where our sound should sit. Especially after we released 'On My Knees' and then followed up with 'Dumb', which was far more pop. The decision to head back towards a more urban sound with 'Teardrops' felt like they were trying to keep us that little bit cooler. At the end of the day, pop sells far more units than R&B in the UK, so they were brave to do that.

Tisha: 'Teardrops' was a song none of us wanted and then when it didn't land in the top five we lost the label's fire around us as a band.

Carolyn: There were several studio sessions where our A&R visited and announced, 'If it's not top five, you're out.' That says it all really. Everything always had to be done under so much pressure, with such high expectations and within such a short time frame.

Jamelia: My music videos sometimes cost a quarter of a million pounds and people aren't making videos like that any more. I'd had my second daughter in 2005 and so the label basically bought one of the flats near where I lived and all the producers would just come there [to record 2006's 'Walk with Me']. I could go home and breastfeed my daughter and then get back to the studio. I'm sure they're not doing that sort of shit now. That's why I owed the label £11 million after I finished. They wrote it off, so it's cool. But £11 million does not surprise me – I was taking private jets to places.

'In the UK industry, it is not fun to feel like there's this fucking ceiling'

If Born to Do It *had been an R&B album with some of the mannerisms of UK garage, by 2002's second album* Slicker Than Your Average,

Craig had ditched the pretence. In many ways it was a smart move, as garage's success was waning, but for some people Craig was so embedded in the commercial rise of such a quintessentially British genre that a move to a more Americanised sound felt jarring. From the title down to the high-gloss sheen of the video for ludicrous Willy Wonka-tastic lead single, 'What's Your Flava?', people were suspicious of Craig's motives. It felt like the bubble had burst as his success slowly started to morph into caricature.

Chantelle Fiddy: The nail in the coffin for UK garage was Victoria Beckham and Dane Bowers' 'Out of My Mind' [released in August 2000]. Overnight, nobody could fuck with it in the way they used to. I think it was also overkill of Sweet Female Attitude's 'Flowers' as well [released in the same week as 'Fill Me In', it peaked at number two behind it]. That was a very divisive song and a divisive commercial highlight for garage. A lot of the tracks that are synonymous with garage to the mainstream aren't what would be synonymous to the underground.

Ceri Evans: UK garage ruined itself. The music took a darker turn and with that it became more aggressive. It peaked and it was actually quite incredible how quickly it all stopped. For a few years after, it was a dirty word. It was a bit like someone coming out as Tory now – you just don't say it because you'll be vilified. You couldn't say you were anything to do with garage.

Craig David: It was a strange period for me. Everything had been working up to *Born to Do It* and there was also this feeling of how to recreate something that had been my whole life up to this one album. A lot of people were saying, 'Just keep doing what you're doing.' I think me and Mark Hill had done something so special [on that debut] that with everything else we were trying to replicate what we'd done. It felt like we were on the back foot a bit. By that point we knew what worked, whereas before we didn't and that was the fun of it. But I was getting a good rapport with a production team called Ignorants, who were doing a lot of remixes at the time. It was a new energy.

Max Giwa: A lot of the urban artists of that era wanted to have their own identity and the ones that then crossed over felt they had to capture the American market, so when they came back people would say, 'Oh, you've gone American,' but the British sound had moved on. It's about trying to adapt.

Dania Pasquini: Now they're quite proud to sound British. They don't have to Americanise themselves to make money in the States. It's global now.

MNEK: Garage is so British and the British have a weird sense of loyalty when it comes to things like that. They say the same thing about Adele now she's in LA doing her thing and doesn't want to live in Tottenham no more. After a while, especially being a person of colour in the UK industry, it is not fun to feel like there's this fucking ceiling.

Ceri Evans: With Craig, he didn't want to do a weird, quirky dance genre; he wanted to be a global superstar. You don't become that making UK garage. But the attraction of UK garage was its originality; it was ours. At the time, there was some amazing R&B from America, but it was all so clinical and clean. We liked the rough edges over here.

MNEK: When you go to America, where there's ample opportunities for artists of colour, it's appealing. Craig, Jamelia and Mis-Teeq were all acts who were inspired by American R&B because that was the only R&B that was being pushed like that. America is always pegged as the place where things are bigger and better. That is tempting. If they kept doing the British thing it would have been nice for everyone else, but would we still be paying attention now?

Hallgeir Rustan: Mis-Teeq were England's answer to Destiny's Child. It was Girl Power at its best and it shone through in the songs and attitude of the vocals. 'Scandalous' still works on radio and in clubs. When it entered the top forty in the US, we realised it was possible to succeed there as well. It gave us motivation to have more faith in what we were doing.

Su-Elise: In the US, 'Scandalous' was picked to replace Britney Spears' 'Outrageous' in *Catwoman*. Not a big stretch from 'Outrageous' to 'Scandalous', is it? So we got to feature in a Hollywood blockbuster, which really helped.

Chantelle Fiddy: There was this big thing of, 'You have to conquer America.' You get a little bit of success at home and then you start changing your formula to hit the American market. If you look at So Solid's second album [2003's *2nd Verse*], no garage, all rap. It was absolutely awful. I could see exactly what was going to happen, but you got gassed because somebody in the label told you it was a good idea and you're going to crack this market and make all this money.

Max Giwa: We wanted to make glossy, beautiful videos but it would be British and we weren't trying to chase the Americans. If they wanted us, they'd come and get us. We wanted to stand out in the crowd. We wanted to create our own visual stamp so people could identify you and say, 'I want that for my artist.' We made brands out of these people. Craig is still going today and people still talk about 'Walking Away', '7 Days', the hat.

Craig David: I felt like 'What's Your Flava?' was so different that it was going to be a Marmite song for some people. It ended up being one of my biggest synced records in terms of getting various different restaurant chains using it. As you can imagine.

MNEK: Garage is a culture. It's beyond the genre. Craig would have his singles that were R&B but he's known for the garage records because they're quintessentially British and they were distinctive. There was no one doing what he was doing at that time. That's why he got pigeon-holed in that way. To be able to do those records and still maintain your Blackness is a great thing and something he shouldn't let go of, and I think he knows that.

Craig David: The slippery slope you could get into is that if you define yourself by numbers then I could easily look at *Slicker Than Your Average*, an album that sold 3.5 million albums, and compare that to *Born to Do It*, which did 7 million. The record label were projecting [*Slicker Than Your Average*] would be 10 million, so as an artist at the time I was buying into that, like, 'Oh, is it not hitting right?' I look at 3.5 million now and think, 'What the hell are you talking about?' I'd take that all day every day.

Chantelle Fiddy: I was sent to LA to interview Justin Timberlake for *Justified* [in 2002] for *Touch* magazine. I was the only music journalist on the trip. Then *Touch*'s editor at the time, Toussaint Davy – bearing in mind we all knew how big that album was going to be – made a decision to put Craig on the cover instead. For that second album. I remember being in the office going, 'What are you doing?' I think part of Tous's rationale was just wanting someone Black to win, you know. You don't want the white guy in America to win. You want the Black guy in the UK to win. But the music just didn't cut it, sadly.

Jamelia: Eventually, I felt more comfortable being in the indie rock world [than the pop world] because in my head they were real musicians. Coldplay were on the same label as me and our A&R guy told me that Chris Martin wanted to meet me. I was a massive fan so I was like, 'You what, mate?' Chris was in the studio recording and invited me down. I remember at the time Gwyneth Paltrow was banging on about this macrobiotic diet she was on and so the first thing I was astonished by was the fact she was sitting there eating chocolate digestives. I was thinking, 'Well, that's not part of your diet.' Then she said to me, 'I think you're the greatest soul singer alive.' I was like, 'What?' Chris is at the piano and he asks me to sit down next to him and just 'vibe'. I'd never worked like that before, but we built [2004's 'See It in a Boy's Eyes']. To be a Black girl from Birmingham that then goes and picks up a *Q* Award [for Best Single] – are you mad? Looking back now, I was allowed in because I was with Chris Martin. On the wall in my office I've got a picture of Bono kissing my hand at the *Q* Awards. The

Mercury Music Prize nomination [in 2004, for *Thank You*] – what? I know now you have Black artists being nominated, but at the time we weren't in that space.

'I got the feeling he wanted to show off the ways I was failing'

First broadcast in 2002 on Channel 4, comedian Leigh Francis' surrealist sketch show Bo' Selecta! *was an instant hit. Built around celebrity stalker Avid Merrion, it saw Francis don (both white and black) latex masks to appear as everyone from Mel B to Elton John to Kelly Osbourne. Michael Jackson was represented as a foul-mouthed hospital patient. The central character, however, was Craig David, played as an egotistical Yorkshireman with a plastic kestrel called Kes. The show, and its various spin-offs, ran until 2006, before returning for a two-part special in 2009 following Jackson's death. For Craig, no longer a commercial powerhouse, the show quickly turned him into a figure of ridicule. It also represented the public face of how Black artists were being treated behind the scenes, with a long-standing assumption – that Black faces don't sell magazines – now contorted into fact.*

Craig David: There was a relentless onslaught from [Leigh Francis], which I could never quite understand. The show was obviously called *Bo' Selecta!* and it was referring to one of my biggest hits, 'Rewind'. So what had been – well, it still is, because the song has stood the test of time – a cultural reference to when people were getting really hyped in the club and they wanted the DJ to rewind the song – something so entrenched in the culture and garage music that we were celebrating – had this guy continuously poking fun at it. But then also at me.

Chantelle Fiddy: I think [*Bo' Selecta!*] really undermined him as a person and him as an artist and him being taken seriously.

Ceri Evans: There's an amazing video online of his manager at the time, Colin Lester, blowing his stack because people were saying that *Bo' Selecta!* ruined his career. We just thought it was a bit funny. We thought it was amazing that mainstream shows were talking about someone we knew.

Craig David: The impact it had on me was I was trying to save face and trying to hold it down and be like the music is the thing. But it wasn't like I didn't feel it every time someone was shouting my name in a northern accent. I got the feeling he wanted to show off the ways I was failing. Like when he went to America it wasn't about success, it was about how it wasn't working. I was thinking, 'Did I do something to you?' I had to just ride the storm and I'm so thankful that the second wave of my music happened and that made it more poignant for me. Not sweeter because I'm not one to hold onto grudges or sip from the poisoned chalice, because I'm done with that. That's so dead in the water now. People recognising the music and who I am as an artist is a blessing.

Chantelle Fiddy: Let's also not forget these were the days where most magazines would be like, 'Well, we've got one Black artist in this month.' Forget the fact you've got twenty white artists in. It was very hard to get people to expand their view of Black music and all the different styles around that.

Craig David: I actually missed [the *Melody Maker*'s controversial 2000 'UK garage, my arse' cover, in which a Black actor dressed as Craig is pictured sitting on a toilet]. Thankfully. I saw the image, but years later. The music was doing such moves that there was nothing that could change that.

Hannah Verdier: I don't think it was [difficult for Black artists to get on the cover of *Smash Hits*] and that pleases me to say because when I've worked on women's magazines you wouldn't have anyone Black on the cover. The publishing director would actually say, 'If in doubt put a blonde on because that sells.' It was out-and-out racism. *Smash Hits* had a history of putting anyone interesting on the cover. I don't think I'm looking back idealistically, because I can see the misogyny, but when it comes to race it wasn't a problem.

Chantelle Fiddy: I used to work for *Smash Hits* on an ad-hoc basis and they were one of the more liberal publications and didn't go, 'Ooh, have we got too many Black or brown faces in?' It was more like, 'Whatever is cool and of the moment then we're putting them in.'

Simon Jones, former Mis-Teeq PR: I can remember an editor of a magazine telling me they wouldn't put a Black person on the cover. Quite openly. Telling me, 'We won't put Mis-Teeq on the cover because they're Black girls and they won't sell.'

Su-Elise: We would be featured inside magazines, but in terms of that coveted magazine cover we did struggle, definitely. Especially in the beginning. The general consensus in that world back then was that three Black girls on the cover of a UK magazine wasn't going to sell the magazine. We had a lot of barriers to break down and a lot of doors to knock on in order to get that changed. We just took everything back to the music. With the music came the sales and with the sales came the fame and the acknowledgement in the industry. Then people were like, 'Okay, maybe we can do this, maybe this will work.' Attitudes did start to change. But in those early days it was a little bit disheartening.

Chantelle Fiddy: It was more the style press and the newspapers that were the issue. If you did put somebody Black on the cover it had to be a woman; it couldn't be a man because that would never sell.

MNEK: I heard this podcast with Celena from the Honeyz and she was talking about how on magazine covers people would purposefully cover her and Heavenli's faces and leave Mariama's because she was lighter. They would cover the Black faces.

Simon Jones: I can remember one magazine saying, 'We'll do an Alesha cover,' which was a big deal because Mis-Teeq hadn't had any covers at that point. So they'd shoot the three girls inside but only Alesha on the cover. Obviously the label wanted to do it because these magazines were so important. That must have been very hard to swallow for Su-Elise and Sabrina [Washington]. It definitely created tension within the band.

MNEK: Because Alesha and even Su-Elise were very much the more palatable options. Sabrina, who was the singer, wasn't even given half the limelight. Those things were happening and no one would be commenting on it but now it's so different. We've come too far for that to happen again.

Simon Jones: The label would be applying pressure like, 'Why are Atomic Kitten on the cover of every magazine?', and I remember sitting in a meeting and someone saying, 'Well, they don't put Black people on the cover of magazines.' It was just talked about like it was normal. We did the shoot but I think it was done begrudgingly.

Su-Elise: Alesha was a female MC, she had something different about her and she is so friendly and outgoing that maybe her personality put her in front of the right people.

Jamelia: I was encouraged to wear my hair like Naomi Campbell's. Obviously I was a fan so I said yes. They didn't want the Jamelia that walked into the label office all those years ago; they wanted a certain version of me. By the time my record deal ended, I was being pushed into being very sexualised and very European-looking. I remember saying to them, 'What's wrong with me as I am?' I was probably a size ten, but sample size was a six. So around that time I was a matchstick because I thought that's what I had to look like to be successful. Not eating? I'm Jamaican. We eat. There's this double existence, especially when you're Black and Jamaican, because I'd go out into the world as a celebrity and then I'd go to Grammie's house and she'd be like, 'What is wrong with you? Let me feed you.' I just got to a point where I was like, 'This is exhausting.'

Su-Elise: We'd actually started recording tracks for a third album. But the label went under, they owed us a lot of money, so financially that was a big strain on us. We lost out. But in business, shit happens. We shopped around trying to look for a third deal with the management we were with at the time, but we were being told that what we were looking for wasn't out there. Now, in hindsight, whether we were being told the right information, I don't know. I wasn't in the room when those meetings were being held but I have an inkling that there was other stuff on the table that didn't get to us. Also, Alesha specifically had said she was quite tired and was having second thoughts at the time. I remember thinking, 'Well, Mis-Teeq is all three of us so if it's not going to be all three of us then maybe this is the end of an era and a journey.' And what a journey.

Craig David: So many of the old systems and things that were 'okay' or 'you just laugh along' have changed now. It's unfortunate that so many people have to suffer before you see change, but we are in a place where the conversation is a lot different to what it was in the '90s and early '00s.

★ ★ ★

In 2015, after his mash-up of 'Fill Me In' and Diplo and Skrillex's 'Where Are Ü Now' on 1Xtra went viral, Craig experienced a cultural and critical renaissance among a younger generation who had never heard of Leigh Francis. In 2016, his sixth album, *Following My Intuition*, peaked at number one, giving him his first chart-topper since *Born to Do It*. In 2020, *Bo' Selecta!* was removed from Channel 4's All4 streaming service in the wake of the Black Lives Matter protests following the murder of George Floyd.

8

The slow rise of pop outsiders Xenomania

UK pop in the early '00s was split into two strands. On the one side there were songs built around pastiche that gleefully recalled vintage pop hitmakers such as ABBA or Chic and wedding-reception-proof genres like disco or funk. On the other side was a Scandinavian approximation of US R&B spear-headed at first by the likes of Denniz PoP and Max Martin with Five, then later owned by Norwegian trio Stargate, whose work had graced albums by the likes of Hear'Say, Blue and Atomic Kitten. For Brian Higgins, a musician and songwriter who'd followed up a global hit in the shape of Cher's 'Believe' with radio silence, pop was in desperate need of a riotous kick up the backside. Alongside songwriter Miranda Cooper and a host of musicians drawn from every corner of the music world (including an ex member of KLF's touring band), Higgins built hit factory Xenomania and set about re-wiring pop's brain chemistry.

The songs Xenomania would create for Girls Aloud and the Sugababes were often sutured together from a handful of different elements; verses from song one were fused with a chorus from song two, while a bridge from song three was reworked with an element of song four to make song five. Individual lines were often sung by each band member, in various different keys, before finally being pieced together like a brain-frying jigsaw puzzle. Genres were also gleefully spliced together, reflecting Higgins' own disparate music tastes. The roaring return of guitar music via early '00s preeners the Strokes et al. was reflected in Xenomania's ability to make guitars in pop fun rather than purely an exercise in authenticity box-ticking. But their success wasn't overnight. Failed bands, false starts and a huge amount of time spent unpicking and rebuilding pop's constituent parts meant they were close to missing their moment.

'It was ahead of its time in terms of what was going on'

Brian Higgins, songwriter and producer: I hated the pop sound at the time. I couldn't stand it. I detested it. It was just so sugar sweet and so similar to itself. There was also the clean-cut, Swedish R&B sound. I started to really analyse these records just to hone my dislike of them.

Miranda Cooper, Xenomania's chief songwriter: I don't know if there are many people who have come from dancing into songwriting. Dannii Minogue spotted me through the window at Pineapple Dance Studios in London and went, 'You're new, do you want to be my dancer?' I also did loads of stuff for PJ & Duncan and then Gina G. At the time, Peter Loraine was the editor of *Top of the Pops* magazine and he used to do a fun thing like, 'Who snogged who?', and I was always in there somewhere. When I first started writing for Girls Aloud, I remember passing him in the Polydor offices and he was like, 'Miranda, what are you doing here?'

Peter Loraine: She had a name – Miranda the Dancer. When she went to Eurovision [in 1996] to dance with Gina G, she became our Eurovision roving reporter.

Miranda Cooper: Yes, I did. When I was younger I didn't know you could be a songwriter. I loved dancing, but it was just being moving scenery. I did have a nagging feeling that maybe this wasn't going to be what I was going to do forever.

Peter Loraine: That year, Morten Harket from A-ha was the presenter of Eurovision and I remember he was hanging out with them and then, when Gina G didn't win, he didn't want to know.

Miranda Cooper: But it was there that I met Steve Allen from Warners and he said, 'Oi, love, have you ever thought about being in a pop duo?' I think it was Brian [Higgins] and Saint Etienne who had come up with this idea of doing this cool, kitsch, pop duo. They saw me and this other girl Chloé [Treend] on *Top of the Pops* and we became T-Shirt. We covered Hot Chocolate's 'You Sexy Thing' and somehow it became this big hit in Australia. In the UK, we were doing PAs in Romford and *Mizz* magazine roadshows. It was the really fun but not massively elegant world of pop.

Brian Higgins: Xenomania actually started in November 1995. That was when Steve Allen offered me a record deal as an artist, but really it was to cement my creative relationship with him. I would make records for the label, so Dannii Minogue's 'All I Wanna Do' was the first hit for Xenomania. Cher's 'Believe' was the second. I was working in the day in another job through all of that. Although my song had become what it had become I was still in a suit and tie. I didn't leave that job until 'Believe' went to number one in America [in March 1999].

Miranda Cooper: T-Shirt were asked to tour Australia but I had started going down to Brian's studio. Brian had a backing track that he asked me to write on. So I took it home and I don't know how I knew what to do, but I came back with a full song called, 'Hey I'm OK'. I grew up listening to musicals, mainly, but then my brother was into punk and indie. He'd give me lots of the Cure and the Sex Pistols and Blondie. I was massively into Transvision Vamp, as well. This splurge came out, which actually I feel like somewhere in there is where Girls Aloud sits. I also wrote another song with the line 'I've got a cherry red scooter, with a hot pink hooter'. Brian, bless him, was like, 'This is awesome.' So I turned down the chance to tour Australia [with T-Shirt] and they got another blonde in to replace me. No one even noticed.

Brian Higgins: I got into a project with Miranda Cooper at the time 'Believe' was successful called Moonbaby. That was really the sound of Girls Aloud in its newborn state. It was ahead of its time in terms of what was going on.

Miranda Cooper: I'd always been the one on stage so it didn't enter my head that I might not be the best person to be the vehicle for my songs. I thought I should be the artist. We were in Brian's little garden shed; it was me and Matt Gray, Brian, Tim Powell. I would get the 4.20 p.m. train down to Kent from Victoria every day, because Brian had a normal job. There were rumbles of things happening with this song 'Believe', but we were in a bubble. That's all we did for three years from 1997, basically, doing the Moonbaby thing and not realising that actually it was the blueprint for Sugababes and Girls Aloud.

Brian Higgins: Pete Tong signed it [to London Records], so I worked very closely with him. It was an invaluable working experience for me because he taught me an awful lot about how I could make it better. He was a very hard taskmaster. He was also the coolest man on the planet at that time, the number-one tastemaker.

Miranda Cooper: It was a really exciting, big deal. And then it was awful. They said, 'You can either be Natalie Imbruglia or All Saints.' We thought we were making this wonderful art and it was reduced down. Also, I just wasn't good enough. What they had signed was the writing and the chemistry we had together. When I got dropped, I was pretty broken. I wasn't even sure I wanted to do music any more. Pete Tong used to say, 'She won't be there, will she?' when he'd come down because I was a reminder of this great black hole of debt. I'd never met anyone like Brian; he knew exactly what he wanted to do. I was just holding on to his coattails. Obviously 'Believe' had happened and all these people were phoning him saying, 'Can you do this?

Can you do that?', and he'd say, 'No, I've got this amazing girl, Moonbaby, it's going to be a huge hit.' Then when it went tits up, he thought, 'Shit, I better get my house in order.' He brought in this girl, Lisa Cowling, who he'd worked with at Reed, the publishing company. I thought, 'I don't want some fucking girl coming in.' She was there to build me up and make me feel better and it was just a meeting of pure joy. We wrote tonnes and tonnes of songs.

Brian Higgins: I think working on the Moonbaby project moved me away from purely dance-pop. I had made a record in 1992 which was about making multiple versions of the same thing that I'd then piece together again. The first version took about eighteen months to make. So that idea of [crafting songs from various other bits of songs] had been kicking around in my mind for a while.

Miranda Cooper: [The end of Moonbaby] meant that when we did get our first opportunity with the Sugababes, we were ready.

9
Sugababes: The sweet and the sour

While not as buoyantly in your face as 'Wannabe' four years earlier, 'Overload', the debut single from the teenage Sugababes – AKA north-Londoners Mutya Buena (aged fifteen), Keisha Buchanan (fifteen) and Siobhán Donaghy (sixteen) – was equally revelatory in terms of the evolution of the British girlband. For a teen audience whose teeth were set on edge by the post-Spice Girls sugar rush, 'Overload', which nonchalantly fused breakbeat rhythms, flamenco guitar and a cacophonous middle eight, represented something genuinely cool. The fact that the band themselves eschewed dance routines, matching outfits and smiling, AKA the era's three pop mainstays, only made them stand out more, with their diffidence and grunge-y aesthetic a siren call to equally 'whatever' teenagers unmoved by DayGlo motivational anthems. Lyrically, 'Overload', like much of 2000's *One Touch* album, represented a snapshot of teenage life: a time of confused emotions, heightened hormones and on-the-surface yearning.

More of a critical than commercial success, *One Touch* was the only album to feature that first line-up of friends. From there, new members – Heidi Range (2001–11), Amelle Berrabah (2006–11) and Jade Ewen (2009–11) – were airlifted in almost with each new album. While the top-tier, attitude-heavy hits continued to pile up – the Sugababes' six UK number ones are second only to the Spice Girls' nine when it comes to the most chart-toppers by British girlbands – their personnel troubles eventually started to overshadow the music. Their revolving-door policy when it came to members, mixed with pop's inherent mission statement that the song is king, meant most fans invested in the Sugababes brand as opposed to the individuals.

At the start, however, were three girls gleefully skipping school to hang out in a studio and partake in their favourite hobby. That they were formed almost by accident – initially as the Sugababies – only added to that early sense of alchemy.

'Some days we'd be in the studio until the sun came up'

Siobhán: Ron [Tom, manager] was my best friend at school's brother-in-law and she said to him that I could sing. He had also met Mutya's dad in a supermarket. So he was managing the two of us as solo artists. Me and Mutya had met before and so we wanted to do a duet. Then Mutya brought Keisha to the studio from school.

Keisha: I just really liked singing and so I begged my mum, asking if I could go to the studio so I could be around it. Originally I was just there to support Mutya as a friend.

Siobhán: It was totally not on anyone's mind that we would be a group. Ron just announced it to us; not, 'Would you like to . . .?' or 'How about this?' It was more, 'This is what we're doing.' We were so young that we were like, 'Okay then.'

Mutya: We became the Sugababes on that day. It didn't feel real. We were just three teenage girls trying to sing and do school at the same time.

Siobhán: Ron always said that he thought the three of us individually were amazing but that we were really exceptional together. We were quite shy and from regular working-class families. We weren't media trained, which quickly became obvious to people when we came out.

Keisha: We'd do half a day at school and then go straight to the studio afterwards. Sometimes we'd skip days. We didn't do much by the books. Some days we'd be in the studio until the sun came up and then we'd go home and we would jump in the shower, change uniforms and then go back to school again. And then we'd leave before lunchtime. We were Energizer Bunnies.

Siobhán: I think Mutya and Keisha were actually expelled because of how little they were attending at one point. Ron used to come down [to the studio] with all his mates, which annoyed us because it would be a party and they'd be opening booze. It wouldn't be for us – we were only interested in the music and the singing. The rest of it was just noise going on around us.

Keisha: I'm always going to hold dear the early days of us being berated by our teachers for missing homework, but just not really caring. It was my absolute dream and my absolute joy to sing and create music. It came with a lot of long nights, but when I look back, hats off to us.

Mutya: We had such a fast childhood but I guess back then it didn't seem like that.

Keisha: My mum would always double-check, like, 'Are you sure you're not tired?' I think we were all just really adamant that it was something we wanted to do.

Mutya: My parents were overly supportive. I had already been touring Europe when I was nine, doing Filipino dancing and singing. For me it just felt normal. I also went on [Michael Barrymore's ITV show] *My Kind of People* with a Filipino group doing some dancing. Then they called me back to come and sing. I had already been on the *Royal Variety Show*, doing Hawaiian dancing to 'Under the Sea'. So when we were in the Sugababes I was so comfortable performing and travelling around.

Siobhán: My parents never guided me down a certain path. It was never like, 'Wouldn't it be amazing if you were a doctor?' Ron used to come and visit the house a lot and my parents loved him. They were happy we were in safe hands. It always used to flabbergast me because he'd go out into our garden and spark up a spliff and I'd be looking at my parents like, 'Is this alright?' But I always felt quite disconnected from my friends [at school] and felt so jealous when they were doing their A levels and going off to university. We just went down a different road.

Mutya: We definitely had people who explained [financial] stuff but I feel like it still went over our heads. We were too young to be bothered about a contract and sitting down trying to figure out what was going on. I would like to turn back time and read everything properly.

Siobhán: We had a really good lawyer and our parents always had to be in the room when things like that were being explained to us. It really was explained to us too; how many albums the deal was for and what was expected of us. I remember at one point they said that as an indemnity against me not fulfilling my part of the contract they could come for my parents' house. They'd worked for it their whole lives.

Mutya: We were paid monthly. You couldn't give a fourteen-year-old a card and be like, 'Here you go, do what you want with it.' We were all very disciplined with the money, but also you just want to go out and have fun and forget about it.

Siobhán: I remember we got transferred £3,000 but I think it was a million-pound deal. That's a whole other conversation.

'They hung out like a little girl gang'

The credible space the Sugababes would eventually settle into was one carved out by London Records labelmates All Saints. Billed as the cool alternative to the Spice Girls, they'd arrived in 1997 with 'I Know Where It's At', a swaggering amalgam of R&B and pop that mixed delicious harmonies with untouchable, cool-older-sister attitude. While other pop acts looked like they were trying very hard, All Saints made every element of the pop game look effortless, even revitalising slam poetry via the spoken-word intro to classic second single, 'Never Ever'. As with the Sugababes, however, it had taken a while to find the right sound and for everything to click into place. For both bands, the catalyst was Massive Attack and Neneh Cherry collaborator Cameron McVey and his team of grumpy misfits.

Cameron McVey, songwriter and producer: London Records had All Saints and loads of people had worked on their stuff but they couldn't get anywhere with it. I used to get those kind of projects; they were usually a quarter of a million pounds in the hole and they'd be like, 'Send it to Cameron and he'll sort it out.' Then the same thing happened with the Sugababes. I was like the Red Adair of the music industry, putting out fires. You never get me in when things are going well. It's always when you're in the shit and there's nothing else left to try.

Felix Howard, songwriter: What [Cameron] did with All Saints is nothing like what he did with the Sugababes. On All Saints, they had some really good people. He didn't have to do a rescue job like he had to on Sugababes. All Saints had Shaznay, who is a great songwriter, and they were more of a together unit.

Cameron McVey: As far as I was concerned, like with All Saints, [Sugababes] had people who could really sing and who had a real personality. I can't do anything that's not real. I can't do any of that fake stuff where some rich guy wants his daughter to sing and they can't. I trained at PWL and we worked with a lot of people there that couldn't sing and I had a real problem with that.

Mutya: All Saints opened up the urban side, the cooler side of the girl groups. Obviously we all looked up to the Spice Girls, they opened up doors for everybody, but All Saints as a British group was my ideal. If I wasn't in the Sugababes I would love to be in something like All Saints. Of course I wore combat trousers like them. Of course.

Siobhán: They were probably the only all-female group that showed us we could be alternative and work. I didn't have it in me to do choreographed dance routines. I was just too awkward. I still am. Somebody with a bubbly personality and a gorgeous smile – that just wasn't me.

Keisha: Normally for a lot of bands you'd go in the studio and before you even make a record there will be whispers of, 'You're going to be the next this or that,' but we were three girls from north-west London who were into R&B and indie.

Cameron McVey: We'd all come off a really long project, so everyone was in a bad mood. We were all working in different rooms and everyone was grumpy because nobody wanted to do pop. My daughters [amazing pop artiste] Mabel and [amazing pop artiste] Tyson were in the studio and they really liked the girls. They were basically A&R-ing it. I didn't know anything about it; I was like, 'What do you think of this one?'

Jony Rockstar, songwriter and producer: I used to work for a producer called Howie B, and then Cameron [McVey] scooped me up. I worked with him on a Neneh Cherry record that never materialised, but I was part of his production team.

The [Sugababes] gig came in to Cameron and he likes to remind me that I didn't want to do it because I hated the name.

Siobhán: The name came from Ron Tom. We hated it. When you're that young, you want to be grown-up. I think we assumed we'd think of something else.

Cameron McVey: Jony was one of the grumpy ones saying, 'I don't want to fucking do this.' We gave him a couple of spliffs, locked him in the room and he came up with the beat for 'Overload'. By the end of the first day, he said, 'I told you I should do this, this is the best project ever.'

Felix Howard: Jony hated everyone. And smoked weed all fucking day. If he didn't want you in the room, he would keep turning the music up really loud.

Jony Rockstar: It was like, 'What? Why are we doing this?' They were also fourteen-year-old girls. Obviously it was a great move in the end. I absolutely loved their vibe and they had phenomenal voices. They had that new-world, multi-cultural identity that was far more authentic back then. It didn't feel staged or contrived. It was organic. They hung out like a little girl gang.

Cameron McVey: The great thing about the 'Babes is they're like the Supremes in that it's three voices that don't clash. They can sing over any noise and just make it work. All three of them have perfect pitch.

Jony Rockstar: Their tones were so different but so complimentary. Like an act of God.

Siobhán: All of us were into the big American R&B scene. The first song I sang to Ron Tom was by En Vogue and we loved Monica and Brandy, Aaliyah, Missy Elliott. Garage was also a massive part of all of our lives. Me and Mutya used to go to the under-18 raves. You'd get your mixtape at school on cassette. You'd learn the songs in the week and then go out on the weekends with probably a quarter bottle of vodka.

Cameron McVey: They were so naughty, the three of them. They were devils.

Keisha: We were adamant we wanted to have a garage sound. Me and Mutya – not many people know this – we started a garage girlband with two other members. Briefly. And we were rapping by the way. I'll take full credit for that because Mutya's going to dive under the table with embarrassment when she finds out I've shared this news.

Mutya: Wow. I was Little Miss Naughty and she was Curvy K. We used to pretend we were garage MCs.

Siobhán: That was kind of behind the scenes. I don't know what I thought of that.

Mutya: My household was full of all different types of music. My dad would play the guitar every night and I would sit with him and sing. So we all had something to add to the mix. As the Sugababes we were able to jump into different types of music while still sounding very soulful. That's the thing about it; we could go pop but there'd still be a bit of soul in there.

Jony Rockstar: It was the Blair years, it was Britpop, it was celebrating British culture, being proud of that. The music was art imitating life in that respect. We were all really having a great time. There was no political upheaval. It was pre-9/11. They were some very golden years, so people wanted to hear uplifting, fun, cool music. They didn't want depressing music.

Siobhán: I think we were cooler [than a lot of other pop acts at the time]. But, funnily enough, Keisha was a massive pop fan. She loved S Club 7, A1 – that was totally her thing. I don't know if she admitted to that.

Keisha: My first ever CD singles I bought were Jay-Z and Foxy Brown's 'I'll Be' and Robson & Jerome's 'Up on the Roof'. I was the person who was listening to both S Club Juniors and 2Pac.

Siobhán: She fancied Bradley from S Club 7. Me and Mutya refer to Keisha as Disney. All that happy pop stuff, she loves it.

Keisha: We knew we were different but it wasn't above me to buy the pop classics either.

Siobhán: The way the *One Touch* album evolved would never have been intentional for us. To a certain extent a lot of it would have gone over our heads. Even some of the lyrics we came out with, I don't think we understood the connotations around some of it. And how grown-up it was.

Mutya: When you're singing or writing when you're so much younger, you never question things. I look at stuff now that I wrote back then and think, 'What was I thinking?' I knew that our lingo and everything was different.

'Everyone said they couldn't write and that they were a bunch of idiots'

The liner notes of a pop album quickly became a battleground in the '00s. If the act's name wasn't featured in the songwriter credits then it became a stick to beat them with. Being a 'manufactured' pop act was the antithesis of authentic guitar music typically made by white men, whose names would often still appear next to a list of seasoned hitmakers and songwriters-for-hire. To the gatekeepers of credible, a lack of input conjured up ideas of conveyor belts, songwriting committees and old men putting words in teen-age mouths. While that's not entirely inaccurate, it also ignores the will of the artists and the bigger industry framework they were working in. For the Sugababes, being given the opportunity to write unlocked their sound and allowed them to capture a moment.

Keisha: At first [producer/songwriter] Don-E was writing a lot for us. However, he really set the tone for how we sing – he pretty much taught us where to stack our harmonies. The sound you hear when you call it 'the Sugababes sound' definitely came from him. When it came to writing, Cameron McVey was really encouraging about us sharing our thoughts. I remember saying, 'I don't write songs, I write poetry,' and he was like, 'Well, let me hear it.' We all felt so good having to vent on paper.

Cameron McVey: Everyone said they couldn't write and that they were a bunch of idiots and I was like, 'What are you talking about?' I just said, 'Write about what you want to write about because you're writing tunes for young people.' We were excited to work with kids because we were so jaded by all these people doing this pompous left-field music.

Siobhán: One day Cameron sent us home with a backing track. He wanted it to be from us. I'm a bit of a perfectionist so I took it really seriously, like that was my homework. I actually tortured myself. I wanted to be really good at it, because of imposter syndrome. There are all these musicians out there who are natural songwriters and I've always felt that I wasn't, but that if I tried really hard I can put something good together. In my head I always felt like I had to try harder than everyone else.

Felix Howard: Cameron would have said, 'I don't talk like a fourteen-year-old girl therefore I need this fourteen-year-old girl to tell me how to talk.' Which is hardly ever the case in the music industry.

Mutya: It was just nice to have that creativity on that first album. Writing was the first thing we knew. Then after that with every album people would always know that we wrote our own music, so they allowed us to be open and free with what we wanted to do. We've always been open-minded about taking songs that have already been written for us, but it's quite nice to know that people would be like, 'Okay, cool, we know the girls can write, let them get on with it.'

Cameron McVey: On the first day, Siobhán basically wrote most of 'Overload' and we mixed it that day. The board mix from the end of day one is the version they released.

Jony Rockstar: A lot of my life is quite hazy but I do remember those 'Overload' sessions vividly. Originally on 'Overload' we had the verse melody as the chorus and the chorus melody was the verse. I switched them around. I was using breakbeats and I had this sampled bassline that I'd cut up. It was very organic. We didn't reference other music or say, 'Let's do a song like this.'

Felix Howard: [Jony Rockstar] would sit there in a marijuana cloud and he would work on this tiny piece for hours and hours. In this green smoke and terrifyingly loud music, Siobhán and I fashioned the skeleton of what became 'Overload'.

Siobhán: I loved that day. It was very relaxed. I don't think I really understood where we were going with the lyrics in the room. It just felt like a series of random stuff we were saying, but I remember the first time I sang my bit I did know how special it was.

Felix Howard: At the time, 'Overload' was called 'Ragga Train', which is a Cameron McVey-ism. It was not thought to be a single. [London Records founder] Tracy Bennett, to his credit, picked that one out of the crowd and said it was the single. It sounded nothing like what was being made in pop at that time. And still doesn't. It's a curate's egg – you couldn't ever make it again because it was made in such a weird way.

Cameron McVey: There's a big thump you can hear when the middle eight comes in because there used to be an electric short on the desk in that room, so you can hear this bang where it was me making it come back to life again. I never send anyone into a booth. There's the sound of one of them complaining about their homework in the background. We were more strict about their homework than we were about the recording. Like: 'You've got to do your homework or we're not recording.'

Mutya: I never thought about ['Overload' entering the top ten]. If I could turn back time now, I feel like I would appreciate everything a hundred times more. I probably would have taken things a little more seriously than I did then. But I can't help the fact we were so young and a lot of people forgot about that, too.

Felix Howard: Brian [Higgins] was inspired by 'Overload'. He is a fabulous magpie. He takes tiny bits of tunes and sticks them together and makes songs out of them. He works in an incredibly unique way. 'Sound of the Underground' is pretty close [to sounding like 'Overload']. It wasn't as close as the Christina Aguilera tune 'Make Over' [from 2002's *Stripped*], which we successfully sued them over and now have a piece of.

Jony Rockstar: If you listen to the *One Touch* album it's pretty lo-fi. It was just authentic. We live in such a contrived reality now that when things are authentic they really do shine and that album was made with pure love. You know, we were a bunch of rowdy guys. We were loud party guys, we were going out after and it was kind of rock 'n' roll back then, in the music business. They were just lovely sweet girls, who fucking delivered. So we loved them.

Cameron McVey: We were nuts. I had bought the house behind the studio so I was trying to bang a hole in the wall so I could go straight into my front room. Then one day Madonna turned up and [producer and mixer] Mark 'Spike' Stent said to me, 'You've got to move; M is coming through the room.' I was eating my breakfast at the time. I was like, 'Fucking good luck moving me, mate. I'm having my sausage and egg. Fuck off.'

Siobhán: From the get-go, and especially because of the single choice [with 'Overload'], we felt in a very alternative music world rather than pop.

Cameron McVey: I had [late iconic stylist] Judy Blame involved with them, so that meant it sat in a really good place. The visuals were really good, the videos were really good. I got to choose the singles. We just got total free rein, which you never get out of a record company unless they're in the shit.

Siobhán: Our first showcase was at Ronnie Scott's. Our first tour was with *NME*. And the crowd was so much older than us. If we had expected teenage screaming fans, we were thoroughly disappointed.

Keisha: At our shows we'd be like, 'Why is everyone fifty years older than us?' We knew we were different.

Alexis Petridis, former *Select* magazine editor: They seemed to me to be like a mixture of All Saints and a bit of that Massive Attack sound. They seemed to be a cut above. 'Overload' was a record that got played a lot in the *Select* offices when it came out.

'Doing anything that was like acting was alien to all three of us'

There's a shocking moment, watching now, about forty-five seconds into the minimalist video for 'Overload', shot by fashion photographer Phil Poynter. After a couple of attempts at a smile, Mutya breaks into a full-on, teeth-baring, eyes-twinkling giggle. In fact, all three members smile at various points, almost despite themselves. Performing the song later on Top of the Pops, *viewers used to peppy, mimic-in-the-playground jazz hands were met with the incongruous sight of three teenagers sitting on stools looking at their laps while a propulsive, forward-motion breakbeat rhythm chugged out around them. In lieu of the standard high-octane arm choreography, Mutya, Keisha and Siobhán would occasionally turn to look to the left or the right, a shrug of acknowledgement at industry norms. It meant they were often called moody or sullen, an accusation that would later underpin conversations around the various line-up changes.*

Keisha: We had performance training because they said we were really shy.

Siobhán: There was a guy that did the choreography for 'Overload'. He would also do mock interviews so we could practise answering questions. That was it. No one ever said, 'You look a little bit moody.' I almost wish someone had said that to us.

Mutya: I knew how to do interviews but I was too young and a bit, 'Hmm, okay.' Quite unbothered. But it was weird because that unbothered look really appealed to people. I would get a lot of *NME* journalists wanting to do interviews with me because they thought I had attitude. To be honest, that wasn't the case, it was just because of how I grew up in my area. I was a little bit cooler, if you get what I mean. I looked like I was moody or rude, but, at the same time, people took it in and people liked it.

Keisha: We weren't moody. Even with our friends, if we were all laughing and joking, as soon as a camera came on us, everyone would have straight faces. Now it's seen as a cool thing, whereas we just naturally didn't smile. And we didn't realise how that was coming across.

Siobhán: I remember having to have a glass of wine on the 'Overload' shoot because they had to loosen me up. I think someone in the glam team suggested the wine, so we can't blame Phil. All I had to do was walk in a straight line, pull my sunglasses down and look over my shoulder, but for me it was so big. Doing anything that was like acting was alien to all three of us.

Mutya: We came from an era where there were a lot of pop groups. The *Smash Hits* days. There was indie but you also had your Girls Alouds, your Atomic Kittens, your Blues, your Blazin' Squads. Everything was a bit more upbeat then, so having the Sugababes where people think we're moody and don't know how to take us, I found it funny. We'd be walking in and people wouldn't know whether to say hi or not.

Siobhán: The other girls would go and chat [to other bands] a lot more than I did. I was just really awkward. I think we were somewhere one day and A1 were there, and this is really mean of me, but I ignored them. I just totally didn't think they were cool.

Christian Ingebrigtsen: We had fun with most of the bands but we weren't the most popular. We were a little bit too squeaky clean for a lot of them. We didn't feel like the most popular band on the road.

Siobhán: They had that 'Take on Me' cover out and I thought that was horrendous. I remember *Smash Hits* magazine would try to get us to laugh. All we would do was lift the corner of our mouths for the photos.

Keisha: I wish people had given us a bit more slack because we were kids.

Siobhán: We just didn't want to be fake. We'd have to go back to our friends and we were worried they would laugh at us. Who walks down the street grinning ear to ear? No one. It was more normal what we were doing.

Laura Snapes: They weren't like their really slick pop peers – I don't want to call them bratty, but they were just sixteen-year-olds who sometimes just couldn't be fucking bothered and they didn't hide that.

Siobhán: It's such a complicated time in your life to navigate something like [being thought of as moody]. I realise now how much that has affected me moving forwards in terms of my anxiety. I was super confident before I entered that band and definitely didn't come out of it that way. I don't think anyone is going to come out unscathed when you start your career at such a young age.

'I packed my bag and I went home'

The band's ingrained laissez-faire attitude also meant it was easy for genuine sadness to go unnoticed. Or ignored. On 22 August 2001, while on a promo tour in Australia and Asia, Siobhán quit, less than a year after One Touch*'s release. A swirl of false information followed, ranging from the mundane ('management tried to say I had a kidney infection') to* *the ridiculous (no, she didn't climb out of a toilet window, never to be seen again). Relationships within the band had turned sour, often escalated, they say, by the adults around them.*

Siobhán: There was definitely a disconnect between myself and Keisha and so there was an element of the people working with us that was a bit 'divide and conquer'. I just felt isolated and lonely and so I just focused on doing a good job.

Keisha: We weren't encouraged to have a relationship with each other. I guess there's more power in having the upper hand. Some people prefer discord because then you're the person who always fixes it. Create the mess and then we all come to you to fix it. It's a tricky subject because it's had so much impact on my life. I don't really like to dwell on it. Mainly because I have younger nieces and nephews and whenever there's an issue or a problem I always want to empower them and tell them how special they are. I have a passion for helping young girls and it's a shame that wasn't embraced in our situation.

Siobhán: We initially signed a production deal, which wouldn't have been great for us. We should have been on a standard management contract, so when we communicated successfully and spoke to our lawyer we were able to negotiate it to a better place. We changed our contract. They don't want you doing that. We were so in the dark about a lot of things. I do think they kept us in a way that made us suspicious of each other. That meant we made people in our team our confidants rather than each other, so it wouldn't have even crossed our minds that those decisions were ours to make. And actually we were paying for everybody.

We didn't have that understanding back then so we just behaved ourselves and did pretty much what we were told.

Keisha: At that time, I feel like none of us were happy. Unfortunately towards the end of that era there was so much darkness.

Siobhán: I had been warning the team for a while. I needed more support. I didn't feel like I was being treated very well and I needed the adults to monitor that better. But they didn't; they were too busy off out. Even when we were away, especially on that tour, any minute they could, they were off doing fabulous things while we were working. It just meant that some of the stuff going on went unchecked. So I was like, 'Okay, if this is what we're saying, that I am on my own with this, then I can tell you that I can't deal with it.' So I packed my bag and a flight was arranged for me and I went home.

Mutya: I feel like a lot of adults could have done better. There could have been a lot more communication and there didn't need to be all the dividing. But that's the industry. It's very divide and conquer. It's very snake-y and shark-y; you just have to work out who you can and can't talk to.

Siobhán: Communication had broken down to the point where I didn't even think [sitting down with the band] was going to be helpful. In a sense the decision had been made for me. I was so isolated. And I knew I would be replaced. There had been conversations about replacing another member as well, before I left, which I found unacceptable. It was also a conversation before I left the band that we were going to go to another label. So there was definitely an onward journey and in someone like [lawyer and new manager] Sarah Stennett, it was hardly going to be the end of the road. She is a force of nature. I totally made the right decision for me and I have never looked back. Even when 'Freak Like Me' went to number one I was happy for them, but I was also happy for myself.

'Heidi's a true Liverpool trooper; she just got on with it'

Aged just seventeen, Mutya and Keisha had already experienced a lifetime's worth of music industry highs and lows. As quickly as they were let go by London Records, however, they were snapped up by Island Records, and a new member in the shape of ex-Atomic Kitten member Heidi 'Queen of the middle eight' Range was brought in. It was another period of adjustment, but one that this time felt tinged with hope.

Keisha: I remember thinking, 'Ugh, I just want to be happy.' We wanted to continue and have some fun because everything felt so heavy.

Mutya: We didn't even have enough time to be like, 'Oh, it's over,' because we had an offer for a new deal. It wasn't that long after we got dropped that me and Keisha got re-signed and then Heidi came along.

Keisha: That's when the fun really started. Not in terms of the loss of [Siobhán], but it was a brand-new start; a brand-new label, a brand-new member.

Mutya: I remember not being sure how old [Heidi] was. I was like, 'She doesn't look our age, that's not right.' I thought she was older. I remember asking to see her passport and everything.

Keisha: Originally one of our friends wanted to join but I think she was fifteen at the time. And we'd just got out of the age group where the rule was you could only work a certain amount of days a year, which meant we missed out on touring. We didn't want to take a step back now that we were of age. We were told that we were going to be looking at a girl from Liverpool called Heidi, and she came in, pretty girl, lovely smile, great energy, upbeat. I taught her this horrendous dance routine because by then I'd started developing myself as a choreographer. I taught her this whole routine and she went along with it. Years later she was like, 'That routine was horrendous.' Lots of rolling on the floor.

Mutya: I was very sceptical [about Heidi coming in]. I had been in a group with Siobhán for so many years so to have some new person come into her place felt weird. I felt like me and Keisha had worked so hard to get to where we'd got to, so to let someone just jump in for me felt a bit not right. But obviously it was the best thing to do in that moment and I don't have any regrets. I was happy with how it went.

Jony Rockstar: [Them having a new member] was of no consequence to me. Heidi could really sing, so that's all I cared about. I felt a little protective of Heidi while working on [second album *Angels with Dirty Faces*] because I could tell she was a bit intimidated. I'm sure it was very weird for Keisha and Mutya, but they were lovely to her. We all knew each other, we all had a working relationship, and then here's Heidi. But she's a true Liverpool trooper; she just got on with it. And she wrote the middle eight of 'Stronger', the whole thing. She delivered.

Keisha: In the early days we all had the same resting bitch face and so we all had that same vibe. Under the circumstances Siobhán left in, there were obviously things said. So when Heidi arrived, she was sunshine, biggest smile, she came from a background where she had done all these dance competitions, so that perfect pop picture so to speak. When you put that in the middle of our stone faces it just highlighted it even more.

Mutya: Heidi did bring the pop factor and I can never fault her for it because she did her job within the Sugababes.

Keisha: Sometimes I look back and I'm like, 'Just smile! Please, for the love of God!' So when you pair that with us two and all the controversy that surrounded the breakup of Sugababes 01, people just judged us.

'The band were very suspicious of me because I hadn't done anything other than a trendy single'

While One Touch *had gone gold and eventually peaked at number twenty-six, it was hardly an earth-shattering success. The Sugababes were cool, which carried credibility, but they weren't a household name. If they were written about at all in the tabloids in 2001, it was because of in-fighting and accusations of bullying. So Island knew they needed a Big Song to re-launch them – one that would build on 'Overload''s critical consensus as 'Pop it's Okay to Like', while also blowing the minds of people who don't care about the moronic concept of 'guilty pleasures'. While work started immediately with then relatively unknown songwriters and producers Xenomania, the raw, semi-illegal single that would save them was being played in sweaty nightclubs in east London by a mysterious bootlegger called Girls on Top.*

Darcus Beese, former A&R Director, Island Records: My lawyer at the time, Sarah Stennett, was also representing the Sugababes. Sarah told me the Sugababes were getting out of their London Records deal and when I went to see them with my boss, Nick Gatfield, they were doing rehearsals with Heidi. At that point I think Sarah had them in with Brian [Higgins]. [Future single] 'Round Round' was there as a real rough demo, well before 'Freak Like Me' happened.

Brian Higgins: I really liked them and I thought 'Overload' was a fantastic record. Their voices were incredible. I think they had just been dropped the first day they came down to work with us. I felt like [Sarah] knew what she was doing and that there was a record deal up their sleeve.

Darcus Beese: I loved the *One Touch* album. 'Overload' gave you the template of how to make records in terms of the Sugababes. I'd like to think we extended what they were doing on *One Touch* into what they did with *Angels with Dirty Faces*, then obviously they went stratospheric. But initially 'Freak Like Me' and 'Round Round' were an extension of what I thought was cool coming out of the *One Touch* era.

Keisha: We were recording and trying to get the new single and our A&R said, 'Hey, there's an underground track called "Freak Like Me".'

Darcus Beese: At the time, Ross Allen and I were in the Island A&R department. In a meeting one day, Ross played the 'Freak Like Me' bootleg 7-inch. The samples hadn't been cleared but it was just this fucking amazing piece of music. I think it was [Island President] Nick Gatfield that said, 'This would be great if the Sugababes cut it.'

Richard X, 'Freak Like Me' producer: I don't think anyone thought it was going to be big; it was more like, 'Here's a girlband who were quite cool, AKA they were in the *NME*, but then they were dropped and could we just do something with this?' It's funny, I don't think anyone thought that would be a very successful record. Even in the industry. It just didn't seem to make any sense.

Darcus Beese: At the time, Richard X was this kind of bootleg kid doing his shit under the radar [as Girls on Top] not wanting to be found out. So Ross either knew him or got hold of him. At first Richard was really cautious because he thought we were coming to bust him.

Richard X: I was buying those odd electronica singles, or IDM as they were called, in the late '90s and that was quite an interesting area for a while, but then it got really up its own backside. I think what I was doing [with 'Girls on Top'] was a reaction to that po-faced-ness – I was reaching back to the pop electronica, so sampling the Human League or Kraftwerk. My stuff fitted into a bit of electroclash, a bit of that [trendy London club night] Trash scene, into indie discos.

Darcus Beese: We ended up meeting him in a café in Brixton and we were like, 'All above board, how do we work together?

We'd love the Sugababes to cut it.' Ross and I convinced him. Off the back of that, Richard X went and signed to Virgin but we got 'Freak Like Me'.

Richard X: The reason Virgin signed me is because I was a very cheap deal and it was an interesting scene. The Soulwax record ['As Heard on Radio Soulwax Pt 2'] hadn't come out yet, which is another benchmark of the bootleg era. Also, Virgin thought they could clear my Kraftwerk and Whitney Houston bootleg ['I Wanna Dance with Numbers'], because they had contacts with Kraftwerk. Then I got this report back from Kraftwerk that said they thought it was the worst record they'd ever heard but in the best-looking sleeve. That for me was great.

Keisha: The moment we heard ['Freak Like Me''s] first verse me and Mutya started jumping up and down screaming because we knew the song back to front. We'd been singing the R&B version by Adina Howard since primary school. They printed out lyrics, which we threw to the side. Heidi had never heard it before, but we were old-school R&B heads. We just wanted the mic. We didn't know anything about 'Are "Friends" Electric?', all we cared about was that our friends at school would know we'd finally done an R&B track. We wanted to be accepted by our peers so much.

Mutya: I wasn't sure at first. I loved Gary Numan but I didn't see how it could work until we did it. No one had brought anything out like that so it was quite risky. The label knew, the management knew. Then when we did the video it made more sense.

Cameron McVey: The girls went off to work with Darcus at Island and he called me up to work on [*Angels with Dirty Faces*]. But then I heard the first single and said, 'I can't top that, it's a number one,' and that's what happened. The only place I could go was down.

Felix Howard: When I came back [to work with the Sugababes], there was no Cameron. He'd decided to take Siobhán's side on everything. Jony and I were told, 'Don't work with them, fuck them,' and we were like, 'Shut up.' So we worked with them again. I liked Heidi. I wanted to stay out of all that shit: people have fights; it's showbiz. I didn't think it had anything to do with me.

Richard X: The band were very suspicious of me because I hadn't done anything other than a trendy single. They were in a difficult position, too. Heidi had joined and she was obviously finding her feet, so it was like a new beginning for everyone.

Keisha: I remember us arranging our parts [with Richard X]. We were so excited because there'd been this shift in energy. Lots of optimism. It felt really good.

Richard X: [We recorded] in Shepherd's Bush for one session and then another in Kilburn. It was a vocal recording to a backing track, so it wasn't like we were making the music, so labels would put you in any little studio then. Especially if they didn't have to impress the band.

Mutya: It wasn't hard for us to go into the studio and lay our vocals down.

Richard X: If you've ever been and listened to a singer you know on record and they just open their mouths and it's them, that's what they're like. They're characterful. That's what makes them great.

Darcus Beese: I was always a voices man. The fact that there was a girl group who had those vocals was probably the success of the group in terms of credibility.

Richard X: There's three or four different versions of 'Freak Like Me'. My one was used in the video and for some radio releases, then there was another one that I didn't know had been done. I was in a club and heard it for the first time. They'd changed the drums and I remember being like, 'Why would you do that?' My whole purpose was that they were raw records. You're deliberately making things a bit crushed, which is that annoying low-res sound that's very much the sound of terrible MP3 players. I wanted crunchy and horrible. By the time they got it to the Sugababes, it wasn't my record, ultimately. You do your work on it and then it becomes theirs.

Darcus Beese: Clearing the publishing was a fucking nightmare, but Gary Numan was amazing. He liked the idea that another generation was discovering it. I remember we did an early version that I ended up cutting onto 7-inch and we called it 'Are Freaks Electric?' by Sugababes vs Girls on Top.

Richard X: I don't remember that being a conversation either. I wasn't bothered about it; it's just out of your control.

Darcus Beese: We put the bootlegs in Rough Trade and off the back of that I think Sara Cox played it on Radio 1 and it all exploded from there.

Mutya: Then it went to number one – imagine that!

Alex Needham: In terms of pop music, that was definitely the stuff to focus on. You wouldn't do all the TV talent show stuff. Also, electroclash basically turned into that sort of pop music, with the same sounds and to a certain extent the same aesthetic. The bootleg things Erol [Alkan, DJ and producer] was doing at Trash, that was a cool indie thing, but then Kylie did it at the BRITs [in 2002, with her mash-up of 'Can't Get You Out of My Head' and 'Blue Monday'] and the Sugababes did it with 'Freak Like Me'.

Brian Higgins: I think 'Freak Like Me' was a very important record. It's also a very aggressive pop record, especially at that time. I think it showed the extent to which Radio 1 were prepared to back the Sugababes and were prepared to back an excellent record. I think it informed a lot.

Richard X: The Rough Trade wall was where you had a certain type of pop music before the '00s. It was often indie-infused. Then suddenly those sounds were in the charts or being used by bands. There was a need to freshen things up. Pop's always picked from the underground and the influence of dance music on pop was a big one. Also, the Americans were doing better records. I remember that early part of the '00s you had Timbaland and Missy and all this exciting stuff. They were massively weird, big records and every other month seemed to be them flipping everything on its head. It does make a certain pop mentality that it's just about little boybands or little girlbands just seem a bit . . . square.

Keisha: We had something to prove. We wanted the industry and our peers to embrace us. At first it was really difficult. Even with 'Freak Like Me', I remember we had done the BRITs and I was watching an interview and they were like, 'They've got the number one, but do we honestly think they're going to have another album?' I was quite a stubborn little mule when I was a teenager and I was like, 'You'll see!' To say you've won a BRIT for any girlband is amazing. I was always confused about the category in which we won [Best Dance Act]. Whoever was on the committee that year clearly lost the plot.

Mutya: Oh my God, imagine. I actually forgot we won one! I still don't believe it. I have to pinch myself and say, 'Mutya, these are your achievements.'

Keisha: I remember we did the *NME* but we also did the MOBO Awards, then we also did the Trevor Nelson show and then we were on the *Smash Hits* tour and then we were doing the BRITs. We were covering so many bases, so it was like, 'Are we an R&B band?' No. 'Are we a pop band?' I guess, but it wasn't straight pop. So I can understand why someone was like, 'Just put them in the dance category.'

Darcus Beese: That was so random. We were crossing genres and banging styles together. Later on I got them to cover 'I Bet You Look Good on the Dancefloor' [by the Arctic Monkeys] and all of a sudden they were appearing at the *NME* Awards. They could inhabit loads of different genres.

Keisha: I think we were seen more as a Black band because I think Mutya's race was ambiguous – people didn't really know where she was from. I think people thought she was mixed race, as in Black and white, whereas she was Asian and white. I think people assumed because of how she was and how she was raised that that helped us be more embraced on the urban side because it looked like there were two Black girls in the band.

Mutya: For most of my life, until people started knowing where the Philippines was, a lot of people used to call me Black-Japanese, Black-Chinese, mixed-race. I was never the race I was. For me, I found it irritating because I've always been very open about what race I was, but people weren't listening. Or they didn't understand. I used to get attacked a lot for being a race that I wasn't. I'd get people coming up to me being quite rude, then when I would correct them they'd be cool. It made no sense. It was so racist. Then Myleene Klass came out, who is the same race as me, and Vanessa from the Saturdays, too. Then people were like, 'Oh, the Philippines, okay, I know where that is.' It was hard back then because everyone looked at me like I was an alien.

Myleene Klass, Hear'Say: Mutya was the only Filipina that I knew of in a band. She has one of the best voices in pop. An outstanding talent and is hugely respected in the Filipino community. It's clear to many that I'm mixed race but no one ever knew where I was from. It shows the importance of visibility. If you can't see it, you can't be it. And music opens that door to everyone.

'You weren't allowed dogs in the hotel, so Heidi would smuggle it in in her handbag'

The success of 'Freak Like Me' in April 2002 helped prove that UK pop acts could hold their own when it came to weird. It solidified the idea it didn't need to all be pastiche or gloriously one-dimensional. By helping push an underground sub-genre into the mainstream, the Sugababes appeared, to the general public at least, to be at the cutting edge of something cool once again. It also gave them a platform to go anywhere next, having proved they could easily handle R&B, pop, indie, soul and, according to the BRITs panel, dance. For Angels with Dirty Faces*' second single, 'Round Round', they collaborated with Brian Higgins and Miranda Cooper, whose careers had yet to be sky-rocketed by Girls Aloud. Equally weird and unexpected, 'Round Round' (just about) fused together an obscure drum-loop sample, two separate verse melodies and a middle section swiped from a different song. It was the start of a creative relationship that saw them collaborate on five more top-ten singles across 2003's* Three *and 2005's* Taller in More Ways *albums.*

Darcus Beese: On first meeting when you went down [to the Xenomania studio in Kent], the energy was off the scale. It was something I hadn't seen before in my young A&R career.

Keisha: They work in a strange way but I actually embraced that. Sometimes you don't want to spend sixteen hours on one song. I would write maybe ten different verses, the other girls the same, and Brian would just pick the ones he felt were the best. Sometimes the beats were completely different because they were different genres – so 'Round Round', there's a whole ballad in the middle eight that was from a completely different song.

Darcus Beese: ['Round Round'] was a brave choice but it was so compelling as a record. And you were coming off the back of a huge record like 'Freak Like Me', so you were starting to own the lane. I think Sugababes dictated rather than followed.

Miranda Cooper: Brian and I used to go to Paris for the day – very extravagant, but he had all the 'Believe' money – and we used to go around the record stores and pick up CDs based on their front covers. Then we'd come back and go through all of it. Most of it would be complete dross, but he found this beat ['Tango Forte' by German production team Dublex Inc.] on a compilation, which was the start of 'Round Round'. We didn't have computers in those days so I would write down every song I wrote. Brian would say, 'Bring out the list,' and I would sing every chorus I'd ever done over this beat and see what went with it. We got the chorus for 'Round Round' and they came in and sung it and it sounded ace.

Darcus Beese: There were these real obscure samples that we had to clear and that was the exciting thing about how Brian put his stuff together. Across a couple of records he made some real compelling, best of breed songs. I think the girls' voices helped as well in terms of keeping it Sugababes. Brian just facilitated this pop landscape for them that was just off the scale.

Jon Shave, former Xenomania producer and songwriter: I remember going down [to the studio] and they had the first, eight-minute version of 'Round Round', which was just a chorus on a loop of the sample. But it immediately jumped out as this vital idea.

Miranda Cooper: I remember being in Amsterdam really stoned and coming up with the first verse. The Sugababes were involved in the writing, so we'd normally start with a chorus idea and then they'd be involved in the verses. The whole thing was quite an abrasive sound, probably because we were quite abrasive people. We wanted it so much. We were really sick of being unsuccessful. After all that time, the first song we put out went to number one.

Mutya: We'd stay down there for a week or so and just have so many songs on the go, it was very confusing, but then when he'd put it together it was like, 'Ah, okay.'

Miranda Cooper: They were so cool. I remember going back to London with them and feeling like they were in the upper sixth form and I was in the fourth form.

Brian Higgins: I knew that with Mutya's voice we could make incredible records.

Jon Shave: She was one of the best singers I've ever been around. As soon as she opens her mouth it just sounds like a record. She manages to communicate endless amounts of charisma and attitude and intrigue in every syllable.

Felix Howard: Mutya has the best voice of all of that girlband generation. She is absolutely the number one. She's wildly ahead of everyone else.

Darcus Beese: It was always the battle over who would start a Sugababes song. You can guess where the issues rose because it was always Mutya. They were great at ballads because of

Mutya. She could emote like nobody's business. She was the one that gave ballads like 'Stronger' and 'Caught in a Moment' the weight in terms of emotion. Heidi was the 'take it to the bridge' person. Keisha could give you the power and the ad-libs and the runs. Mutya would give you the depth and the truth.

Keisha: The only hard thing around that time was staying down where [Brian] was, because it was in the middle of nowhere. I remember we stayed in this little cottage across the street, but for any teenager once you're done for the day you want to go and hang out with your friends. Instead we were in the middle of nowhere.

Mutya: Kent was so far and we were so young so no one was driving. They put us in this creepy hotel. I would sneakily get my friend who drove to come pick me up and get me out of Kent and bring me back the next day. Or I'd get my friends to come over to the hotel and we'd have a party there.

Darcus Beese: Brian tells a brilliant story as to why the album is called *Angels with Dirty Faces*. It's because Mutya would disappear. She once turned up a day later after going missing and Brian said the car rolled up, there was this music playing, all this bass banging out of the car, the door opens and all this smoke comes out and Mutya steps up like butter wouldn't melt. That's where the title came from. Did you ever hear the story where she walked out of the Shepherd's Bush Empire gig? They were just about to do their encore and it's like, 'Why haven't they come back on?' The story was that Mutya had just walked out. She had the hump. Just walked out the stage door and fucking went home.

Miranda Cooper: One time the girls wanted to stay in London and Brian said, 'Well, sometimes we go to hotels.' We used to go to the country for two or three nights and turn our phones off and just write and write and write and make ourselves silly with weed and God knows what. So he said, 'Let's do something in London.' They ended up choosing the Dorchester hotel. We were in this suite and I remember Heidi had a pug, and you weren't allowed dogs in the hotel, so she'd smuggle it in in her handbag.

Jon Shave: And it would poo all over the carpets.

Keisha: Of course we wanted to be in London, because we wanted to see our friends, which is kind of normal for a teenager. As an adult now, I can't think of anything better than a sleepy village.

Mutya: I love the quiet now.

'The Blazin' Squad boys fancied us lot like crazy'

Angels with Dirty Faces *was followed by* Three, *which also went multi-platinum, establishing the Sugababes as a proper Q4 act, i.e. their albums were locked in for the music industry's September–December sales jamboree. It also meant an escalation in their workload, with that check-list of TV shows, magazines and tabloid interviews becoming increasingly important. While in the past they'd always been too young or, in Siobhán's case, too unwilling (poor A1) to hang out with other bands, now they relished being on the same promo loop as acts, including their newly created peers in ludicrous pop bangerdom, Girls Aloud. The increased success, however, also brought with it unwanted attention.*

Keisha: People think that when you're in a band it's just you three, but it wasn't; there were always about ten other people travelling with you but they were all adults. If you ever go on the internet, any events that the Sugababes and Girls Aloud were at together it will be Girls Aloud and then me next to them. I would ditch my bandmates. I loved being in their presence.

Mutya: When we were doing the *Smash Hits* tour, we had so much fun. Blazin' Squad were there, Blue, Big Brovaz; there was Gareth Gates, A1, everyone that you can think of in pop. We all hung out. We used to cause mischief in the hotel, play Knock Down Ginger. The Blazin' Squad boys fancied us lot like crazy. We chilled with and hung around so many amazing people like P!nk, Black Eyed Peas. Once we were on the same stage as Britney Spears.

Keisha: The only band we had a bit of a weird thing with was Atomic Kitten, but I think the press kind of built that up bigger than it needed to be. It was because Heidi used to be in that band and I think a couple of things were said between one of their members and Mutya. But that was the most gangster it got.

Mutya: Back then, all I remember was being flown from one place to another to another. One time we did *CD:UK* and I did an interview alongside Cheryl and Posh Spice, Victoria. [Heidi and Keisha] had left to go to the airport before me, so when it was done I was flung on a motorbike straight to the airport. Another time I had to get a helicopter down to somewhere near the sea to do a festival. It was very 'move, move, move'.

Keisha: I'll let her tell her story but it was also a really difficult time [for Mutya] because [the way the tabloids wrote about her] affected the band. It affected her even wanting to have her picture taken. There should have been more done to protect her at that time. There was a TV show and they were counting down Britain's mingers or something and they billed it as me and Heidi as the soft pop princesses and then there's Mutya. She experimented with her style and she's always been that way. We laugh about it now, but when you're young it's not nice at all. Who wants to go out on stage when you think people are laughing at you?

Mutya: It was depressing. I feel traumatised by these people. I never understood why they had such hate for me. I literally would say boo and they'd make it into a story that got really personal. It was how I looked and things I didn't like talking about in public. I was always in the paper for something and most of the time it was bullshit. I never understood why they wanted to talk my name. Today it's even worse because of the internet and social media. Thank God we didn't have that back then. I don't know how I'm still standing. But I will not let them affect me now.

'We all felt like we wanted to support her whatever her reasons were'

By the time fourth album Taller in More Ways *– which saw the band work with American super-producer Dallas Austin – became the band's first UK number-one album in October 2005, Mutya was already contemplating her future. Now with a nine-month-old daughter and suffering* *from postnatal depression, her focus had shifted and she officially left the band on 21 December. The contentious Xenomania-created 'Red Dress' was then lined up as the first release to feature new recruit Amelle Berrabah.* Taller in More Ways *was eventually re-released with new artwork and Amelle's vocals replacing Mutya's on three songs.*

Mutya: I didn't like 'Red Dress'. I hated it. But then I had left by the time they released it as a single, thank God.

Jon Shave: Around the time there were other struggles going on and it was bigger than just 'Red Dress'. It was difficult to get [Mutya] to the studio and it was difficult to keep her in the studio.

Miranda Cooper: She sounded amazing even though she sounded absolutely over it.

Brian Higgins: Mutya was very laid-back [in the studio]. We'd teach her the chorus and she'd go into the room to sing it and I was always waiting for the moment she was going to say, 'I'm not singing this.' Literally waiting. I could feel our career in the balance, just waiting for her to sing. Then the music would start and you'd think she was going to sing and she wouldn't. Then the music would come back around again and then she'd start singing and it was like, 'Fuck me, it's incredible.' Horrible getting to that point.

Darcus Beese: It was always a fight as to what the singles were. Apart from 'Freak Like Me' it was always a fight. But Mutya really hated 'Red Dress'. Although by that point I think she was starting to hate the whole scenario.

Mutya: If I'm going to sing a song I have to make sure it makes sense to me and it makes sense to you. I don't want to go up and sing anything. That's not what I'm here for. If I don't like it I won't just go, 'I'm not doing it,' but I will say that I'm not sure. 'Red Dress', for me, was just no. The chorus didn't make sense. Everyone was like, 'It's amazing,' and I'd be, 'What are you even talking about?'

Miranda Cooper: That Sugababes album [*Taller in More Ways*] was difficult to make. It was quite chaotic. I remember once Mutya went out to get lunch and never came back.

Darcus Beese: Listen, the girls were never 100 per cent trusting of the situation in terms of the process. They were very headstrong and when you're dealing with three different people you've got to deal with their different personalities. If X thinks you're talking to Y and Y thinks you're talking to Z, then that creates a dynamic. With the girls, they could have enjoyed it a lot more. There was always in-fighting in the group. Whether it was Siobhán, Heidi, Keisha or Mutya, there was always something going on. It's about how long you can keep them together. There's going to come a time when it's going to implode.

Mutya: There were a lot of things going on. There were deeper things. At the same time, me having my daughter didn't help. Not having any time off, still being in the studio breastfeeding until 5 a.m. That took a lot out of me. Then I got baby blues and depression is a bitch. Having no one understand you during that time can really be hard. Just feeling like I was alone in my head. Don't get it twisted: the label were supportive, but not in the way of 'You can have some time off.' I was seven or eight months pregnant in Atlanta recording the album. Then, two weeks after I gave birth, I was back in the studio finishing the album. Within a few months we did the video for [lead single] 'Push the Button' and it was the skinniest I've ever been in my life because we were just working, working, working. I was only twenty.

Keisha: It was such a heavy load. Extremely hard, both personally and professionally. Personally because I'd been with Mutya every day at that point since I was nine years old. Even though we started to have a lot of distance between us as we got older, it was like my arm wasn't there. But I understood that it was necessary at that time for her to go. We all felt like we wanted to support her, whatever her reasons were. So the actual split was amicable. Then, professionally, I felt like there was a lot on my shoulders. I felt like I had to carry way more, both behind the scenes and publicly. Everything that used to be on Mutya – any name-calling, anything – it just shifted automatically onto me and only me. I felt the weight of that.

Darcus Beese: What management were always really good at was being ready to flip something. Mutya was one person that you couldn't let leave the Sugababes. I had many evenings trying to convince her not to go. We got through the pregnancy, she had her baby, but she just wasn't enjoying it. Her relationship with the other two had gone south. At some point you've got to start thinking [about the future]. We'd released 'Push the Button' and she'd done the video for [second single] 'Ugly' and then she said, 'I'm gone.' As we were trying to convince her we had to go, 'Fuck, what's plan B?', and they had Amelle.

Mutya: To be honest, before I'd even left the band, [Amelle] had recorded six songs of mine. It was weird. She came in forty-eight hours after I left and then they had my album cover up on the shelves for two more weeks and then took it down. She already had six songs on that album that she had covered, so you do the maths. I don't need to tell anyone what happened. That tells you that she'd been doing it from a long time ago, as in before I said I was leaving. It should never have been done that way. No one wants to be a back-up. I found it very sneaky.

Darcus: I remember [management] playing me Amelle's voice and being like, 'This is a bit too spooky.' We were guided by Mutya just going, 'I'm out.' But the narrative on the outside starts to go, 'Oh, she was in the wings waiting,' but it wasn't like that.

Keisha: For any member who's entered the band, we've always been told there's been extensive research and 'we happened to find this person' or 'we didn't know this person'. You can read between the lines for yourselves; I won't say anything else. But later we did a *CD:UK* interview and Mutya was there to support us on our first TV appearance with Amelle.

Mutya: I came and said hello because people were trying to say I was hating. How could I hate? I left the group for her to take my space, so that makes no sense. I walked in and said, 'Hi, pleased to meet you,' like, 'We're cool, we're cool.' Then I got banned and was told I couldn't perform under the same roof as the girls because I made them feel uncomfortable. That was fucking bullshit. I was in the Sugababes my whole entire life; no one's going to tell me anything else. That's my baby regardless. It was pretty deep. For a long time I didn't see Keisha because obviously I was upset with the things I was hearing. Me and Keisha are always going to be close because we grew up together and obviously they did her wrong too later on.

'It felt like the Hello! *magazine end of the Sugababes'*

Now becoming adept at brushing herself down and carrying on, Keisha found herself as the sole original member of the Sugababes. Having lost the edge that Mutya gave them, the band re-grouped via 2006's Overload: The Singles Collection, *which featured twelve UK top-ten hits, and 2007's spectacularly unpleasant Girls Aloud collaboration 'Walk This Way' (it was for charity). That was followed by the shiny* Change *album (another UK number one) and then quickly by 2008's patchy* Catfights and Spotlights. *At some point in September 2009, after work finished on the disastrous* Sweet 7 *album, Amelle briefly quit, before Keisha was ousted instead and hastily replaced by Eurovision Song Contestant 2009 fifth-place runner-up Jade Ewen.*

Keisha: It was the first time for Heidi to have a member leave, but for me I was seasoned in what to do. It was about embracing [Amelle]. I was given the role of teaching her the ropes and making her feel as comfortable as possible with this shitstorm going on around us. Again it was about having to prove ourselves. Every article was, 'That's it, they're done, Mutya has such a prominent voice in the group,' and we had to read those things. Again, I was like, 'Well, you'll see!' ['About You Now'] is the biggest song we've ever had. It was number one for a month.

Darcus Beese: I convinced Dr Luke and Cathy Dennis to come and do a writing session and the girls cut 'About You Now'.

Keisha: [With *Change*] I understood the assignment, let me put it that way. Is it my favourite album? Definitely not. 'My Love Is Pink' was probably my least favourite song of all time. I actually deny my voice is on that to anyone who asks. I don't know that song, I don't know who sang it.

Darcus Beese: I love 'My Love Is Pink'. 'Never Gonna Dance Again' is amazing too and there's a demo of that song somewhere with Mutya's vocals. The original.

Keisha: I feel like the songs [on 2008's *Catfights and Spotlights*] were great but just not for us. I remember conversations where they were trying to recreate *One Touch*. They were trying to go dark and cool because they felt like everyone was saying it was going a bit too pop.

Darcus: I had just been made co-president of Island, which brings a lot of different responsibilities. I knew Klas Åhlund from all the stuff we were doing with [Swedish pop icon] Robyn, so I got him to come in and start working with the Sugababes. He had some Robyn demos that him and Max [Martin] had done, so we used those records as a jump-off. That album probably signals the end of the Sugababes. When we picked the singles it just felt like we were running out of ideas. It was all a bit starting to push water up a hill.

Keisha: Unfortunately someone from management was given the position of the lead and he was making decisions that I can only describe as extremely naff. Never in my life have I been in a creative process where someone had come in and said, 'We've got to do this' or 'Radio wants this'.

Darcus Beese: They were starting to reach the end of their cycle. The artwork for *Change* felt like the *Hello!* magazine end of the Sugababes.

Keisha: Then there was the album *Sweet 7*, which technically I recorded. We had the first single [the Bruno Mars-assisted 'Get Sexy'], which I think had gone to radio, and they had to pull it and re-do my vocals. The one thing I will say is that up until that point I had the most fun with Heidi and Amelle and it's the most horrendous music I've ever recorded in that line-up. I absolutely loved [that time], which is so ironic because that's the line-up I got booted out of. I don't know what happened there.

Mutya: I was shocked. I didn't see it coming. I remember going on GMTV when I found out that she had been kicked out. They were asking me about her being a bully and I was like, 'I didn't leave because she bullied me.' She's definitely not a bully. I know how it feels when people are doing the most and lying and it's not nice. I felt sorry for Keisha. It was crazy. They just thought the name was bigger than the people in the band and unfortunately for them it's the group of people that makes it. It's vocals.

Jony Rockstar: They became a commodity. So many people were relying on their success for their own wage packet and that's when it just goes horrible. Music isn't about that.

Felix Howard: There's an allegory about a boat – if you have a ship made of wood and gradually you substitute each plank out but you keep the structural integrity of the boat, by the time you've removed all the planks is it the same boat?

Siobhán: It was definitely a step too far for me. But then even when Mutya was replaced, sure, they went on to have their biggest hit ever, but it just didn't mean anything to me. The whole point was that it wasn't manufactured and here it was about as manufactured as it could be.

Mutya: Over the years I'd always bump into Siobhán.

Siobhán: We would see each other at random fashion parties and we'd always be really excited to see each other, which was nice. Even when myself and Keisha finally ran into each other, it was just so obvious that being so young and not being supported in the way we needed had been so detrimental to our relationship. It just didn't need to be like that.

Keisha: Me exiting the group will obviously be the lowest point [of the Sugababes journey], but there were so many positive highlights. There's finally seeing Michael Jackson at the World Music Awards [in 2006]. Then to be introduced by Whitney Houston at the Fashion Rocks event, that was amazing. We got to go to the afterparty and she was performing in front of only about thirty people. Then there's always going to be the highlight of me jumping offstage and giving Simon Cowell the most embarrassing lap dance of all time at a corporate Christmas party. I had a Sasha Fierce moment and forgot myself.

'If I touch hands with another fucking icon, I'm going to drop on the floor'

While Keisha remained the Sugababes Recruitment Agency's longest employee, Siobhán and Mutya both released solo material. Continuing with London Records and working with some of the same team as One Touch, *Siobhán released the* Revolution in Me *album in 2003. That was followed in 2007 by the bewitching alt-pop cult classic,* Ghosts. *Mutya, meanwhile, leaned into her love for R&B on 2007's top-ten* Real Girl, *an album that featured two legends. Oh, and she also supported Prince on tour.*

Siobhán: The one takeaway I had was how much I loved making music and being in the studio. London Records reached out to me to see if I wanted to do anything on my own and I did. I just rolled with it.

Cameron McVey: It was so much fun; it was such a laugh. She's just got this killer voice. When you're writing with her you can say 'sing this' and she'll just do it. The only other person I think is like her is Michael Stipe – he is one of those people you can say 'sing me this' to and he'll do it there and then.

Siobhán: It was very therapeutic but so much damage had been done that really until a good few years later I hadn't really bounced back completely. I've been left a bit of a nervous wreck by it all. It's much easier to look back on it now because it is so different. And how nice it is that the three of us have been able to be back together and operate on such a different level with each other. Most people don't get the chance to have that. But with [second album] *Ghosts*, in my naïvety I thought that if you made something that to you sounds great then that is the best thing you can put out. Rather than it having to be a certain BPM or a certain sound. Obviously I've always shot myself in the foot in that sense.

Darcus Beese: Mutya had George Michael [on 'This Is Not (Real Love)'] and Amy Winehouse ['B-Boy Baby'] on one album – who does that? [*Real Girl*] was probably where I really learned how to dig an album out of an artist that doesn't want to come to the studio.

Jony Rockstar: I didn't write [*Real Girl*'s 'Strung Out'], I just produced it. I think I may have been sent the vocal.

Felix Howard: I have a song ['It's Not Easy'] on that record and I'm very grateful for it but I had no creative input in that album really.

Mutya: Basically, with George Michael, he approached the Sugababes' management while I was in the group and said he wanted to record a song with me. And my manager said no. He said I was busy with the girls, which was crazy. It's George Michael! I will make time and drop the girls for five seconds. So I was like, 'Okay, what will be will be,' but I was upset the opportunity had gone. Then when I left the band I got another phone call and it was like, 'I know Mutya's not with the girls now, would she be interested in coming to the studio?' I thought it was a joke. But we set a date and I went into the studio and there he was, swivelling in his chair. I was like, 'Argh!'

Darcus Beese: It was mind-blowing. I don't even know if she realised at the time how off the scale [it was] and how lucky she was.

Mutya: Because I thought it was a joke I didn't tell my mum I was going and she's the biggest Wham! and George Michael fan. He was probably the nicest, most genuine person I've ever met in my life. I'm not just saying that because he's George Michael, you're fucking crazy, but he never did anything to make me feel insecure about how I was singing. I was talking to someone and they were like, 'You know he's only worked with four female artists' – that would be me, Whitney Houston, Mary J. Blige and Aretha Franklin. Only four females and I'm one of them. I cherish that like it's my party trick.

Darcus Beese: I remember I said to Amy about this hook that she never used, which was 'B-Boy Baby', and she only said yes because it was Mutya.

Mutya: We were friends as well as labelmates. She had such a kind soul. Whenever we'd see each other at award shows we'd go for a sneaky cigarette. I feel blessed that I was able to work with two legends.

Darcus Beese: There's a story where Prince invited Mutya to do an afterparty gig to jam and sing some songs and she looked at her watch and was like, 'Nah, I'm going out with my mates to a club.' Sorry, Prince, I'm out.

Mutya: I opened for Prince. I got to meet him and he told me that his favourite song of mine was 'Suffer for Love' and he wanted to sing it with me at the afterparty . . . then my manager said no, I had to go somewhere else. They were ruining my life! The next day I was doing something in Leicester somewhere and they wanted to leave straight after the show. I didn't understand it. Then I heard that I was Prince's screensaver on his laptop, like my album cover. I was also told not to look at him, so I came offstage at the O2 at rehearsals and while I'm walking towards the dressing room I see this smallest little thing ever. I'd heard he was always with his security so I was expecting to get jumped by somebody but it was him talking to me. If I touch hands with another fucking icon and legend, I'm going to drop on the floor. I was so blessed to work alongside any of them.

Tom Findlay, Groove Armada: We had an A&R man called Jonnie Blackburn and I think it was his idea to work with Mutya [on dance behemoth 'Song 4 Mutya (Out of Control)']. I think he got where the record was heading, which was quite pop. I still to this day think Mutya has got one of the great UK female pop voices that there has ever been.

Mutya: Groove Armada are amazing. We wrote that with [songwriter extraordinaire] Karen Poole.

Tom Findlay: Mutya did it all in my funny little basement studio in Stoke Newington. It was really surreal. I always fondly remember Mutya having a battered sausage for lunch. I enjoyed that as a detail. It made her feel very human to me. She brought a really stinky battered sausage to my studio.

Darcus Beese: [Making the album] was like getting blood out of a stone.

Mutya: I was dropped for some of the strangest reasons and it wasn't because I wasn't selling music. I was definitely dropped on a personal reason. I was selling music. I was number two [with lead single 'Real Girl'] behind Rihanna's 'Umbrella', so that's just dumb.

Darcus Beese: Hopefully she's proud of that album because she should be.

'Here we go again'

The enduring legacy of Sugababes' debut, One Touch, *is buffeted by ideas around what could have been. Of potential lost. So rumours in 2012 of a reunion of the original members – or 'Origibabes' as website Popjustice called them – caused mild panic in pop fans of a certain age. A major stumbling block was the right to use the Sugababes name, given an earlier legal attempt by Mutya in 2010 – just before the release of* Sweet 7 *– led to her only being able to use it on stationery, paper gift wrap and paper gift-wrapping ribbons. To that end, their first release after the reunion, the depressingly prophetic 'Flatline', was released as Mutya, Keisha, Siobhán and, annoyingly, sans Sugababes wrapping-paper tie-ins. After parting ways with label Polydor after that one single, the original trio disappeared again, only to return as the Sugababes for 2021's delayed twenty-year celebration of* One Touch. *In 2022, they embarked on a sold-out UK tour following a rapturously received Glastonbury performance and, that Christmas, finally released a range of Sugababes wrapping paper, alongside an album,* The Lost Tapes, *featuring MKS songs that never officially saw the light of day a decade earlier.*

Siobhán: It was exactly because Keisha was no longer in the Sugababes [that we reunited]. Never would I have thought there would be something that would happen to so unite our feelings. How could we not get together and have that conversation? It was just too tempting. Then of course the minute we were together we were like, 'I wonder what it would sound like if we sang together,' and by that point the curiosity is too strong. The minute we got into the studio and did a three-part harmony it was like, 'Ahh.' It was almost annoying that it was so good because how can we not carry on? Then it's, 'Here we go again!'

10

From Boyzone to Busted: How the boyband evolved

Louis Walsh: You just need a good band and good songs. Why do people like you always try to over-analyse things? It's just a boyband with good songs.

Boyzone, Westlife and the rise of the stool-botherers

Boyzone, AKA Ronan Keating, Stephen Gately, Mikey Graham, Keith Duffy and Shane Lynch, were formed in the shadow of Take That. Or, rather, they were formed by manager Louis Walsh in 1993 as Ireland's answer to their UK counterparts, who, by the time Boyzone released debut album *Said and Done* in the summer of 1995, were already on their way out. Take That's final musical gift, however, had been 'Back for Good', an immaculate ballad that seemed to aim straight at the hearts not just of teenagers but their mums, too. For

Boyzone, this slower tempo was the template for their 'oeuvre', eschewing the usual 'banger, banger, ballad' pop singles strategy and picking instead to chuck in an up-tempo for charity or perhaps as a fourth single. Covers would also be a mainstay, as would chunky-knit rollnecks.

'Boyzone were like a pound-shop version of Take That'

Holly Jade-Johnston: Me and my friend flew to Dublin to search for Boyzone. I was fifteen. All we had was an issue of *Smash Hits* as it had a guide to which part of Dublin they lived in. The first house we tracked down was Stephen Gately's. We knocked on the door and his wee mum was stood in her bathrobe. He wasn't there but she invited us in anyway. His *Smash Hits* awards were on the mantlepiece and she allowed me to have a picture taken with one of them. Mikey was my favourite so we went and met his mum. We met Shane's siblings. Nobody was at Ronan's house.

Colin Barlow: It was a glorious time for pop music when *Smash Hits* was the great influencer. I'd worked on East 17 when I was in publishing and they were the rivals to Take That, so all of a sudden there was a market in pop music. Boyzone came from nowhere – they were signed to the Irish company, had a hit in Ireland and then we picked the record up.

Louis Walsh: I was the driving force of Boyzone. I put them together, I picked the name, I picked every single song they ever had. I was involved in every single thing.

Holly Jade-Johnston: What I liked about Boyzone was they were like a pound-shop version of Take That. Boyzone were attainable. They weren't quite as polished. You felt like you could touch them.

Lee Brennan: The first time I met Boyzone [at a club gig], we didn't have any songs to perform so I had to pretend I had a sore throat and the other two guys just went on and did their crazy dance routines. When Boyzone went on we put our hoods up and walked into the club to see if they were any good at dancing and Spike was like, 'Nah, they haven't got the dancing vibe at all.'

Gregg Masuak, director, 'Baby Can I Hold You': They were pretty boys. Ronan was the Gary Barlow of Boyzone in that he's sensible, he's professional, he's kind. Mikey was just there for the ride, just a nice average bloke. Shane always looked so lovingly at the camera. He was stuck in wanting to be the sexy one so he'd spend a lot of time brooding. He turned up with weird braided hair and it was like, 'Oh, for fuck's sake, why do you do this to yourself?'

Alex Needham: Boyzone were a classic example of people that didn't really want to do it particularly. The three guys who weren't Ronan and Stephen were really grumpy about it. Shane was the grumpiest of the lot. Boyzone were never good, were they? When you went to see them, it was never a good performance.

Holly Jade-Johnston: Boyzone opened up the Ice Blast [a ride in Blackpool Pleasure Beach] and I remember my friend phoned me on the landline to tell me. I just happened to have a banner I had made that said 'Mikey' on it. So I got there and watched them on the ride holding my banner. That's when everyone started calling me 'Mikey Banner'.

Colin Barlow: I think in our lifetimes [Louis Walsh and Simon Cowell] were brilliant strategists for that market. They got what that pop audience wanted and they were brilliant at understanding the marketplace.

Louis Walsh: [Both Boyzone and Westlife were] for girls. Girls and gay guys. They like boybands. There wasn't any plan or plot, it was just 'do a boyband' and that's it.

Holly Jade-Johnston: As well as Boyzone, I also loved OTT with all my heart. I was on MTV Select once with Donna Air, asking her to play OTT. I remember it cost my mum about £50 in calls. But before social media, [the fans] were penpals; you'd write to each other. We used to have Friendship Books that were basically made out of index cards. You'd put down your favourite bands, so OTT, Take That, Boyzone, then underneath you'd brag about all the things you'd done with the band like 'chased through a carpark'. Then you'd pop it in an envelope and pass it on to your friend. It was always lesser bands like Orange Orange, Upside Down, Ultra. We loved them because we could meet them.

Lee Thompson: Somebody once referred to the audience of regional radio pop shows as 'the council estate girls'. Not in a disparaging way. What they meant was they were the most loyal pop fans. You could have an evening show interview with

NSYNC – who I remember coming to Viking radio in 1999 – but a band like Code Red, for example, would have more people waiting outside. They could speak to them directly, whereas the American boybands were more aloof superstars.

'Simon Cowell would always tell me: "Nothing's cooler than selling a lot of records"'

By 1999, with six UK number-one singles under their Burton belts, Boyzone were ready to 'try out new things', AKA Ronan was keen to go solo. For fans of immaculate balladry performed by five Irish men this was clearly devastating news, but thankfully Louis Walsh had a plan. Initially formed as 'pop vocal group' Six as One in 1997, and featuring Kian Egan, Mark Feehily, Shane Filan plus three others, Walsh took them to BMG. After an audition, they were rejected by Simon Cowell, who called them the ugliest band he had ever seen in his life. Three members were dropped and swiftly replaced by Nicky Byrne and Brian McFadden, the latter initially changing the spelling of his first name from Brian to Bryan to help with the look of his autograph. Satisfied with the genetic make-up of the newly named Westside, later Westlife, Cowell signed them to BMG and Walsh cleverly employed Ronan Keating as their 'co-manager'. Cowell and Walsh also put them in the studio with British songwriters Wayne Hector and Steve Mac, as well as flying them to Sweden to work with the likes of Max Martin, Rami, Andreas Carlsson, Per Magnusson and Jörgen Elofsson. Like Boyzone, they favoured ballads, but also leaned into the late '90s surge in post-Cheiron mid-tempos as favoured by the Backstreet Boys and Britney. The formula worked, with Westlife's first seven singles all debuting at number one in the UK. By the time they went on hiatus in 2010, six years after Brian 'Bryan' McFadden's departure, they'd doubled that tally.

Alex Needham: [Westlife] were just Boyzone: the second generation.

Holly Jade-Johnston: They were a lesser Boyzone.

Louis Walsh: [Simon and I] thought about the punters. People. We were never trying to be trendy or be in the *NME*. Or at the *Q* Awards. This was just aimed at people. That's why Westlife are still selling out arenas. We couldn't care less if Radio 1 liked it. We had TV and regional radio. We had all the magazines. The Saturday TV shows were very important for Westlife.

Lauren Cochrane, senior fashion writer, *The Guardian*: There was a bit of a thing about white around the millennium, including white parties, and Westlife definitely plugged into that in their style – as well as bringing a not-very-subtle reference to heaven and angels complete with pray hands long before emojis. Their hair and the nice shirts were also all about making sure they had broad appeal – beyond teenagers to a more grown-up demographic who would like the smartness.

Savan Kotecha, songwriter and producer: [Simon] was so good at putting these projects together – they weren't the cool projects; they were the projects that sold. [Westlife] were smart and they listened to Simon. He just had his finger on what the punters would like. He'd always tell me: 'Nothing's cooler than selling a lot of records.'

Louis Walsh: [Westlife] had these great producers and writers including Steve Mac. He writes ballads and that's his thing – he's really good at them. We didn't get any better than him or the

Swedish people. It was Simon Cowell and me that decided what they were going to do. It just worked.

Savan Kotecha: Everything I was doing at that point was with [Swedish producers] Quiz and Lorossi and they were pitching solely to Simon. We would basically be writing for Simon Cowell rather than the particular artist. He had a very specific pop taste and we just happened to be some of the people able to nail that. He was really good at taking care of songwriters and producers and very loyal.

Steve Anderson: My feeling on Simon Cowell is he is literally one of the best A&R men ever. Simon has what I call punter's ears. He's not technical but he can hear the general public, basically. When I was working on Westlife's 'Where We Are' [in 2009], he would call me up and say, 'There's something that happens at fifty seconds in, I don't know what it is, it just doesn't sound right to me.' I'd go to fifty seconds in and he would be right.

Savan Kotecha: [2001's 'Bad Girls'] was meant for [future 'Despacito' hitmaker] Luis Fonsi. He then decided not to use it, so Quiz and Lorossi played it to Westlife. This was the time when Simon wanted Westlife to be what Westlife was, which was doing ballads, but they were young guys who went out and partied. They were like, 'This is an edgy song for us, we're going to do it,' and it was my first big break. It was a bonus track [on *World of Our Own*], but I was getting royalties off an album that sold 5 million copies. Suddenly I could pay my rent.

Louis Walsh: Absolutely [the songs are more important than the band]. Look at the Backstreet Boys – the songs are better than any of them. There was no solo career there. If you have Max Martin or Brian Higgins or Steve Mac committed to a band then that's all you need. I was lucky with Westlife because I had Simon Cowell. His day job was A&R and he really worked – he picked all the covers with me and I'd be on the phone to him every day. We picked 'Mandy', 'I Have a Dream', 'You Raise Me Up'. We picked all those songs ourselves. That's why it worked. It was just me and him and them.

Savan Kotecha: The pop artists had a lot less control in general than they do now. Back then you had Simon Cowell at the peak of his powers, creatively. There was a lot of record-label influence on the songs and they found great songs. We don't have that as much nowadays.

James Masterton: During this period of colossally high record sales, [songs] didn't necessarily stick around long enough to have a huge cultural impact. Westlife were the poster child for this kind of phenomenon because they managed to get the marketing absolutely down pat. You can say what you like about Louis Walsh, but he certainly knew how to time releases. He could almost guarantee Westlife getting to number one.

Lee Thompson: [The Box] were the most important when it came to Westlife videos. [The label] would always give it to us first to see how it performed over the weekend and then it would go to MTV on the Monday. The reason The Box was so important to the labels was it was the first line of promotion when it came to doing your pre-sale at Woolworths. Bearing in mind Woolworths were huge – if you weren't stacked at

Woolies on a Monday morning then you weren't going to be in the top twenty.

James Masterton: During this whole frantic era there was a great phenomenon of the Woolworths six. The guy who was the chief music buyer at the time instigated this policy that Woolworths, who accounted for a sizeable proportion of CD sales on the high street, were only going to stock six of the new releases each week. If you weren't one of those six, that put a huge dent in your chart position in week one. Shops were the gatekeepers for all of this.

Lee Thompson: Bookers at *CD:UK* would see how songs were performing at The Box and then decide whether to have them for Saturday morning TV. It all worked in tandem. The Box, *CD:UK* and Woolies were the three most important linchpins to all of those big pop hits in the late '90s and early '00s. More so than Radio 1 and commercial radio.

Steve Anderson: There is no frontman [in Westlife]. I think the rule of boybands and girlbands is that there really shouldn't be a singular front person.

Louis Walsh: If you have two or three lead singers then you're fine. With NSYNC they had Justin and with Take That it was Gary and Robbie. You always have one or two better singers, but everyone has to be featured if you want the band to last and you want a happy band. They all have to have a role.

Nigel Dick, director, Westlife's 'Swear It Again' (US version): When you're doing a boyband you're promoting good-looking young men so that girls can scream at them. Just show me more boys, really. If there are five guys in a band then you have to cater to all the fans of each member – this girl loves the blond boy, this one loves the short guy – so if they don't get to see their guy a lot, there will be complaints.

Dania Pasquini: Westlife were the band your mum would listen to and they knew that. They had to work that. They were good lads. We threw rain on them. And a wind machine to get those clothes rippling.

Max Giwa: The thing about Simon was he was open to any idea. It was like, 'If you can do it, make it happen.' He's very in tune with the public outside of London because his thing was, 'If the mother in Leeds is sitting in her kitchen washing the dishes listening to this then we've cracked it.' That was his ethos with the music and the videos.

Brian Dowling: I interviewed Mariah Carey [on *SM:TV*] once. She was singing that song with Westlife, the Phil Collins cover [2000's 'Against All Odds'], and it was almost like she'd never met them before. It was so odd. In my mind I'm going, 'She has met them before, right?' Westlife loved [*SM:TV*'s often rowdy band vs band football match] Eat My Goal. They put a fucking gay Irish man in goal and I was like, 'This will not be happening.' Westlife wanted to fucking batter me every Saturday morning.

Lucie Cave: During the *Smash Hits* tour, we'd be in the bar until 4 a.m. and I remember saying to Brian McFadden, 'I've got to go and wake you up in your room in half an hour' [to film for Trouble TV]. So I'd have to quickly go to bed, they'd have to climb into bed having had no sleep and then I'd knock on the door with the camera crew like, 'Wake up!' I remember at one point they had condoms on the bedside table – not used ones – and we had to pixelate them out because it was kids' TV.

Savan Kotecha: All pop artists want to be cool at some point. They want to be edgier than their music. That's sometimes the downfall.

Simon Jones, former Westlife PR: [Westlife] wanted to be in *i-D* magazine. I was called into a meeting because they weren't happy. They wanted to do fashion and ideally they wanted to do *i-D* magazine or the cover of *GQ*. I was like, 'That's never going to happen.' I was just trying to be realistic. Then they said they wanted to be on the cover of *Cosmopolitan*, but they'd only done one guy on their cover and that was David Beckham. And they were like, 'Yeah, and . . .?'. Why would they be bothered about those things when their fanbase was Julie in Norwich, and they don't care about those magazines? You have to hit your fans and let them know there's a record out. They were never going to be in the fashion world.

★ ★ ★

In 2019, after dabbling in solo careers, the four members of Westlife regrouped for their eleventh album (and eighth UK number one), *Spectrum*, which was followed in 2021 by *Wild Dreams* and another stadium tour. As for Boyzone, they went on to release the 2010 album *Brother*, named in memory of Stephen Gately, who tragically died the year prior from a pulmonary oedema.

In 2018, they released the fairly self-explanatory *Thank You & Goodnight* album.

A numbers game: 911, A1 and Triple 8

'Ben A1 came in for a shoot and had to get his curtains ironed down'

While Boyzone aimed to heal the hearts of broken-hearted Take That fans via soppy ballads, 'Bodyshakin'' hitmakers 911, AKA Lee Brennan, Jimmy Constable and Spike Dawbarn, were keen to move them onto the dancefloor. As with early Take That, 911 battled for attention early on, initially releasing their debut single independently in 1996. For Ben Adams, Paul Marazzi, Christian Ingebrigtsen and Mark Read, AKA A1, who emerged two years later, their focus was also seemingly on defining late '90s boyband traits, be it curtain hairstyles, retina-burning all-white outfits or hi-NRG pop. By 2003, in a post-Justin-Timberlake-goes-solo world, however, that boyband iconography was starting to look as staid as a white sleeveless tee, with major label certainties Triple 8, AKA David Wilcox, Iain James, Jamie Bell, Josh Barnett and Justin Scott, attempting a harder-edged sound to general indifference.

Lee: Spike and Jimmy were on [late-night dance show] *Hitman and Her*, which was presented by Pete Waterman and Michaela Strachan. At the time, I was working in a ten-pin bowling centre in Carlisle. I wrote a letter one night and took it to my local radio station Sea FM basically saying I'm looking to start singing, are there any roadshows I can do? My letter was faxed to the guy looking after Spike and Jimmy. He rang me at Hollywood Bowl and said he was looking to put a boyband together, do I want to come and meet him? A few weeks later I met Spike and Jimmy in a Burger King. I left my full-time job and told my family I was moving to Glasgow to be in a boyband. I just go for it, me. I don't worry about failure. We moved into our manager's house and signed on the dole basically.

Christian Ingebrigtsen: I went to the Liverpool Institute of Performing Arts, and I studied songwriting and vocals. In December of 1997, I got an email from my songwriting teacher saying, 'If you want to be in a boyband, this could be your big break.' I immediately turned to my friend sitting next to me and said, 'What's a boyband?' I had no idea. He explained to me: 'It's like the Backstreet Boys.' I replied and said I could do it. Vicky Blood and Tim Byrne had this vision of creating a boyband where all the members were songwriters and musicians, rather than actors or models or dancers. They auditioned 3,000 people initially but then they realised that songwriters and musicians don't go to auditions for boybands, so they started looking at performing arts schools.

Alex Needham: [A1] had the same management as Steps. I remember doing one of Tom Watkins' bands, North and South, and by the late '90s, early '00s, I think you just had a generation of bands where the record companies and the managers had taken control. You've not got a Bros or Pet Shop Boys situation where you've got a pretty strong creative force saying, 'No, we're not going to do that.' The managers have really taken over completely and these people will put up with being moulded. Then you end up with something like A1, where they're very bland and embarrassingly super gay. It's just a middle-aged gay guy's idea of what a pop band should be and there's something that's inauthentic about it.

Iain James, Triple 8: We formed the embryonic part of the band in Bristol between myself and Justin. We were really into music and it was a really good way of getting ourselves out of trouble. We were really dedicated and committed to making it work. We lost a few members along the way and then we came to London and got spotted by some producers. Before we knew it, we were making demos and looking for more members. We felt that having five people just looked better than four. Three doesn't work. Remember 911?

Lee: Straight away when Take That split our manager said, 'There's a huge gap for a new boyband,' which is why he put it together so quickly. That was the angle we approached major labels with at the start, but they weren't interested. Our manager was adamant there would always be an audience wanting boybands doing their pelvic thrusts. He looked at the blueprint of Nigel Martin-Smith and what he did with Take That. And Nigel used to get Take That doing the full circuit of under-18s, over-18s, the gay clubs, all of it. So we did that for the first fifteen months before we got signed. It was crazy.

Christian: I sent a demo I had made and they asked me to come to London to meet the other boys. That was Paul and two other guys from the initial auditions who weren't the songwriters and musicians they were looking for. I met Tim in Steve Mac's studio. This was at the same time as Westlife were being made as well. Initially Tim had organised for Steve to do all the writing with us, but because I didn't really want to do [A1], I immediately said I wanted to write the songs. And if not I wasn't interested. It was a bit of reverse psychology that kind of worked. In the end, when

Steve Mac realised we wanted to write all the songs ourselves, he focused on Westlife, where he could get his songs placed.

Iain: I knew [Chris Herbert] had worked with the Spice Girls and Five and as soon as he sat down with us and gave us his story we were like, 'Okay, I think we're in good hands here.' We were doing everything on our own, for years, and we didn't know what the hell we were doing.

Chris Herbert: I loved Triple 8. That was the culmination of everything I had learned up to that point. They were so hard-working; they were so well-rehearsed. They were great songwriters.

Iain: I remember at the time Polydor really liked this idea of us as a sort of 'lad band'. I think because we hadn't been to performing arts school, we were just some kids from the street with no experience, it was easy to tag us with that. A bit naughty and a bit rough. We liked having arguments and airing our dirty laundry.

Christian: For a while I rented a cupboard in Bow, which was a very scary area back then. It had a single 90cm mattress on the floor, but that had to be lifted up in order to get in and out of the room. I lived there for six months and then I stayed at a mate's house until the management decided we should get a place together. They rented a place for us in east Acton, which I'm sure we paid for.

Lee: Our manager secured an investor called Frank. He invested about £10,000 initially so we set up our own label for our first two singles. After Take That, a lot of bands were put together by labels, but we did it really organically. Our first single went in at number thirty-eight and then we did twenty-one on the second single. Suddenly labels were like, 'Who are these guys getting in the charts without any TV behind them?' Then it was a bidding war and we signed with Virgin and released our third single.

Lauren Cochrane: You could see the remnants of Britpop in 911's look – from the haircuts to the slightly retro T-shirts. They also occasionally played into a rave moment with the dummy around the neck and the baggy silhouettes. They were aiming for a slightly edgier look than a lot of the more polished boybands from this era.

Christian: I wasn't into the pop scene in the way the other guys were. I hadn't heard of Steps until I joined A1 and we went on tour with them. That was really instrumental in creating an audience for us and also the *Smash Hits* tour we did with Westlife. We did quite a lot before we got signed and that was one of the advantages of Tim coming from the world of television. We were on *SM:TV* and *CD:UK* before we were signed by Sony.

Iain: I remember doing gigs with [Westlife] and being like, 'Make the most of it, lads, your time's up soon.' Which obviously it wasn't. I remember having a very strong feeling of confidence slash arrogance. But you needed that. The main aim was to knock Westlife off of those stools. To try to be the anti-that.

Lee: Virgin put us up in a hotel in Maida Vale, so we had little apartments each in there. I remember I wanted to go to the West End so I'd ring my tour manager and he'd get a car and a Merc would turn up. What a lifestyle. You'd have your driver waiting for you outside the club until you were ready to leave.

Holly Jade-Johnston: I remember we went on a rollercoaster with A1 in Blackpool.

Hannah Verdier: Ben A1 came in for a shoot and he was having a fag outside and his curtains were all over the place. He had to get them ironed down. It was like the dream was over; it was shattered.

Lauren Cochrane: The curtains were very much of this era too, the kind of hairstyle seen on David Beckham and Michael Owen.

Hannah Verdier: We had A1 on the *Smash Hits* tour. It was carnage. Always in the middle of the night the hotel alarm would go off because the fans wanted to see Paul A1 in his knickers outside.

Christian: We realised we liked the train much more than cars, so the label would rent us a whole carriage. Once we were going to Nottingham and I'm on the phone to a friend and a person comes in from the car in front of ours. I'm like, 'This guy's the spitting image of the prime minister.' And it actually was Tony Blair. He was joking about how his security detail had told him there were several hundred young people at the platform and he wondered if we might have something to do with that. Then he asked for our autograph for his children. This was at the time when George Bush and Tony Blair were the most important people on the planet. It was a big deal. So we were all calling our family. Later he was waving to us from the platform and we're waving back from the train and then suddenly we see our head of security going, 'Wait, wait, get off.' We were so excited we had forgotten to get off the train. All the fans were watching us leave. Security had to drive and pick us up at the next train station.

Jordan Paramor: I went to LA with B*Witched and I remember getting in the lift with Lindsay and someone else and one of them said, 'Oh, God, what will Lee say?' And that was the moment I realised Lindsay was dating Lee from 911. We all suspected. She quickly said to me, 'You won't put that in [the mag], will you?'

Lee: The last thing a fan wants to see is their favourite boyband member with a girlfriend. It loses something for fans is what we were told. Towards the end of 911, my now ex-wife Lindsay was in B*Witched and we slowly started coming out as being together. After a while we were like, 'Right, that's it, we're together.' [B*Witched] were very sweet and innocent.

Jordan Paramor: When you're young you genuinely think you're going to marry these people. You think you're in with a shot. Lee was a big heartthrob so for him to be dating someone from B*Witched, not only would they be asked about it in every interview, but it might turn some fans off.

Iain: [The label] spent over £2 million on us and we didn't even release our album. Management should have sat us down, but I think they just wanted us to cause trouble and spend money we didn't have. It's almost like a mad professor behind it with the puppet strings going, 'What can we conjure up here?' Financial ruin? Maybe some fights? Drug and alcohol abuse? Getting a female pop star pregnant? I remember doing *CD:UK* and it was the biggest budgeted debut performance. The buzz around it was huge, you could feel it. All the other bands were whispering.

Peter Loraine: I had this idea with Triple 8, which was kind of a very naïve version of what Twitter would become, where we made tens of thousands of little business cards. Each boy had their picture on it and on the back was their phone number. We gave them mobile phones and you could text them or ring them and they'd speak to you. We'd have these days when it would be marked in their diary 'Triple 8 to spend all afternoon texting people'. They'd be giving out these cards at *CD:UK* like, 'Anyone want my phone number?'

Iain: It was a way of interacting with fans in a new way. We always used to get told off for not answering them or for turning them off. Or just phoning our mates. I didn't really want to speak to Julie from Grimsby at 3 a.m. It was constant.

Peter Loraine: It was a good idea until the mobile provider presented us with a bill for £25,000 for these five phones. One of them had a friend who lived in America and they'd been on the phone with them night after night, just whizzing up the bill.

Christian: When we won the BRIT Award [in 2001], Noel Gallagher was outraged that they'd awarded that to a boy-band like us. Looking back now, I'm immensely proud we beat Coldplay to British Breakthrough Act.

Pete Selby, former music retail buyer: I was working for Our Price and at that point I was still rather dazzled by the sheer pomp of the event. I remember standing at a Portaloo urinal next to one of the A1s just after they had won their award. He was on the phone to his mum. It was rather touching. But I also remember thinking, 'Enjoy this moment – you in the Portaloo with a BRIT on your new tiny Nokia . . . this is the pinnacle.' It seemed very bittersweet.

Lee: We were just about to switch on the Christmas lights in Birkenhead and it was literally about ten minutes before we went on stage. There'd been so many arguments and conversations over the weeks, so we went into the broom cupboard backstage and me and Spike said, 'We think it's time to end it, Jimmy.' He didn't want it to end. Our deal was finished and we weren't getting on well and mentally we were wrecked.

Christian: Sony was really trying to break us in America. NSYNC were the big band over there, so they were the inspiration. We had been in America for three months at that point and had to go back to Asia so we didn't lose those markets that we actually had. That's when the horrible thing happened and four girls died at a stampede at our signing in Indonesia. That just stopped everything. We wanted to honour their custom by observing a period of mourning for five months. Then when we started over again that's when we decided to go in a completely different musical direction [via 2001's immaculate, soft-rock opus 'Caught in the Middle'].

Lee: We just [announced we were breaking up] live on Chris Moyles' radio show. I remember fans crying outside Radio 1. We all got into our separate cars and didn't speak to each other again for about a year.

Iain: Lucian Grainge, the head of Universal, called us into a meeting and pretty much said, 'I expect your first three singles to go in at number one and then we'll release the album.' I was like, 'Okay . . .' He justified it by saying, 'So you guys have got to work really hard.' We *were* working hard. When [first single, 'Knockout'] went in at eight and ['Give Me a Reason'] went in at nine, I don't think Lucian was best pleased.

Chris Herbert: I thought those singles were really representative of that time. They straddled pop and also N.E.R.D and those kinds of bands. It was brilliant. I really put my whole heart into that band but it just didn't connect quick enough. I think if the label had stuck with it we could have grown it.

Iain: We were due to release the album and he just said no. That's when the ground gets pulled from underneath you. It was a killer. We'd worked our bollocks off. I'd written the majority of [the album] myself and it just didn't see the light of day. As quickly as it all blew up, it just disappeared.

Lee: I had to check out of the hotel that I'd been living in. They were happy to get me a car and then the train back home, but after that it was like someone had pulled the rug away. I was completely lost for a long time. I became very low and depressed in 2001, very sad about lots of things. I hated being recognised because I felt like a failure. You're the guy that *was* in that group, you're not the guy that *is* in a group. I'd always be recognised in the supermarket. Kids used to shout stuff and it really affected me mentally.

Christian: We had time in that period [of mourning] and so the studio was our playground. 'Caught in the Middle' would have been number one in any other week that year, but it was beaten by 'Hero' by Enrique Iglesias. But follow-up 'Make It Good' was our lowest-charting single ever and it was number eleven. I think it went over the heads of some of our fans and a lot of people that would enjoy that song wouldn't listen to us because we were a boyband. We fell between two stools. We had a song called '2:59', which is a very rock-pop thing, and the management hated it. We could see that's where things were headed and McFly did that exact sound after us. We were all very exhausted, but it was just going to be a break. But that break lasted for eight years.

Iain: I'm still buddies with a couple of Westlife guys and we laugh about it now. Mark and Shane will say, 'Ah, bless you, guys, you really did try but you just couldn't beat the power of the fans.' Which is true. Blue knew what suited them, Busted knew what suited them and Westlife what suited them. Ultimately that was our downfall – we didn't quite know who we were as a brand and a boyband.

Chris Herbert: There was another band we were launching up against called D-Side. We specifically set ourselves up to be the antithesis of them. They were going to be the new Boyzone and we were going to be the new Five. Their launch didn't quite happen and neither did ours, so they switched [style] and came into our lane. No one won at the end of the day.

Peter Loraine: It was too formulaic by then. What was really sad was that I don't believe they had the songs. Iain is the most phenomenal songwriter and at that time we had people in Sweden writing tunes for them. It was a shame we didn't tap into what we had with him.

Busted, McFly and using guitars for good

'For Kerrang!, *it almost felt like they were spoiling our bands'*

As the new millennium marched onwards, surviving a non-existent 1 January bug and barely surviving a very real existential crisis post-9/11, pop in the UK started to look for something more 'authentic' to rub up against the march of TV talent shows. Taking its cues from the likes of Green Day and Blink-182, pop-punk landed its first superstar in the shape of Canadian grump Avril Lavigne, whose debut single 'Complicated' arrived in March 2002. Six months later the choreography agnostic Busted, AKA teenagers James Bourne, Matt Willis and Charlie Simpson, released their debut single, the very-much-not-okay-in-the-modern-era 'What I Go to School For', a Daily Mail *headline in song form about a school boy being groomed by his teacher. Its follow-up, 'Year 3000', featured lyrics about triple-breasted women, a wank fantasy that put a PG spin on the crude lyrical template of their American heroes. The genesis of 'What I Go to School For' was started by Matt and James years before Busted's creation, with the pair eventually joined by exceptionally eyebrow-ed Charlie, who beat a certain Tom Fletcher to the final place. Later, Busted's management, Prestige, would give Tom his own band, the equally guitar-obsessed McFly, alongside Dougie Poynter, Danny Jones and Harry Judd, who would arrive in Busted's slipstream but eventually outlast them. Prestige also decided to have their cake and eat it via V, AKA Antony Brant, Aaron Buckingham, Mark Harle, Kevin McDaid and Leon Pisani, a very old-school boyband simultaneously being destroyed by their creators.*

Iain: I remember Busted exploding right next to us at the same sort of time. I'd studied pop's cyclical nature. You've only got a few years before the next sub-genre kicks in.

Chris Herbert: There was a switch. You were getting more guitar bands and then you had a boyband come along that played guitars. I could see it happening.

James Bourne: There was a lot of music around I didn't like – I didn't like S Club 7, for example. I liked Westlife's songs but I thought they weren't as cool as the Backstreet Boys. It wasn't exciting.

Ashley Bird, *Kerrang!* magazine editor, 2002–05: I was the editor of *Kerrang!* that had to fight the authenticity battle for a couple of years. The spoiler alert is that I didn't feature Busted in the magazine. Or McFly. Or Avril Lavigne. *Kerrang!* was always about real bands – people who had got together, played in a garage, practised, done a load of gigs and then maybe somewhere down the line a label signed them and said, 'You should get rid of your drummer,' and the band said, 'No, we're a real thing.'

James: I played guitar from a really young age. I would play songs by Green Day, Oasis and Nirvana all the time. I had this understanding of guitar bands.

Jonathan Bown, former assistant editor, *Smash Hits*: We were really used to super-groomed boybands at the time. We were starting to see a lot of groups coming out of shows like *Popstars*. At the same time that was happening there was this super-produced R&B sound coming out of America, then you also had bands like Blink-182 that were providing something different. Something like Busted was a real response to that.

Ashley Bird: Authenticity was always a thing for us until Linkin Park came along in 2000 and made us start to question everything. The rumours were that the label had brought in the singer at least, if not the rest of the band. It was the first time *Kerrang!* had faced this 'Are they a label creation or are they not?' question. The conclusion we came to was they were alright to appear in the magazine. What was happening at the same time was that authentic pop-punk was getting more commercial. So for the first time we had readers and bands who were – not to sound disrespectful to *Kerrang!* readers because I absolutely was one of them – pretty. And looked after their hair. Of course that gets the attention of a major label world for whom that works. We had to ask, 'How much is *Kerrang!* going to accept in terms of this commercial side of things?'

James: Back then the pop music business and the alternative business felt like two separate entities. Everyone wants to be successful, I don't care whether you're indie or pop. People [in the indie world] wanted the success we had and were trying to find reasons to bring us down – they couldn't believe sixteen-year-old kids wrote these songs. I really felt like we had the makings of a real band but we were marketed as a boyband, so there was this weird thing where we were like a boyband but we had this knowledge of real music.

Ashley Bird: For Busted, a band who had grown up listening to Green Day and Blink-182, this new concept came up, which is a label-created pop-punk band. That, for *Kerrang!*, was an existential crisis. I think Matt and James from Busted initially met at another audition for another boyband. I think the whole process came about via auditioning for label creations.

James: [Before we signed to Island] we went to Simon Cowell's office at BMG. The beginning of the meeting with him was really cold. He scanned the room and I was at the end and he went, 'So what's the story?' He didn't say anything. Before you knew it the ball was in your court and you had to respond. Simon wanted us to add a drummer as a permanent member of the band. Which probably was a really good idea, but we didn't want to at the time. Before the Simon Cowell meeting we did have people say, 'Look, we don't know what this is and we don't know where it belongs – you're not a band, you're not a boyband, you're not anything.' But I think Simon Cowell saw the potential, and because he saw it, it meant other people started to as well. Word had gotten around the music industry.

Jenessa Williams, journalist and McFly super-fan: Listening back to Busted now, I can't hear much in it that couldn't have held its own among any of the pop-adjacent artists who do get that kind of rock coverage now. I think McFly in particular definitely fell foul to that long-established sexism that dictates that artists who are broadly loved by girls can't be any good. I was always really enraged by that, wishing that I could read 'proper' interviews that gave insight into them as artists as well as the fluffy 'what's your favourite colour?' pop magazine stuff.

Hannah Verdier: The first time I saw Busted was when their record company asked a few of the *Smash Hits* staff to go to the rehearsal studio to check out their new 'rock boyband'. It was clear the record company had a firm idea of what they wanted. Busted played a couple of songs, including 'What I Go to School For', which had a bit of sauciness, delivered by Mattie, who was like a baby Robbie Williams, with a wink for the mums. I think using us as a focus group was a smart move. As was putting on a showcase with loads of free booze and school dinners.

Pete Selby: Some of the more important media partners were invited to the studio to watch a nascent Busted. Retailers were lower down the pecking order so a colleague and I were invited to Island head office and plonked on a sofa in the tiniest kitchenette, while the three lads – pre-pop-punk makeover and in very sensible knitwear – performed a few energetic numbers acoustically. Only Matt didn't have a bass guitar so he sort of jigged about on the spot and did things with his hands while James and Charlie did all of the musical heavy lifting. Oh and there was no free booze.

James: Matt had an early idea of a song but it wasn't about what 'What I Go to School For' is about now. I made one of the lyrics he had rhyme with 'member of staff' and I was like, 'We have to take this down the school theme.' We started laughing about our experiences at school. We drew on experience but it was done in a way that wasn't completely autobiographical.

Jonathan Bown: It must be tricky for them to perform that song now. You'd have to inject a heavy dose of irony. At the time, they were young enough for it to seem okay. You certainly couldn't have got away with a teacher character going, 'That's what I go to school for.' I think people liked that cartoon-y element. It helped broaden their appeal. They were a much edgier alternative to your Westlifes.

James: I liked Westlife songs but I thought they were boring lyrically. After a while, a lot of the lyrics start to look the same: 'I need you', 'I miss you', 'You make me complete'. Very predictable. I felt like we had a way of keeping our lyrics fresh and you never knew what our next song was going to be about.

Ashley Bird: Singing about triple-breasted women and fancying your science teacher is the kind of thing that goes down quite well in *Kerrang!* world. Blink-182 are the massive bridge between that authentic world and the pop one.

James: We followed up 'What I Go to School For' with another song ['Year 3000'] that was better and bigger. I think that's the reason Busted had the effect it did and why we opened the floodgates for more. That was a trend that no one had really seen.

Jonathan Bown: The acts coming out of the talent shows were so groomed and so micro-managed. They could perform but could also say very little. The good thing about Busted is that you had three very different personality types. Charlie went to [public school] Charterhouse, he was clearly from a privileged background. You had Matt, who was almost the exact opposite, who had had quite a difficult upbringing and at one point was living with James. Then you had James, who was the Gary Barlow type. That was an interesting dynamic.

Ashley Bird: For us, it almost felt like they were spoiling our bands. Every band that is a real band that we cover, every time they do a star jump on stage it was like, 'This has all been spoilt.'

Lauren Cochrane: In a way, you could put Busted in the indie sleaze moment. Their style was meant to signify that they were an alternative boy band from the peroxide hair to the caps and the vacant stares, which were quite Damon Albarn via John Lydon. It was all quite on the nose.

Jonathan Bown: I remember one interview that was quite difficult to do. We hired a location house that had a nice pool outside and I had to interview them while I was sitting on a pool inflatable. As we were talking to each other we'd start floating in opposite directions. I'd have to try to paddle my way back to them. They were much more up for a bit of a laugh.

James: In those days our tour manager had our passports so often I would get in the Addison Lee and genuinely not know where I was going. We had management do our schedule and we'd be told we were being picked up at a certain time, but there would be so much in our day we wouldn't be told about. I would get in the car with nothing and we'd go to the airport and fly to Denmark and then do four Scandinavian countries in one day.

'Nobody seemed keen to give a band like McFly the same degree of praise as Arctic Monkeys'

By the middle of 2003, Busted were firmly rooted as one of pop's biggest acts. Matt and James were living in pop's very own village, AKA Princess Park Manor, alongside members of Girls Aloud, Blue and the Sugababes (Charlie had quickly left to move in with friends). On long lonely nights, James would write songs while Matt slept on a La-Z-Boy sofa post-pizza slump. Idyllic, right? Not quite. Keen to have another songwriter to collaborate with for what would become Busted's second album, A Present for Everyone, *James asked his management to call in Tom Fletcher, who had very briefly been part of Busted. Signed as a songwriter by Busted's management, Tom would later meet Danny at the auditions for V before the pair would audition bassist Dougie and drummer and former Charlie schoolmate Harry. McFly's debut single, '5 Colours in Her Hair', emerged in March 2004.*

Tom Fletcher: I went to the Busted auditions and saw Matt Willis there. I'd known Matt from Sylvia Young and it wasn't that we didn't like each other; we just weren't compatible. He was this cool kid, super popular, and I was a bit more of a teacher's pet. I asked if he was there for the audition and he was like, 'No, I'm in the band already.' I just assumed there was no way I was getting in. But the audition went really well. I was at the same audition as Charlie, so they told us we were both in the band. I remember really clearly my younger sister had a Halloween party and the phone rang and it was Busted's manager and he was like, 'Hey, Tom, so we've decided we're just going to keep it as a three-piece so you're no longer required.' I was heartbroken. But he said he really liked my songwriting and that he really wanted to work with me.

James: I called management and said, 'Can you send Tom round? I wouldn't mind writing songs with someone.'

Tom: We were just inseparable. The first group of songs we started writing included 'Air Hostess' and 'Crashed the Wedding', songs that would become number-one singles for Busted. I left college and went on tour with Busted, too, and shared James's hotel room. Me and James are both super nerds. We'd stay up until 6 a.m. but we weren't doing the rock 'n' roll thing of throwing TVs out of hotel windows; we were ordering vanilla milkshakes and watching movies. I was aware that that kind of stuff was going on, maybe with some other bandmates, but what was genuinely exciting for me was I suddenly had a friend who was as into songwriting as I was. And who also loved *Back to the Future* and *Star Wars*.

James: Tom was definitely down about not making it into Busted, so I said to him, 'You can have your own band, write the songs, and you can basically dress the same [as Busted], but we can make your songs you. We can set your music apart and can add major sevenths and minor chords.'

Tom: We both had this love for the Beach Boys and the Beatles, so we had a few songs that had those influences. Those songs became the basis of what would become McFly.

James: All these songs like 'That Girl', 'Memory Lane' and 'Obviously' started happening quickly.

Lauren Cochrane: Style-wise, McFly felt like they were playing into the Abercrombie bro look that was popular in the '00s. They were British but they have the look of Californian surf and skate kids from the Quicksilver T-shirts to the backwards caps and sun-kissed hair.

Jonathan Bown: I thought some of the songs on [debut album] *Room on the 3rd Floor* were incredibly mature. They'd write songs about adults going through midlife crises. It certainly felt like '5 Colours in Her Hair' was an entry in and then after a few more singles they found their groove. But it also struck me as slightly unfair as a pop fan that you had a band like the Arctic Monkeys, who were in their teens and played their own instruments, but who were heralded as lyricists for a generation and put on this pedestal as amazing songwriters. But nobody seemed particularly keen to give a band like McFly the same degree of praise.

Tom: I remember getting booed at rock events. If we went to see bands like the Used or Green Day we'd have to take security with us because people would want to kick the shit out of us. Just to say, 'I punched a guy from McFly.' One of the first times we were written about in the *NME* and – please excuse the language – they had a picture of us and they captioned it: 'Wanker, Cunt, Dickhead, Twat'. We were sixteen- and seventeen-year-old kids, so seeing a magazine with your idols in put that under a picture of you was heartbreaking.

Jenessa Williams: I really appreciated how off-path they were willing to wander, how non-patronising that kind of experimentation felt to a young listener. Also, MySpace had happened and there were tonnes of bands I discovered both through McFly's networks and just the wider sense of genre-blurring discovery. It was a really, really great time to be a music fan.

Tom: People said that we were the reason they'd moved on to bands like the Arctic Monkeys. People that were looking for the next thing. That also came with its own frustrations because we were growing up and we wanted to be a credible band, too. We didn't just want to play to thirteen-year-old girls for all of our lives.

Jordan Paramor: Busted and McFly's rockier sound and honesty about their lifestyle also set them aside from other boy-bands. While other bands were creating anodyne 'appeal to everyone' personas, they were more open about being flawed and acting like twats. I remember Dougie telling me a particularly horrific story about the time he pooed into a cup on their tour bus and he wasn't in the least bit worried people might fancy him less because of it. They smoked and drank and openly had girlfriends, instead of rolling out the classic 'I'm looking for the right girl' line every time they were interviewed.

Paul Flynn: I went to the McFly house and I've never ever been more depressed in my life. It was like the modern-day equivalent of *Brookside*. A new-build estate on a London ring road so they can get everywhere easily. No delineation of them having personalities.

Tom: Logistically it all made sense to live in London together, but we didn't want to live in that apartment complex that Busted and Girls Aloud lived in. There was a house ten minutes around the corner. That was the best decision I'd ever made because suddenly we were four kids – Dougie was fifteen, he'd just dropped out of school in Year 10 – and we had no one with us. At the time, it was the biggest house I'd ever seen. This huge five-bedroom house in north London. We were all disgusting in terms of hygiene and cleanliness. In terms of the rock 'n' roll lifestyle, Harry was pretty bad. He was a public-school boy from a very different background and he introduced some of the more stereotypical rock 'n' roll elements that I was against bringing into our house. He grew up in dorms where they'd always shower with each other all the time. When we're on tour, even now, if you're in the shower, you can guarantee Harry will get in with you.

Paul Flynn: Harry Judd was absolute kit off at *Attitude*. He was the ultimate paragon of how bands a bit later would have members for the gay press.

Tom: Playing at G-A-Y was amazing. They would fill you with alcohol before you'd go on stage and it's this amazing, electric atmosphere. It was so much fun. Normally, we were playing to young teenage girls wearing bunny ears, so suddenly we'd be in front of nineteen-year-old gay men at 2 a.m. and we could get naked and swear.

'I remember standing outside the venue afterwards and Charlie speeding off in his Porsche'

On Christmas Eve, 2004, Charlie – who by this point had started his hard-rock side project, Fightstar – called the band's management to inform them he was keen to leave Busted. On 14 January 2005, at London's Soho Hotel, the band announced they were eschewing the Sugababes option of switching in a new member and instead were splitting up. As quickly as they'd arrived, all chunky Vans, frayed sweatbands and checkerboard belts, Busted were gone, swallowed whole by a quest for authenticity that had gotten out of hand.

James: Charlie got some shit from a band he went to see live and he had a hard time dealing with the attention he was getting. He's two years younger than me and Matt, so back then he cared very much about what critics said. I personally didn't care. When you're getting number ones that often and you're writing songs for your own band and McFly and you're getting seven number-one records in a year, people can say what they want, it doesn't bother you.

Jonathan Bown: We went to the press conference. I was a fan as much as anything else, so I was really sad when they split. I remember standing outside the venue afterwards and Charlie speeding off in his Porsche. I thought that was a good analogy for the fact that Charlie was going to be alright, but I did feel for the other two. For them it was very much their lifeline.

James: I was sad for it to end but it wasn't like I was this suicidal weirdo. I was partly excited, actually. It was an adjustment because you're losing something that has been an amazing thing in your life but you're also getting back time you didn't think you were going to have.

Tom: Busted didn't have a super tight friendship – they were three very different individuals. The management knew with [McFly] that they had to let it seem like we were organically choosing each other as friends. That was a career-defining decision because the core of our longevity is that we haven't killed each other because we're still mates. You can't just shove three completely separate people in a band together and expect it to last twenty years. They will self-destruct.

Jonathan Bown: It was clear from our engagements with them that Charlie was getting increasingly unhappy. And increasingly unhappy at the thought of holding a silly prop or answering questions about snogging someone or whatever. Plus he had another creative avenue with Fightstar. He felt very compromised by the boyband label. But it did feel like a shock and it did feel like the knives were out for Charlie from the Busted fans after it happened.

James: If someone doesn't feel like they're being represented creatively in their own self, it's like, 'Okay, if you can do both, do both.' He was working around the clock to do both. So, when he just wanted to do Fightstar, that was interesting to me because you're literally in this band that's killing it and you could use that to fund your really amazing other thing. He had it all. But I understand why he wanted to focus on what he wanted to focus on. That wasn't hard for me to understand because Busted was my Fightstar.

Ashley Bird: We [at *Kerrang!*] had to think about it and it was like, 'Okay, so we didn't do Busted but now he's doing this.' The point was he found his guys for [Fightstar]. In the beginning they weren't very good and it took them a year or so to work it out. I said, 'Most of the bands we do cover got together in their late teens, it's just that Charlie's day job wasn't working in McDonald's, it was being in Busted.' Obviously he had a leg up straight away, but you could tell he loved that music. We saw it as a different thing. So we did cover Fightstar.

James: Busted have made so many bad choices in our career. But I do think us splitting up was a good thing. I think it preserved the integrity of what it was. It was the reason we were able to come back with a bang. A lot of people have tried to come back and failed and I credit that to the way we ended it. In the beginning I think people really thought we were these sell-out, manufactured, commercial pop stars and that couldn't be further from the truth. We were turning down these huge Argos offers to make these shitty acoustic guitars with our faces on the boxes. The three of us went, 'Well, fuck that, our fans are going to go and buy a real guitar from a real guitar shop.'

Hugh Goldsmith, founder, Brightside: It definitely felt like pop was moving in the direction of a more guitar-driven sound at that time and both Busted and McFly were highly successful in capitalising on this in a big way. [Pop-rockers with excellent fringes] Rooster were the first artist I signed to Brightside, my new JV label with Sony/BMG, and there's no doubt that the success of Busted and Maroon 5 led my colleagues and I to think that a more rocky-sounding band could be successful in the market at that time. However, it was never our intention for the band to be as mainstream pop as groups like Busted or McFly because the guys in the band would not have felt comfortable in that lane. Their influences were artists like Led Zeppelin, Cream and others from that era.

Tom: Following on from us there were a few bands that tried to do it, like Rooster, but for some reason they just missed the bus by ten seconds.

Jenessa Williams: I think both Busted and McFly have laid incredibly clear foundations for future acts – without Busted, there would be no McFly, but without McFly, there would be no 5 Seconds of Summer or the Vamps. Even One Direction;

a lot of the styling and cheeky presentation in the early days really borrowed from that beachy-Britannia 'everylad' image that McFly did on their first album.

James: We had a bigger impact on this era of pop than any other band. We changed it. One year at Christmas I went to buy a guitar and a guy came up to me and was like, 'We've sold so many guitars and it's because of your band.' McFly were part of the Busted ripple effect. You've got these people that have been in the manufactured bands, the Simon Fuller bands, but Busted was this different thing. Given the time we were together – two years and three months – the impact of that is pretty unrivalled.

'They were creating the devil that was killing us'

While Busted were re-shaping the boyband parameters, their management team were keen to not just make another band in their mould via McFly, but to also get more mileage out of the more traditional boyband setup. Inevitably, it proved tricky, but not for want of trying, with V's only album, 2004's actually-very-good You Stood Up *(a number-86 smash), featuring production from the likes of Stargate, Xenomania and Mark Taylor.*

Peter Robinson: There'd been attempts [by Prestige] at a boyband before Busted called Skandal, with a K. They were a really old-school boyband and it hadn't really worked. Busted ended up being a huge success, McFly ended up being launched off the back of Busted, so that all fitted in. The management had created this weird situation where they could provide a band who were a reaction to their other band. They'd changed the tone of pop music to being about guitars, so they were like, 'Okay, what if we used one of these guitar bands to launch an old-fashioned boyband?'

Kevin McDaid, V: I saw the advert via *The Stage*. I sang really terribly at the audition because I was very nervous. I think I sang 'Flying Without Wings' by Westlife, which is ironic [Kevin would later date Westlife's Mark Feehily from 2005 to 2012]. I also had to do a little dance, which was the cringiest thing you can imagine. They just put a song on and I freestyled in a room with about fifty guys. Mortifying. I just pretended I was in the club. I was only seventeen so I probably shouldn't have been in clubs, but I was.

James: [Our managers at Prestige] Richard and Fletch were doing V. I really wasn't involved in it at all. I just knew they wanted to do a 'real' boyband.

Kevin: Busted were at their peak of their early success. But they were also the band that changed pop music. Danny from McFly was found at the V auditions. So it was bizarre that we were being put together at the same time. Music was massively changing – it was going very indie in terms of the credible side of things and then within pop music fans were seeing their favourites with instruments. So it was terrible timing for V. It did feel like there was a commitment there from [Prestige] to make it work, but they were creating the devil that was killing us.

Tom: What we couldn't see at the time was that Busted and McFly were helping this little shift in the perception of what pop music was. It was right at the back end of bands like Blue, who were having the last stages of their major success. All the boybands that were coming along like D-Side and Triple 8 were just not working. Busted and McFly just killed that type of boyband off.

James: I never understood [the move to create V] at the time. There were songs I'd written with Tom that they'd try to use to break V. There was one issue of *Smash Hits* that only featured Busted, McFly and V.

Jonathan Bown: I've got a reasonable head for remembering songs, but I'd struggle to name a V song.

Kevin: I literally felt like my dream had just come true. I used to watch *Top of the Pops* and think, 'How do I get from being in this living room to that show and doing music like that?' I just thought, 'Wow, this is it.' Then we moved to London. It was a five-bedroom, five-bathroom duplex modern apartment, but you're paying for it. The cost was taken out of our advance, like everything is. But you're not really told how that works.

Steve Anderson: I was signed to Universal back then and there was a writing camp put together and people were pitching songs. It was going to be the next big thing. It was very classy; it was live strings, it was beautiful production, it was Justin Timberlake-sounding.

Kevin: From the start, we were told, 'Look, boys, this is a phenomenon, worldwide smash, or it's nothing.' All or nothing, basically. We had a fantastic band and we had some great songs and we had what it takes to have gone further, but the timing wasn't on our side.

Steve Anderson: That [V writing camp] was very much, 'Let's just make an album really quickly.' If you have to make an album in three months then it's not the time to sit down with the five boys in the band and say, 'What do you want to sing about?'

Miranda Cooper: I think [V's second single] 'Hip to Hip' was a Moonbaby cast-off. That was very much us still learning how to record that many people. We were still in the trenches trying to be heard.

Brian Higgins: [V's management] were putting nice pressure on us. They were on Island, the same label as the Sugababes, so they would be really persistent about it and eventually we got them down [to Westerham]. It was difficult because we never really had the passion for a lot of these other projects. There was no passion like there was for Girls Aloud.

Kevin: We were on the road promoting [third single] 'You Stood Up' and we just knew it was done. We felt a pull back from the label straight away. Then the album came out and it bombed.

Felix Howard, co-writer, 'You Stood Up': I vomited something out in five minutes and it ended up on their album. I was very confused about that. It was a strange song anyway and it was even stranger that they sang it. By that point I was moving into A&R.

Kevin: We were dropped by our label and we literally had a week to move out of our home. It was as harsh as that. Nothing prepares you for when that rug is pulled from underneath you and how you deal with that on every single level. And with zero support. I refused to move back home, so I moved in with our choreographer Kate and stayed with her while I found my feet.

★ ★ ★

While McFly carried on until 2010, ironically scoring their lowest-charting album with *Above the Noise*'s dance-pop experiment, a career resurgence occurred when they joined forces with Matt and James in 2013 to form unholy pop-punk hybrid, McBusted. The success of their arena tour seemed to catch the attention of Charlie, who returned to Busted in 2015 for the knowingly titled Pigs Can Fly tour. A new album, 2016's *Night Driver*, saw the trio move into soft-focus synthpop. It didn't last long, with 2019's *Half Way There* leaning heavily into pop punk. McFly, meanwhile, reunited in 2019, releasing a new album, *Young Dumb Thrills*, a year later.

'It's kind of like being in school and school is not the place you come out in'

While the boyband evolved across the first half of the decade in terms of sound, style and success, one depressing constant remained. For gay band members like V's Kevin, it was decided it was much easier for them to stay in the closet, with the pressure of their bandmates' livelihoods resting on their shoulders should the 'inevitable' happen and a band's young, female audience turn their backs en masse. Even within the context of reality TV slowly breaking down barriers in terms of showcasing the full gamut of human existence, the pop industry, be it within bands or on music-focused TV, seemed to still be caught up on a decade-old falsehood.

Kevin: I had a conversation with my management and they asked me how I wanted to deal with my sexuality publicly. It was decided that we would almost neither confirm nor deny. But really that means you're denying it. By then, all the people interviewing me, whether it was mags or TV shows, all knew I was gay because I'd have drinks with them in bars afterwards. I wasn't hiding it. If journalists asked me who I fancied [in print], I just used to say Christina Aguilera because I was genuinely obsessed with her.

MNEK: The limited media and the limited knowledge was instrumental in [people staying in the closet]. *Smash Hits* and all the teen mags were appealing to young girls. That's what the research was saying. With that research and those results the label was like, 'Well, we're in a heteronormative world,' and obviously their aim is to sell shit. Some of these pop artists, it wasn't about expressing their soul or saying everything on their spirit, they were just trying to sing and dance and get this bag real quick. They're not trying to ruin a business, which they're constantly being told they will.

Brian Dowling: When I was first asked to present *SM:TV*, I was like '. . . the fucking show? On a Saturday morning? That's live!' I thought, 'Well, I'm a gay guy, this is a kids' television show' – I genuinely thought, 'Am I allowed?' I know that's a stupid thing to say. It hadn't been done before.

Kevin: We had a really interesting moment on *Popworld*. I've had this conversation with Simon [Amstell] since and it's a pretty bizarre moment to be put into because you wouldn't get away with it now. [Two of us from V] were doing an interview and Simon said, 'Oh, it's okay now to have gay members in a band, it's not an issue.' Then he was like, 'Now would be a good time if someone wanted to come out now, on TV.' We froze. He went on to say, 'Not both of you, just one of you.' I didn't get it at the time, it went straight over my head, but it was naughty because he knew I was gay. And they aired it on the show.

Paul Flynn: I always hated that Simon Amstell thing of 'tell me you're gay'. I would suspect that he regrets it now.

Brian Dowling: If you were a guy in a band, teenage girls had to fancy you to buy your records. But gay guys also buy pop music. I think it is so naïve of people. Also, if you have five guys in a band, chances are at least one of them would be bisexual or gay. It was record labels that were run by straight men that didn't think outside the straight box.

Kevin: I didn't know what to fucking do, I was a kid. I also had a responsibility for the boys' lives and careers; it wasn't just me. I didn't want to ruin the dreams of four other guys in my band. At the same time, I was unashamedly gay and I was very confident that I would not be going back into the closet.

Brian Dowling: [The producers] were very mindful of my private life, let's put it that way. They wanted my private life to remain private, even though I was openly gay and hosting a TV show. When I would go on a red carpet I'd be told, 'You can walk a red carpet on your own or if you want to bring a girlfriend.' I was dating my now husband back then and it was never acknowledged that I was in a relationship.

MNEK: I think about Mark Feehily and Stephen Gately and how for both men in those groups there was no safe space. It's kind of like being in school and school is not the safe space where you're ready to tell everyone you are gay because you don't know what's going to come next.

Brian Dowling: Back then it was label board meetings – 'Should they come out?' Sometimes people were forced to come out because newspapers had the story. People should never have done that.

Simon Jones: I was asleep and [Blue's] Duncan [James] called me about 4 a.m. He said he had something to tell me and said, 'I like boys as well as girls.' I was like, 'Okay, that's fine.' He was worried it would be a really big deal. Later a showbiz journalist called and said, 'I have a story that Duncan James is gay.' It was for the *News of the World* and they had a kiss-and-tell from this guy he'd been seeing. They did that age-old trick of, 'We don't want to run this story, in fact we're not going to run it, but we think it would be great if he came out and did it with us.' It is blackmail. Why have you done the interview if you're not going to run it? The reason is because you've got all the facts and you can hold it over us.

Brian Dowling: You had to conform to what gay version they wanted you to be. We'd have to go on CITV to promo *SM:TV Live* but my clothes were carefully picked for me. I'd be told to rein it in or don't be so excitable. And 'excitable' to me meant camp. It doesn't bother me now and I wouldn't hold those people accountable because they didn't know. I once got a chance to interview Britney Spears. Britney fucking Spears. I remember the next day in *The Sun* they removed the page-three girl and they had a huge picture of me and Britney and it said, 'Queen of

Pop meets Queen of TV'. I don't care how offensive that was. I did not fucking care.

Simon Jones: It made Duncan feel very unsettled that they had this interview in their back pockets. He hadn't come out; he hadn't told his family. You've started a chain of events now that can't stop. We didn't want to do it with the *News of the World*, but imagine if we hadn't. They'd have started a hate campaign. That's what these papers do. They rely on a culture of fear where the PR and celeb are too scared to go against them. If we had gone somewhere else their entire mission would have been to bring Duncan James down. We did the coming-out interview and it was fine. But would he have come out at that point? Probably not.

Brian Dowling: It was very much like I was taking on a different character. They were fearful. I remember someone locked myself and [co-host] Tess [Daly] in a room to stop me from shooting *Celebrity Streetmate* for Children in Need. They had said, 'We can't really see you being gay,' etc. and then I'm booked on a show looking for men. Tess and I were howling. But also really panicked. I was banging on the door saying, 'You open this mother-fucking door now.' The door was opened and I went and did it. It was a very odd situation to be in. In a way, I found that I couldn't express myself any more. I wanted to live my best gay life.

11

'Have you ever been hungover on morning TV?'

Drinking isn't big and it isn't clever, obviously, but it can be amusing to think of pop stars utilising a mask of respectability to hide a monstrous hangover on, say, *CD:UK*. While their indie counterparts were almost assumed to be having wild nights out and living the rock 'n' roll lifestyle to the fullest, pop's coterie of early twentysomethings were either shamed for doing the same or assumed to be tucked up in bed learning their songs. For some there simply wasn't time to have a proper night out, while for others an early morning start was the perfect excuse not to go to bed. All rise? More like one (more) for sorrow.

'Someone was trying to give me an injection to make me stop throwing up'

Louise: It's one thing that people don't always know about me, but I love a tequila. Always have, always will. I have been totally hungover on *CD:UK*. People thought that if you were in the world of pop you didn't go out and party, but of course you did. The Met Bar had my name written all over it.

Bradley, S Club 7: I partied enough for two lifetimes. I'd party until 3 or 4 a.m., get home and my driver would be waiting outside my house. I'd literally run in, have a quick shower – or a cat lick as they say – and then get in the car, have a nap, get to the TV studio and crawl under the table with a pillow I'd brought with me. Then I'd do it all again that night. I don't know how I'm still alive, to be honest with you.

Mutya, Sugababes: I was the worst. How I looked at things was, 'Okay, my call time is 4 a.m., I'll do hair and make-up at 5 a.m., so if I want to go out I can go straight from the rave to the *GM:TV* studio, there are showers, and then get ready.' If I'd have gone home I would have just gone to sleep. That was the lifestyle back then. You'd go to the clubs in central London and you'd bump into everybody. I went [to the Met Bar] a couple of times but I was more about Propaganda, Pop, Chinawhite. I was in the in-crowd.

Christian, A1: They worked us so hard that there just wasn't time. It did happen – we had parties and got drunk – but most of the time I would look at the calendar and think, 'If I drink tonight, when is the next day I can sleep in?' It would be in two months.

Nadine Coyle, Girls Aloud: Back then I couldn't hold my drink – it was like two drinks and I was done for. Do you remember [ITV's] *Grease Mania*? I was throwing up on the stage during soundcheck. Oh, God, it was horrendous. Someone from LWT was trying to give me an injection to make me stop throwing up. Something to relax my muscles because I was just vomiting and vomiting. But it made it so that I just threw up really relaxed. I can see the hangover when I watch those clips.

Kelli Young, Liberty X: Most people were hungover on *CD:UK*.

Tony Lundon, Liberty X: I definitely recall being badly hungover on *This Morning*. It was the day after we'd done our number-one celebrations [for 'Just a Little'] and Lorraine Kelly was interviewing us. I vaguely recall Kevin [Simm] closing his eyes on live TV beside me.

H, Steps: We didn't go home. *SM:TV* was like opening a dressing-up box on Saturday morning. It was hangover TV, for the viewers and for us.

Brian Dowling: One time I got drunk and fell down a flight of stairs at a party. I was so shit-faced. I had done a tan and I didn't have time to wash it off. So I had to go to Cat [Deeley]'s dressing room and use her shower – don't think mine had a shower. Tess [Daly] was like, 'You fucking stink of alcohol.' I only did it once in two years because it's just not worth it on live TV.

Una Healy, the Saturdays: We never really went out. We were always fresh and bushy-tailed because we never had time to go out. We weren't a hungover band.

Ritchie, Five: You think about it, you're seventeen. Prior to this you've been raiding coin jars in your mum's house to get a couple of Hoochs or Mad Dog 20/20s. Then all of a sudden you're going to these industry parties where the whole bar is just free wine. You're downing it. I probably should have thought, 'I'm in a band, there's media here, I should probably not have too much to drink,' but it was the '90s, man!

James, Busted: Those 5 a.m. starts meant we hadn't gone to bed. You'd just get in the car and go. I had an Addison Lee driver shout at me once because he thought I was a slob. I was asleep and we got to the studio and he was like, 'WAKE UP! GET OUT OF THE CAR, YOU'RE HERE.' He was telling me off.

Kevin, V: I actually went out with my TV plugger of all people to a party and I had *Blue Peter* the next morning. I went on without a wink of sleep and reeking of booze. I felt like death all day and then we had to walk through this paper thing and smash it. When I watched it back on TV it didn't even show me. I could have just been in bed.

Lee, 911: I wasn't a really big drinker, so I wasn't hungover, but I was just terrible with mornings. So we'd park our tour bus outside *The Big Breakfast* or something at 2 a.m. and then get woken up to go on the show. They used to want you in really early, even if we weren't on for four hours.

Natalie Appleton, All Saints: I had a very embarrassing morning on *CD:UK* once. We were talking to Ant and Dec and we all had sunglasses on because we couldn't see. We went to a commercial break and I had to go because I couldn't breathe, it was really bad, and I got this phone call from my mum being like, 'What's the matter with you!' Then they came back from the break and I wasn't there. Our hairdresser was throwing up in the toilet. I was throwing up before we actually went live. Mortifying.

Daizy Agnew, Girls Can't Catch: We did a Radio 1 interview the day after a night out with JLS. We partied with them, then we went back to the A&R guy's house and got a car home at 5 a.m. Then I slept in until about 2 p.m. and did a Radio 1 interview. We were a bit wild, to be honest. We'd go out loads. We bumped into Dane Bowers quite a bit so we'd go to his afterparties. I was literally living the rock 'n' roll life and I do not regret that.

Liz, Atomic Kitten: It wasn't always because we were leading the party lifestyle; it was more because we had the chance to grab a drink after an insane day. Then you'd only have two hours' sleep. There was one night where we were allotted forty minutes for sleep. That included G-A-Y and a *CD:UK*.

Natasha, Atomic Kitten: Either me or Jenny would be asleep under the make-up table or trying to find a dark corner to sleep in.

Jenny, Atomic Kitten: Oh my God, I used to be unable to speak. I wouldn't have slept. I'd go there absolutely hungover. Honestly, I'm so embarrassed by some of the states I got in. I remember the doorbell went once and we'd all be partying and I'd be like, 'Oh, the neighbours are complaining again,' and it would be, 'No, it's your driver, you're going to work.'

Claire, Steps: I might have been [hungover on TV] a couple of times. One year, I think it was the year we got our award [in 2000], the BRITs were on a Friday and we had to do *SM:TV* the next morning. I'd had an hour's sleep and I was absolutely hanging. I was still drunk. We were performing 'Deeper Shade of Blue' and wearing leather and studs and stuff. I remember feeling really hot and very aware that I must have stank. I have this memory of being there that day and standing next to Geri Halliwell. She looked up at me and went, 'Oh, you're really pretty, aren't you?' I thought that was nice at first, but then I thought it was a bit weird. Did she think I was some kind of monster before?

* Natalie Appleton quotes taken from my interview for *Guardian Guide*, 21 July 2018

12

Popstars, *Pop Idol* and the explosion of TV talent shows

Originally started in 1999 in New Zealand and eventually sold to fifty countries, the *Popstars* format revolutionised British popular culture when series one launched in January 2001. Suddenly pop music was Saturday-night entertainment, and everyday people – already tabloid catnip thanks to the emerging *Big Brother* – were being transformed into superstars on a weekly basis. Unlike the plethora of other TV talent shows that followed in its wake, from *Pop Idol* to *Fame Academy* to *The X Factor*, *Popstars* was presented as a rudimentary documentary as opposed to a glittering live show that required a voting public. All the decisions in regards to who would make the winning band were to be made by its three judges: TV producer and proto-Simon-Cowell, 'Nasty' Nigel Lythgoe; Polydor A&R Paul Adam; and the Spice Girls' former PR, Nicki Chapman. While the first six episodes followed the audition process and the eventual creation of Hear'Say, AKA Myleene Klass, Kym Marsh, Noel Sullivan, Danny Foster and Suzanne Shaw, the second half of the series followed the band living together, doing interviews and recording. The final episode, the only one shown live, captured their reaction to debut single 'Pure and Simple' crashing into the charts at number one.

'I still have the odd person telling me they voted for me'

While the show's format dictated there would only be one ultimate winner, its success soon created a splinter group. For Kelli Young, Michelle Heaton, Tony Lundon, Kevin Simm and Jessica Taylor, who would form Liberty (later Liberty X), they represented another soon-to-be-TV-talent-show-staple; the lucky 'loser' who, outside of the full-beam glare, could quietly make success work for them.

Craig McLean, journalist, *The Face*: Obviously the paradigm now is that TV shows make pop stars but back then TV shows had not made pop stars. *Pop Idol* hadn't come, *The X Factor* hadn't come, so *Popstars* was the first one. Suddenly mainstream television was making bands and the show was shining a light on the hitherto secret backroom behaviour of your Svengalis.

Colin Barlow: Lucian Grainge had been approached by Granada television and a guy called Nigel Lithgow who had put *Popstars* together. Lucian agreed to do the deal to be the record label. Then Paul Adam, who worked with me at the time, was asked to be one of the judges. I don't think we realised at the time that it was a life-changing thing. Pop music was big but it had never got to that level of becoming Saturday-night television. It was a phenomenon. The single sold a million copies in two weeks.

Myleene: I had initially seen the auditions in *The Stage*. It later transpired that when I was working at LWT as a backing vocalist on *The Lily Savage Show*, the auditions were happening in the same building. I had to go.

Kelli Young, Liberty X: At the time, I had been auditioning for *Lion King*, the musical. I was down to my final recall for the main part and so I knew when the *Popstars* audition date was but it clashed with my recall. Then on the morning I just woke up and felt that I had to go to the *Popstars* audition. Proper *Sliding Doors* moment.

Myleene: I was told by one of the producers of the show I would definitely have guaranteed work for the next six weeks minimum and over Christmas, which for a jobbing musician was brilliant news. I turned down the role of Mary Magdalene in Andrew Lloyd Webber's *Jesus Christ Superstar* as I had just done a year in the West End in *Miss Saigon*. I wanted a new challenge away from doing the same thing every day.

Tony Lundon, Liberty X: I was living in London and the plan was to learn how to write and produce music. I was running out of funds because it wasn't really working. Before I went back to Ireland to go to university to study law, my mum called and said, 'You should check this *Popstars* thing out, as your last-ditch attempt.' So I did.

Myleene: My family thought I was mad; one job was guaranteed, the other wasn't financially stable. Then the TV company started making dolls of us and it felt like it could go on a bit longer than six weeks.

Peter Robinson: You think about what TV talent shows are like now, and then you look at an old episode of [*Popstars*], it was like it was shot on zero budget. It's also the pacing of it and the colours in it and the personalities. The whole thing is incredibly flat for what was early Saturday-night television. It's just a documentary.

Myleene: People have forgotten how crude and bare the initial shows were. A real reflection of true auditions; makeshift chairs, extendable tables, grotty rehearsal rooms. They've forgotten the original format to the extent I still have the odd person telling me they voted for me and I haven't the heart to break it to them. The shows are so ingrained in how we understand and consume this form of media, these talent shows, that they are endlessly parodied and all get lumped into one.

Colin Barlow: I also did *Fame Academy* [in 2002], which was more like *Big Brother*. The BBC had them filmed in the house so you watched them doing loads of things as it went on. I think *Fame Academy* is one of the most underrated talent shows. Lemar, Alex Parks, David Sneddon – there were some really great people on that show.

Tony: I wasn't experienced with auditions – I'd only done one before. I had no reference point or expectations. I was definitely impressed with the level of production we were dealing with. I got a sense that if a broadcaster is placing that much of a priority on it, it's going to be a big TV show. I obviously had no idea it would help spawn a whole host of other TV shows and a whole generation of pop acts.

Kelli: We all had to sing '. . . Baby One More Time', hence why Darius [Danesh] did that. We all had to sing it but Darius's version obviously became the most famous.

Tony: I remember we all had to sing a track of our choosing and I hadn't done very well in the previous round and so I sang a U2 song that I felt comfortable with. I definitely did not do a rendition of '. . . Baby One More Time', that much I can tell you.

Peter Robinson: I was at *NME* at that point and running the pop part of their website. At the time, we were around the corner from LWT so they'd bike over the VHS tapes and we got a call once saying, 'Darius is around, do you want to interview him?' He'd just been kicked out so we did a video interview with him. I bumped into him a few weeks later on the Underground and he was struggling with a suitcase and he'd broken his arm. It just seemed like the really sad decline of Darius . . . Then the next thing you knew he was back on TV [being amazing on *Pop Idol*].

Lucie Cave: It was all about the underdogs with *Heat*, so we put Darius on the cover. He was one of the biggest talking points. In the same way that later on we'd put the Cheeky Girls on the cover.

'I would say the politics that lie behind that decision can't have been too pretty'

It's easy to argue the near irrelevance of the actual music when it comes to TV talent shows. For decades prior, pop acts had clamoured for attention via magazines and performances on more niche TV shows aired early in the morning or just after tea on a Thursday night. Personalities would have to leap off the pages or emerge instantly during a three-minute performance, but in the world of TV talent shows the fame game was flipped on its head; instant exposure meant you were famous before you'd really done anything. Still, the show's winners would need a song and something that would chime with a pop world shuffling away from the brightly coloured hues of Steps (who were on the verge of splitting) and S Club 7. The answer, as it turned out, lay not in the vault of some super-producer or on the nib of a white-hot songwriter's pen, but as an album track on pop flop Girl Thing's debut album.

Kelli: I remember the second round of auditions they put us into groups and everyone had to sing 'Never Ever' by All Saints. And when you listen to 'Pure and Simple' and 'Never Ever' they're not a million miles apart.

Peter Robinson: 'Pure and Simple' was on Radio 2 recently and I thought, 'This is better than I would expect it to sound now, but also not very good.' Both those things at the same time. In that kind of weird post-Spice Girls, pre-Girls Aloud era of pop music, which in hindsight wasn't always very good, when I first heard 'Pure and Simple' I thought, 'That's good.' It's just not amazing.

James Masterton: The talent shows helped to ensure that the end of the CD single era had one final huge exclamation point. It's interesting that it was timed to climax in the spring, because that was considered a nice easy, fallow time, when there wasn't much competition around.

Craig McLean: There was feverish anticipation for that single, but from *The Face*'s point of view they were still trying to be the place that would tell you first about things. Which was slowly being eroded by the early arrival of the internet. While we couldn't be the first to tell you about *Popstars*, or indeed the band, we could be the first people to tell you the story of what these people were like. That's why I spent a week with them; going to *CD:UK*, on the video set and some dance rehearsals. It felt like a cultural phenomenon and we could be the first people to pick it apart.

Myleene: I remember [first hearing 'Pure and Simple'] really well as it wasn't even our song. It belonged to a band called Girl Thing. I would say the politics that lie behind that decision can't have been too pretty. I also remember a lot of the producers we worked with couldn't read music and thought it was mad I could hear what notes were missing for harmonies or chords. I couldn't believe I'd tortured myself at music school for so long when maybe I hadn't needed to.

Chris Herbert: [As well as managing Girl Thing and, later, Hear'Say] I also managed 'Pure and Simple''s songwriters, so Pete Kirtley and Tim Hawes, who wrote it with Alison Clarkson, AKA Betty Boo. So I put them to work with Girl Thing and they came up with 'Pure and Simple'.

Peter Robinson: I'd brought the Girl Thing album on import on CD – great days – and their original version of 'Pure and Simple' on that sounded like a 'Never Ever' rip-off. I guess that was the point of it. It does strike you as strange that for the most focused-on and most exciting pop band in the country at that point, they just found a song that already existed.

Jodi Albert: 'Pure and Simple' was earmarked as our third single.

Chris Herbert: [Simon Cowell] was in limbo, deciding what the next [Girl Thing] single was going to be or whether there even was going to be a next single. I was lobbying for 'Pure and Simple'. This went on for ages and the writers were getting frustrated because they knew it was a hit and it was going to end up sitting on a shelf somewhere. Meanwhile, I was managing Hear'Say and we were looking for a first single, so we played 'Pure and Simple' to Paul Adam and he was like, 'This is brilliant, this is the first single.' The songwriters were like, 'Yeah, absolutely.'

Colin Barlow: [Girl Thing] were not doing that well and I think the songwriters at the time got the opportunity to put a song on the biggest TV show in the country.

Peter Robinson: The song was already out there, so if a song's been released you can cover it. It's also what happened in America with 'Year 3000' and the Jonas Brothers [who released a cover of the Busted song in 2006].

Chris Herbert: That was the thing. Simon Cowell could have blocked it if it hadn't come out on the Australian album. He held the master. But we just rerecorded it as a cover. I was under massive pressure from Simon Cowell saying, 'You need to take control, this can't happen,' and at that point I was like, 'I'm in complete conflict here: I manage the songwriters,

I manage both bands, I'm going to have to step away and you guys can fight this out yourselves.' Anyway, Simon didn't win; the songwriters did. It went on to be the fastest-selling debut single.

Peter Robinson: Thinking about it from Girl Thing's label's perspective, if you wanted to drop a band and avoid a difficult conversation, saying to them, 'Ooh, yeah, we were going to put a lot of money and effort behind this but, sorry, that song's gone so we can't do that now' would be a nice way of getting out of the conversation.

'We had people pranking us, going through our bins and putting hexes on our lawn!'

Before 'Pure and Simple' could be released, the process of whittling down the brave young souls continued. By episode five, with the final ten chosen, ratings reached 11.35 million. Episode six, shown just a few hours later, was watched by 12.63 million as the final band was unveiled and the members of what was becoming Liberty X were told the bad news. The TV phenomenon was also rapidly becoming a tabloid one, a state heightened even more when Nasty Nigel started earning that moniker via some appalling comments about Kym Marsh's body. As a documentary showing the mechanics of the music industry, Popstars *was also succeeding in showing some fairly unsavoury aspects of its treatment of women.*

Kelli: For the final section of the auditions, we had to stay in a hotel in London for a few days. I remember forming real friendships with certain people. Tony was one of them. I started putting my dream band together in my head.

Myleene: At the time, we were running alongside *Big Brother* and the formats of getting to know real people on a 24-hour basis felt new, risky, cutting edge. It was a completely alien idea for me. At music college you're drilled that whatever happens, the show must go on, keep up a professional front, smile even if everything is crumbling. Suddenly I was in a world where everyone was crying in the auditions or in the waiting room, revealing their vulnerabilities, their fears, their family's personal predicaments. We were being followed by cameras all the way home as we gave a blow-by-blow account of whether we'd received a callback or not. The anticipation, the cliff hangers, the added adrenaline of our fellow auditionees and our own families was like a pressure cooker. If you messed up the words, you didn't just make them up and carry on. It was dissected and a massive drama was built around it. It went against everything I knew.

Tony: The crew came over to Galway. They were with me for at least a day before they gave me the news. In that twenty-four hours it was pretty evident I wasn't getting in the band. Nasty Nigel came over with a director from the series, who was this heavy-set guy. I remember my mum put a plate of freshly baked scones on the table when they arrived and they couldn't really eat. They were all picking at it. My mum said to me, 'Well, the big lad's not eating, you're not getting in the band.' Nasty Nigel was well versed in hiding his emotions, if he had any, which I'm assuming he did.

Myleene: I got my break in the band when the rehearsal pianist didn't show up one day. People were panicking in front of me that they couldn't run their music, they didn't know the key, they were tail spinning. I went back to my day job and started rehearsing with them. It was then that Nicki Chapman said, 'You never told us you could play the piano.' It had never occurred to me to mention it. Getting into the band was an amazing feeling but I still didn't really know what it actually meant or what was ahead of me.

Kelli: I personally was disappointed [not to be picked for Hear'Say]. However, when they started to put stuff out, I understood why they didn't pick me. They had a vision for what that band was going to be and I didn't fit into that. It was not the kind of music I would have wanted to do.

Myleene: We moved into 'the *Popstar* house' and lived together for months. It was brilliant for us to do as a band but we were vulnerable. Overnight fame and no security at the house meant we had people pranking us, going through our bins and putting hexes on our lawn! It was also a crash back to reality when you turned over a painting or picture hanging on the wall to see a number written in sharpie because it was all from a prop company. We were literally living on a set with microphones hidden in teapots. It was surreal.

Kelli: They didn't know each other and they were thrown together really quickly. Having to gel as housemates as well as professionally. Kym felt she had to lie about having kids throughout the whole process otherwise she would never have been chosen to be in the group, which I think is probably accurate.

Lucie Cave: Now that would be a reason to put her in the band. You'd want that inclusivity. Things have changed so much. Remember Jade in *Big Brother* and people calling her a pig? The newspapers were saying 'burn the pig' and even Graham Norton would dress as a pig on his show talking about Jade. That would never happen now. It was just that sort of cultural landscape at the time and I guess the outcome of everyone being able to be famous meant that everyone could own a piece and say what they wanted about them.

Craig McLean: [Before *Popstars*] we'd never seen ordinary unknown people have their lives suddenly blown apart on stage. Kym Marsh taken to task for being a single mother and being told her bum's too big on television. We'd never cared about quote-unquote ordinary people. Pop artists before the show were extraordinary, but *Popstars* the TV show made the ordinary extraordinary.

Hannah Verdier: Hear'Say were an example of the way women were treated. Nasty Nigel saying, 'Kym, Christmas is coming and the goose is still fat.' It was abuse. The way the girls from Hear'Say were treated was shocking.

Colin Barlow: It was a time when those situations were mass tabloid news. We had this fantastic office in Chiswick and you'd have blacked-out cars driving them in for meetings because you'd have *The Sun*'s photographers outside.

Hallgeir Rustan: [Working with] Hear'Say was madness. Viewers who had followed *Popstars* didn't know the final line-up, so before it was announced the whole band was staying in Trondheim, recording the songs in Stargate Studios. Some British paparazzi had figured out the plan and set themselves up outside the studio. We had to smuggle the band in and out the back doors of the studio and we had to have security guards at the front doors.

Myleene: For a couple of weeks we wore masks as we jumped in and out of our Previa – the car of choice for all bands – going from studios to meetings to shoots. It was like regressing, being a kid again. I get why youngsters in the music industry lose their minds. You get treated like a child and so you start acting like one. We were told we were the fattest band in pop countless times so we made a point of eating numerous bars of chocolate and fast food in defiance. We played Knock Down Ginger on No. 10. It was Tony Blair's time and his son Euan opened the door while we stood there covered in face paint feeling a bit stupid, then slid down his banisters when they let us in. Less rock 'n' roll, more juvenile. We were idiots. We had a tribute band, Near'Say, that would follow us around in their own van. Can you imagine our Previa, a secondary van behind us of 'lookalikes', then paparazzi on bikes and sometimes police outriders, too? Crazy times.

Tony: Going back to normal life [after not making the band] for me was going back to London. I was working part-time, but we were put on a retainer and asked in return not to speak about the results. I suddenly had a few months where there was a wage coming in for doing nothing apart from keeping my trap shut.

Craig McLean: They were waiting in the wings to take the place of anyone who failed.

Tony: We were in a contract with LWT and so there must have been an option to swap us in if something went wrong [with a member of Hear'Say].

Kelli: As [the show] started to get more and more popular we started getting approached a lot by journalists or people in the street asking if we were in the band. We'd signed NDAs so we couldn't say anything. But it was getting harder and harder to keep it a secret. We were starting to become famous, so it was a really weird experience because week by week, the ratings were massive but we were just not protected at all. I was getting paparazzi outside college taking photos of me. I had experiences of paps going through my bins at home. We were just watching it all unfold like the public were, but with all the knowledge.

Craig McLean: Everybody in the country was watching the TV show. This was before social media, barely any internet, so you could only go by TV ratings and this was the dominant thing. It felt like it was a pop culture revolution happening on a Saturday evening.

Tony: It was weird when the show started airing because I definitely didn't realise our faces would be in *The Sun*. I was really uncomfortable at that time about not being in control of how people perceived me.

Kelli: The only people we could speak to about what we were experiencing was [the members of what would become Liberty X]. We started calling each other: 'This just happened to me,' or 'Oh my God, Michelle's just been chased down the street.' Then we were getting interview requests and ITV were sending us out in twos and threes to do little interviews.

Tony: As soon as the [Hear'Say] reveal happened, we were brought out as the 'flopstars' and I remember feeling pretty used. We were essentially promoting the show while Hear'Say were in with stylists.

Peter Robinson: Thinking about it, is *Popstars* not only the first but also the last true exciting pop show like that? Because there was genuine jeopardy; you either win or you can fuck off. Later it would become the narrative that actually you don't want to win *The X Factor*, you want to come second. Because then you don't have to do all this stuff and you can find your own voice. With *Popstars* it genuinely did seem that you'll either win it or you're nobody. I suppose all game shows need to have some sense of jeopardy.

Tony: I remember it being written into the contract that if anybody did go off and sign a record deal that you would be under the umbrella, shall we say, of LWT. I don't know if I'm still under an NDA, but I'm going to presume no one gives a shit and that they won't come after me.

Kelli: Tony and I were the only ones who lived in London, so there were a couple of occasions where I invited everyone to stay at my place. Through that we bonded even more. One time we were booked to go on *Lorraine* and the night before Kevin had a radio interview to do. He happened to say, 'Well, I'm staying at Kelli's, there's a few of us here,' and they asked us to sing something all together. So we did and we just looked at each other like, 'Wow, we actually sound really good.'

Tony: The level of profile we had been afforded gave us an opportunity.

Kelli: They'd done all the hard work for us. They'd picked ten people that included a baritone, an alto, a soprano, like all the pieces of the puzzle were there. We ended up going on *Lorraine* and she asked us what we planned to do next and one of us just blurted out that we were thinking of being a band ourselves. ITV went mad because that was not part of their plan at all. At that time, Hear'Say hadn't even released a single, so the last thing they wanted was competition. What was lovely about forming what became Liberty ourselves was that we were able to steer the ship. We didn't have that manufactured pop bubble situation. We were real rebels because we did it all on ITV's time. It was mortifying for them that we used the platform to announce we were going to be a band ourselves.

Colin Barlow: Hear'Say was a phenomenon. I don't think anyone at Polydor appreciated how big it was.

Chris Herbert: We didn't know what to expect. We knew it had a decent TV audience but none of us knew that would convert into sales. It felt like uncharted territory and so bloody exciting. I remember the morning the single hit radio, I was driving at the time and I flicked through four stations and it was playing simultaneously across all of them.

Colin Barlow: It was that big that Hear'Say performed on the BRITs.

Myleene: I remember the booing from the music industry got pretty loud. We just sang louder. I also remember that someone said our styling was dreadful and that we looked like we'd just left an office party. For me it was next level. I met Beyoncé, got an autograph from Eminem – he signed it 'To Marlene from Marshall Mathers' – and seeing as I was actually booked to have sung backing vocals for Robbie Williams but was now appearing in my own right, I had the time of my life.

Kelli: All of us are northern, bar Tony who is Irish, and I remember we couldn't think of a band name and someone said, 'We're just us five, aren't we?' So we toyed with being called Us Five for a bit but it didn't sit right. I can't remember where Liberty came from. It stuck because we felt free.

'I really like Will Young, but you can't mention him in the same breath as the Jam'

While the members of Liberty X navigated record-deal meetings with some of pop's biggest players, their victors were starting to deal with the first waves of a backlash. While Big Brother *allowed the viewers control,* Popstars *presented its winners fully formed, encouraging a sense of, 'Who do you think you are?' when the inevitable pop-star makeover took place. Meanwhile, Simon Fuller, a keen fan of* Popstars, *was tweaking the format for his own TV talent show,* Pop Idol. *Arriving seven months after the release of 'Pure and Simple', the first season of* Pop Idol *– which, like* Popstars: The Rivals *after it, did include live shows and public votes –*

gave the world Will Young. An auditions-circuit veteran, having previously auditioned for future Pop Idol *judge Simon Cowell on* This Morning *alongside Lee Ryan, Will would later stand out not just for his silky voice but for his ability to stand up to Cowell. Unlike* Popstars, Pop Idol *was keen to not only find one winner, but as many acts as possible. It's where* Popstars *reject Darius Danesh finally came good, finishing third behind Will and Gareth Gates and eventually scoring that coveted number-one single with 'Colourblind' in 2002. Sadly, Darius died in August 2022, aged forty-one.*

Tony: We started being brought [by LWT] to various meetings, the most memorable of which was with Pete Waterman. I remember we were with Pete and he was talking to us at length about his success with Steps. We were played some tunes that as young people we wouldn't really have bought into. We made a point that we didn't want to be another Steps because Pete kept referring to them. Essentially it didn't end well.

Kelli: We had a meeting with a particular, now very famous, A&R. He asked us our vision for the group, what kind of music we wanted to do and how we wanted to look. Tony tended to be more of the spokesman of the group, so he said we wanted to go more down the R&B/pop route. We left the meeting and our representative at the time came out to talk to us and said, 'He's really enamoured with you, he's really interested in signing you, however, he'd rather sign the group without Kelli as he feels like she is steering things down the R&B route and he doesn't think that's where you guys sit in the marketplace.' Then it was, 'But don't worry, we can find opportunities for Kelli, she can do her own R&B thing, but for the rest of you I think it would be better if you went your own way as a pop group without Kelli.'

Tony: The assumption Kelli was behind our sound happened a lot. I don't mind naming names; we went to see Simon Cowell. I very much remember Kelli answering some questions and I answered some. Simon referenced the Spice Girls and that most recent R&B album [2000's *Forever*] that hadn't performed well commercially. I was quite surprised to learn afterwards that Nigel had taken Kelli aside and said there was a solo opportunity for her and that maybe the other four [of us] would have a separate deal. Pete Waterman was mentioned in regards to producing [the band]. I definitely didn't want to do the Pete Waterman thing.

Kelli: I remember saying to the others, 'If that's what you guys want to do, I'm not going to hold the four of you back.' That was a real bonding experience for us. It was a collective vision we had. That was one of the experiences that made us realise we were all on the same page. No one was going to separate us from one another.

Tony: We would have been malleable and open to experienced producers and people we respected. Not that we didn't respect Pete Waterman or Simon Cowell, but they were of an era. The stuff they were playing us didn't feel like we would be more than a one-hit wonder. A quick hit and then consigned to the dustbin. I would rather do something else and fail than a Fast Food Rockers song.

Myleene: The first time I ever appeared on *Top of the Pops* it was as a backing vocalist for Cliff Richard and that blew my mind. To go there in my own right, not standing behind anyone, was next level. Being in *Smash Hits* and all the mags we shot, can you imagine, growing up reading and watching it all and then actually standing in your own dream. It doesn't feel real. We also learned about the snobbery of publications or their readers. The uproar when we were on the cover of *The Face* and *NME*. The biggest band of its time, the dawn of a new era of music, and grown men were complaining and sending letters of complaint and death threats. Mad.

Craig McLean: We did Hear'Say at *The Face* in that sweet spot where anticipation was everything, but it was moving so fast already that you could see the sweetness turning sour. They'd been in the bubble of a TV studio and a TV show and suddenly they were being thrust into the public arena. At that video shoot there was a video crew filming the video and there was a *CD:UK* video crew filming the video crew filming the band. Pop was eating itself very quickly.

Peter Robinson: The *NME* were already doing [Hear'Say on the cover] and they came to me because I'd been covering them a lot on the website. The headline from it was, 'The band that killed pop'. That it would change the way pop worked. And it did. Because it had been made like a documentary and so therefore happened in the past, it was more like a *Masked Singer* thing of it all being this secret. *Pop Idol* built on that by turning it into more of a live thing and doing the battle-bus stuff around the country with Will and Gareth, but what was happening on *Popstars* felt, in the world of pop music, like an incredibly exciting thing. What people didn't realise was that it was going to pretty much put in motion the decimation of pop music A&R in this country and the pop music press.

Pete Waterman, judge on *Pop Idol*: [TV talent shows] were very new then. Very unusual. I guess we really didn't know what we were doing. But once we got the gist of what was going on, we really enjoyed it. It was bloody boring though, Christ. Being there for fourteen hours some days listening to absolute crap was a bit difficult. Some days you'd go in and sit there for six or seven hours without seeing one act that was any good.

Lucie Cave: With Hear'Say, the boys were really boring and the girls were much more interesting and they became celebrities in their own right. The soap opera of their love lives quickly overtook what they'd done music-wise; Kym and Jack Ryder, there was Suzanne and Love Rat Darren Day. We'd always coin names for people and that would stick. Darren Day was always Love Rat Darren Day and whenever we talked about Will Young it was What Ho Will Young because he was so posh.

Paul Flynn: Gareth was so perfect, so no one expected Will to win.

Pete Waterman: [It was always] Will for me. This is the reason *Pop Idol* was such a good show because Simon was fully convinced Gareth was his man and I always knew that Will was going to be the winner because I saw the public's reaction.

Dania Pasquini: We directed Gareth Gates' 'Unchained Melody' video. He ended up being the runner-up. Here's the thing, though: Simon gives us a call and says, 'I want you guys to film either the winner's video or the runner-up's video and you're going to go to Florida and I'm going to let you know who has won while you're flying over there.' So we get the call and we're doing Gareth Gates. Then we're told it's 'Unchained Melody'. So we basically came up with the idea on the plane. We landed and Gareth was flown in.

James Masterton: Will Young's debut single ['Evergreen/Anything Is Possible'] was released a full week after the final had aired, simply to give the label enough time to manufacture enough CDs. He then became the first person to sell a million copies of a single in the first week. That was the final exclamation point of the CD era pre-downloads.

Chris Cowey: I thought [TV talent shows] were a useful source of manufactured pop music. It replaced stuff that was in the same genre, that was pure pop. We did lock horns once when Will Young had won *Pop Idol* and the record company wanted to have Will on the same [episode of *TOTP*] as Gareth Gates, but they wanted him to do two songs. I just said no. The plugger who was looking after him said, 'But, Chris, this is the first act since Frankie Goes to Hollywood or the Jam that has had this kind of effect.' I really like Will Young, but you can't mention him in the same breath as the Jam. I said no and management withdrew his availability.

Paul Flynn: Will came out the first week *Pop Idol* finished [in March 2002]. But he'd sort of outed himself very cleverly on the show. They asked that classic 'who would you most like to go on a date with?' question and Will said the Queen Mother. The gayest answer ever.

Brian Dowling: He was out to all his family and friends. There was no secret and there was reassurance in that sense. I remember the first time we met we didn't talk. It was odd. I think we were aware we were two gay guys that had come from two huge reality TV shows. I was very mindful of people getting the wrong idea. I remember seeing him and thinking, 'I have felt everything you are going through.'

Paul Flynn: The thing with Will was he was very rare in the pop market at the time. He had a university degree and nobody did. Finding your way in the music industry was university for those kids. So they hadn't had that contemplative time to lose themselves and find themselves. Will knew who he was. And his identity was a gay identity recognisable from that time. He knew the sadness of being gay at that time and he knew the happiness of it. I think at that time he was the first person to have the first release coincide with him being out. Laws were changing around that time for gay people, too [Section 28 was repealed in Scotland in 2000 and three years later in England and Wales]. Equality was on its way to happening in Britain and that has real-world consequences. I remember having a conversation with my mum about Will and thinking, 'Oh my God, you want him to be my boyfriend.' That was the role he had for Marks & Spencer's Britain.

Pete Waterman: By [*Pop Idol* season two], Simon had lost it. He didn't want to do it any more. That's why I walked off [after Michelle McManus was announced as the winner]; it was a joke. The public could see it was nonsense and there's a point where you can't cheat the public. You have to take it seriously. As Bill Shankly said, 'It's more serious than death.' You're asking people to give you their pocket money. If you don't take that seriously then you shouldn't be doing it.

'What started to happen was this pendulum swing and we became the antithesis to Hear'Say'

Hear'Say's fall from their pedestal was vertiginously steep. While their chart-topping debut album Popstars *had shifted 300,000 copies in its first week, second single 'The Way to Your Love''s first week sales of 75,000 were substantially down on 'Pure and Simple''s opening gambit of 500,000. While that sort of decline made sense given they were no longer being beamed into living rooms every week, to the media it was a clear sign their time was over. Nine months after their debut, the band released their second album,* Everybody, *which peaked at number twenty-four. In January 2002, Kym Marsh quit, replaced for one single by Lisa Scott-Lee's husband Johnny Shentall, who won his place via, you guessed it, a televised audition process. It was while promoting that single, 'Lovin' Is Easy', that the band started to receive abuse from the public, with one man arrested after threatening the band at a motorway service station in Leicestershire. As Hear'Say's fortunes started to dip, Liberty X landed a record deal with Richard Branson's V2 label.*

Myleene: Everywhere we went, people would wave their CDs out the windows of cars or cry and scream in our faces like scenes reminiscent of the Beatles or the Spice Girls. It didn't feel real. We had a number one and were the most famous band in the country but we were all pretty broke and I was still paying off my student debt. In fact, my first Hear'Say cheque – and it was a cheque – paid off my student loan and bought my piano. I had to wait for the next pay day for my piano stool.

Peter Loraine: [Polydor] literally couldn't manufacture the CDs quick enough. It was crazy. They must hold some strange record for the quickest jump to success and the most dramatic fall from grace afterwards. They sold a million copies of that album.

Kelli: After Hear'Say released 'Pure and Simple', they were quite unpopular. So from a press perspective it was, 'Well, we don't like them so we're definitely not going to like the rejects.' We were on the back foot. Behind the scenes, wonderful things started to happen, like Richard Branson had seen that *Lorraine* interview and he got in touch trying to sign us. Plus we were getting into the studio and realising we could write our own stuff and engineer our own sound. Behind the scenes things were going beautifully, but to the public everybody just thought we were going to be rubbish.

Malcolm McLean: For bands that weren't created in front of us on telly it was a much slower decline. Even with B*Witched, when most people were saying, 'They haven't done anything for years,' we were like, 'Oh, we saw them at the airport and they do gigs here and there.' But with Hear'Say we went to see them around 'Pure and Simple' and they literally stopped traffic. It was total gridlock outside the *Pepsi Chart Show*. So that gave us the impression that they were the new Spice Girls; they're going to take over the world, look at how many people are here. But that lasted for all of that single.

Jamelia: My real first single was 'Money', which went top five when I was eighteen. This is why I really empathise with artists of today because I still felt, even after having three years of development, like I was propelled into the limelight. Now it's one day nobody knows you and the next day you're famous and you're supposed to be a star.

Myleene: I still have copies of the day diaries and there was one time in three months that we had just two days off. In which I did my laundry. We were often broken. Anyone that thinks pop is a world of bubblegum has no idea how hard these bands actually work. The hours are brutal and schedules are like no others. No rock stars would be able to keep up with what these pop bands do, namely because they probably couldn't or wouldn't. It's hardcore.

Malcolm McLean: We went to see them promoting the second single ['The Way to Your Love'] and we could already tell it was over. Even though they got another number one, we would see the fans on the ground and it was like, 'Well, there's six of us now and there used to be six hundred.'

Myleene: We were hated by most. Booed at the BRITs and constantly heckled and criticised for our weight and looks. The music industry didn't feel we'd earned our right to be there. It wasn't enough that we'd gone to music school – most of the music industry can't read music but I was getting heckled – and other members had done the club/pub circuits, others were trained, incredibly talented performers. To many in the industry it wasn't okay that we hadn't made the journey as a band and worked what in their eyes was the hard, long way up. We hadn't earned our stripes. We hadn't publicly suffered enough to get there. Basically, they were jealous.

Colin Barlow: I think with Hear'Say, because they were the guinea pigs, they took more pressure than anyone. The general public felt like they knew them.

Myleene: It was extremely hard on us and our families. They were equally thrust into the spotlight with no idea of how to deal with any of it. Phones ringing through the night from fans. People sleeping under the windows of our homes or taking pics through the gaps in the curtains. Old friends or exes selling out. The good was great, phenomenal in fact – my mum and dad stayed longer than I did at a famous pop star's party once as I was too tired. But there were very testing, very pressured times. We often found it frustrating that people assumed we had changed and would treat us with that assumption in mind, not realising *they* had changed.

Tony: At the time, it was more, 'You're on your journey, best of luck to you, but we don't really care.' But, in hindsight, [Hear'Say's demise] was horrible. I feel grateful that I wasn't in an entity that got built up only to be torn down as fast as possible. I don't think there's a cabal of media types in sync with each other to spin narratives and then spin the opposite, but I think there's this tendency towards that that's a bit weird to me. There's almost this vacuum where the narrative stalls and you know it's going to reverse. With that kind of band, where they're not in control, it feels inevitable. The speed with which it happened was really harmful.

Chris Herbert: It was driven by the media. This was a mad experiment of how the media can elevate a band. The press had got behind them and it was all really positive, but like any soap opera story there has to be a start, a middle and an end. The media, the papers, the tabloids – they wrote that storyline. They wanted to create the stories about the in-fighting and then they wanted to write a lot of negative press about the demise of the band. It was a rapid rise – record-breaking single, record-breaking tour, record-breaking merchandise sales – and then it just dropped off a cliff. It was a really harsh experience.

Malcolm McLean: There was a backlash because people saw them at their most raw [on the TV show], being called fat or crying, so there was this impression that people thought they owned them. If it was S Club 7, you'd be like, 'Well, I had nothing to do with your creation and I don't own any part of you,' but with Hear'Say, and other acts that followed like Gareth Gates, it was like, 'We created you.' Even though we hadn't with Hear'Say specifically. I saw a girl outside a studio once, she was a Blue fan and she had it in for Noel. She called him every name under the sun, just screaming it at his face like, 'You fat gay cunt.' It was so horrible.

Dean Piper: I got sent to Amsterdam and I was put in the Grand Hotel. I was told that Robbie Williams was going to be there and I had to follow him around. So I had to sit in reception with my photographer and hope that he came out and went on a bender. But he didn't come out. Instead Gareth Gates did. He was like seventeen and I followed him all night, watched him walk past all the strippers and prostitutes. I look back on that and think, 'Hang on, this was a seventeen-year-old kid.' We had no qualms about plastering him on the front page.

Craig McLean: It was a democratising of pop culture. Suddenly it was a gladiatorial arena where normal folk could have a shot at stardom. You risked getting ripped apart by lions or the judges, but there was a way for them to do it. There'd always been star finders, but this was something that was primetime entertainment. That also created a generation who were happy to go on TV and think, 'I don't mind if Nasty Nigel is mean to me or Simon Cowell rips my family and me apart – in fact I'd rather do that than never have a go.'

Tony: There's something really quite horrible about the fact you're given this opportunity to transform but because that transformation is visible it induces jealousy. When you hide that transformation people just receive the finished entity and buy into you as an otherworldly star. Even these successful entertainers who do this transformation behind closed doors, they really believe they are that person too and they never want to go back.

Kelli: What started to happen was this pendulum swing and we became the antithesis to Hear'Say. I think the image we came out with was a little bit edgier, a bit more real. Less bubblegum.

Craig McLean: The legacy of *Popstars* is every other TV talent show. It showed that those kinds of shows could be successful in terms of TV viewers, it proved that in terms of being in pop magazines that these bands were smash hits and it showed that there's a huge appetite for seeing how the ugly duckling becomes a swan. It showed a generation that actually getting on TV could be a way to pop stardom.

'We had to change our name and do it quickly before we released another record'

Released in September 2001, the debut single of the so-called 'flopstars' Liberty, 'Thinking It Over', peaked at number five. Just as they were about to start working on what would become their debut album, however, a legal notice was sent from representatives of another musical act called Liberty. The case went to the High Court and the band had to rethink. Having arrived at this point the hard way, they weren't about to stop now.

Tony: Nobody wanted to give us any tracks. The one decision we did make was to hire a manager, Gary Wiltern, who had managed a band called Worlds Apart. They had created a nice career for themselves in France and Germany. Our thinking was, 'Fuck the UK, if we're flopstars here then that doesn't mean we don't have what it takes.' He got us set up in some writing sessions and Kelli and I were doing them. The very first session we did, we wrote 'Thinking It Over'.

MNEK: If they had been under Syco or the 19 management umbrella, for example, they would have been told to just make teeny-bopper stuff or anything like Hear'Say was making at the time. Here they had 'Thinking It Over,' a garage-lite song. It was current, it was fresh, it wasn't appealing to, you know, Phil and

Jill in Doncaster. It's a great pop record inspired by garage music. They had a longer career than Hear'Say because they had more time to develop and cultivate their sound and their vibe.

Kelli: When we put out 'Thinking It Over' we actually released it anonymously on a white label because we didn't think anyone would play it if they knew who it was by.

Malcolm McLean: The first time I heard 'Thinking It Over' we were on the Hear'Say tour, seeing them everywhere, and I was livid because it was really good. People would laugh and call them 'flopstars', then they did that and everyone loved it.

Kelli: The success of 'Thinking It Over' attracted another band called Liberty, who sued us in the High Court. They filed a case against us for basically trying to harness their fans and popularity, which obviously we did not do.

Tony: It was a pretty ridiculous claim. There was an opportunity for a settlement between them and V2, but it went to the High Court and the version of events I was given was that because we didn't provide much of a defence the case was awarded to that group.

Kelli: They had the smaller outfit and we had these London lawyers, a big law firm, so they didn't want to be seen to be hammering them. But then when the judge made his ruling he said because we hadn't argued our case fully he had no choice but to rule in their favour, so they won.

Tony: They weren't awarded any damages. It was pittance. But we had to change our name. I do remember a poll [in *The Sun*, allowing readers to vote on a new name] and people saying, 'Let the people be involved in it all.' I thought it was a great idea as long as we weren't wedded to the results, like if they wanted to call us Flopstars.

Kelli: They voted on Ex Liberty. But we preferred the X on the end.

'We felt like we never had anybody on our side until that moment'

While 'Thinking It Over' was a hit, it wasn't a career-defining smash. In a period where pop acts would enter high and drop like a stone, it was hard to make a song that would stand the test of time. For the newly named Liberty X, however, their defining moment was waiting for them on a CD-R, ready to turn them from TV talent show runners-up to credible, BRIT Award-winning superstars. That led to a collaboration with producer Richard X on mash-up 'Being Nobody', before the dream started to fizzle out.

Tony: We got lucky with 'Just a Little'. Our first single did well, then the second one, 'Doin' It', got to number fourteen. We knew we were in trouble. Everyone agreed, label included, that we should record a few more tracks. In that period, Michelle went to a writing session and they played her 'Just a Little'. As I understand it, it was intended for Anastasia and she turned it down, which is why they played it to Michelle. She came back and was like, 'They played me this song that was quite cool.'

Kelli: Michelle Escoffery, who wrote it, had done the demo vocal and she's got a really amazing R&B voice. I remember thinking, 'It's a massive song, it's wicked, but we are going to have to really do it justice.'

Tony: I took a photograph of Jess, Kelli and myself holding the track and I think we had our fingers up as in this is a number one.

Kelli: Once we recorded it and added bits I was like, 'Oh my God, this is banging.' Then it just all snowballed. Everyone at the label was so excited and it was just meetings and chats about the video.

Tony: We had an incredible stylist, Michelle Clapton, who went on to become the costume designer for *Game of Thrones*. She had a contact in the fetish fashion world and the girls were like, 'Yeah, fuck it, we can pull this off.'

Kelli: The song is so sexy. We just had to be sexy in the video. It couldn't be us coming out in baggy trousers. We weren't afraid to be risqué. We didn't want to be seen as a bubblegum pop outfit; that's not what we are. We all sat around a table and came up with the *Entrapment* idea for the video. Everything just rolled from there, like, 'What if we danced with canes?'

Tony: Another word for a cane is a crutch, so if you'd taken that cane away from me I felt more exposed. Our poor choreographer saw myself and Kev and thought, 'Fuck, what am I going to do?'

MNEK: We think of Liberty X's records more now than we think of Hear'Say's. 'Just a Little' is a classic. It's not a classic in the way 'Pure and Simple' is, which is ironic. 'Just a Little' is a genuinely great record.

Tony: Winning a BRIT [for Best British Single in 2003] was crazy. We could hold our heads up high – we had a number one and a BRIT Award. It changes the way you feel about yourselves. From that moment onwards you get to say, 'You know what, I don't have to worry about how I'm perceived – it just is what it is.'

Kelli: I remember the whole day. We were rehearsing for our tour and then we had hair and make-up arrive to get us ready and the label had put on a limo. It was probably one of the most pop star-y days of my life. Then to actually win, it was totally mad. That was voted for by the public, so it felt all the more special. We felt like we never had anybody on our side until that moment. We'd really achieved something.

Tony: [The workload] was constant. We had our own limited company because our manager and tour manager had instilled some good practices in us so we voted on things. We knew that our finances were such that we had to go out and gig because that was our money, because back then touring earnings belonged to the band. We knew that whatever happened with the records we wouldn't do very well because of the way the deal was structured. So we did our promo during the day and then we gigged in the evening.

Kelli: We just didn't sleep for seven years. I'm being genuine about that. We used to have two weeks off at the start of January, because that was when the music industry pretty much shut down. We worked non-stop, fifty weeks of the year for seven years. Then we started to get international success around

2003 and it just multiplied. We made time to have fun. Michelle made time. She really didn't sleep.

Tony: 'Freak Like Me' was absolutely banging, so the possibility of working with Richard X made me very excited. We were at the point where we needed a producer who had the chops to take it to the next level. We got the feeling that we needed a superstar producer or someone with designs on becoming one. Finances at the label dictated that we weren't going to go in with a superstar producer for a whole album, but we did get to do a few tracks with Richard. To me he was in line with that 'Just a Little' and 'Thinking It Over' sensibility. Pop stuff that isn't too sweet.

Richard X: I liked that Liberty X were the underdogs who'd done well; that chimed with me. Also with my anti-glamour stance and trying to diffuse everything that Virgin wanted me to do. I was never going to be all 'look at me' or be hip. I was hip for like a week. Even using the word 'hip' tells you a lot. My thing was a reaction to that glamour, so Liberty X suited my mindset. The success of that song was down to them. My friends were very confused seeing me on *CD:UK* just doing a little dance.

Kelli: He used to come and do performances and stand in the back with his grey boiler suit, pretending to press buttons. We'd be there giving it all the moves. We did some of the promo trail with him, which was quite funny. I think he liked seeing all the madness and then going home.

Richard X: They tolerated me. I was always the weakest link in the album campaign. They were really nice and funny and I was really dour and pretentious. They would be happy to play along with any pop star chat.

Steve Anderson: I remember we did a writing camp with Liberty X. You'd work with individual members of the band and so it would depend really on who you got. Obviously from the band's point of view, mainly financially, but also a little bit creatively, they wanted to be part of the songwriting.

Hannah Robinson, songwriter, 'Everybody Cries': I'm sure they won't mind me saying but that single came with the worst video I've ever seen. They're walking down a railway line and there's rubbish coming out of black bin bags falling from the sky. I was gutted because it didn't really do that well, but looking back now, if I had that chart entry today [number fourteen], I'd be over the moon.

Tony: Even my kids rip the piss out of me when they see that video. One of them said it was the worst music video he'd ever seen. It's hard to disagree.

★ ★ ★

After scoring eight UK top-ten singles and three top-thirty albums, Liberty X called it a day in 2007. In 2012, they joined a number of their '00s peers on ITV's *The Big Reunion*, before disbanding again in 2014. In 2016, Kevin Simm won the fifth series of *The Voice*, before later replacing Marti Pellow in Wet Wet Wet. Tony, meanwhile, moved into TV and film production. Jessica, Kelli and Michelle still perform as Liberty X.

13

What will the neighbours say? How Girls Aloud tore up the rulebook

By the summer of 2002, TV talent show formats were springing up faster than you could say 'singing is my passion'. *Pop Idol*, launched in late 2001, had ditched *Popstars'* documentary-style feel and, looking to chime with the democratisation of everything boom post-*Big Brother*, opened the outcome up to the viewing public via live shows. Keen to expand on this further, *Popstars: The Rivals* drew from one unexpected result of the original *Popstars*: the tabloid-created rivalry between winners Hear'Say and 'losers' Liberty X. This was cleverly built into the show, with a boyband and a girlband created to go head-to-head, with the winner (hopefully) landing the coveted Christmas number-one spot.

Looming over the show was the spectre of Hear'Say, who, despite only releasing their first single in March 2001, had acrimoniously split by the time the first *Popstars: The Rivals* live show aired in October 2002. Of course, the realities of the music industry don't matter when the promise of something life-changing is at stake, and so it was that hundreds and hundreds of hopefuls joined queues in London, Manchester and Glasgow for a chance to be critiqued by judges Louis Walsh (who earlier that year had completed a stint as a judge on the Irish version of *Popstars*, which featured a certain Nadine Coyle), Pete Waterman and 'Heaven and Hell (Being Geri Halliwell)' hitmaker Geri Halliwell. From there, the two bands were whittled down to ten boys and ten girls, with each group chucked in a big house together during the live shows. While both Kimberley Walsh and Nicola Roberts missed out initially on the final ten, fate saw that they would eventually take their rightful place in Girls Aloud, AKA one of the UK's biggest and best girlbands.*

'It was a bit more like panto'

Louis Walsh: I never wanted to be on TV, ever. But the fact I was there with Pete Waterman and Geri, that sounded fun. I was very naïve to television. I'm a lot wiser now. But I think it helped, the fact that I was naïve.

Nicola: I used to do all the local competitions and my mum and dad subscribed to *The Stage*. I remember seeing this advert saying, 'TV auditions to make a group on ITV'. So I recorded myself onto a CD and didn't really think anything of it. It felt

* Kimberley replaced Hazel Kaneswaran, who was disqualified for being ten days older than the maximum age limit, while Nicola replaced Nicola Ward, who quit the show over what she considered the 'exploitation' of the contestants.

like such a long shot. The auditions fell while I was on holiday in Devon, so I had to be driven to Manchester and then driven back to Devon to continue my holiday.

Kimberley: My dance teacher at the time handed me the application and was like, 'I've half filled this out, you've got to send it off.' I didn't know if it was for me. It seemed a bit terrifying, the whole thing. But she gently persuaded me.

Nicola: The year before, when I was watching *Popstars* with Hear'Say and Liberty X, it all felt quite far removed. It was just something I'd watch in my very normal living room at home; there was no correlation.

Kimberley: I thought *Popstars: The Rivals* was going to be the same as the previous *Popstars* format, so I did get a sharp shock when I realised what the actual process was going to be. But I was in it way too deep at that point.

Nicola: Even with *Pop Idol*, I was just watching while getting ready to get drunk in the local place that used to let underage people in. That was it. Watching Will Young win, like, 'Oh, yeah, great, he's won, pass the lipstick, how much money have we got? Am I going to be able to afford a WKD or a Smirnoff Ice?' That was where I was at.

Kimberley: I wasn't thrilled at the idea of doing a show that was live on TV to millions of people. It seemed like a higher level of anxiety. I was pretty confident that I would find a way of making singing a big part of my life, but these shows do require a bit of luck and a bit of drama. I didn't bring any drama.

Nadine: I had been on Irish *Popstars* [in 2001]. They had an over-18s limit and I'd just turned sixteen at the time. I didn't know they had an age limit when I applied and then when I found out someone there was like, 'Oh, it doesn't matter.' Then I got disqualified.

Louis Walsh: I had kept in touch with Nadine. She was very damaged after the Irish *Popstars* thing because it was front-page news and it made out she was lying. She was never going to sing again.

Una Healy: I actually met Nadine [on Irish *Popstars*]. The night before we auditioned we all sat together in the living room and went around the circle and sang a bit. I just remember Nadine singing and going, 'Oh my God, she's amazing.' Then she was removed from the show because of her age, which was actually a bit of a blessing in disguise for her.

Louis Walsh: I knew I was doing this show [*Popstars: The Rivals*] so I called her up and said, 'You have to go for it.' She didn't want to. I told her she had to and that she was a great singer, so she went for it. That's the truth.

Nadine: That is true. It wasn't that I was close to giving up on singing, I just didn't like that type of show. It was very much about making a TV show rather than singing. A friend of mine was auditioning for the Girls Aloud version and Louis was like, 'You must audition, you must, I will never speak to you again.' So I went to Scotland to audition. You don't think you're going to win these things.

Nicola: Initially it was just about getting myself through the process. It was, 'Do I know my song? Can I sing my song? Am

I happy with my song? Will the audience like my song?' It was self-contained in that way. Once we'd made it into the group, you could zoom out and it was about how do we beat the boys and get to number one?

Nadine: You were seeing people's dreams ripped away from them. I was sixteen or seventeen. There were people there older than I was and their dreams were being shattered and I found that hard to deal with on a day-to-day basis. I had loads of random illnesses that I haven't had since being in that process.

Kimberley: [The chart battle element] felt like it made it all a bit more light-hearted. It was a bit more like panto, that side of things.

Nicola: There were definitely some stronger characters in the house. Older girls, more experienced girls, that liked to dominate. I'd never lived away from home – I'd just done my GCSEs. I was quite nervous around new characters.

Kimberley: It wasn't cameras in your face the minute you wake up in the morning, but you were being filmed rehearsing and stuff like that. It was just about to the level I could cope with. I'd done quite a bit of TV acting so I had done jobs that meant living away from home, so that side of it was okay for me.

Nicola: I was late to the house and so I joined just before the live shows. I remember one of the other girls saying, 'If she gets through after we've been in the house for weeks, it's going to be a joke.' This girl wasn't a very good singer. So I was thinking, 'Well, we'll see.' And then she was the first one out.

'Let's go and do something so exciting that even if we lose we've got a career'

For the as-yet-unnamed girlband, who were still having their numbers whittled down, second place seemed inevitable. As with the Spice Girls six years earlier, the industry thinking was that there wasn't really an audience for a girlband and that pop fans would always gravitate towards a band of cute dimples and swept fringes if given a choice. It was going to take a very special song to change that fate. Unbeknown to everyone, an undeniable banger – the drum 'n' bass meets surf guitar curio that is 'Sound of the Underground' – was sitting on producer Brian Higgins' computer. The only problem was that while it was always meant for a girlband, it wasn't Girls Aloud.

Brian Higgins: [Xenomania] had a girl group, Orchid, that we'd put together. I'd thought long and hard about what sound we needed to break a girl group in the UK.

Miranda Cooper: I remember being really cross. Moonbaby had gone and then Brian was like, 'We've got this girlband,' so I remember seething about it. When I wrote 'Sound of the Underground' I definitely thought it was for Moonbaby part two.

Brian Higgins: 'Sound of the Underground' was written to a very dark piece of drum 'n' bass. The process of turning it into a pop song started in around April 2002. I made the initial version of the record with the surf guitars and imported that record into the studios of two Tims – Tim Larcombe and Tim Powell. I was walking up the stairs between the three studios and hearing everything that was going on with these three versions – my original, what Tim Larcombe was doing with it and what

Tim Powell was doing with it. I heard the record coming out all mashed together. I literally said, 'Bassline from that one, this bit from that one, then add that to that, and that's the record.'

Miranda Cooper: I wrote it with Niara Scarlett in my little flat. I would go round with my notepad and just write words and concepts down. Anytime we would write we'd have lots and lots of backing tracks. We'd have our dictaphones and we'd press play and then we'd just sing over the top. Just a stream of consciousness. Then I would go through all of my lyrics and try different ones and the same lyrics would pop up over loads of different tracks. But with 'Sound of the Underground' I was singing, 'The wheels on the bus go round and round' over and over.

Brian Higgins: Colin Barlow heard the record and said, 'That's the record of the year in my opinion.'

Colin Barlow: As we started to do *Popstars: The Rivals*, I just knew that was the song I wanted to use. I took the mantle of helping scout for the girls.

Peter Loraine: Colin called me into his office and said, 'Here you go, it's your dream, you can go and do the new Bananarama.' There was a video tape with loads of footage of different people that had entered and we sat and watched it together. There were maybe about twenty girls that were in consideration. At that point, they didn't have any members, obviously, or a single, so it was like, 'What is this going to be? What are we going to try to do? Are we going to do something like Eternal? Or Atomic Kitten?' Musically it could have gone in any direction. Visually it could have gone in any direction.

Brian Higgins: Colin phoned me up out of the blue and said, 'You know that song, I think we have a vehicle for it.' He told me what it was. The truth is I never really believed him. I thought, 'There's no way you're going to put that out as the first single [from a TV talent show] because it's always a dreadful song.'

Miranda Cooper: I remember at the time Brian and I thinking that reality TV was over, it was just saturated, and that maybe we shouldn't do this. It was either going to be a cover of 'Stay Another Day' by East 17 or 'Sound of the Underground'. We just thought there was no way they were going to go with our song.

Brian Higgins: Did I watch the show? No. I'm not interested in things like that. I don't understand things like that.

Colin Barlow: Towards the end when Pete [Waterman] had his classic boyband [One True Voice] with the nice mid-tempo ballad, I sat with everyone and played them 'Sound of the Underground'. They thought I was absolutely mad. I said to them, 'The odds are we're never going to win – the boyband should win by a mile, so let's go and do something so exciting that even if we lose we've got a career.' I felt the song was that good.

Miranda Cooper: Later, Brian and I were invited down by ITV to the big house called Horizons, where all the girls were, and we played the song and they totally didn't get it. They were into Mariah Carey and thought they'd have their beautiful moment song.

Nicola: A few weeks before the end of the show, I found a CD in the house and it had all these potential singles on it. Someone had said to me, 'Oh, "Sound of the Underground" is the one they're going with.' I remember putting it on and thinking, 'No one's going to understand this. *I* don't understand this.' I was quite concerned. As a teenager, as a music listener, it was all about those sweet melodies, being able to connect to the song, like, 'Does this reflect my life? Does this remind me of the boy I like?' And it couldn't have been further away from anything I'd been listening to. It felt like a risky move.

Peter Loraine: Colin said, 'We've found the first song,' and he played it and from that moment onwards everything fell into place. Straight away you could picture who would work with them, what it should look like. Never before has there been such a defining song. There was no getting away from the fact they were a manufactured band. What you're getting is five very different people who all potentially would have their own ideas, but no experience whatsoever. No time to learn, no time to grow, no time to experience how anything worked. They were very reliant on a team who would say, 'This is what it's going to be like.'

Colin Barlow: That's when the genius of Peter Loraine came to the fore. Naming the band, coming up with the whole punk ethos [around 'Sound of the Underground'] and then really creating something edgy. It was exactly the right group.

Kimberley: Everything would have led you to believe [the boys would win]. For sure. But then when we heard the songs I did think, 'Ah, maybe not.'

Peter Robinson: I was doing the book [*Popstars: The Rivals: The Official Inside Story*] and it had a split cover, so one with One True Voice on the cover and one with Girls Aloud on the cover. I think

I'm right in saying they printed more copies of the boys' one. *Smash Hits* got me to do a cover story but it was with One True Voice. The whole thing was 'here come the boys', basically.

Louis Walsh: I thought I was going to get the boys. But then they gave me the girls and it was like, 'Oh, God.' But Colin Barlow found 'Sound of the Underground' and Brian Higgins gave them all their hits.

Nadine: As soon as I heard the songs, I didn't worry about [us losing] at all. The boys were super talented, great singers, but I knew from hearing our song that there wouldn't be much competition.

Nicola: I don't know why Colin went with Brian and that song. Why didn't he go with somebody who had done a load of Atomic Kitten records? Or straight to Biff, who had worked with the Spice Girls?

Peter Loraine: There was one member, who didn't make the final band, who when we went to play all ten of them 'Sound of the Underground' she said, 'No, no, no, that's not the song that will be launching my group.' I remember thinking to myself, 'I really, really hope you're not in the final line-up.'

Kimberley: I was so relieved that it wasn't going to be this generic pop ballad. We were coming out of that era so I would have known then that it was probably going to be a short-lived thing. I just remember not really knowing if I loved the song itself but just being glad it was something different. A bit edgier.

Keith Semple, One True Voice: I remember thinking ['Sound of the Underground'] was a catchy song. I remember liking the mix of the song better than ours and thinking it was more edgy and current. As an already touring rock musician, I was not interested in boybands. However, I thought we had established ourselves on the show as competent musicians and singers and would not be considered a boyband going forward. Of course that turned out to be wrong!

Louis Walsh: I knew it was going to walk all over radio and kill Pete Waterman and his group. I was happy with that. It was a great song.

Alexis Petridis: It keyed into a much wider tradition of brilliant, trashy, balls-out, British pop music. It wasn't watered down R&B. It felt really British for a start, because it had that drum 'n' bass undertow to it. They were making records that were far better than they needed to be. Which is not really the ethos of people who make records for TV talent-show winners. Most of the things that have been huge hits off the back of these TV talent shows have been rubbish. The plan works in the short term and seldom works in an extended sense. It was a record by someone who really understood what makes British pop music good and unique.

Peter Robinson: In the space of a week, backstage at where they made it, which was in the same building they filmed *CD:UK*, I got played the One True Voice song by Pete Waterman and then I went into Polydor to hear the Girls Aloud song. That week I placed a £50 bet on Girls Aloud being the Christmas number one and that paid for my Christmas. The odds were brilliant because everyone thought the boys would win.

'Louis made sure Pete always felt that he'd lost'

As the live shows continued, the bands slowly started to form, with the Louis Walsh-managed Girls Aloud in one corner and One True Voice, stewarded by Pete Waterman, in the other. While Pete Waterman had plumped for a mid-paced, vanilla cover of a Bee Gees album track ('Sacred Trust') for the Burton-suited boys, the strappy top and polyester-trousered girls had started recording the upbeat, decidedly edgier 'Sound of the Underground'. Every other week, the band gained a member: Cheryl Tweedy, Nicola Roberts, Nadine Coyle and Kimberley Walsh had all made it through, with the final spot a battle between Sarah Harding and judge favourite Javine Hylton. It wasn't the only controversial moment, with Pete Waterman – who let's remember was sending out his boyband with a cover – furious that 'Sound of the Underground' had existed before the show started.

Brian Higgins: I went to see them when there were ten girls. I didn't watch any of [the show] until literally the throwing-out bit, so then I had to find a way to make sure the five people who made it in fitted. We recorded everyone, all ten girls.

Miranda Cooper: We'd have to delete the vocal of the person who got chucked out. I remember Javine sounded great on it and we were gutted when she went.

Peter Loraine: Everyone thought it was a slam dunk that Javine would be in, so depending on what the line-up was it was 'Version A, send that off,' 'Version B, send that off.' When Javine didn't get in, it was like, 'Oh . . .', because she was all over the song. By this point, we'd also done a photoshoot with six members using every different configuration. There was a photo session that had Kimberley, Nicola, Sarah, Nadine and Javine. And then we'd switch out Kimberley and put Cheryl in.

Nadine: I thought Javine was going to make it into the band. I almost took it for a given. But I truly believe that, without those other four girls, it just would not have worked in the way it did. It was a really nice, harmonious thing. We're all very different – very different backgrounds, very different people in general.

Louis Walsh: I thought [Javine] was going to be one of the stars of the group. The public were in charge of Girls Aloud; it wasn't me. At the end of the day, they are in charge because they decide if they're going to like a song.

Colin Barlow: Thank God Sarah Harding got that last place because she became the heartbeat of that group. It's funny now, putting Sarah into that song made it more pop, whereas the way Javine sang it, it had more of a garage, urban feel. The pop-ness Sarah brought to it made it much more mass appeal.

Iain James: I remember [*Popstars: The Rivals*] very clearly because we all fancied [Girls Aloud] and we were picking which one we were trying to chat up basically. They had that boyband as well, One True Voice, and Polydor were very much, 'That's your direct competition.' We used to watch it and very arrogantly just used to laugh, like, 'This isn't a competition.'

Peter Waterman: [Doing that show] was horrible. Everybody was cheating. They'd made the bloody record three months before the show. And I'm believing that you've got to start when the bands were found. How naïve was I? It's a good record, but I was played it before we started, like, 'This is going to be their single.'

Brian Higgins: He's just a bad loser, I think.

Keith: Their song was simply better, whether it already existed or not.

Peter Robinson: If you know you've got to have a song ready by the middle of December, you start looking as early as possible. You don't go, 'Oh, we've won, shall we think about writing a song?'

Colin Barlow: I love Pete but he wanted to win so badly and Louis made sure Pete always felt that he'd lost. There's a bitterness there that the two of them have always played on. If you put them in a room together now, within two minutes they'd bring it up. They were so desperate to win that the rivalry was beyond intense.

Louis Walsh: [Pete] didn't talk to me for years when Girls Aloud won. He thinks he invented pop music. He told me once that he invented pop music and he believed it. We didn't cheat; we just had a better song and a better group. Obviously. Girls Aloud went on to have twenty hits and he had no hits with One True Voice. Listen, he's a nice guy, he's just slightly out of touch with today's market.

Nadine: Our team, I think it was Peter Loraine, came up with the very crafty thing to do, which was to record their song and put it on our B-side.

Peter Loraine: The Bee Gees were signed to us as well and so we got the girls to record a version of 'Sacred Trust'. We were going to put a sticker on the front of the CD saying, 'Includes

"Sacred Trust"'. It was decided by my boss that that was one step too far. Too dirty.

Colin Barlow: I don't know why we didn't do that. We should have done that.

Peter Robinson: I remember Pete Waterman going, 'We've got an unreleased Bee Gees song.' And it's not; it had come out before as an album track. If you're going to cover a Bee Gees song, don't cover a not very good one. I mean the boys weren't great together. Even when I was doing the *Smash Hits* shoot, one of the members was becoming a problem and needed to get a bollocking from the PR. That was before the song was even out.

'That was the moment of one pop era ending and another one beginning'

By the end of November 2002, the pop cosmos had two brand-new stars, but the show's ultimate prize – that coveted Christmas number one, to be announced on a later show – was still up for grabs. Relishing in their underdog status, Girls Aloud, along with their tight-knit marketing team and despite an increasingly absent Louis Walsh, set about electioneering up and down the country, their genius slogan – Buy Girls, Bye Boys – quickly searing its way into the public consciousness. On 22 December, having sold 213,000 to One True Voice's 147,000 (another Popstars: The Rivals *act, the Cheeky Girls, were at number three with searing polemic 'Cheeky Song (Touch My Bum)'), Girls Aloud were crowned the winners.*

Peter Loraine: We had a week to do everything. There wasn't time to be trying things out. It very much needed to be, 'Here's the song, now go.' And off we went.

Nadine: My mum was crying her eyes out that night I got into the band because we had to leave immediately and go to a hotel. No time for them to have a conversation with me to make sure I was okay. It was extreme.

Kimberley: It was pretty full-on. It was literally like go to a hotel, then start the Buy Girls, Bye Boys promo the next day. We just lived out of a Chrysler for the next however many weeks until it charted. I'd never had sleep deprivation like it.

Nicola: I have never, and I will never, work that hard again in my life. Our feet did not touch the ground.

Jeremy Joseph: When *Popstars* happened, we approached the TV company about putting on One True Voice and Girls Aloud at G-A-Y. I remember Louis and Pete being very competitive at G-A-Y with what they did. Louis brought on someone from Westlife just to try to make sure the girls got more press on the Monday. I'll tell you what the interesting thing was: when you looked in the dressing room, the girls were all sitting together. They were a group. Whereas the boys were very apart. It didn't feel like a unit.

Nicola: I remember we were about to leave somewhere and our tour manager was like, 'The label have just put this new thing in the schedule,' and we were all crying because we were emotionally and physically and mentally exhausted. But it was like we were athletes running for the finish line. We used to do crazy things like we'd stop at red lights and open the car door and be like, 'Buy our single – don't buy the boys' single.'

Peter Loraine: There were certain areas of the media, like *Smash Hits* and Capital radio, who were on the boys' side. Capital were doing a takeover with the boys, so I bought all the advertising spots around their appearance. It was so exciting. We had things where if you went to Asda there'd be someone there to sticker you with the Buy Girls, Bye Boys badge. When you went to HMV, we glued big Girls Aloud footprints to the floor so you followed it to the CD rack where 'Sound of the Underground' was. I had the budget, so we just ran riot. The brief was to win. When we went back for the episode to reveal who would be number one, I remember in the green room Pete [Waterman] saying to me, 'You nailed it because you had time to do two CD singles and we only had time to do one.' I remember thinking, 'What the hell are you on about?' The line-up of the boys was announced a week before the girls. They had seven days ahead of us to get everything prepped.

Peter Robinson: Girls Aloud winning was the moment of one pop era ending and another one beginning.

Pete Waterman: No. No, no, no. Nothing to do with musical trends, we just had five guys who should never have been together.

Keith: Pete was obviously a genius in his earlier career. Although I disagreed with his choices on our style, single release and the band not being allowed to perform instruments live, I understand that in the '80s and early '90s he was on the top of the industry.

Kimberley: I can't actually remember getting the chance to celebrate. We got the number one just before Christmas and so I think that was the first time any of us went back home after getting in the band. Then it was just more about having time to reflect on the madness of the past six weeks. You're sitting there on Christmas Day watching yourself performing the Christmas number one on *Top of the Pops* and it's just a bit of a bizarre moment.

Keith: I still have the gold disc on my wall for a number-two British hit and over 400,000 singles sold. That can in no way be considered anything but an awesome achievement. I will always be proud of that.

Nicola: The word 'whirlwind' doesn't do it justice. You've gone from being nobody to then trying your best to get through a competition to being in a group to then promoting a song and having a number one. You go back home for Christmas to your normal life. It was like being put in a washing machine with loads of fucking red socks and expecting it to all come out white. It was honestly the most crazy, far-fetched few months of our lives.

'Someone said, "Oh, he's at Currys buying Cheryl a Hoover"'

The beautiful thing about early TV talent shows was the genuine rush of seeing a very normal person or group of people stepping, Stars in Their Eyes*-style, through the smoke and coming out the other side as bonafide pop stars. The tricky thing for major labels, however, is that it's hard to then reverse-engineer the years of development most pop acts go through before they're presented to the public. If Nicola Roberts has been voted into a band for her singing but also her feisty attitude, for example, the public don't want her to then reappear months later as someone varnished to a dazzling sheen. For Girls Aloud, a rabble whose debut single and punk-esque marketing had* *underpinned their zero-fucks-given attitude, it was vital they remained true to themselves. Even after they were dumped in an old asylum in the middle of nowhere (Friern Barnet) with no time to buy a vacuum cleaner.*

Laura Snapes: Even though a band like Steps were just as hothoused as Girls Aloud, with Steps, that took place in private. All the edges of their personality were sanded off, so you had this happy-clappy product that was obviously aimed at kids. The journey – 'The Journey' – of Girls Aloud on a show meant you got to know them as people before they became pop stars. You saw where they all came from in a very literal sense and I think that encourages a stronger sense of bonding.

Alexis Petridis: They seemed like souped-up versions of ordinary young women. That was the thing that seemed exciting about them as people. I once interviewed them over lunch at the OXO Tower and I always remember Nicola Roberts looking at the menu and going, 'No, no, no.' She wouldn't eat anything. Then she proceeded to go into her handbag and pull a bag of Nik Naks out and eat them at the table. It was brilliant.

Paul Flynn: I could dress their story up. I could take those kids who I did go to school with and who did come from nothing and who didn't have nice upbringings and who weren't privileged and who didn't go to university and I could treat them with the same amount of dignity as the people who don't fucking deserve it but who went to the right schools. The respect they get automatically, I could give to those pop stars. They're fulfilling something and that something is an escape.

Nicola: The benefit of us not knowing the situation we were in was that we would go into the label and just talk to them in a way that was a lot less eloquent than we are now. We'd just be like, 'Yeah, we're not fucking doing it.' And that's how we'd speak to them.

Colin Barlow: It was hilarious. I don't think they ever knew what any of us did. They knew there were certain people in their lives that they saw regularly but they didn't know what that person did. Peter [Loraine] was very integral in their lives and I drove all the music, but they'd see me once in a while and I'd be like, 'You did the Disney Awards and you didn't perform very well,' and they didn't know why they were being called in and told off. They had this wonderful naïvety to it all. They weren't street-savvy kids in regards the music industry – they were five girls who had just won a TV show.

Nicola: It was [just] us, we had no manager, and the schedule would just constantly change.

Kimberley: I think it's been quite heavily documented, and I've said plenty on this subject, but Louis was very much a manager on paper. That was as far as it went. Me and him did have a few clashes along the way.

Nicola: He did nothing. He wouldn't pick the phone up. He literally did nothing and we just paid him.

Louis Walsh: I wasn't [a hands-on manager]. I was working with Westlife and doing loads of other things. I wasn't able to help [Girls Aloud] with their hair and their make-up and their styling – I wasn't any good at that. They were great at that. And Polydor were great. And Peter Loraine was very much involved. So they did most of it.

Colin Barlow: Louis was the most hands-off manager you had ever met.

Nadine: There were all these people running around doing jobs – tour managers, A&Rs, marketing people, TV pluggers, all of these words put together that I'd never heard before – so it was hard to figure out what people were supposed to be doing. It was like, 'Who is in charge? Are we just aimlessly running around the UK? Who is deciding what's happening?'

Louis Walsh: I didn't have a great relationship with them because I did say [Nadine] was the best singer. So obviously the other four hated me anyway. I shouldn't have said it but she was the best singer by a mile and she sang the lead on every single track.

Kimberley: I was a little bit older so I could stick up for the rest of the girls and try to take control. Just so it didn't get out of hand.

Nadine: Kimberley did a lot. I had to do it at the beginning because for some random reason they had decided that me and Hazel [Kaneswaran] should be the ones flown over to London to pick the lawyers and the accountants. I was seventeen. To this day, I don't know why I was the one chosen. I was also having to deal with Brian Higgins, too. I remember we were on stage at *Top of the Pops* and my phone was going crazy and I was like, 'I cannot do it any more, someone is going to have to take over.' So I said, 'Kimberley, you went to university, did you not? You seem smart enough, could you not take some of these calls?' So she did. Hilary [Shaw, manager] arrived a few years in, before our first tour [in 2005].

Kimberley: I wouldn't say I was the manager but I think the general day-to-day logistics and looking after our wellbeing and finances and stuff, I took that on in a mother-hen role maybe.

Colin Barlow: Kimberley was the boss. She used to have a clipboard.

Nicola: I'd be like, 'Kim, I really want to go out in Liverpool at the weekend, can you tell the label I've got a wedding please?' And she'd be like, 'Nic, you've had four weddings this month, I'm not sure we can get away with another one.' So I'd say: 'Can you tell them it's a christening? That I've got my friend's kid's communion? Tell them someone's turning seventy.' The guys at the label must have just laughed their heads off. Throughout the week, we'd do all our TV shows and promo, whatever they wanted us to do, but we were teenage girls so I did want to be back home chilling in my friend's car [at the weekend]. And I did really want to get drunk because I wasn't supposed to. But then you'd come back on the Monday and have a lawyers meeting, then an accountants meeting, then a stylist meeting. The two worlds just couldn't have been any further apart.

Colin Barlow: There was a point where Kimberley was head girl and she was somebody I'd call up and she'd say, 'Right, we've got a problem, this has happened, these two aren't talking, what do I do?' Kimberley would always pull it together. Now when I look at bands I'm like, 'Who is the Kimberley?' If you don't have a Kimberley, you don't have a group. I don't think Sugababes had a Kimberley and that's why they changed personnel so much.

Peter Loraine: I was overseeing everything for them at that time. Their diary was kept out of our office. But in addition, where are they going to live? None of them lived in London. How are they going to pay for their food when they haven't made any money yet? All those things needed sorting. One particular day, my boss appeared in my doorway and it was like, 'Where's Peter?', and someone said, 'Oh, he's at Currys buying Cheryl a Hoover.' Because she was having a meltdown like, 'There's no time to do anything, I can't even clean my apartment, I don't even have a Hoover.' So I went and got her a Hoover.

Nicola: We all lived in the same building. It was called Princess Park Manor. It used to be an old mental asylum. It was in Friern Barnet and as soon as you came out of the gates of this complex there was just nothing there. I don't know why they wanted us there.

Kimberley: I was with Nadine. Nicola and Cheryl were together and then Sarah was, by choice, on her own. I didn't blame her, to be honest. I think she was happy to have the one bit of time away from us.

Nadine: I was seventeen! My parents had done everything before that. They decided how late I could stay out. I'd never had a job. I had nothing that made me an adult, at all.

Kimberley: It was quite the place at the time. The Sugababes were there. In fact, Keisha and I were next-door neighbours.

Keisha: We literally shared a wall in our apartment block. She probably heard things she shouldn't have – I was in a weird relationship back then.

Kimberley: It was nice to know you had someone living next door that you could call on if you needed to. We'd all go out for a night out and the afterparty would just be back there because everyone was going back there anyway. I feel grateful we were part of that last surge of pop bands because that was the most fun part of being in a band. In this generation after us, I don't think it was quite the same. There weren't as many pop bands and it was all quite separate because of the nature of not having the likes of *CD:UK* and *Top of the Pops*. It was a different vibe completely.

Nicola: We didn't know how to work our heating. We didn't know you were supposed to answer letters.

Peter Loraine: This actually happened with Nicola. 'Peter, our electricity's gone off.' I was like, 'Right, okay, we'll speak to them, but I'm assuming you've paid the bill?' 'What?' 'You must have had a bill?' 'I don't think so, we never get any bills.' 'What do you mean you don't get any bills?' 'We don't get any post.' 'Have you checked downstairs in your mailbox?' 'No, what's that?' So downstairs in their apartment was about a year's worth of correspondence.

Kimberley: The record company took over so much of our lives, so in her defence maybe she assumed they would take care of every part of it.

Nadine: They teach you algebra [at school], but no one teaches you how to live as an adult or pay bills.

'We made a conscious decision that we could listen to that other music in our own time'

While the commercial success of 'Sound of the Underground' was to some degree a given, its critical acclaim was unusual. No debut single from a TV talent-show winner before (or after) had managed to cross over to the likes of NME *and the broadsheet supplements. As work started on what would become the band's debut album, named after that call-to-arms smash, the girls were given a brief taste of working with songwriters and producers who weren't part of the Xenomania stable. In fact, the (slightly patchy, let's be honest) 2003 album wound up featuring input from the likes of Steve Anderson, ex-Westlife member Brian McFadden and 'Pure and Simple' co-writer Alison Clarkson, AKA Betty Boo. Towards the end of recording, with that elusive second single still missing, Polydor returned to Brian and Miranda – who had just returned from working with Britney Spears in LA – who presented the band with 'No Good Advice'. Like 'Sound of the Underground', its core sound – Blondie covering 'My Sharona' – was out of step with pop in 2003. To the point where a brief rebellion was mounted by a band keen to replicate the music they were listening to for pleasure.*

Paul Flynn: I really loved the second single, 'No Good Advice'. All the references were so classic; it didn't sound like the references that were around at that time. American music was so future-facing and exciting, but all the British stuff just sounded like watered-down versions of that.

Richard X: It was 'No Good Advice' that I really loved. I felt like they were kindred spirits. They seemed like the sort of band that could fit in my world.

Kimberley: The second single was the main focus while we were working on the album. We were very mindful that it had to be something equally as strong.

Brian Higgins: There was a bit of vengeance in that song. It was the sound of defiance and that was so integral to how we approached that whole decade. We felt we knew better than anyone else about what was a pop record and how great pop could be. 'No Good Advice' in many ways was proof that Xenomania as a creative unit was starting to fire on all cylinders.

Peter Robinson: Anyone who goes on that sort of show isn't quite sure of what to expect when they go into a recording studio for the first time. Then if you add the fact that you're going down to an old vicarage in some ridiculous village in the middle of nowhere and having these really bizarre sounds thrown at you and lyrics, it must have been hard to work out what the song actually was. It's hundreds of interpretations later that there's this magic route through the whole thing. It's extraordinary. I can't imagine it's very enjoyable for an artist unless you submit yourself to the process.

Nicola: Did Brian mention the time we tried to ditch Xenomania? We went back to Brian about February-ish time and he was playing us all these different tracks, little verse and chorus sections. I think there were elements of 'No Good Advice'. But it was all very different to what we were into. We were all listening to Christina Aguilera, Blu Cantrell, more generic female pop-led stuff. With a little bit more of a narrative lyrically. We sat in his backroom as a group and decided we were going to tell him that we didn't like the music. We were like, 'We'll tell him we don't think it's very us and we just don't want to do it.' He comes in and says, 'Girls, is there a problem?' I think it was me that said it. Maybe it was me and Cheryl. We were always the ones – we'd think it as a group but the others would never say it, so we did. And we'd always get into trouble for that.

Jon Shave: They tried to stage a bit of mutiny. He left them in no uncertain terms that it wasn't quite their place to decide that at that point. He insisted they submitted to the process and, to be fair to them, from that moment they absolutely did.

Nadine: I remember several meetings where they tried to get rid of Brian. Several! I liked what Brian was doing. I did think some of the stuff was a bit too whacky. But I always felt like I could say that. He would ask for our perspective on what was happening in our lives, so lyrically it could be more aligned to how we were living rather than from a man in his thirties or Miranda.

Kimberley: He'd play us a song and it was almost like, 'No, you can't have an opinion on this.' Basically, you've got to sing it like robots and we were never going to be okay with that. So it didn't go down very well from his point of view. He wasn't entertaining it, but we said it anyway.

Nicola: Brian literally gave us this twenty-minute rant about how if we don't like it we can go, but we don't have any options and we don't know what we're talking about and we should be so grateful that we're there. He left the room saying, 'So you just think about all those things I've just said.' Early on we made a conscious decision that we could listen to other music in our own time.

Colin Barlow: The fights I had with the girls at the time were just, 'Trust me, you've got to go with these records because you're pushing boundaries – if we play safe and come out with a really lightweight pop record no one will play it.' They didn't get that. People love the edginess of Girls Aloud and records like 'Love Machine' – which they hated at the time – and 'Biology' were so important because they became a guilty pleasure for an *NME* audience that wanted to be cool. Then the penny dropped and Nicola and the others suddenly started to realise that these records are really beneficial to us.

Brian Higgins: [Xenomania] were indie. We infiltrated pop. I was old enough to understand what Roxy Music meant, fusing guitars and electronics. Depeche Mode, New Order, all of these bands. But pop music at that time of Girls Aloud was dreadful because it was being made by cynical guys who were trying to get themselves into the minds of teenagers and write what they think they like. I didn't want anything to do with that. Half the people who worked at Xenomania would never have generally found themselves working on a girl group from a TV show. Never. Not because they were snobby; they just wouldn't have moved in those circles.

Miranda Cooper: I remember people really urging us after they won to get out, that we'd got the best out of it. Then Colin played the album and we just felt like it wasn't our vision for them.

Brian Higgins: Colin sent me the [*Sound of the Underground*] album and I was in LA because we were working with Britney Spears.

Miranda Cooper: We got a phone call from Britney's team saying, 'We want "Sound of the Underground",' and we were like, 'Well, it's already been a hit here, does that matter?' They said they wanted something like it. So we went out to LA and worked with her for a week. We got her to do the same thing as with Girls Aloud – she sang her twenty-eight different choruses or whatever, and there's a CD I've got of all of her vocals. She recorded 'Graffiti My Soul', which sounded awesome. Brian was like [to Britney's label], 'You can only have it if it's going to be her first single,' and I think they said, 'Fuck off.' So it ended up being a Girls Aloud album track [on 2004's *What Will the Neighbours Say?*].

Brian Higgins: I do look back on that and think I was as bloody-minded about that as I was about everything else, but that's why it sounded the way it did. You can't dilute any of it. You can't suddenly pull off a mask; it has to be real.

Colin Barlow: What became really apparent was that any time we put the girls with anyone else, it just didn't sound like anyone. It just sounded like a bunch of girls singing a song.

Brian Higgins: I was annoyed about [the album]. It was bad. I said, 'The rest of this album isn't worthy of our song,' and I really meant it. So Colin said, 'What can you do?', and so we did six more tracks for about £4,000. Really cheap, just to kill everyone and make the album work. So we got them back in and recorded in a very rough-and-ready way.

Miranda Cooper: I think the thing that turned that album around was 'Jump'. It wasn't a done deal for them at all. The fact that we got the broadsheets and music press was brilliant, and that's what drove a lot of their success until the mainstream came on board.

Peter Loraine: After 'No Good Advice' was number two and 'Life Got Cold' got to number three, it felt like things were going in the wrong direction. Then Richard Curtis called saying they wanted someone to record 'Jump' for *Love Actually*. My boss came to me and said, 'I've told him the girls will do it.' I thought it was the wrong move, that it didn't sit well with what they stood for, and he was like, 'You need to understand that something drastic has to change here financially because we're in the hole hugely.' So begrudgingly off we went to do a cover of 'Jump' and it saved the day, to be honest.

Brian Higgins: I couldn't stand 'Jump'. I hated it. I was trying to find a way to make it more aggressive, because the original [by the Pointer Sisters] annoyed me. I wanted to do something that affected the way you heard that record, because it was too sweet. It gave Polydor a stronger position and the album went platinum. It sort of saved them. I think Lucian Grainge knew that this wave of indie-dom was coming and that pop music was going to die. The official word was, 'Everyone, get out of pop, it's fucked.'

Alexis Petridis: I think Xenomania were able to [own Girls Aloud's sound] because Louis Walsh wasn't interested. Nobody really cared. So somebody had to take the reins that maybe wouldn't have been allowed to do that if the usual dark forces were in motion. Also, Brian had a reason to keep them and for them not to be given the same rubbish as everyone else.

Brian Higgins: Colin phoned me and said, 'You need to make the whole of the second album,' and I remember being a bit unsure. But he was like, 'Nope, you have to do it, that's it.'

Colin Barlow: By the second album [2004's *What Will The Neighbours Say?*], no one could get near Girls Aloud. My view was he'd bought the rights to do everything. He was super tough on the girls. No one makes records like they did.

Brian Higgins: I was just happy to please Colin. He understood that these two entities – Girls Aloud and Xenomania – could not be separated. Some of the covers we did were probably pressure he was being put under to make sure there was some situation where they might get some airplay. Radio 1 wouldn't touch them because of the Guildford nightclub incident [in January 2003, Cheryl was found guilty of assault occasioning actual bodily harm but cleared of the racially aggravated assault of nightclub toilet attendant Sophie Amogbokpa]. The best they ever got at Radio 1 was the B-list until [2006's] 'Something Kinda Ooooh'. But that was good from our perspective because once we realised radio were never going to support them we were able to make more and more strange records and have fun with that.

'Not only did you sing five choruses for one song, you sang all of that in five keys'

Girls Aloud's brief taste of the more straightforward recording studio practices for a pop band soon started to feel like a distant memory. At Xenomania, demos didn't exist. Backing tracks numbered the hundreds, as did Miranda Cooper's bank of lyrical ideas. Songs would often resemble the aural equivalent of magic eye posters, with a chorus from one song morphed into the verse of another or vice versa. It was a process that felt more natural, however, as their run of twenty consecutive UK top-ten singles started to gather momentum.

Brian Higgins: Because the music was constantly being made, there'd be eighty or ninety musical ideas that would have been created from the albums being delivered to them coming round for the next one eight months later. We'd be making music that whole time for Girls Aloud and the Sugababes – we wanted to run the two groups together but keep the sound separate. We'd write about fifteen or sixteen songs and that would be it. And in those songs had to be the singles, had to be everything.

Nicola: We wouldn't have dared ask to hear what they were doing with the Sugababes. Brian controlled his surroundings acutely and I think it was important for him in terms of how he was able to differentiate the two. The Sugababes were very edgy; they were the All Saints to our Spice Girls. We had a blonde, we had a brunette, we had a really leggy one. We were very tabloid-heavy. Also, the Sugababes got to work with other producers as well, whereas for us it was only Brian because our sound was so specific.

Brian Higgins: No one [hears the finished song at the time]. I just can't do that. Nothing sounded like the final version at the start. That's the whole point. The records would be made well after the girls had left. We'd deem an idea a hit and then we'd expand it into a bigger piece of music.

Nicola: I remember being in LA shooting the 'Call the Shots' video and we had *Tangled Up* delivered to us. We were in a room in the Standard, I think, and Hilary played it while we were all sitting around the bed. We were just like, 'Yeah . . .', and we started comparing it to *Chemistry*. Like it's not got what that album had. Little did we know that *Tangled Up* was actually our best one.

Nadine: On that album, Brian and Miranda came out to LA [where I was living] and we worked in a studio in Sunset Marquis. We'd just finished the [Chemistry] tour and I think the rest of the girls were off on holiday and I would get a few days and then it would be straight in the studio trying to get the songs together. The songs would then be chosen by Brian and the girls would come in at a later date and sing.

Nicola: Some people reading this will be like, 'What, you just used to have your record handed to you?', but the way in which the songs were formulated, it had to be that way. We didn't know how a song was going to be curated.

Brian Higgins: The band members weren't picked because of the suitability of their voices together; they were picked by the public based on their personalities. The truth of the matter is to get them to sit incredibly comfortably on one record was difficult. But they also had a rock singer in Nadine, which meant she could sing all sorts of stuff very loudly. Which was thrilling from my perspective because the louder it is, the faster it is, the better it is.

Nicola: We were in the studio a long time doing all of these different sections and we had to sing the songs in five different keys. So not only did you sing four verses and five choruses for one song, you sang all of that in five keys. That was just one song idea. People would say, 'Oh, I bet they don't all stand around the same microphone,' and we'd be like, 'Do you want to try doing a song in eighteen parts that's in five different keys around one microphone?' Someone would have been killed.

Miranda Cooper: I remember Shaznay Lewis on a review show on Radio 1 saying ['The Show'] sounds like four songs gelled together and I remember thinking, 'Yes, basically.'

Nicola: One day I took my sister to the studio and when we left she was like, 'Is that what you have to do every time?', and I'd be like, 'Yeah.'

Miranda Cooper: We had five or six different studios set up and, when I say 'studio', we had these screens made and then we'd put a duvet over the top. And sometimes it was in the loo because it would be a better sound in there. We'd have a list in each studio of what needed to be done and the girls would go around each one. Then we'd get everything loaded into Brian's computer and we'd give the individual bits stars out of five and put what key worked. It sounds like it was a special formula but actually it was hugely creative.

Brian Higgins: In the songwriter industry, everyone was like, 'Let us at Girls Aloud, let us in,' and so I thought that if we lose one single slot we'll lose it all. We were motivated every year to make them better and to make us better. It was very creatively greedy. It was a sickness really.

Peter Robinson: You could tell that a lot of the people around the band were really excited by the band. Thinking back, maybe that was one of the big differences compared to a lot of pop music that had come before that. Like, say, with Atomic Kitten – who around that band was excited by it? Were the label excited? They might be excited by the success, but that's not the same. Or management? Or the songwriters and producers? They did some efficient music, but were they really excited by it? The members of the band – did they find it exciting? Girls Aloud showed it could be something people should be excited about.

'It would always be "I really like Xenomania" or "I'm not saying I like Girls Aloud"'

In 2006, Sheffield indie saviours the Arctic Monkeys appeared on BBC Radio 1's Live Lounge where they covered Girls Aloud's 2004 opus 'Love Machine'. At that time – let's call it peak joyless 'guilty pleasure' syndrome – it was par for the course for indie stalwarts to strip back a pop bop to highlight the song's apparently hereto untapped brilliance using their weapon of choice: the acoustic guitar. With the Arctic Monkeys cover, it served to double down on what a bonkers song 'Love Machine' was and also how Girls Aloud's best moments often used guitars in far more interesting ways than most indie bands. (In 2008, they'd poke fun at some of their NME *Awards drinking buddies on caustic B-side 'Hoxton Heroes'.) It was also just one of many moments in which Girls Aloud transcended their pop bubble, often appearing in the pages of the* NME *or reviewed in* Q *or given space in broadsheet supplements such as the* Observer Music Monthly. *That Girls Aloud had done it via a TV talent-show route just made the whole thing more surprising.*

Brian Higgins: Girls Aloud started as the real underdogs and then the Guildford incident happened and they were literally hated. That's why when the *NME* adopted them it was like, 'Yes.' Everyone else thought they were this racist pop group, which was absurd.

Nicola: We were aware that we had cool press. We knew that critically it was working, which Brian must have loved.

Brian Higgins: It felt like we'd found a community. I felt great about that. They understood it, intellectually. Around *Tangled Up* we were still in our creative zenith. Franz Ferdinand were flirting around us, Arctic Monkeys were, Coldplay covered 'Call the Shots'. The whole world seemed to understand what we were doing.

Miranda Cooper: We agreed to do the Franz Ferdinand album [in 2007] but the reality was they were too much of their own entity. They were taking hours EQ-ing one drum sound and Brian was just like, 'Write with us, let's collaborate.'

Brian Higgins: I invariably found getting people to realise the material just isn't very good too painful. I would eventually feel like they were dragging me to the place where the worst ideas existed. I was used to going where I wanted to go, to where the best ideas were, and no one would stop me. I would invariably resign from these projects and say, 'I can't do that.' That was certainly the case with Franz Ferdinand. We were blurring the boundaries between pop and indie so well that it was inevitable those groups would come in to try to work it out. I think we were really our own band and we needed to work with artists that didn't write their own songs. The most undiluted, best version of Xenomania was that. When people came in to break off the bit they wanted, the inspiration they no longer had, I would find that difficult because I would start seeing through them creatively.

Alexis Petridis: The Girls Aloud songs felt futuristic at a time when 'alternative music', or what was being presented as alternative music, was feeling ever more like a re-hash of stuff that had come before. If you look at the history of indie music, it's always had an element of the past to it, but you'd sprinkle your own thing on top of it. And that sprinkling of your own thing had just ceased to happen. [Girls Aloud's music] just seemed more futuristic and exciting than, say, 'She Moves in Her Own Way' by the Kooks. It didn't seem peculiar to me or out of the ordinary to say these records were good. I didn't feel like I was fighting for pop music.

Peter Robinson: That's kind of why I started Popjustice. This idea that you don't have to love the band in order to be able to love the music. Even though I did love a lot of pop bands, at the heart of it I always loved the music and I think that's what happened throughout the 2000s with Girls Aloud and Sugababes – people began to have a grudging respect. But then it would always be 'I really like Xenomania' or 'I'm not saying I like Girls Aloud.'

Laura Snapes: In the '90s, Britpop reached a critical mass where rock stars were being invited to No. 10 and what was underground went totally overground. So in the '00s you see publications like *NME* trying to re-entrench the idea of an underground and a cool alternative to the mainstream that's not just what has come before. But by the end of that decade stuff like Kaiser Chiefs and Arctic Monkeys were the mainstream again, so the alternative look and the whole hipster thing went mainstream, too. I wonder if pop reflexively gains a new sort of appeal because it's like we don't need this dumb separation of mainstream and alternative any more, it just started to seem really false.

Alexis Petridis: People always revere early '80s new pop, but it only works if it's popular with people who aren't going, 'The semiotics of this are very interesting.' It's got to be popular with kids. That's the point. Whatever you see yourself as doing, unless you're actually in the charts and unless the people buying your records are not *NME* readers, they're tweens, then it doesn't work, no matter how clever you're being. I interviewed Girls Aloud for *GQ* magazine and they were gratified by it. But it was not part of the game plan. Like, finally the man we were attempting to reach with our music is here!

Colin Barlow: When we did the Girls Aloud *Greatest Hits* album [in 2006], we did market research and they were such a guilty pleasure that we didn't put their pictures on the sleeve. We created more generic imagery so that anyone could buy a Girls Aloud best of and it sold a million copies. If you were a guy, it was alright to have a Girls Aloud album.

Peter Robinson: There was something quite chaotic about the band. Peter Loraine and Sundraj [Sreenivasan, the band's PR] did a really good job of harnessing that and channelling it in the right direction. It was quite messy and unsanitised. The way Sundraj was choosing the journalists he was taking the band to and the places he was positioning them in. It was about keeping the *Smash Hits* side of things ticking over but also going, 'Okay, this music doesn't sound like a lot of pop, so therefore this band doesn't have to do everything other pop bands always have to do.'

Peter Loraine: It was such a collaborative thing. There was a big debate over what was going to be the third single from *Tangled Up*, then it's decided it's going to be 'Can't Speak French', so we get them to sing it in French [for B-side 'Je Ne Parle Pas Français']. But no one can speak French, so we have to find someone who can teach them.

Peter Robinson: I guess there's something exciting about a big stupid pop band doing something exciting and edgy. Compared with a band like the Sugababes, who as soon as they came out went straight to *NME* and straight to *The Face*. They were cool from the start, so the idea of a big pop band being cool is more exciting than a cool band being cool.

Paul Flynn: The thing is, Girls Aloud weren't amazing. They were sort of ephemerally amazing. People would say, 'Oh, Girls Aloud are the new Spice Girls,' but they're nothing like the Spice Girls. The Spice Girls were driven, ambitious, they had this demonic energy to them. Girls Aloud reminded me of Bananarama. That sort of 'can't be arsed' attitude.

'It was very much stiff upper lip and we just got on with it'

The rise of Girls Aloud chimed not only with the rise of celebrity magazines, but also with the explosion in reality TV. Suddenly a new stratum of celebrity had been created, one that seemed more accessible and attainable.

That in turn made for a blurring of the lines between what is up for grabs and what isn't, with the blunt, critical language used towards celebrities in print often mirroring the chats viewers would have at home. Gobby, opinionated and frank, Girls Aloud were a tabloid dream, with Sarah, Cheryl and Nicola singled out for specific attention as the years went on. For Nicola, this focus soon morphed into personality takedowns following bullying by the likes of Busted's Matt Willis and DJ Chris Moyles (the then Radio 1 breakfast host called Nicola '[the] ropey-looking ginger one', 'horsey chops' and a 'sour-faced old cow' on air).

Nicola: The media were more interested in girls having cat-fights than pillow fights. We definitely weren't wallflowers and if somebody said something nasty we'd say something. Plus we were always being asked about it all in interviews. We didn't have the decorum to go, 'We're not getting involved in that.' Being a little rough and ready, if someone says, 'Oh, Lily Allen's slagged Cheryl off,' your natural reaction is to get your back up as a tough girl.

Kimberley: [The label] never encouraged us, but anything that was in there was natural. I don't think the label minded it because it was all promo at the end of the day. Nothing was fake.

Nicola: Our tour manager used to put newspapers in the car, God only knows why because it was so unhealthy. We'd have *The Sun*, the *Star*, the *Mirror*, the *Sport* – Christ – and then *People*, *News of the World*. We'd be in every single one. It would be one of us on the cover of the *Sport* coming out of a night-club or someone saying something nasty about me or Cheryl spotted here. It just felt like that was life. It was a time when we didn't really talk about our mental health, we didn't talk about bullying, it was very much stiff upper lip. So no one ever came to me and said, 'I can see you're struggling.' There was none of that. We didn't talk about it. It wasn't a rallying-around situation, it was just, 'That's happening.'

Kimberley: It was difficult to watch [Nicola struggling with negative coverage] but you were never quite sure how much she'd seen and she was so young we just wanted to protect her [from it] as much as possible. Now in retrospect I feel like she was holding it all inside and suffering in silence. I probably should have dealt with it differently. You just wouldn't get away with it now – she was a seventeen-year-old girl.

Nicola: We didn't necessarily have the emotional intelligence to be able to have a perspective on it, whereas if that was happening now I'd be strong enough to say, 'This is a load of shit, why are you doing this?' Back then we just had to take it.

Nadine: I didn't take much nonsense from anybody. People would say, 'Nadine's difficult' or 'Nadine's a diva,' but I'm not. I'm just not going to let somebody talk to me like shit. If that makes me a diva then so be it. I thought everyone in the band should have that 'fuck it' attitude. If someone's being abusive then the floor is open for you to snap back. I remember someone [Matt Willis from Busted] called Nicola a rude ginger bitch and so I told her to paint it on her skirt [for a performance at G-A-Y in 2003]. I was like, 'Fuck them, write it, don't let them intimidate you.' Who are these people? FUCK OFF.

Lucie Cave: Girls Aloud represented a cross-section in the same way you had with the Spice Girls. With Cheryl, the stories just didn't stop coming and she was a showbiz journalist's dream really in terms of who she was and where she'd come from. She was stunningly beautiful and she obviously still had that grit about her. Then there was that story in the papers about her and the toilet attendant, which is something she took ages to shake off. Inevitably that makes her even more interesting as a celebrity.

Alexis Petridis: It was at a point where everything was becoming increasingly streamlined and media training had become a bigger thing. I can see why – people kept saying really stupid things. Like Lee Ryan. But as a journalist it's really boring and actually as an audience it's really boring as well. I'm not in any way condoning what Cheryl did, but fights happen in nightclub toilets all the time to ordinary people. People get drunk and do stupid things all the time. Girls Aloud felt a bit uncontrolled. There was always this mad stuff around them.

Dean Piper: Girls were always on the front of the papers. Guys would only get on the front page if they were really doing something bad, like drugs or affairs or an arrest, but girls could get on there if they wore an outfit or if they were thin or if they'd pulled a Posh Spice and got a footballer boyfriend. It was an opportunity to have five bits of fresh meat in the celebrity circuit. Girls Aloud were the first proper TV talent-show pawns for the papers to play with when they came out of a show like that. It felt like a big deal.

Nicola: We felt misogyny from the media in what women are supposed to do and what they're not supposed to do compared to a male artist. But in our own world we felt really powerful in being five women. It's nice that we weren't media-trained because we were able to have a voice and were never silenced.

Kimberley: We did *Blue Peter* and they made us dress as nurses from different eras. We didn't kick off about it at the time – it's *Blue Peter*, it's an institution – but we were in a band trying to be cool. Some things you just knew you had to do. Any of the tabloids you were just like, 'Oh, God, do we really have to?' In one sense they're asking us to do a piece of promo, but you know that the next week they're going to be writing some rubbish about you so you'd feel resentful you had to play the game.

'No, help the Pet Shop Boys out on somebody else's time'

By 2008, Girls Aloud were in a curious position of being a cult pop band with four top-twenty albums under their studded H&M belts. While the top-ten hits had kept coming, it still felt like their music was perhaps a bit too left-of-centre to have properly infiltrated the 'two albums a year from Tesco' portion of the mainstream. That all changed after Cheryl replaced Sharon Osbourne as a judge on the fifth series of The X Factor *in the summer of 2008. Suddenly, the band was being mentioned in front of millions of people each week. Keen to harness this new audience, Xenomania knew the band needed a big first single to launch fifth album* Out of Control. *In the end, they came up with two: 'The Promise' and 'The Loving Kind'. For the girls, however, there was only ever one choice – and they were keen to make their voices heard.*

Nicola: We definitely felt a gear change. The TV shows we were doing were bigger, our outfits were way more expensive, we were selling out more shows. We didn't have social media [to gauge], so it was more, 'How many times do we see ourselves on TV? How many times are we on the radio? How many times are we in the newspapers?' I think Cheryl being on *The X Factor* introduced us to a bigger audience – the show was getting 10 million viewers every weekend. It opened the doors for us as a group.

Brian Higgins: We knew they were ready to be a supergroup, so therefore they needed a supergroup sound. A step up from everything we'd done before. And more commercial really. The minute the piece of music that went on to become 'The Promise' was identified it was ring-fenced as the first single. So me and Miranda sat down and planned strategically how we were going to write the song, where we were going to write it, what time of day we were going to write it. Everything. To have an appointment with a number-one record.

Miranda Cooper: We were so sure of ourselves at that point. We were moving so much into the mainstream – actually, about to be chucked out the other side. One day Brian said, 'Let's write our number-one hit for Girls Aloud.' I said I didn't feel like it – could we do it tomorrow? And we did it. It was weird with that song because it wasn't spiky, it was mainstream, and it wasn't shocking lyrically. We were a bit nervous about it: is this what people want?

Brian Higgins: We couldn't mess it up. We went in at 5 p.m. on a Wednesday, a beautiful sunny day, and we wrote 'The Promise' in about seven minutes. We sat at opposite ends of the room and sang our ideas and threw them all in together. 'The Promise' has an intro, then the chorus, then there's verse one and pre-chorus one. Then there's another chorus. Then there's verse two, which is different from verse one, pre-chorus two, which is different to pre-chorus one, and another chorus and a middle section. So seven different melodic parts. That's their more commercial sound.

Nicola: Because I used to write a little bit I knew how to work the computer in the writing room. I've never told Brian this, but I'd go into the computer and open the folder that said 'Girls Aloud – options' and I'd click through everything. I remember hearing all these parts for 'The Promise' and saying to the other girls, 'There's a song that I like, it feels retro, almost like Motown, it's so cool.'

Miranda Cooper: I remember 'The Loving Kind' was difficult because that was going to be the first single.

Nicola: They were like, '"The Loving Kind" is the single we're going with,' and we all categorically said, 'We will not promote this song, we won't do any press, we basically will not work for you if this is the song you want to put out first.'

Nadine: I said, 'Well, I'm going to fly back to LA, phone me whenever "The Promise" is the single and I'll come back.' It worked. Literally within an hour it was 'The Promise' and we all continued with our days.

Kimberley: We'd got to the point in our careers where we were like, 'We're the ones that have to go and front it and if we don't believe in it then that's crazy.' So we dug our heels in.

Nicola: We were calling each other saying, 'If Colin rings you or Brian rings you, don't you dare buckle, stand strong with the group!' Colin was like, 'This is career suicide if you go with this song as your first single.' But we felt it was right, and it was. It was a huge machine around us but it also felt really close-knit. Because of the foundations that we built early on, we were still able to communicate personally with the label. We never felt like we couldn't have an opinion, because we'd started off with that dynamic between us and them.

Nadine: It was a strategic play as to why they wanted 'The Loving Kind'. They were working with an act that had written it. Was it Duran Duran? No, it was somebody anyway. Pet Shop Boys? And I was like, 'No, help the Pet Shop Boys out on somebody else's time.'

Miranda Cooper: I think probably Colin loved the idea 'The Loving Kind' was [co-written by] the Pet Shop Boys. It was a good story. 'The Promise' was my favourite and it was the right choice.

Colin Barlow: The fact they were so passionate about it was the reason to do it. It was good to see because sometimes I'd have moments with them where I'd be saying, 'You've got to be more passionate about your music, you've got to have ownership.' I think 'The Promise' is a magical moment for that group because it felt like it was their song. Maybe 'The Loving Kind' would have been that classic thing of going safe, while 'The Promise' wasn't safe. The girls had realised that to go with something risky was a bigger look for them. 'The Promise' was them growing up.

Peter Loraine: To win the BRIT [for Best Single for 'The Promise' in 2009] was brilliant for them, because they deserved it. I absolutely can't bear music snobbery. I would find it hard when people who liked indie bands would diminish the achievements of pop acts.

Miranda Cooper: On *Out of Control*, Nadine was living in America and wasn't that reliable about turning up to the studio when she was supposed to, so Sarah really stepped forward. Her moments on 'The Promise' were obviously amazing. She was very much taking over that lead role.

'We understood it was beautiful'

Five months after signing a new record deal, in July 2009, Girls Aloud announced a hiatus, a move eventually delayed slightly so they could support Coldplay at Wembley Stadium. Solo albums followed for Cheryl, Nicola, Nadine and Kimberley, while Sarah dabbled in acting. In 2012, to celebrate their ten-year anniversary, the band reformed, releasing stomping single 'Something New' and another greatest hits album, Ten. *On the final date of the accompanying hits tour, the band (minus Nadine) posted a TwitLonger announcing they were to split.*

Kimberley: I don't know [what Girls Aloud's legacy is]. I don't really think you can objectively look at yourself in that way. I'd love to know how other people see us and what we are and what we stand for.

Nicola: I think our legacy is how lawless our songs were. How we paved our own way in our own lane. We really did take risks and against the odds we as five very normal girls managed to achieve incredible things with an incredible team around us. We weren't moulded within a Sylvia Young-type situation so we all had different personalities. You can kind of see me awkwardly dancing around to the song, then you've got someone like Cheryl who's a born performer, and then Sarah's quirky personality . . . I just think the different ingredients of the five of us meant you didn't have this static image of the group.

Nadine: A lot of people took a lot of strength from those songs and from our journey. And still do. Also, the songs haven't aged. They still sound as fresh today.

Brian Higgins: We understood it was beautiful. Everything about it was beautiful. There's the tension in the sound, which is us not wanting to cock it up, but it was a beautiful sum of its parts.

Alexis Petridis: It hinged on them as much as it did the producers. If it hadn't, Xenomania would have gone on to launch loads of other amazing artists, and they didn't. They tried to launch people like Mini Viva [in 2009] and it didn't work. There was no one that came out of a TV talent show that was remotely like them. Girls Aloud seemed like a blip, an aberration. Something that happened almost by mistake.

Miranda Cooper: People would ask, 'Do you think the best songs would have worked with anyone else?', and they wouldn't. It's a special alchemy. With Girls Aloud, we got close to finding this magic.

★ ★ ★

Tragically, in September 2021, the band's heart-on-the-sleeve force, Sarah Harding, died aged just thirty-nine from breast cancer. In the months before her death, the band reunited for sleepovers, re-living a whole lotta history.

Nadine: Whenever we all met up recently with Sarah, she just wanted to watch [2006's documentary series *Girls Aloud: Off the Record*]. Every episode. We sat and watched them all in our PJs.

14
The saga of Rachel Stevens' 'Some Girls'

How did a glam rock-inspired song alluding to blow jobs and dangerous power dynamics in the music industry recorded by an ex-member of S Club 7 become a charity single? And why did it (allegedly) cause a former Spice Girl to lock herself in a car by way of protest? If these are questions you've ever asked yourself, then I don't believe you, but please read on regardless.

The ludicrous 'Some Girls' is one of the more storied singles of the '00s. It also represents the way songs would ping-pong around labels before settling on a home. Having plied her trade as one-seventh of acting/singing/smiling triple threats S Club 7, Rachel Stevens was in a strange position as a solo artiste by the start of 2004. While her debut single 'Sweet Dreams My LA Ex', an intoxicating mix of tabloid-ready drama (albeit someone else's – it was co-written by Cathy Dennis for Britney Spears as a response to Justin Timberlake's

'Cry Me a River') and Swedish experimentalists Bloodshy & Avant's skeletal production, had crashed into the charts at number two in September 2003, the David Bowie-sampling follow-up 'Funky Dory' stalled at a disastrous twenty-six. In an era where you were only as good as your last single, Stevens was seemingly headed towards the dumper. She did, however, still have S Club 7 overlord Simon Fuller in her corner, a man who could sniff out a hit from 100 miles away.

Thankfully for Rachel, in a small studio in London, Richard X and his rebellious songwriting cohort Hannah Robinson had started work on something completely bonkers that would be strangely perfect for her.

'The idea was the casting couch'

Richard X: 'Some Girls' was about making a pop record with my sounds and my ideas and my slightly odd sense of humour. I like that multi-layered thing; I like records about records. That's kind of what 'Some Girls' is. It was the first time I met Hannah and it was a fortuitous meeting.

Hannah Robinson: We hit it off immediately. He liked the melodies I was singing and we were always talking about topics that could work for lyrics.

Richard X: I think it was done with Girls Aloud in mind.

Hannah Robinson: It definitely wasn't 'This is for Rachel.'

Richard X: It had this glam rhythm and there was a lot of German electroclash influences, Goldfrapp was doing that stuff, too. I made the demo of 'Some Girls' pretty much as you hear it but with Hannah singing it. It's quite a dark story.

Hannah Robinson: I don't even know how we got on to what we were talking about. It's one of those things where it could have been more ordinary but we took it somewhere else. When you think about Epstein and Weinstein, the song is probably ahead of the curve in terms of its subject matter.

Richard X: The idea was the casting couch. Hannah was on board with that and she brought a lot of ideas to the table, so we had her lyrics and my lyrics. I would never have done a singalong melody like it does in the chorus, that was Hannah's idea, but it was perfect because it just sounds quite insane.

'I didn't have any other thoughts than, "Geri is going to ruin my song"'

The mythology of 'Some Girls' is a glorious hotchpotch of gossip, misunderstandings and truths stranger than fiction. As is the way with these things, the demo – still featuring Hannah's vocal – had managed to work its way out of Richard's studio and on to the stereos of various A&Rs and managers – including Geri Halliwell's – keen to dabble in a more experimental pop world post-'Freak Like Me' and Girls Aloud. Even after the creators of 'Some Girls' had settled on the perfect vehicle for their song, there were still fights to be had, revenge songs to be written and a few rumours regarding Geri to settle.

Hannah Robinson: 'Some Girls' ended up being a song that people liked and wanted.

Richard X: Actually [underrated Norwegian pop star] Annie wanted to do 'Some Girls', but it had already gone. It wasn't important to me that Rachel Stevens had done the music she'd done in S Club; it was just important that she'd been in a band. It fitted so well with what we were doing.

Hannah Robinson: At that time, I was working on Geri's album with [songwriter and producer] Ian Masterson. She came in and I had no idea she'd had the track sent to her – as far as I knew, Rachel was cutting it – and the first thing she said was, 'I'm so excited about recording this song, I've got a new middle eight.'

Simon Jones: I feel certain that I heard her version. I definitely know it was the plan to release it. And I remember the conversations of, like, 'We don't have that song any more.' It was awful.

Richard X: I've never met Geri Halliwell, but I just thought [her version] was going to be rubbish. You stand and fall by your records and I was saying things about left-field pop, so you can't do something rubbish at that stage. You can't have something so out of your control. My publisher at Warner Chappell had played it to whoever and it was like, 'Geri is doing this.' *Is* doing this. They already had a director for the video. I think it was David LaChapelle. It was like, 'Geri's got some good ideas for it,' and then, 'Has anyone asked Richard about this?' The answer was no.

Hannah Robinson: Then she said she wanted to change part of the song and I rather naïvely said, 'Oh, that song's gone.' It didn't go down very well.

Richard X: It was dangerous ground for Hannah.

Hannah Robinson: A phone call was made while I was standing there. She called her manager and said she was unhappy and then the next minute my manager was being called. I remember the quote from her manager to mine was, 'Can you let Hannah know she'll never work in this town again.' I then have this relayed to me later and I am absolutely beside myself, I'm in tears. Geri is an icon. I was lucky to be working with her and I'd already upset her by saying she couldn't have the song she wanted. It was snowballing. I thought my career was in the bin. It wasn't Geri who relayed that information, it was her management, which is completely different.

Richard X: I did not give any thought to the commercial value of Geri doing it. I didn't give any consideration to what Hannah thought either. I didn't have any other thoughts than, 'Geri is going to ruin my song.' I didn't want Geri hamming it up.

Hannah Robinson: Time passes and Ian and I are invited to LA by Geri to continue writing. There was this huge element of pressure because they wanted 'Some Girls', but it had already happened. Songs don't happen like that every day.

Richard X: I think because they'd presumed the whole campaign was a cert, they had the song, they'd just forgotten to ask me. But with Rachel it felt perfect. We fit in this world; this is '00s world, this is not patronising pop, and she'd be great for it. Also, the song projects so well onto her. It made so much more sense. Later I was told Geri had locked herself in her car in protest. I would have loved to have seen it, obviously.

Hannah Robinson: In LA there was a situation where Geri was in the car. That did happen. There's been a few stories that have merged, so I just want to set the record straight. It had been a really strange morning that day anyway because I'd been sick in her car. She had to pull over while she was on her phone. We arrived at the studio and there was something in the press that day that had upset her. So she said, 'I'm going to sit in the car for a bit.' This is at 11 a.m. Ian and I were in this amazing studio and there were security cameras everywhere so we could see Geri hop into this SUV. We sat there having a coffee, still watching the CCTV to see when she was coming back. I think the car door opened at 6 p.m. It transpires she'd fallen asleep. So somewhere along the line that's morphed into it being about the 'Some Girls' thing, but that's not the case.

Richard X: She did write a reaction song.

Hannah Robinson: Didn't it say, 'excuse me Mr X' or something? I feel like I did get to hear that but I don't know how.

Richard X: It was a glam song, so it was a bit like 'Some Girls', but it was like, 'Excuse me Mr X / Let me kiss your lips / Unwind my knickers from this twist'. I think I probably turned it off at that point.

'I was trying to evoke this glam era and the idea of post-industrial wastelands'

Rather than focus on the more everyday lyrical motifs of the era, the pair quickly started transposing their passion for black humour into pop songs that didn't rely on comforting relatability. Songs were formed via studio-based gossip sessions or from tabloid whispers or, in the case of Annie's excellent 'Me Plus One', from a Geri saga that was still unravelling. Remixes, meanwhile, were inspired by the post-industrial 1970s and necessitated Richard asking Rachel Stevens questions about the Winter of Discontent.

Hannah Robinson: We would take inspiration from all sorts of silly stuff. For instance, a producer friend of mine once invited me to a Cathy Dennis party. I idolised Cathy. So I went to Richard's studio and I said, 'You'll never guess what, I'm going to Cathy's party.' Then the next day my friend calls and says, 'Oh, Han, you can't come, she's only celebrating having a new kitchen so it's just a few of us.' The next day I went back in with Richard and said I was really disappointed, so we wrote a song called Cathy's Party. The chorus goes something like, 'Everybody's going to Cathy's party, everybody's going but me'. The songs that have less meaning always felt a bit more meh. 'Me Plus One' by Annie, for example, was loosely based around Geri [and the 'Some Girls' saga]. It was very jokey and it wasn't meant to be unpleasant at all.

Richard X: When we did the recording of 'Some Girls', I took [Rachel] to one side and said, 'Look, I've got this idea for the remix.' It was just a way of getting some off-the-cuff stuff and if you've ever met Rachel she's really guarded. So I sat her down for this Q&A and she went along with it. I was trying to evoke this glam era and the idea of the 1970s, the post-industrial wastelands of the north. She was very confused. The idea behind it was ZTT. They used to have these very long B-sides where they'd cut up interviews with Frankie [Goes to Hollywood] or Paul Morley. So I wanted to do that. No one questioned it. It was only when the Sports Relief thing came along that my plans for it all fell apart. That was quite scary. 'Richard, I've got really exciting news for you . . .' It always starts like that.

'No one ever asked what it was about – they just heard it as a fun thing'

Launched in 2002 as part of the biennial Friday-night charity event Comic Relief, the more energetic Sport Relief came with an accompanying fundraising single. In 2002, this meant Elton John re-working 'Your Song' as a duet with opera singer Alessandro Safina. In later years, acts like McFly, JLS and Little Mix would all release songs tangentially linked to either the charity's get-up-and-go spirit or the event's prevailing mood of offering hope and emotional support to those in need. But in July 2004, for reasons unknown, a song about the dark machinations of the music industry set to a glam rock beat was selected. It peaked at number two.

Hannah Robinson: Half the time you'd deliver a song like that and [the label] would not hear what you were writing about. 'Some Girls' has a really dark subject with a really pop melody. I didn't worry until I heard it was going to be a charity record. That did feel a little bit inappropriate.

Richard X: Maybe the song was just there on the desk and it was like, 'Oh, this will do.' You know that feeling when you've done something a bit naughty at school and you're just laughing hysterically because the naughtiness is continuing.

Hannah Robinson: No one ever asked what it was about. Rachel didn't ask either. The lyrics were there in front of her. The oral sex stuff is implied in regards to the Champagne making it taste so much better, but that could also be about making something more palatable.

Richard X: I think a journalist brought up [the fact the song alludes to blow jobs] with Rachel in an interview and she was horrified. I didn't tell her because she didn't ask. If she'd asked what she was singing about, I would have said about the idea of the casting couch being prevalent in the industry. In the era we're in now, we wouldn't have done that. But at the time it was the up-and-down world of showbiz.

'It's telling a story – it just happens to be a rude one'

While 'Some Girls' took on a life of its own, unwittingly causing problems everywhere it went, another Richard X and Hannah Robinson curio was still waiting for a home. Once again, what had started out as a playful, black-humoured lyric meant to poke and prod at a standard lyrical trope – this time the rubbish boyfriend – had quickly gone down a very different road.

Richard X: One person who had a narrow escape was Paloma Faith, because she was also signed to [Simon Fuller's management company] 19 at that time. She was going to do some electropop with me. But Frankie [Bridge, neé Sandford] cut a couple of songs we'd already done. One was called 'Birthday', which is quite unsavoury. Ask Hannah about that one. Ask her why we would do that to someone like Frankie.

Hannah Robinson: It's really important that you know we did not write this with her in mind. It was just the result of something I said. Basically, Richard and I were talking and I started waffling on about men who insist on having anal sex with women. There was some joke flying around the room like, 'only on your birthday', that kind of thing. This turned into, 'Let's do a song, it will be hilarious.' Some of the lyrics are 'You tried to turn this girl around / You tried to do me over'. When you first hear that, it could just be about a rat bag, but as the song goes on there's lyrics like, 'Something's up and my earth isn't moving'. We had so much fun coming up with all these little double entendres. In the second verse it goes, 'You said it was a compliment underneath the covers / You said that we could make a change and put it all behind us'. Basically someone heard it and wanted Frankie to do it. All of a sudden it felt really wrong. It's telling a story – it just happens to be a rude one. I'm relieved nothing happened with it. I mean she did record it, but it was never released.

15
The X Factor's journey to cultural domination

By the mid-'00s, pop music felt intrinsically linked with Saturday-night television. After two seasons as the pantomime villain on *Pop Idol*, Simon Cowell, resplendent in ludicrously high-waisted stone-washed denim, was itching for something new. In fact, what he wanted most was more control, with the consensus being that 2003's second, and final, season of *Pop Idol* had somehow settled on the 'wrong' winner in Michelle McManus. In conjunction with Sony Music, Cowell successfully pitched a new talent show, *The X Factor*, to ITV in 2004. Scrapping *Pop Idol*'s age limit of twenty-six, *The X Factor* would further differentiate itself from Simon Fuller's creation by splitting its contestants into three categories: 16–24s, Over-25s and Groups. The show's winner would then be awarded a million-pound contract with Cowell's new label, Syco.

By 2007's fourth series, the 16–24s category had been split into Boys and Girls as – surprise surprise – the younger contestants started to dominate. Keeping the added competitive frisson between judges, as initiated years before in *Popstars: The Rivals*, each of *The X Factor*'s industry overlords – Simon, Louis Walsh and Sharon Osbourne, initially, with more added and subtracted throughout the show's fifteen series – were handed a specific category to 'mentor'.

The shiniest of shiny floor Saturday entertainment shows, *The X Factor* launched on 4 September 2004 with 5.25 million viewers. By the time Steve Brookstein was announced as the inaugural winner on 11 December, the show had peaked at over 9 million. While everything was going swimmingly from a TV point of view – and the 6 million votes logged for Brookstein alone in the final must have been music to ITV's ears – 35-year-old Brookstein's win felt like a disappointment. His brand of sensibly suited Pizza Express jazz undermined the brazen confidence of the show's title. While Brookstein's look and sound may have slotted into the post-Bublé boom in nice men doing nice covers of nice songs, Brookstein himself seemed unwilling to play nice. He would be the last winner from the more worldly wise 'Overs' category for nine years.

'We didn't have a band name on the day so we put "the Smiths" down on our application'

Each series of The X Factor *was split into four distinct phases: auditions (thousands of people, lots of 'joke' contestants); bootcamp (fewer people, more tears); judges' houses (swimming pools, yet more tears); and, finally, the live shows (long-winded 'controversies', proper guest pop stars). As the decade wore on,* The X Factor *continued to hunt for stars who could not only prove the show worked in the UK but also on a global stage. Along the way, it found contestants that could easily slot into what was successful at that time (Shayne Ward's mix of Robbie Williams' cheeky sex appeal and Justin Timberlake's sleek sophistication), while also conjuring up ones that felt like old-school throwbacks to an era only half a decade old (step forward, Jedward and the Steps-esque Same Difference). It was at the audition stage, however, that acts got an early taste of what they were letting themselves in for.*

Paul Flynn: Cowell was like Malcom McLaren or Tony Wilson suddenly had a pop iteration. There was something so 'I don't give a fuck' about him. His idea was so simple – let's just put people on television each week doing karaoke and tart it up. He was really canny.

Steve Brookstein, winner, series one: I was on my way to a gig and I saw [*The X Factor*] advertised on TV. I took a note of the number, called it and they said they'd send me a form. The funny thing was I completely forgot about it. Three days before my audition, I found the letter among my other unopened letters that always accompanied me and I was like, 'What's this? It's not brown, it's not threatening.' I opened it and it was ITV talking about an audition date. I was like, 'Oh, when is it? Ah, it's three days away, that's lucky I opened it.' Or not. Depends how you look at it now.

Shayne Ward, winner, series two: I actually missed my first audition. You get a letter sent but I had gone on holiday. So they suggested I go to the open day. You get a lot of scouts now who see you online, but back in my day – during the war! – you just turned up and queued.

Paul Flynn: Shayne reminded me of every working-class lad that went to my comprehensive school. He is much more archetypal Manchester than Liam Gallagher. He worked in a shoe shop in the Arndale. He was that lad that you'd go in and you'd buy your shoes there because he served you. Absolute heartthrob.

Sean Smith, Same Difference, third place, series four: At the time, I was doing a show called *Dancing Queen*, which was touring the UK. I was loving it, but I had been doing that level of show for years and I wanted my big break. The year before we did *X Factor* was Leona [Lewis] and Ray [Quinn], and Leona went on to have a huge multi-platinum album all over the world, so I think we felt like it was at a peak time to give it a try.

Joe McElderry, winner, series six: I was a massive fan of the show. To transition to being part of it and winning it was a surreal process. I auditioned first in 2007 when I was fifteen. It was the first year they lowered the age categories. I got to bootcamp and on the second day I absolutely freaked out. I didn't feel ready for it. I was just overwhelmed. I don't think they'd ever had anyone go, 'Actually, I'm not doing this' before. Everyone said I was an idiot and that I'd made the biggest mistake ever. But I trusted my decision.

Steve: I was at an age where I had been involved in music for a long time. I'd been writing, producing and working with artists, but I'd also had a lot of things that had gone wrong. So I had very low expectations that things would work out; that's how I am. I've always been a pessimist. I suppose that's why things go wrong, because I think they're going to go wrong. Funnily enough I had a Rolodex back in the day and it had all the record labels and A&R men in it. And Simon Cowell was in there. I remember I called his office a couple of times and he never answered.

Sean: I wanted to go for it [as a solo act] and my sister Sarah came along for the day to support me. We kept having to do all the cheering for camera and it was getting a bit monotonous. Sarah was thinking about leaving and all of a sudden a guy appeared with a clipboard and a camera and focused on Sarah. She was all bright and bubbly in the queue so they were like, 'What are you singing today?' She said she was just here for me and brought me in like, 'Hi.' All of a sudden they brought us to the front of the queue. She filled out an application and they asked us to sing together. We did probably the worst rendition of Bryan Adams and Mel C's 'When You're Gone' I've ever heard. We looked at each other like, 'That's game over,' and they said, 'You're through!'

Oritsé Williams, JLS, runners-up, series five: We had been a band for a year before, doing everything we could. People think that JLS was put together on *The X Factor* and that's definitely not the case. Anyone that would hear us sing, we would sing to. It got to the stage where it felt like no one thought a band of Black men had an opportunity in a commercial market coming from the UK. But we believed. After exhausting all these opportunities for a year, I remember we got in Marvin's car and we all just said the same thing, which was '*X Factor*'.

Marvin Humes, JLS: My experience in [2004 mixed-gender also-rans] VS was a large part of the beginning of JLS because we were all so naïve and wet behind the ears, but I'd had a bit of experience. I'd had two top-twenty singles, I'd toured with Blue and had a little taste of the pop industry. So to carry that into JLS and no one knowing that much about VS was a positive thing.

Sean: We didn't have a band name on the day so we put 'the Smiths' down on our application. The producers were like, 'I'm really sorry but you need to change the name.' That's when Sarah came up with Same Genes, which I thought was a bit weird. We loved *Friends* at the time and I remember a joke on there where Ross says, 'Same difference.' So I suggested that and Sarah went, 'Yeah, because we're the same but different, that works.' Of course they filmed us at that moment and it made us look really ridiculous.

Steve: [Sharon and Louis] knew I was a good singer and I was going to go through. They'd filmed me prior to my audition chatting and singing for [host] Kate Thornton. Then I went in and at the time the impression was that Louis and Sharon weren't meant to like me and it was Simon who could say, 'No, I think he's got something.' Then Simon gets me in his group and he takes me and shapes me and turns me from this rough-and-ready not-very-good vocalist into this superstar and Simon wins again. And it went to plan. That's the bit that annoys you – from day one it was all a farce. I knew a lot about the industry and how it worked in terms of the deals people do, but I never knew it was that bad.

Sean: There were people that were clearly not good singers but they were telling them, 'You're fantastic, you're going to go through, they'll love you.' They were setting them up for a fall and it was obvious they weren't there mentally sometimes. With us it was more, 'Come on, guys, you need to ramp it up, you're really excited, hug for the camera!' Of course when you step out there and you look that crazed, the first reaction from the judges is going to be, 'Woah.' One of the big lines Simon said was, 'You are possibly two of the most annoying people I have ever met.'

'There were little things I noticed them doing to get reactions'

Having survived the audition process, the wannabes were then put through their paces via seemingly endless rounds of singing in a line on stage in an empty theatre. For the producers, bootcamp was an early indication of who the real stars of the show were going to be. For the contestants who didn't make it, however, it was a nice excuse to get drunk and perhaps snog someone you'll likely never see again.

Marvin: The difference with us was that we were so ready for this process. This is the problem with a lot of artists that have been on the show that have had problems since: we were so strong as a band. They tried to throw so much at us – they made a band [Priority] in bootcamp to rival us at Judges' Houses because they didn't want us to be so confident we'd make it through. Simon and the team would say the other band were better than us. They would always put us down even when we knew we smashed it.

JB Gill, JLS: Because we'd been together for almost two years by that point, them trying to throw a curveball saying, 'Here's a list of songs to prepare overnight' didn't worry us – we already knew who would sing what and how to break down the parts.

Yvie Burnett, *The X Factor* vocal coach: JLS knew each other. They had this natural brother mentality so they sang well together and they had similar styles so that worked from the start.

Sean: The other contestants at bootcamp were all a lot cooler than us. That gave us a weird niche. But even then people were saying to us, 'Guys, it was really cheesy but it was good entertainment.' They weren't seeing us as any threat. Even in bootcamp when they're filming you can feel that they're focusing quite a lot on you. But I also remember bootcamp being very sexual among everyone else. Everyone was going into each other's bedroom and me and Sarah were like, 'Right, we're here to focus and win this thing.'

Steve: There are a lot more people in bootcamp than you realise. You get to meet a lot of people and so many of them are really nice. There was a bonding thing going on. The problem was that they don't feed you, they give you some water and people start to get a bit agitated, like, 'Why are we waiting around for so long?' It gets some people's emotions up and so then they start filming people getting upset. There were little things I noticed them doing to get reactions.

Joe: I'd made a pact with myself like, 'If you go back in this show you absolutely cannot leave, no matter how traumatic.' Bootcamp was the most exhausting week of my life in terms of learning new songs and the challenges they set us. All I remember is being sat in the bar area and just continuous amounts of Domino's pizzas being delivered.

Sean: Because of my solo application, we were put into the Boys category rather than the Groups. Our room in bootcamp was in the boys' corner so we had all the girls coming into the boys' room. Everyone's walking around with their shirts off, hoping the cameras would come around. Me and Sarah just wanted to sleep because we had the biggest day of our lives coming up. Once they'd done their filming and been kicked out, they didn't care any more. In the end, we just went out and embraced it.

'I'm not being funny, but my sister's got a better house than Simon does'

Once the contestants had been whittled down to the final fifteen (later twenty-one), they'd be paired up with their (apparently unsuspecting) judges and whisked off to sun-soaked places like Barbados, Dubai or, in Louis' case, grey Dublin. Or, in season one, glamorous, er, London. There they'd fight for their place in the final three (later four) and their chance to sing live in front of millions of people every week.

Louis Walsh: I always got the worst category. We never knew what category we were going to get until we opened those fucking doors. Simon would wind me up sometimes and I would be thinking I was getting a really good category and the doors would open and I'd think, 'Oh . . .' One time I was like, 'I don't want this category.' I was just being honest. Who wants the Overs? Simon was making those decisions but denying he was. He was in control of the whole show.

Shayne: [Louis' Judges' Houses round] was in Dublin and there were people going to Miami or LA. We all went to this empty, cold apartment in Dublin. It wasn't Louis' house.

Steve: We stayed local. Simon had a place in Holland Park. Funnily enough it wasn't very far from where I used to work in a recording studio. It was an area I knew really well. I wasn't impressed. I'm not being funny, but my sister's got a better house than he does. It was in an expensive area, it was fancy, but many years ago I was an estate agent in Wimbledon so I've seen big houses. It had no personality. It looked like a show home.

Sean: Our bootcamp was in a stunning house in Marbella. The grass was all perfectly cut. I remember going to the loo and it had fancy black toilet paper. It was an incredible experience. We were led to believe it was Simon's house, but I wasn't convinced.

Joe: We flew to Marrakesh. We had this beautiful house on the outskirts of the city. This huge villa. But we were there for two days. We flew in, did some filming with *Xtra Factor* on the first night. Then we filmed the performances the next day, found out if we were through and then came back on the last flight out that evening.

Sean: I had to honour my contract for *Dancing Queen*, so I was in Scotland doing the show and then I was going to Judges'

Houses. We had to fly over [to Marbella] and I was so ill and sweaty. When you watch back our performance I'm white as a sheet and I've got a cold sore as well because I was so rundown.

Joe: You didn't sign [a contract] when you won the show; you signed it before you won the show. Everybody signs the contract at the Judges' Houses stage. Then within [the contract] are stages of where you get to in the competition. Would I sign that contract again now? No. I understand because it's a business, but I do think things have changed a lot since then. The welfare of contestants on TV shows is a much bigger focus now. But I do think there should have been an independent person who does not financially benefit from inside that dissects those contracts. I wouldn't have signed that and, if I'd had an independent person, they wouldn't have advised me to. Or they would have said, 'Let's make these changes and then sign it.'

Steve: We didn't have an NDA. They have NDAs now because of me. If it wasn't for me they wouldn't have thought about them. They learned a lesson there. I can say what the fuck I like.

'If people broke some of the house rules you'd usually see them go out that week'

Finally, after months of auditions, protracted 'you're in my final three!' announcements dished out in featureless rented homes and saying the word 'journey' ad infinitum, the show's final nine (later twelve) were ready to face the general public via the Live Shows. They were also whisked away from their lives and jobs and housed in a mansion barely able to contain them let alone the paparazzi swarming outside. Once again, the shadow of Big Brother *loomed, with contestants' activities filtered out via both spin-off show* The Xtra Factor *and the tabloids. The increased attention from the latter – helped by the arrival of new judges, Dannii Minogue in 2007 and Cheryl Cole in 2008 – also led to a reliance on so-called sob stories, AKA anything vaguely traumatic in someone's life that could be used to create a narrative arc within the show. Not only that, but contestants had to roll with the punches when it came to being in the shadows of the previous winner. In 2006, Leona Lewis quickly became the ultimate* X Factor *winner of the '00s, riding a narrative arc of Lewisham receptionist turned proper Global Superstar. Fortunes change, however, and, following Leon Jackson's surprising win, the 2008 contestants were told that rather than the top three being offered a contract with Syco, only the winner would be signed.*

Joe: That weekend we moved into the house was the weekend the Judges' Houses episode aired, so we had to sneak around London with bags over our heads trying to get to meetings. In our year the interest in terms of the media had gone stratospheric. It dominated the front pages of every paper like it never had before. It was intense.

Shayne: [The live shows] were just non-stop. A whirlwind. It was interviews, rehearsals, more contracts – just signing everything – just a tidal wave.

Louis Walsh: I really worked hard on [Shayne]. He had everything that Steve didn't have – he was young, he looked good, he could sing, he could get those high notes. He was distinctive.

Yvie Burnett: I had something to prove [with Shayne]. I had done vocal coaching a bit, but I was basically an opera singer who had changed career. My husband, Gordon, used to work with Louis on some of his bands. They were out for lunch and [Louis] said he needed a new vocal coach for *The X Factor*. Gordon said, 'Oh, my wife's a vocal coach.' Louis said, 'Let me see her,' because my husband was quite plump then and Louis just assumed I'd be this little fat woman. It's so Louis, isn't it? Then he saw a picture and said, 'Oh, she'd be good on telly!' From then, Louis and I really hit it off. I had this bit between my teeth and I really wanted to do it for Louis.

Marvin: The year before our show, Leon Jackson, Rhydian and Same Difference were the top three acts. Let's face it, it didn't work out for them in the long run unfortunately, so Simon sat us all down and said in series five he was only going to sign the winner.

Sean: I didn't realise until afterwards, but the producers all lived in the house with us and then they go, 'Right, come on, guys, we're all going to play spin the bottle tonight.' And you're going, 'What?' 'Oh, you guys don't have to play, but let's get some people together so we have some stories to feed to the papers.'

Oritsé: You've got researchers in the house with you and you think they're your chaperones but really they're also spies. If people broke some of the rules, you'd usually see them go out that week. It was crazy. A lot of stories were coming out and people wouldn't know why or how, so they were panicking.

Steve: We were in apartments. I shared with Verity [Keays]. Rowetta [Satchell] didn't want to share with me and I didn't want to share with Rowetta. She was playing the game so much.

So we didn't get on. When people have baggage, they get triggered by certain people and certain types. She was triggered by me. At the time, I was a relatively confident man in my mid-thirties. I was in a good place.

Joe: The way it worked was if you had a mortgage, or if you had a professional job, they covered all of your expenses and bills for the whole time you were on the show. We used to get a wage of about £60 a week for food and drink. But there was catering everywhere so we didn't even need it, to be honest.

Marvin: What we believed in massively was manifesting our career. Every single night before we did the show we sat down with our list of everything we wanted to achieve – a number-one record, a number-one album, a video shoot in LA. Literally it was 300 things on this list. Out of those 300 entries we probably ticked off 180, which for us was incredible. Aston's mum worked in the sexual health arena and so we'd always discussed being role models for safe sex. We wanted to be ambassadors for guys who looked like us but were younger than us. [So having our own brand of condoms, released in 2010] was a conversation we'd had with Aston's mum from before we did *The X Factor*.

Louis Walsh: I was scared when I first started because I was walking out on a Saturday night with Simon Cowell and Sharon Osbourne. Everyone knows them two, they're household names, so it was, 'Who is that little twat from Ireland in the middle? Who is he? What is he doing there? Why is he there?'

Yvie Burnett: Because Louis can be funny and say silly things I don't think people realise that man's talent. Louis can choose songs for absolutely anyone and he can choose them brilliantly.

Louis Walsh: I do know music and I do pick songs and I'm very good at what I do. That's why Simon had me there because he knew I liked songs and was involved in picking songs.

Yvie Burnett: He used to forget people's names [on the live shows] and he would go, 'Who is that?' during the ad break. I'd have to write their names down and what they were singing and pass it to him.

Marvin: I believe we hit peak *X Factor* because of Leona's success in series three. It just got bigger and bigger because we had Cheryl on the panel, who was probably the biggest celebrity in the UK at that time. It was appointment viewing on a Saturday night. The numbers were incredible.

Louis Walsh: [Leona] was great. She didn't pop for three or four weeks into the show and then she popped. Simon was behind her and we needed an international superstar and later she had the Ryan Tedder song 'Bleeding Love'. That was an international hit.

Lucie Cave: Obviously amazingly talented but quite boring to write about. [It was about] the more personality they had, the more hiccups, the more they went out and got pissed or snogged someone they shouldn't.

Louis Walsh: It doesn't matter about personality – Whitney had no personality. It's all about the voice.

Alexis Petridis: I always remember the series after [Leona] won, people would audition and Simon Cowell would go '. . . but you were doing a Leona Lewis song.' As if it didn't really matter what you were doing to the oeuvre of Frank Sinatra or if you honked your way through 'I Say a Little Prayer' – that was fine. Just don't touch the unimpeachable oeuvre of Leona Lewis, who has now been big for all of six months.

Dean Piper: After [Leona], it did become about who was wearing what, who was bitching. Every week we weren't giving our story to the editor, we were being told, 'This week Cheryl's the splash, so can you find the story.' It worked that way around. That's a really shitty way to do it. That's one of the reasons I stopped doing my *Sunday Mirror* column because I couldn't write about Cheryl Cole every fucking week.

Joe: [Our house] was near Golders Green, on the corner of Hampstead Heath. It was a footballer's house that they were renting out. I went to the Starbucks nearby on the Friday and nobody batted an eyelid. By the Sunday evening, once the Judges' Houses episode had aired, I walked out of the house and the paparazzi were jumping out of cars. When someone says you're famous overnight, it was the exact description of what happened. I thought I was going to be attacked – I'd never experienced paparazzi before. Nobody even said, 'By the way this might happen.'

Steve: [Fame] was funny. It was surreal. I never got excited about it. I'd joke about it. People would ring me up and be like, 'Steve, you're on this bloody show.' The biggest thing I'll take away from it was the *Sliding Doors* moment because I'd just supported Dionne Warwick in Croydon and off the back of that I'd been asked to support Lionel Richie at Wembley. I gave all that up to go on *The X Factor* and now I'm thinking, 'Ah, man, that was a silly move.' A lot of bad things were said about me but I've never been fame-hungry. Never. I wanted success but it wasn't about the fame. It was about singing great songs and doing them well. You want an audience.

Sean: We were different to what everyone else was doing. Amy Winehouse was huge so everyone was trying to emulate that sound or people were trying to be Snow Patrol. It's a Saturday night and people are getting ready to go out, they have *The X Factor* on and we're doing 'Tragedy'.

Louis Walsh: You need [people like Jedward] for the show. Wagner. The chicken man [series one auditionee Robert Unwin, who worked in a chicken factory]. You need everything for a TV show. People just get bored of singers; they want to see and hear something different. *The Voice* has never had a hit artist or a hit record.

Yvie Burnett: It wasn't just about having a Leona Lewis voice. Sometimes Jedward would be what you wanted that night. You wanted the entertaining person. You had to make them as good as you possibly could. Nothing was as fun as *The X Factor* back in the day, when we were allowed to be a little maybe non-PC and laugh at people. Now you'd be like, 'Should I really be laughing?' They did that thing where the bad people would come on during the final and do a medley – it was terrible, but it was so good. Some of them are probably still 'so and so from *The X Factor*' and they can do a little appearance somewhere.

Oritsé: Bands hadn't been successful before us [on *The X Factor*]. People didn't seem interested. Everyone wanted another Leona. Or a solo artist. I say this in the most humble way, but JLS really brought back the era of the pop band. Boybands were pretty much non-existent.

Shayne: I grew up listening to Backstreet Boys and NSYNC and the boyband era, so to be compared to JT [on the show] I was like, 'Yeah, sure.' I had both my ears studded many years before. I think it was cubic zirconia. JT's were likely diamonds.

Steve: Winning it wasn't the issue. As a singer you just want to get through the night. I wanted to just make sure that when I got on that stage, I didn't look like a dick. There was one night where the monitors weren't working and I missed my cue. This is live in front of millions of people! The only reason I got back into the song was because my vocal coach, Annie Skates, started mouthing the words to me. It was that pressure and then on top of that I had Louis Walsh saying I looked like a serial killer. [During an appearance on ITV's *This Morning* ahead of the final, Louis said, 'I think he's just a very average singer. He just stands there and smiles. He's like Fred West.']

Louis Walsh: He was a let-down.

Steve: [Later] I was in a room with Louis on my own and I was fighting back the urge to punch him. It was just me and him and I was going to knock him out. I don't mind saying it – I had history of going to prison. I'd had a night in prison from getting in fights. Maybe that was the reason I didn't knock him out. To go on national TV and start saying that I look like a serial killer . . . He deserved to get knocked out, to be honest.

Louis Walsh: He was a good singer, but he was like a pub singer, cabaret singer, he wasn't going to be international. Ever.

Steve: They've got this thing of undermining hardworking people. And they've damaged our industry. Whereas before people would look at these singers doing these jobs and respect them, now everyone who is singing in a pub is a wannabe, or a failed wannabe, as opposed to people who have a great living and are going out gigging and making people happy. I used to love doing social clubs. Not everyone can spend £60 on an Adele ticket and sit there bored.

Louis Walsh: We were looking for a star.

Steve: Sharon Osbourne called me a cunt in rehearsals. She said, 'You're just a fucking cab driver, you're shit, you're a cunt, you disrespected me.' The reason I disrespected her was because she was a nasty piece of work. There was a duo called 2 To Go and they were a lovely couple. In rehearsal, Sharon's telling them [their performance] was brilliant and they're both smiling and excited and then on the live show Sharon ripped the piss out of them. Later when it came to rehearsals before the final – and she'd been slagging me off all week, every week – Sharon was trying to give me like, 'Steve, that was really good,' and I just ignored her. 'You fucking cunt.' It was really uncomfortable.

Lucie Cave: Steve Brookstein was such a moody shit.

Steve: Simon doesn't want this story to come out about Sharon Osbourne going round calling a contestant a shit. You can't do that. So I go into his dressing room and Sinitta and his ex-girlfriend, Jackie St Clair, are there. Jackie opens her coat up and she had nothing on apart from a thong and high heels. Simon Cowell is sitting there smoking. I'm a bit embarrassed. This was in his dressing room just before the live final. It was absolutely mad. Once it finished, he's sitting there and he says, 'I thought you needed to relax.' He's smiling. And Sinitta and Jackie get embarrassed. I said, 'Simon, what the fuck are you doing?' I lost my temper with him. He didn't like that. Nobody talks to Simon in that way. Our relationship was always a bit edgy afterwards.

Sean: I remember on one of the live shows we did 'Tragedy' and people were like, 'These guys are great,' and we went through. The week after we did a session with Brian [Friedman, the show's choreographer] and we only had ten minutes to learn the choreo. When the cameras came in, we were all over the shop. Then he started doing bits to the camera saying, 'I'm worried about these guys this week.' We were like, 'What just happened? Last week we had two hours for choreo, today we've had ten minutes.' They do it to freak you out and give a bit of drama. I remember going back to the house and saying to Sarah, 'I think they're trying to get us out this week.' Simon was our mentor but the thing with that was you'd barely ever speak to him. Apart from in the semi-final when he was worried we'd go out and he came to us and said, 'Right, what are we going to do with you guys?' We then went into his dressing room and opened a bottle of Cristal and had a conversation. It was so surreal but amazing.

Joe: They didn't try to put a sob story on for me but they did used to try to make me cry. One of the producers, who I really love and who was very supportive of me on and off camera, he used to try to ask me a question and I'd look behind the camera and say, 'I'm not going to cry.' He used to go, 'For God's sake, Joe, we just need a bit of emotion.' I'd say, 'I'm not crying over a singing competition.'

Oritsé: They pulled me aside by myself and started asking about my mum, who has multiple sclerosis. She went through the worst transition when we were on the show. They saw what was going on. They started asking me about my home life situation and they told me I was a young carer and they were looking at me crying. I just kept saying, 'I'm here with my group and I want it to be about us and our talent.' I didn't want my personal life talked about in that way. It was real life, it wasn't something for publicity.

Sean: This is the semi-final now and you're getting to the nitty gritty. Niki [Evans], who came fourth in the end, her big story was that her father had passed away and he left the application form for the *X Factor* in his will for her. They played on it a lot throughout the show. It was a time when stuff on social media was just starting to come in and she was hearing people saying, 'She's only there because of her dad,' which was heartbreaking. The story in the semi-finals was going to be she was going to sing 'Dance with My Father'. But because she was getting trolled she refused. They then needed a sad angle, so they went back to our original application form where you have to write down your best and worst moments in life and at the top of our list was Sarah being bullied at school. They decided to go with that angle instead, which actually really connected with the audience. For that little five-minute VT [they aired] we must have talked to them for about five hours, until they just wore us down. It was like having a therapy session. Our minds were going to really deep, truthful places. It was a one-on-one session with a producer who's going, 'Right, I'm really sorry but today we're going to talk about your bullying, I hope that's okay.' There was a lot of stuff they were coaxing out of Sarah that I didn't know had been happening, so of course we're both trying not to cry. The funny thing was that when it came to the final it was like, 'Simon has a group in the final so he looks great.' All of a sudden they just wanted vox pops of us saying, 'We're having such a great time going back to our home town of Portsmouth!'

Steve: They filmed our dinner [at Simon's house before the final] but there wasn't a moment when I was just sitting down with Simon and Sinitta, his sidekick, and Annie Skates. We didn't have that intimate dinner where we actually had a chat. Simon was off talking to people, then the dinner was laid out. But I saw them dishing it up and it was M&S. I don't mind M&S, but [it was] microwave Chinese just put in fancy bowls and made to look nice. Then it's getting cold and I can't eat because they haven't started filming yet. I'm becoming empty. This food would have been great when it was hot, but because of the situation, I can't complain about it. They start getting into the emotional side, talking to me like, 'You must really want this.' By then I had some negative press about who I was and what I was about, plus there were some other stressful things going on behind the scenes that were getting me down. I got emotional and they did break me for a moment there. It was pretty sad.

Sean: We were getting hammered by Louis Walsh but it would make people vote for us. Then the next year he falls in love with Jedward and signs them – the hypocrisy of that man.

Louis Walsh: I didn't like [Same Difference]; they were too cheesy. It's Butlin's. We're not looking for Butlin's; we're looking for Wembley.

Sean: I remember my nan would always go up to him and say, 'Why are you so horrible to my grandkids?' And he'd say, 'Don't worry, it's getting them more votes.' He'd say to us that he wasn't that nasty. He didn't want us to think it was fake but he also didn't want us to hate him. I got the feeling he was being fed stuff to say by Simon. That whole goodie and baddie thing from a pantomime.

Louis Walsh: I knew Same Difference weren't the reason I was there. I was there to find somebody who was going to have a career.

Shayne: I'm Louis' only win. I know Simon won a couple and then obviously all the judges that came later. We formed such a good bond on the show and then that continued because I was then managed by Simon and Louis afterwards.

Steve: One of the things that was also weird on the *X Factor* final night was my manager came into my room to ask me about my family. My heritage is a bit of a mixed bag. You knew what your family was and you've seen photographs from when you're a baby, so you know what the reality is, but then you'd always have people saying, 'He ain't your dad,' and then my Jewish background meant I'd be called a tight Jew, and then my dad's South African so I'd be called a racist. All these things throughout my life meant I'd always questioned my reality. It was bizarre that my manager would come in and say, 'The *News of the World* are running a story that you're adopted.' I was like, 'Er . . . no.' But I still thought that journalists had done their research and knew what they were doing. They were saying, 'Your real parents are from Birmingham and they're drug dealers.' This is before I'm about to go on stage. I've got my manager telling me I'm adopted and my parents are from fucking Birmingham. *News of the World* are going to run this story. Before my mum and dad turn up for the live final, I call my mum and say, 'This is going to sound really weird, and please be honest with me, but am I adopted?' And she went, 'Of course you're not.' Even twenty years on, it still fucks me up.

Louis Walsh: I wanted to beat Simon and beat Sharon no matter what I did. And, later, I especially wanted to beat Cheryl. That competitiveness is 100 per cent real. But Simon was always helping Cheryl.

Steve: Looking back, I don't think I was meant to win it, ultimately. This was all about [the Louis Walsh-mentored runners-up] G4. You've got Coca-Cola and Pepsi. McDonald's and then Burger King. You've got Greggs, you've got Pret a Manger. Well, you had Il Divo, a male opera group doing pop songs, and then you had G4 doing the same old bollocks. People love it, let them love it, I don't care. There's a certain market for that. But the fact was they had been the bottom two; I was never in the bottom two.

'I had to speak to Beyoncé because Alexandra couldn't'

While Steve Brookstein and Shayne Ward had to convince the public of their respective talent all alone, from series three onwards, the top-three finalists would be supported by some of pop's biggest superstars (and Westlife) in order to encourage those all-important votes. As the show's viewing figures increased and the number of music TV shows shrunk (both Top of the Pops *and* CD:UK *had finished in 2006), artists looking to promote their latest single were drawn to* The X Factor*'s live results shows. Knowing the viewing figures would peak for the final, the producers were able to nab some actual proper legends looking to impart some of their wisdom to the contestants – therefore seeming more down to earth, a new character trait for pop superstars the show itself had helped usher in – while also flogging their latest single. It reached its apex in 2008 when Alexandra Burke snotted on Beyoncé's shoulder after an incredible version of 'Listen'.*

Shayne: One thing I did understand from the get-go is that it is a conveyor-belt industry. You always want to aim for longevity but you know that by the time you get to the label the next show is coming. The next year of the show you had the duets, but we didn't have those. I wish we had because George

Michael was on one year with Joe McElderry and I would have loved that.

Joe: On the Monday they'd said to Olly [Murs] and Stacey [Solomon] that they were getting Robbie Williams and Michael Bublé respectively. For me they were like, 'We're still working out a duet partner for you.' I assumed no one wanted to sing with me. But they were in full-blown negotiations to try to get George Michael. It got to the Thursday and I still didn't have a duet partner. It was like, 'Am I going to end up singing "The Climb" with Simon?' Then they rang me at midnight and said, 'George Michael has agreed to come on the show and sing with you.'

Malcolm McLean: When I look back to these years we would be spending all our time watching music channels. You didn't need to see an exclusive video on a TV show like *Top of the Pops* any more. It didn't have the power it used to have and they wouldn't be able to get the biggest stars.

Paul Flynn: I always feel like *Big Brother* took over from *Top of the Pops*. *Big Brother*, especially the Friday-night evictions, were so *Top of the Pops*. They had that energy and rush. The crowd were a cross between the audience on *Top of the Pops* and a quite shit nightclub. It felt like it had that similar energy and ultimately there was that coronation at the end of it; who is number one? It was, 'Where does the public stand this week on the issue of the day?'

Alexis Petridis: The decline of *Top of the Pops* suggested there was a breadth of places you could get information about pop music from. I think the charts were becoming increasingly irrelevant as a straightforward marker of success. *Smash Hits* as a whole idea was predicated on irreverence. You could tie its demise in with the end of Simon Amstell and Miquita Oliver [who left *Popworld* in 2006], who both seemed to be operating in that irreverent way that *Smash Hits* did towards pop stars. It became increasingly difficult to be like that towards pop stars [post-*The X Factor*] because everyone was so on message that you couldn't ask them daft questions and get a revealing answer.

Jonathan Bown: I left a few months before *Smash Hits* closed. To be there for almost three years was incredible, but I did always feel like I'd arrived at the party after all the sausage rolls had gone. It went through quite an identity crisis in its final years. It was clear the landscape was changing. Things were narrower after *The X Factor* started. What appealed to me about *Smash Hits* as a kid was you'd have an interview with A-ha next to an interview with the Cure. I think there was an element of losing that. Everyone we were interviewing was from quite a small stable.

Louis Walsh: JLS would have won but Simon pulled a fast one and got Beyoncé to sing a duet [with Alexandra Burke] in the final. It was changed.

Marvin: Initially we heard we were going to sing 'Umbrella' with Rihanna. Because we did 'Umbrella' in the semi-final and we won the public vote for the first time. We don't know what happened. We were thinking there was going to be this Rihanna versus Beyoncé moment, you know, JLS versus Alexandra. Listen, I'm a big fan of Westlife, I've got mad respect for them, so I was buzzing to sing with them. I wouldn't want Rihanna now; I wouldn't change anything.

Yvie Burnett: We went into Beyoncé's dressing room and Alex was just a mess. Literally couldn't breathe. I had to speak because she couldn't. I remember Beyoncé's people were filming us, which we found a bit ridiculous. I said to Beyoncé, 'Look, Alex wants to do this particular line [in 'Listen'], it's her favourite line,' and Beyoncé said, 'Ooh, I don't know, I love that line, why don't we do it together?' So I said, 'Right, deal.' I'm doing all the talking. Then we went out and rehearsed it and I was coaching Alex through it from the stage and Beyoncé's saying, 'Coach me on that, too.' I thought, 'Yeah, okay, Beyoncé.' She was just being funny but it was such a surreal moment, like I'm standing here coaching Beyoncé doing a duet. I think [the show] finished at the right time because you're never going to emulate that again.

Louis Walsh: Anyway, JLS were great and they've had a great career and if Beyoncé hadn't appeared with Alexandra they would have won. But it's fine.

Dean Piper: If you became a judge on that show, you had to realise you were Simon's bitch. The puppet master had hold of you. You couldn't just have one slice of the pie, you had to eat the whole damn thing. I feel like the female judges were scrutinised, played with and toyed with in the public arena far more than the men were. Cheryl, Dannii and Sharon knew they had their money coming in and it would give them a platform for other things – like would Cheryl have had a solo career as sparkling as it was if it wasn't for that? Probably not. But they really had to give up a shitload.

Louis Walsh: Simon never told us the votes. We never knew who was in the bottom two and we were always trying to find out. He knew, but he was pretending he didn't. It's his show, it's his world. We're all lucky to be breathing the air. They never told us. We were standing there like pricks on the stage waiting. That was absolutely real. Waiting and hoping we were going to get through. We were all very involved and we all wanted to beat each other.

Joe: George made the whole thing about me and not him, which not a lot of stars do. I hadn't rehearsed that famous high harmony line from 'Don't Let the Sun Go Down on Me' because I assumed he would want to do it, but at the end of the first run-through he was like, 'Why are you not singing the harmony?' He said, 'It's not about me, it's about you, you need all of the moments in this song. I am coming to sing with *you*.' So we changed. He was very humble.

Shayne: Everything around you is so fast [after you win]. You essentially become part of the machine then. There was a press conference straight away on stage, then a quick hello to my family. I performed six songs at G-A-Y and then the next morning was *Top of the Pops* to record the Christmas special. It was the first time you could download a winners' single that night so I knew quickly that I was en route to number one with 'That's My Goal'.

James Masterton: *The X Factor* hit on the gimmick of making the single available as quickly as possible – sending Andi Peters to the printing plant and showing him holding up a copy of the single. [In an era of digital downloads] *The X Factor* was still a way of focusing people on buying pop music even if at the time people didn't necessarily do so. Shayne was the first *X Factor* winner to have his single released with the aim of having the number one on the Christmas chart. Steve Brookstein's single didn't come out until early the next year. Although Shayne's single was immediately available as a digital download, it still wasn't a mass-market product. It was, 'Yes, you could download it now but wait until Wednesday when the CD will be ready.'

Joe: I remember standing behind the double doors before they announced the winner and Simon turned to [Olly and I] and said, 'Guys, I have no idea what's going to happen here, but I genuinely wish you both the best of luck in the world.' Then the doors opened and I can't remember anything until the next morning being on *GM:TV*. It was like being drunk.

Steve: For the after-show party, I was only given two tickets. So all my family couldn't come. It's packed with press and all these people – nobody I knew. I don't think they liked that I only stayed for a few minutes and then went to a restaurant across the road with my family and friends.

Sean: It literally flipped the second we finished third. It was like it was over as far as the producers were concerned. I'll never forget it: we were driven around by fancy Addison Lee cars at the time and then the day after the final it all came crashing down. They said, 'Well, can you get your grandad to pick you up?' We were like, 'Okay, yeah, sure.' It was just so painful.

'Can you imagine people listening to "Killing in the Name" on Christmas Day?'

The long slog of a TV talent show can make its culmination feel like the pinnacle. But of course the hard work, as Cowell was always quick to state, actually starts once the show finishes and you're thrust into a music industry that's already gearing up for the next load of contestants. Like with Popstars *and Hear'Say back in 2001, it can also give a distorted reading, one in which 'winners' become 'losers' and acts given more time to breathe outside of the full-beam spotlight eventually start to come good. For some, external forces beyond their control can upend careers, be it a recession that closes Woolworths or, in the case of Joe McElderry, an online campaign keen to deal* The X Factor, *and Simon Cowell, its first real blow as the decade came to an end.*

Shayne: The problem is that if you believe when you get somewhere that you are the finished product then you're setting yourself up for the biggest fall. I am a sponge. I am not afraid to ask questions. I want to learn and soak stuff in. They were in control, so for me as a 21-year-old on a million-pound, three-album contract, I was happy to let it be that way.

Savan Kotecha: I would say back then, in general, the artist's point of view was almost irrelevant. They were pop songs that could be released by any artist and they would be the same song. It didn't matter. What I've noticed in the past decade, and that's been a big lesson for me, is that the artist's point of view is very important and you can't deny them that. Back then the artist's opinion didn't really matter to the record label that much.

Steve Anderson: There were lots of writers in lots of big studios just writing songs. There was a massive need for songs back then, especially when it came to the TV talent show. Anyone that was in those shows did ultimately need a record.

Sean: We went on the *X Factor* tour and the reason we got signed [to Syco] is because we sold loads of merchandise. More than anyone else. So they started seeing that the people who liked us really did buy into it. Literally. The other great thing was Steps' manager Tim Byrne was a creative director [on the tour] that year and he knew what to do with us. So Simon was saying to him, 'What did you do with Steps and how can we emulate that here?'

Steve: Given the demographic of who watches the show, every week I was told I was the housewives' favourite. This is what really pissed me off because that was my demographic and yet my album comes out for Father's Day. What the fuck was that about? G4's album came out for Mother's Day. I was thinking, 'But I won and their album comes out before mine?', and it's at the biggest time of the year. The best week for selling records back then was Mother's Day. They were purposefully fucking with me.

James Masterton: In mid-2006, to balance up this demand for digital songs with the demands of the high-street stores, the rule was changed so that a download could count towards the charts a week before the CD single. So in 2007 the high-street stores were consigned to history because all legally downloaded songs could now count towards the chart with or without a physical version. That's when Woolworths and the supermarkets realised the CD single era was very much over. From that point onwards, the digital download became the dominant force. It was the great democratisation of the pop charts because before then there were always gatekeepers.

Joe: They sat us down quite early on in the show [to talk about the Rage Against the Machine campaign], so we were aware of it. They were like, 'When the next set of journalists come in, they might mention this campaign, it's nothing to do with the contestants, it's about Simon and the show and I'm sure by the time the show's over it will be gone.' I've got the attention span of a gnat so I probably wasn't listening anyways. Never got asked about it, but then on *GM:TV* it was mentioned and I'd forgotten. The person interviewing me had said, 'It's tight in the midweeks so far,' and I didn't have a clue. They had to explain that the single was doing really well but we needed to get it higher because of what's happening with this campaign.

James Masterton: Joe very nearly wasn't the first victim. In 2008, Alexandra Burke released her version of 'Hallelujah' to general eyebrow raising. And it did indeed make the Christmas number one that year. But at number two was Jeff Buckley's version and it was the first time two versions of the same song had been numbers one and two that week. His version was behind it by a long way but it's interesting that it was this spontaneous outpouring of support for what is not hard to argue is the superior version of the song.

Peter Robinson: The question is: Do you want to hurt Simon Cowell or do you want to hurt Joe McElderry? I was going to say Simon Cowell probably didn't give a shit, but then it was maybe one of the first times where there was a bit of a wobble for *The X Factor*.

Louis Walsh: It was just publicity for the show. It was fine. It didn't really matter. Both of them had hits. It was like Blur versus Oasis, or Take That versus East 17, or the Spice Girls versus whoever it was [All Saints]. It didn't matter. Joe was good. He's a good singer, a good performer. Not a star, but a good performer.

Joe: Two things. One: I was too exhausted to care. And two: I was so excited by what had happened I was just like, 'I've got a song out and I've just won the biggest show on television.' Everything else was irrelevant to me. Also, there was something quite exciting about it. People were saying, 'There's never been a chart battle like this in about ten years.' It was the first time where people genuinely didn't know what was going to be Christmas number one. *The X Factor* had had it in the bag for the past five years. It was a proper battle.

Peter Robinson: There's something in this kind of idea of going against *The X Factor* and saying, 'It's a popularity contest, it's not about the music,' but then at the same time trying to get a song to number one, which is equally not about the music. It's about making a point. The question there is, what point are you trying to make? Also, you're using music that wasn't intended to be number one.

James Masterton: It was inevitable that this backlash was growing because people were getting tired of Christmas being ruined by *The X Factor* putting out their latest song and it would go to number one regardless of how good it was. You could make good use of Facebook to bring people together for a common cause. You can argue 'til the cows come home about how genuine that was because people were so invested in the idea of getting this Rage Against the Machine song to number one that people were boasting that they brought forty or fifty copies at one time. There wasn't any real barrier to do that. There were rules in place to prevent chart hyping, but it always worked on the basis that it was labels themselves doing it. Nobody had conceived that the general public would try to engineer getting a song to number one.

Joe: They hated the idea of reality television creating number-one singles. The ironic thing is both songs were owned by Sony BMG. By making this point, all you're doing is making everyone more money. It baffles me now. I'd never heard of them. Not really my genre. Can you imagine people listening to that song on Christmas Day? We helped each other sell way more records. There was no loser in the end and I was able to get to number one the week after.

Shayne: Recording the first album happened straight away. This is where the craziness comes in because that's when I found out I had vocal nodules. I came offstage after G-A-Y at 2 a.m., all the adrenaline, and I said to my then tour manager, 'Paul, I've done something to my throat.' We spoke to the label, did *Top of the Pops* and then went to Harley Street and they said I had nodules. I was terrified. When you watch the show as a viewer and someone gets a sore throat, you always get people who say they're doing it for show, but they really have. It's all the interviews, all the talking, it's non-stop work.

Yvie Burnett: Some people have just got a voice that naturally has a lot of stamina. Then there are other people who will literally lose their voice just like that. A lot of it is other things that will make you lose your voice. For example, Alexandra Burke. She would talk really loudly with her mates and so then she'd lose her voice. I had to get her to shut up and look after her actual speaking voice. Her singing voice wasn't the problem.

Shayne: I remember recording my first album on cortisone injections and it was the scariest thing. I guess it was scary for the label too – I'd just won the show and now I had problems with my throat. The first album doesn't feature any of my falsetto because I lost it.

Yvie Burnett: It's something that is a lesson for all of us within these big juggernaut shows. We had worked constantly together every day then suddenly he had to go off on his own without me. He was tired and he was travelling and he was partying a bit, I suppose – he'd just won *The X Factor*. Then he got ill and had to sing on an infection. With hindsight maybe there's a way within these shows that you keep going with them for a little while after.

Steve: ['Against All Odds'] wasn't the song I wanted to release. I appreciate that they had to release it. But there was so much damage done in terms of my perception of reality and what people had tried to do to me and say about me. The lies. It was still fresh in my mind about the Fred West thing. I found it hard to smile.

Sean: There was a mistake early doors with us. Butlin's came in for us and they were paying such good money that our management team agreed to it. I think it made us too accessible, so when we did come back a year later [with 'We R One'] we were holiday camp entertainers rather than massive pop stars. Also, the year after us was so great with JLS and Alexandra Burke, and JLS didn't sign with Syco, so that gave them an extra layer of coolness. We were then doing gigs with artists on the line-up from that year's *X Factor* who had finished tenth, but because people had only just seen them on TV they were bigger stars.

Jamelia: As an artist who felt like they were slogging their guts out, there was an element of jealousy that these people got to have this huge promotion on a show and they weren't even necessarily going to have longevity. People like myself, and other artists around at the time, we practically disappeared because you can't compete with an *X Factor* winner. Doesn't matter if they're good, bad or ugly. It became dispiriting because every song I wrote was a labour of love. It wasn't about just getting the songs from people. As an artist it was dispiriting to see, but not as a person – I'm always happy to see people succeed. But it stopped me feeling confident enough to put out music because I couldn't compete with that. It got to the point where the label would say, 'We can't release around Christmas or January,' but then that little timeframe would keep expanding.

Paul Flynn: I interviewed Shayne for *The Observer* and I went to Manchester to watch the *X Factor* live show. His girlfriend turned to me and said the last time they were in this arena was to watch Justin Timberlake. I did that story with Shayne and wrote it sympathetically, so [Syco] played me his debut album and I hated it. It sounded like a Westlife album and I wrote as much. It didn't sound like the pop star he wanted to be. He wanted to be Justin Timberlake and they'd made him sound like Richard Clayderman.

Savan Kotecha: I was having success in America so when it was time for Shayne's second album [2007's *Breathless*] Simon called me and said, 'Hey, the second album's yours, whoever you want to work with.' Simon wanted to make Shayne the UK's Justin Timberlake and that's what we tried to do. Then at the end [of recording] he said, 'I'm not going to release [the album] without a reggae song.' It was like, 'Oh no!' That's why we had to write 'If That's OK with You'. I love that song but I think it might have hurt the whole campaign. It was such a Marmite song. Simon just had it in his head that if you can crack a reggae song then it's usually a global thing. I want this to be phrased positively towards Simon because we're still close and I love him, but we were so against the reggae thing that we thought that if we made 'If That's OK with You' overly cheesy Simon would understand and be like, 'Oh, okay, never mind, we won't do a reggae song.' But it was the opposite and he was like, 'This is a smash! We're going with this.'

Steve: I did an interview with *Closer* magazine [in 2005] and the female journalist said, 'You're a hit with the ladies, what about with the men?' I said, 'Well, if they like me they like me.' And she said, '. . . but do you like them?' I knew what she was implying. I'm not an idiot. I said, 'Yeah, I've questioned my sexuality.' I was actually quite upfront and said, 'A guy sucked my dick,' and she was like, 'Oh.' It was like, 'This is *X Factor*,

ITV, primetime family viewing, they don't want to know this kind of shit.' I was like, 'All I'm saying is that I tried it and it wasn't for me.' I was in a threesome with a girlfriend who was always having me with other women, and once she said, 'Do it with another guy,' and I said, 'Oh, alright then.' Anyway, there's absolute panic and my manager is having a go at me, saying we have to do an interview with *The Sun* to sort it out. I was a brand and that wasn't my branding. My branding was macho man, likes the women, pals with Simon. So I did an interview with *The Sun* and they basically presented a double-page spread with lots of quotes that weren't from me. They let me look at it [before it ran] and it was all about my shame. It was an apologetic piece about how I regret doing what I did. But I don't regret it. I was a survivor of abuse. This had nothing to do with shame. I got really angry about that and told my manager, 'I can't believe you're fucking doing this. I want this piece pulled.' It never got printed. But soon after I was told my record deal was over and the narrative was I couldn't sell records and that G4 were the real winners.

Sean: We were obviously earning good money and everyone kept asking us, 'So how's the recession affecting you?', and we were saying, 'We'd not really noticed it.' We'd never earned so much money! It was like, 'We're in a recession?' But then it affected us in the biggest way possible because when Woolworths went under they took a lot of our [album] stock with them. We went to our management saying we needed to get the stock back and sent to HMV or whatever. They said that if people wanted it they'd be able to get it. But it's not the same when you're going to be a big cardboard cut-out as you walk in the shop. Even our TV adverts were all geared towards Woolworths.

Shayne: Looking back and being a lot older now, I had a great many years with [Syco] and it was a three-album deal. I never took it for granted. Yes, it's always going to be upsetting and sad when you part ways with a label, but then I'd already come to peace with it when there was a three-year gap between albums two and three. I kind of knew. You part ways on good terms and that's the best way to be because you'll meet these people again. I walked away with the masters for my third album [2010's *Obsession*], which is a rarity.

Louis Walsh: He should have done better. I would still be working with him but Syco dropped him. He had hits in different places and he ticked every single box.

Steve: I wasn't dropped; I asked to leave. I said to them, 'I want to leave the record label, this isn't working, is it? I know what's going on, you're just going to bury my career over time.' We just needed to come to some arrangement. The reason I picked the time that I did to leave was I had to make my stand before the second season of *The X Factor* because they'd want me to come back on the show and say, 'It's so great.' I said to them that I would do that but they had to let me out of the record deal and pay me off. I said, 'You've told everyone it's a million-quid record deal, you've not even spent £300,000 and I've not even released a video.' My second single was pulled. There was no effort being put into my career. They offered me £12,500. So I told them to stick it up their arse. I didn't even ask for much – it was a million-pound deal and I asked for £50,000. Simon then went on TV to say I couldn't sell records and that they might have to let me go. Once he'd done that, I knew they were going to have to bite the bullet and not have me on the show [in 2005] and just ruin me.

Sean: When we got dropped, the management company called and said they'd decided not to take up the option and do the second single. We wanted to call Simon and thank him for the opportunity, but we couldn't even get hold of his PA. That was the saddest thing – we only wanted to say thank you. But of course that would have been awkward for him, building someone up to then drop them. The other bad thing is you're still famous, but you don't want it to come out that you've been dropped. You're waiting for it to be in the papers. That was really tough. I really wish I'd enjoyed it more. I was too serious about it all. Now I'd give a lot to have some of those experiences we had again. I'd lap them up for all it's worth.

Steve: I was going to go to the press and tell people I wanted to leave the label and I got a phone call from Max Clifford. He said, 'Steve, I'd love to see you at this event and doing this and that, but it ain't going to happen if you talk to the press. If you try to tell people what's happened, we will bury you.' They had the power. Every time I would go to the press the journalist would say, 'Don't worry, I'll get the story printed,' and Simon would have the story pulled. I did one with the *News of the World* and I showed the journalist all the evidence of what had been going on and he couldn't run the story. It was replaced with a pro-Simon Cowell story and me getting totally slammed. I had that for over a decade.

Joe: [Splitting with the label] was amicable but I was told about it via email. They were like, 'We're not taking up the second album option but if Joe wants to come in for a cup of tea to chat about it we can.' I remember reading the email and thinking, 'Well, what have we got to chat about? Are you just going to list all the reasons you're not taking up the option?' That is part of the demise of the show – they didn't look after the artists in terms of creating a career, they just stuck with whatever made the most money at the time. In a short term that is always going to work, but for longevity and a long-term brand it won't. The audience start to think, 'What's the point of me paying to vote if you're just going to drop them in six months?' Which is why the viewing figures dropped as the years went on. I love the show and I had a great time on the whole. There are parts of the industry that are wonderful and parts that are dreadful. But that's like any job you do. But do I regret any of it? Absolutely not.

Steve: I go through periods of regretting [doing the show]. But you can't regret because the one thing I have got is my wife and my children and you don't know where you'd be if you made different choices in life. Where it would have led you. I've become more in touch with my faith and I believe the reason I've gone through this is because I had lessons to learn. I'm a better person now than I was when I was younger. Life isn't meant to be easy.

Paul Flynn: What Cowell sold really beautifully was this idea of a better life. They didn't deliver on it but they fulfilled the fantasy of it and we all need to see that fantasy.

Peter Robinson: It's funny looking back on *The X Factor* now because, while it was a really big TV show, how useful was it really? There was a lot of noise and shouting for a handful of decent pop stars.

★ ★ ★

After Joe McElderry's Facebook-instigated attack left *The X Factor* bloodied and bruised at the decade's end, the show rebounded in 2010 with One Direction, who, despite finishing third in season seven, went on to become a Spice Girls-level global phenomenon for the next half a decade. In 2011, Little Mix, who became the first band to win, went on to release six multi-platinum albums across a decade-long career. From there, despite flashes of brilliance (Misha B, Ella Henderson, Fleur East), the show increasingly became less about the acts and more about changes in hosts and judges. In a music era that had switched from CDs to digital to streaming during the show's lifespan, launching a brand-new act with that all-important number-one single was becoming increasingly tricky. In 2015, winner Louisa Johnson became the first contestant signed to Syco not to release an album, a move replicated in 2017 by Rak-Su and the show's final winner, Dalton Harris, in 2018. In 2021, ITV announced they'd axed the show after seventeen years.

Annoying fade-out

By 2006, every single one of UK pop's cultural markers had disintegrated. *Top of the Pops* aired its final episode – aside from the Christmas specials, natch – on 30 July, five months after *Smash Hits* published its final issue. In March of that year, a recently Ant & Dec-less *CD:UK* aired for the final time, while a month later Simon Amstell and Miquita Oliver quit *Popworld*. The ecosystem that had housed the late-'90s and early-'00s pop boom in the UK had vanished, with the grip of the so-called media gatekeepers loosened by the rise of the www (over 50 per cent of UK households had internet access by 2005).

There were other factors, too. The success of digital downloads had shifted the chart rules, making it all seem unnecessarily complicated (things would get worse when streaming hit in 2014) and therefore less of a direct marker of a song's success. Downloads also meant that songs were starting to be released quicker, with none of the exciting six-week build-up that therefore necessitated pop stars doing the rounds of morning TV shows and magazine photoshoots. Releasing digitally also meant singles could be retroactively switched to 'buzz tracks' if things weren't taking off, with videos downgraded to a lyric video if necessary. Speaking of videos, YouTube arrived in 2005, while music TV channels like The Box started to chime more with the democratisation of culture kickstarted by reality TV. Why wait to see if your favourite song was going to be on *Top of the Pops* when you could just punch it into a keyboard or vote for it from your couch?

The success of *The X Factor* by 2006 meant that new pop stars were being found via an annual conveyor belt, with the idea of off-screen auditions or club tours etc. seeming almost perverse. On the flip side, the rise of social media, and specifically music platform MySpace, gave us a whole new breed of pop star, spearheaded by Lily Allen, who arrived that summer. The internet – which had tried to kill off the music industry altogether via illegal file-sharing sites such as Napster – was opening up a new avenue for beleaguered A&Rs. Positioned in direct opposition to the world of manufactured pop, Allen was the figurehead for its move towards the Very Real, assisted by social media's reliance on solipsism. Gone were broad-stroke generalities or high-gloss emotions and depthless platitudes, replaced by text-speak sentiments and sweary, diaristic tales of complex youth.

Suddenly fans also had a direct relationship with pop stars like Allen, with MySpace and Facebook allowing them to message and chat with their idols. Fans could also watch their faves progress in real time, becoming part of that all-important Journey, far removed from the inauthenticity of a Saturday-night TV show. *The X Factor*'s dominance meant that for a raft of new pop-adjacent artists – La Roux, Little Boots, Florence Welch –

being positioned clearly as the alternative was hugely important. This re-entrenched the idea of a more defined alt-pop strata, which then slowly became all-encompassing in the 2010s as pop the genre moved away from its meaning as 'pop as in popular'.

What *The X Factor* had also done was sanctify vocal prowess. This then cast the manufactured pop that came before it in an even worse light. Acts who harked back to that era, à la Same Difference, were viewed as frivolous relics. Even within the very inauthentic world of *The X Factor*, the idea of credibility was being fostered as this new bastion of pop. Sensible hat-botherer Matt Cardle beating One Direction in 2010 is evidence of that. His win also chimed with the rise of singer-songwriters like Adele, Sam Smith and Ed Sheeran, who, despite being teenagers and early twentysomethings, made music aimed at a much older audience. Pianos and guitars replaced synths and drum machines, and glorious escapism via a so-called 'throwaway' pop song was surpassed by a need to earnestly wallow in reality. Performative sadness had replaced choreography, and 'meaningful' lyrical content was now way more important than being emotionally moved by a top-tier melody.

In 2006, Twitter arrived. Seemingly utilised at first as a nice way to enjoy *The X Factor* in a large group (down a shot for every time Louis Walsh says, 'You're like a young [insert famous Black artist here]'), it quickly became an often negative feedback loop. It also focused on the personalities of pop stars, a part of the pop game that hadn't always been as crucial post-Spice Girls. There were now fewer places to hide as camera phones arrived and pop stars could be spotted in clubs, in supermarkets or, say, weeing up against a cash machine while on their phone. Tweets were also picked up by tabloids and celebrity magazines, with frustrated missives fired off in anger now used as official statements.

This focus on relatability had its positives. Popstars were able to reiterate that actually they were human too, which in turn led to important conversations happening around representation, race and mental health. Initially empowering self-empowerment anthems ruled the roost, as did positivity bangers aimed at undoing decades' worth of one-sided narratives. Over time, however, Twitter became imprisoning for pop stars, with their professional and personal lives entwined in the palm of their hands. If the workload for '00s pop stars was exhausting, they could at least switch off. Nowadays, it's difficult to see when anyone can take a breath.

All that reality can be overwhelming and recently, as the world has literally started to burn, a yearning for the late '90s and early '00s has started to grow. It's piping-hot nostalgia for a time of big, dumb (but not actually dumb) pop, made by disposable (but not actually disposable) pop stars that you could choose to either fully love or keep at arm's length – that seem frozen in amber; happy (but not actually always happy) and dressed in all-white everything.

At the heart of all of this nostalgia, though, for me at least, are the songs. This was, after all, the era where the single was key. While writing *Reach for the Stars* I gorged myself on a playlist of this decade's top-tier bangers, bops and ballads. Immaculately constructed for optimum pop culture dominance, the best songs from this era – 'Say You'll Be There', 'Just a Little', 'Keep on Movin'', 'Don't Stop Movin'', 'Whole Again', 'If You Come Back',

'No Good Advice', 'Fill Me In', 'Overload', 'Day and Night', 'Some Girls', 'One for Sorrow', 'Thank You', 'Colourblind', 'Pure Shores', 'Flying Without Wings', 'Scandalous', 'Caught in the Middle', the list goes on – feel laser-focused to deliver pure, unadulterated serotonin every single time.

Who doesn't need a huge gulp of that in their lives?

Acknowledgements

A huge, chart-topping, platinum-selling thank you first of all to everyone who gave up their time to speak to me for the book. This weighty tome would have been about 400 pages shorter if you hadn't, and I hope I've done your stories justice. To the pop stars, thank you for the music, which sustained me during lockdown and led to this idea bubbling up in the first place. Thank you to Pete Selby at Nine Eight Books, who asked to meet me to see if I had any book ideas and then sat slack-jawed while I ranted at him for about an hour about '90s and '00s pop. I'm sorry for all the emails! Thanks also to Melissa Bond for her eye for detail and unwavering enthusiasm and to Lizzie Dorney-Kingdom for handling the press. Big shoutout to my agent, Matthew Hamilton, and to Steve Leard for the amazing cover.

Special thanks to all the PRs who helped organise the interviews and to the videotelephony software programme Zoom for making my life easier. I also want to give an extra shout out to Peter Loraine, Simon Jones, Gemma Cutting and Jordan

Paramor for going the extra mile when it came to landing some of the interviews.

I also want to thank all the people who helped keep me sane during this whole process: Candice Carty-Williams, Hattie Collins, Harriet Gibsone, Priya Elan (extra special thanks for reading an early, 25,000-word version of the Sugababes chapter), Stephen Churchill, Kasia Churchill, exemplary advice-giver Paul Flynn, Peter Robinson (thanks for the date framework idea), David Goggin, Fiona Goggin, Laura Snapes (extra special thanks for reading an early, 25,000-word version of the Girls Aloud chapter), Alim Kheraj, Owen Myers, David Russell, Holly-Jade Johnston, Duncan Hammond, Holly Hammond, Georgia Fazan-Clarke, Luisa Gibbons, Kate Grinnell, Dave Grinnell, Michael Hann, Hanna Hanra (and for lending me Pam the dog when I needed her) and Gwilym Mumford. If I've forgotten anyone, it's because my brain is now mush.

Thanks to my family: Mum, Ian, Sonya and Lottie-Joy (can't wait to play you Girls Aloud's classic album *Tangled Up* on a loop as you get older). This book is dedicated to the memories of two amazing women: my nan, who unashamedly loved pop; and my auntie Karen, who was a complete icon in every sense of the word.

My biggest source of inspiration throughout this process, more so than 'Some Girls', 'Scandalous' or 'Just a Little', was my love, Ben Gazur, who I first bonded with over Busted. None of this would have been possible without you. It's also important you know that I have finally forgiven you for constantly getting Girls Aloud and the Sugababes mixed up, even while we were attending a gig by the latter. Thank you for always being there for me, and for being you.